BISHOP'S WALTHAM
Parish, Town and Church

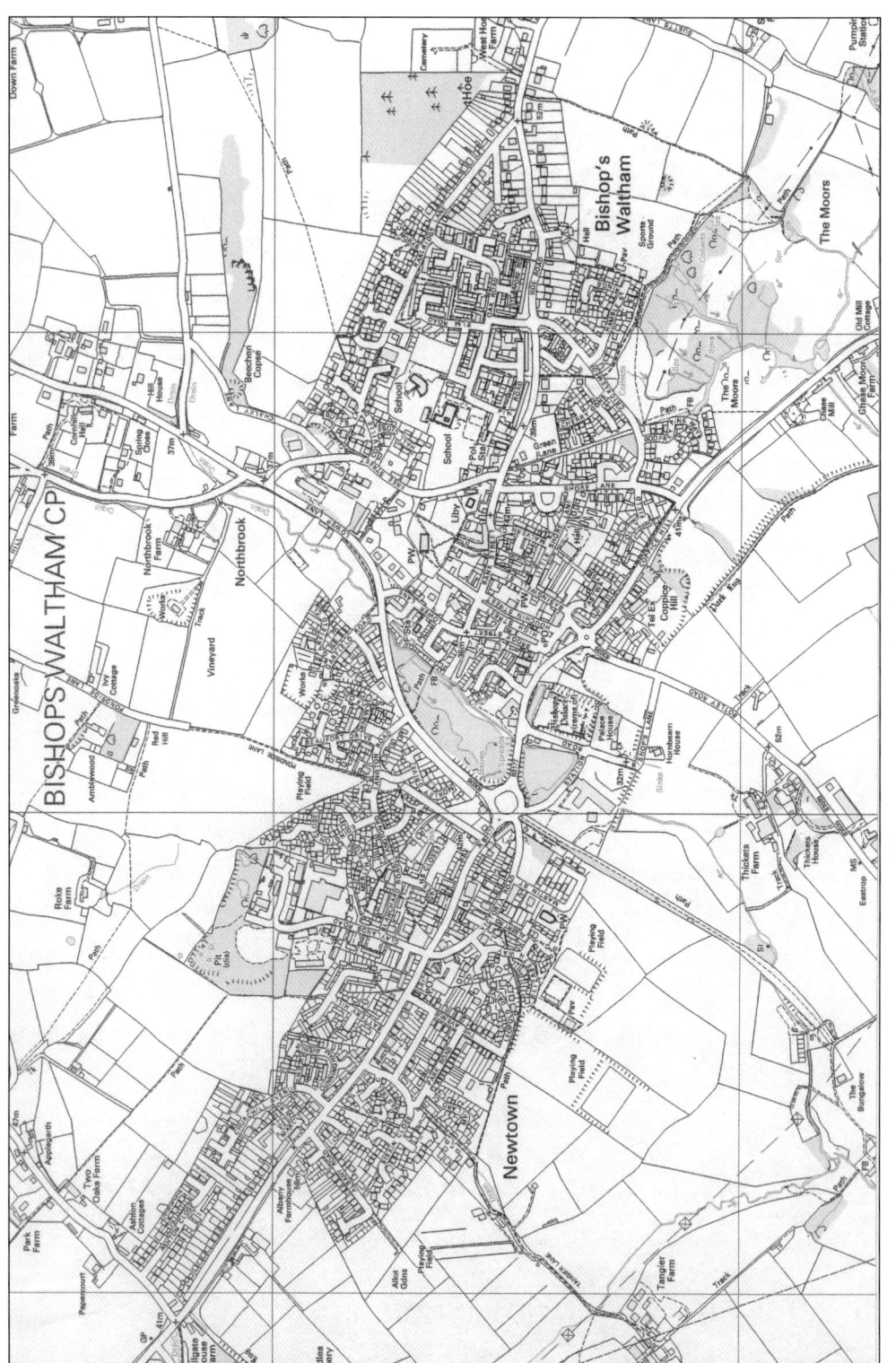

The town of Bishop's Waltham

BISHOP'S WALTHAM
Parish, Town and Church

PETER R. WATKINS

SWANMORE BOOKS

Published by Swanmore Books
7 Crofton Way
Swanmore
Southampton SO32 2RF

© Peter R. Watkins 2007

The author has asserted his rights under the
Copyright, Designs and Patents Act 1988,
to be identified as the author of this work.

ISBN 978-0-9541566-2-6

Peter Watkins is also the author of
Swanmore since 1840
ISBN 0- 9541566-0-9

Designed, typeset and produced by
John Saunders Design & Production OX13 5HU
Printed in Great Britain by Biddles Ltd, King's Lynn

Contents

Illustrations	vii
Preface	xv
Acknowledgements	xviii

Introduction		1
1.	Palace, park and ponds to 1644	3
2.	Manor, town and church to 1644	18
3.	After the Palace 1644–1760	31
4.	Poverty, pestilence and fire 1650–1850	43
5.	The turnpike roads	55
6.	From the French wars to the Census of 1851	64
7.	Registers and rectors 1737–1833	77
8.	From the Grammar School to the Educational Institute	87
9.	From the National School to the County Mixed School	97
10.	The Gunners of Bishop's Waltham	109
11.	Arthur Helps and mid-Victorian enterprise	119
12.	William Brock and the Victorian church	132
13.	Primitive Methodists, Congregationalists and Roman Catholics	140
14.	The Enclosure of Curdridge Common & Waltham Chase	152
15.	Houses, people and places in the late nineteenth century	156
16.	Pleasures and pastimes 1870–1914	168
17.	The restoration of St Peter's 1896–7 and the pre-war church	178
18.	The Parish Council and the town 1894–1914	191

19. The First World War and the inter-war years 1914–1939   201
20. The Second World War and after 1939–1965   215
21. Growth and renewal since 1965   231

Appendices

A Landmarks in the history of Bishop's Waltham   247
B Population of Bishop's Waltham   252
C Rectors of Bishop's Waltham   254
D Chairmen of the Parish Council   256

Abbreviations   266
Sources   261
Notes   265
Index   281

Illustrations

Source of illustration and where applicable author and copyright is indicated in brackets. Where reference only is shown the source is Hampshire Record Office. Other abbreviations appear in full except the Local Studies Library, Winchester (LSL) and the National Monuments Record Centre, Swindon (NMRC).

Front cover Bishop's Waltham Palace 2004 (NMRC No.23628/11)

Back cover Aerial photograph of Bishop's Waltham with reconstruction complete – central car park, road across the pond, traffic island on site of old station and new Corhampton road. (NMRC)

Frontispiece The town of Bishop's Waltham (Ordnance Survey Licence No. 1000035877).

1. Bishop's Waltham Parochia. (P.H.Hase 1975)
2. Charter of Bishop Henry of Blois undated but probably between 1153 and 1171. (Winchester College muniments No.10629)
3. Reconstruction of Bishop's Waltham Palace as it may have appeared about 1450. (*Three Palaces of the Bishops of Winchester* by John Wareham p.29 English Heritage.)
4. Bishop's Waltham Palace: the Bakehouse & Brewhouse built by William of Wykeham, 1378-81. Upper floor added by Henry Beaufort 1439-41.
5. Bishop's Waltham Palace: the West Tower built late 12th century, altered by William of Wykeham and fourth storey added by Henry Beaufort. The bishop's private apartments.
6. Plan of the Bishop's Park. (Edward Roberts 1988)
7. Park Lug near Tangier Farm. (2006)
8. Plan of the Bishop's Great Pond. (Edward Roberts 1986)
9. The Parish Registers kept from 1612. Entries for 1626 & 1627. (30M77PR1)
10. Extract from Poor Rate Book 1656 containing signatures of Joseph Goulston, Rector, John Woodman and James Hampton, Churchwardens. (30M77 PO1)

11. List of Churchwardens, Overseers of the Poor and Surveyors (incomplete) 1709-1713 from Poor Rate Book. (30M77PO2)
12. 'The New Key' made on the instructions of the Bishop of Winchester 1688.
13. Vernon Hill House rear garden. (2007)
14. Title page of the Act of Parliament for enclosing arable fields at Ashton 1759. (45M69/17)
15. Map of Hampshire Taylor, 1759 Sheet 11
16. Accounts prepared by William Ledwell, Master of the Workhouse 1756-57. (30M77PO4)
17. The Barleycorn Inn, Basingwell Street c.1895 – the parish workhouse from 1762.
18. The eighteenth century fire engine in use until 1910 on an occasion when it was brought out as a curiosity.
19. Diagram to show turnpike roads round Bishop's Waltham.
20. Thomas Milner map of Hampshire 1791 sheet 17 showing the Coldharbour and Waltham turnpike gates, the Gibbet on the Chase, Coppice Hill brickyard, the Mill on the Chase, Curdridge Lane as the main road from Curdridge to Bishop's Waltham and Green Lane continued to join the Gosport road.
21. The Waltham Turnpike House on the Gosport turnpike.
22. Milestones on the Gosport turnpike and the London to Southampton turnpike.
23. Table of Tolls at Park Gate on the Bishop's Waltham to Fisher's Pond turnpike, 1834. (Bishop's Waltham Museum Trust)
24. The Palace ruins across the pond, 1784.
25. Title page of *Our Town* Volume I by Peregrine Reedpen, 1834.
26. Parish Register – christenings for the year 1758 signed by Joseph Challoner Bale, Curate. (30M77PR3)
27. Parish Marriage Register for 1767 – bride and groom often make their mark. (30M77PR3)
28. Parish Banns Register for 1786 – banns signed by Charles Walters, Curate 1785–1811. (30M77PR4)
29. Brownlow North, Bishop of Winchester, 1781–1820. (TOP Portrait N5)
30. Plan of the South Gallery erected in St Peter's Church 1797. Names of pew holders include No.5 Jemima Jones (girls' school in Church Lane), No.10 Ezekiel Donniger, organist, No.29 the Revd Charles Walters curate, No 30 the Revd John Vodin Walters. The amount each occupant paid annually in pew rent is also shown. (5M54/73)

31. Tablet in the chancel of St Peter's church erected in memory of the Revd Charles Walters.
32. Cover of printed prize poem entitled *The Remains of the Episcopal Palace* dated 29th May 1839. (261M86/10)
33. Termly account for Master James Ridge, a boarder at the Grammar School, payable to the Revd. Thomas Scard, c.1840. (Harry Gunner)
34. The Old Grammar School on the corner of Lower Lane and Brook Street shortly before demolition in 1962.
35. The Educational Institute built partly from the grammar school endowments, opened 1899. (LSL 495/5/5)
36. Diagram to show elementary schools in Bishop's Waltham.
37. The demolition of the school in the churchyard, October1907. (30M77/PZ11)
38. The British School opened 1866, often referred to as 'The School on the Hill'. (LSL 397/1/1)
39. Group of pupils in the boys' department probably before 1910. (LSL 416/2/4)
40. Group of senior girls outside the School on the Hill c.1953. (Diana Gibson, nee Chamberlain)
41. William Gunner II 1777–1857 founder of Bishop's Waltham and Hampshire Bank. (Harry Gunner)
42. Holm Oak and part of Gunners bank, Bank Street.
43. Caroline Gunner 1829–1906. (Harry Gunner)
44. Licence for a male servant 1905. (Harry Gunner)
45. Licence for a carriage or motor car 1905. (Harry Gunner)
46. Charles Richards Gunner 1853–1924. (Harry Gunner)
47. Some of the children of Charles and Jessie Gunner c.1892 – Charles James, Daisy May, John Hugh, Thomas Ridge, Walter Robin and Benjamin George. (Harry Gunner)
48. Family tree of the Gunner family of Bishop's Waltham.
49. Ridgemede House built 1897 by Charles Richards Gunner. (Harry Gunner)
50. Arthur Helps. Portrait by George Richards, 1858. (National Portrait Gallery, London).
51. Workmen at the clay works in Claylands Road 1922.
52. Bishop's Waltham Railway showing sidings leading to the clay works and gas works.
53. Timetable of the Bishop's Waltham railway June 1863.
54. Bishop's Waltham station. (LSL 397/5/3)

ILLUSTRATIONS

55. Prince Leopold laying the foundation stone of the Royal Albert Infirmary 1864. *Illustrated London News*. (TOP31/2/13)
56. The Priory, 1912. Built as the Royal Albert Infirmary but never used as a hospital. It became a private house until it was bought by the White Fathers in 1912.
57. Charles Sumner, Bishop of Winchester 1827–1869. (TOP Portrait S6)
58. William Brock, Rector 1833-91 wearing the academic gown and bands which he wore when preaching. (Val Short)
59. The Primitive Methodist Mission Hall (white building centre) 1871–1909.
60. St Paul's Primitive Methodist Church opened in Basingwell Street 1909. Now the United Free Church.
61. The Congregational Church (United Reformed from 1972) Lower Lane, built 1862, demolished 1979. (LSL7/7/2)
62. Our Lady Queen of Apostles consecrated 1998.
63. The enclosure of Waltham Chase 1870 showing the triangle of land allotted to the parish as a recreation ground. (Q23/2/14)
64. The Padbury clock, High Street. (WEWalmsley)
65. The Palace House. (LSL148/7/1)
66. Agnes Blanche Hemming, diarist. (Val Short)
67. Page from the census return of 1861 showing the entry for Northbrook House with eight living-in servants. Not all entries in the census are as legible and beautifully written as this one.
68. Richard Austin III 1866-1945 wearing the bowler hat for which he was well-known, with his wife and recently widowed mother c.1905.
69. High Street c.1916. G.T.Floate was a photographer who published photographs of the town still available in 1944. (LSL 43/5/3)
70. The town pump, Basingwell Street c.1912.
71. Two views of High Street before the road was tarred c.1910.
72. The Liberal Party campaigning in the General Election of 1906. The Liberals claimed to stand for cheaper food – the large loaf – and gained a landslide victory.
73. The Revd Edward Falconer, curate 1884–7, the cause of the Beer Riots. (Val Short)
74. The Bishop's Waltham Cycling Club outside Eastway House c.1898. (Dorothy Westbrook)
75. Bishop's Waltham Cricket Club no date.
76. Bishop's Waltham Football Club 1907–8. (63AO4/81/2/84)

ILLUSTRATIONS

77. Bishop's Waltham Scout Troop with Thomas Swinnerton-Hewitt, scoutmaster and the Revd Noel Stubbs, curate and assistant scoutmaster c.1910. (10M99/B1/8/21)
78. Singing the National Anthem to celebrate the Coronation of King Edward VII 9th August 1902. (Paul Desa).
79. St Peter's church choir c.1892.
80. Two early Parish Magazines, the first shows the dormer windows placed over the south aisle to light the south gallery in 1797 and removed in 1896–7.
81. A page of advertisements in an early Parish Magazine.
82. Thomas Graham Jackson (later Sir) architect of the restoration of St Peter's 1896–7, in his early 60s. (Portrait in possession of Wadham College, Oxford reproduced with permission.)
83. Plan of St Peter's church prepared by T.G.Jackson, showing the organ and choir in their original place and as Jackson proposed – organ at the end of the south aisle and choir in the chancel. He also proposed to move the pulpit steps but this was not achieved until later. (30M77/PW35)
84. The south gallery built 1797, before its demolition in 1896–7. (30M77/PW36)
85. Interior of St Peter's before the restoration of 1896–7. Note the distorted chancel arch with scriptural text, the old reading desk and central heating pipes above floor level.
86. The Rectory from the rear garden.
87. Result of poll for the first Parish Council 17th December 1894 from the Council Minute book. (150M85/PX1)
88. The front garden of Mount House, Little Shore Lane with Thomas John Brown, Chairman of the Parish Council 1894–1915 and his wife. (LSL478/2/6)
89. Dick Richards and the tank used to water the roads in summer.
90. Station Road looking towards the Square c.1900. (LSL 398/1/6)
91. St George's Square c.1900.
92. Two First World War fatalities: Midshipman Edward Gunner drowned in HMS Bulwark 25th November 1914 and Sapper William Henry Richards (right) who died of wounds in the military hospital at Etaples, 1916. Three members of each family are commemorated on the War Memorial in the churchyard. (Harry Gunner & Val Short)
93. Bishop's Waltham postwomen 1917. Postmistress Mrs Wensley with Kit Askew, Polly Aburrow and Sis Weavill.
94. Northbrook House used as a hospital during the First World War.

95. Miss Wright's school for girls at Lithend House, Free Street, 1920s. (Harry Gunner)
96. Advertising cards for two well known businesses from *Hampshire and the Isle of Wight by pen and camera* 1907.
97. Bishop's Waltham fire brigade first motor engine 1930.
98. Civil Defence workers marching to St Peter's for Warship Week service March 1943. (W.E.Walmsley)
99. Admiral Andrew Cunningham 1942. (Michael Simpson)
100. The Mill Pond and the Mill on the Chase. (LSL 403/3/1)
101. Aerial photographs c.1938. a) The Palace in the foreground and Coppice Hill brickyard in the background, b) Palace and Pond in the foreground, also includes the railway station.
102. The Rectory and Northbrook House c.1958. Rectory land bordering on Lower Lane was then intended as an extension to the graveyard, later sold for houses. Also shows Ridgemede House with drive from Free Street.
103. Demolition of last brickworks chimney (130 feet high) Claylands July 1958.
104. Aerial photograph of reconstruction in progress 1966. Central area has been cleared for a car park. Building of road across the pond, traffic island and new Corhampton Road in progress. (NMRC)
105. Boundaries of the parish of Bishop's Waltham after the 1967 adjustment. (Ordnance Survey Licence No. 1000035877)
106. The Church Hall, Free Street opened 1910 enlarged 1964.
107. *Parish News* June 1976. Former rectors.
108. St Peter's church with dais for nave altar completed 2005.
109. The Jubilee Clock and St George's Square, 2002.

Dedicated to the memory of my mother and father
Mary Gwyneth Watkins (nee Price) 1900–1997
Frank Arthur Watkins 1903–1990

Preface

In the second half of the twentieth century Bishop's Waltham was fortunate to have three people who made significant contributions to the written history of the town. Frank Sargeant was rector of the parish from 1949 to 1962 and an historian. He wrote a series of articles in *The Parish Magazine* (as it was then called) which he subsequently published in three small books about St Peter's church, the Bishops' Palace and the town. They have all been out of print for many years.

Barbara Biddell, the wife of Christopher Bidell who followed Frank Sargeant as rector in 1962, began research on the records in the Parish Chest, then kept in the upper vestry in St Peter's Church. Though the Biddells left Bishop's Waltham in 1975, Barbara continued research on the parish records and in retirement was able to complete the work. In 2002 she published the first full-length history of Bishop's Waltham.

John Bosworth was an historian of an entirely different sort. By profession he was a photographer. History was his hobby and his passion. Over many years he made a huge collection of photographs of Bishop's Waltham and the surrounding villages. He had an encyclopaedic knowledge of people and places over the whole of the twentieth century and published a number of books of photographs of Bishop's Waltham, Durley and Upham whose captions incorporate his knowledge and often draw on the reminiscences of local people whose folk memories went back to the nineteenth century. He was also the founder and life curator of the Bishop's Waltham Museum which moved into enlarged premises negotiated by him just before his death in 2005.

I have also made use of the only nineteenth century history of the town entitled with Victorian prolixity *The History of the Town, Church and Episcopal Palace of Bishop's Waltham from the earliest period to the present time* by Charles Walters published in 1844. The author had been master of the grammar school and curate of the parish church. His book, based on a lecture he gave to the Bishop's Waltham Literary Institute, runs to only 96 pages. It is however the work of a scholar, at times pedantic and opiniated but also painstaking. It has the advantage of being 160 years closer to the events which it describes than we are today. Without these I could not have attempted to write a history of Bishop's Waltham and readily acknowledge my debt to all four. I have however written with a rather different focus from theirs.

First, my emphasis is on the history of Bishop's Waltham since 1644 and in particular in the nineteenth and twentieth centuries. I have devoted only two chapters to the first 1000 years of the town's history up to the destruction of the Palace during the Civil War and its subsequent abandonment as a residence by the Bishops of Winchester.

Second, I have made fuller use of some additional primary sources, in particular the Census returns from 1841 – 2001, the Parish Council minutes from its creation in 1894 to 1953 and *The Parish Magazine* (later *Parish News*) from its first publication in 1890. I have also spoken to people in Bishop's Waltham whose memory goes back as far as the 1920s and drawn on earlier memories published in the *Parish News*.

Third, I have tried to relate events in Bishop's Waltham to what was happening elsewhere in Hampshire and in the country and I have drawn attention to evidence of the history of the town which survives in its contemporary landscape. I have at times strayed on to the borderland between history, economics and sociology, touching on such topics as unemployment, the provision of services such as electricity and mains sewerage, as well as literacy rates and infant mortality.

I am aware that I have written a perhaps disproportionate amount about the parish church of St Peter. This is partly because it is better documented than some aspects of the secular history of the town but also because it lay for many centuries at the heart of the life of Bishop's Waltham. Its rector and churchwardens were until 1894 responsible for both the church and many aspects of welfare. After the Palace was deserted it was the most prominent, the oldest and the only stone building in the town. The list of rectors is continuous for over 700 years. For almost the whole of that time the parson (person) was its leading citizen known to all in the town.

Local history is usually descriptive rather than evaluative or critical. There are however judgements to be made even if for lack of evidence they must be tentative. There are many aspects of the history of Bishop's Waltham which fascinate because things could have been different. It is for example remarkable that a town as significant in the locality as Bishop's Waltham with a population at least twice that of anywhere within eight miles radius, should have no provision for education beyond the age of eleven within its boundaries. Second an extraordinary feature of Bishop's Waltham is how long it took for mains sewerage to arrive in the town. Although concern about the spread of disease from open drains was expressed as early as the 1830s it was not until the early 1960s that complaints about overflowing effluent and the unpleasantness of emptying toilet buckets, ended with the building of the sewage works at Brooklands Farm. Yet mains sewerage was on the agenda of the Parish Council from the beginning of the century until the First World War and again in the 1930s but in each case economy was preferred to amenity.

The same was true of recreational facilities. The Enclosure of Waltham Chase in 1870 provided four acres on the Chase for a recreation ground. It was of course inconveniently remote from the town itself yet neither the Parish Council nor a town meeting was prepared to support spending the necessary money to exchange land on the Chase for a town centre site which would cost money to buy, drain, fence and lay out football pitches and cricket squares.

History happens chronologically. It is however difficult to write local history chronologically rather than topically without fragmentation and repetition. I have retained a broadly chronological framework but have sometimes started or finished a story even though part of it falls outside the period with which I am chiefly concerned.

I am grateful to all the people who have shown an interest in the work I have been doing and indulged my fascination with many aspects of the town's history. I have acknowledged many of them elsewhere.

Peter Watkins
Swanmore
October 2007

Acknowledgements

Many people have contributed, sometimes unknowingly, to this history of Bishop's Waltham. The list is far from complete since I have benefited from conversations and snippets of information picked up by the way for which I have later found a use but whose source I could no longer recall. Information comes both from people whose families have lived in the town for generations or even centuries, and from people who have moved away but still look back with affection and nostalgia to the days they spent in Bishop's Waltham.

I am particularly grateful to older people whose reminiscences go back as far as the 1920s and have helped me to capture something of a vanished world. Many people have contributed reminiscences, lent or given me documents, articles, books, photographs, family diaries and letters as well as sharing their knowledge and enthusiasm for the history of the town

Those from whom I derived assistance include: Arthur Apsimon, Harold G.Barstow, Barbara Biddell, Margaret and Reg Bunyan, Sybil Churcher, Don Cole, John Cornell, Barry Cross, Betty Daysh, David Ellis-Jones, Peter Ewence, Helen Franklin, Priscilla Fryer (formerly Lady Newton), Diana Gibson, Harry Gunner, Jean Hammerton, Dr Charles Hemming, Diana and Tony Hunt, Gilda Jacobucci, Hazel Josey, Ian Lees-Smith, Alan Lovell, Jenny Maidment, Ann Pearson, Neil Padbury, Les and Jean Powell, Val Short, Susan Tatton-Brown, Bunny Thornton, W.E.Walmsley, John Watts, David Williams and Kay Young.

I also wish to thank the staff of the Hampshire Record Office in Winchester where I have spent many days exploring the records of the parish deposited there and the Local Studies Library also in Winchester whose staff helped particularly with photographs. Wadham College, Oxford directed me to a portrait of Thomas Graham Jackson, formerly a Fellow of the College and the National Portrait Gallery provided a copy of a painting of Arthur Helps. I have done my best to trace the owners of copyright photographs and am grateful for permission to publish them.

Members of my family have helped once again. Jill and Graham read drafts and made suggestions many of which I have incorporated. Kate, my younger daughter, provided invaluable help transferring illustrations to disc a feat quite beyond me. Needless to say errors of fact and interpretation remain my responsibility.

Introduction

STAND AT the top of the tower of St Peter's church and you will see the small town of Bishop's Waltham below you. It lies less than a mile below one of the sources of the river Hamble, cradled in a fold in hills which are outliers of the South Downs where the chalk meets the valley clays and gravels. Bishop's Waltham is a small town in Hampshire with a larger population than Odiham or Stockbridge but not as big as Alton or Petersfield. It is about two miles across and until 1894, when Curdridge became a separate civil parish, it extended down the valley of the river Hamble as far as Botley, a distance of about six miles. Bishop's Waltham lies at the junction of roads from Winchester, Fareham and Southampton as well as a route from London down the Meon valley and then over Corhampton Down. Its postal address is Southampton, for local government it belongs to Winchester City Council whilst St Peter's church is in the deanery of Bishop's Waltham, part of the Anglican diocese of Portsmouth carved out of Winchester in 1927.

The town's history falls naturally into three periods. The first starts with the Saxon settlement which had probably taken place by 500 AD and includes its acquisition by the bishop of Winchester in 904AD in exchange for Portchester. The second period begins with the building of the Palace of the bishops of Winchester, the erection of St Peter's church on its present site and probably the lay out of the town, all the work of Bishop Henry of Blois beginning about 1136. The middle ages have been described as Bishop's Waltham's golden age. The third period starts with the destruction of the Bishop's Palace by Cromwell's troops in 1644 after which the town was no longer under the shadow of the bishop and his palace. In the first two chapters I have summarised the first thousand years of the town's history before attempting a fuller account of the last 360 years in the remainder of the book.

Bishop's Waltham contains much which reminds the perceptive inhabitant or the observant visitor of its remarkable history. Signposts point to the Palace, making clear that it is a ruin in the custody of English Heritage. It is well kept and open to the public during the summer, a fascinating ruin well worth a visit. There are vestiges of the bishop's fishpond created by damming the river Hamble and of the deer park where he could hunt or where his retainers could obtain venison for his guests. There are remains of clayworkings. Some go back to the fourteenth century others were opened in the nineteenth century though both closed in the 1950s. The large and interesting churchyard of St Peter's church contains gravestones and table tombs, some dating from the eighteenth century and still legible, commemorating the people who contributed to the development of the town in their generation. Along the surrounding roads are milestones set up more than 200 years ago by turnpike trusts as well as two toll houses. At the south entrance to the churchyard is the memorial to the dead of the wars of the twentieth century and in St George's Square the handsome clock placed there to mark the Golden Jubilee of Queen Elizabeth II at the beginning of the twenty-first century.

The centre of the town, despite the drastic development carried out by the planners in the 1960s and 70s, is still recognisably as it was laid out 850 years ago, although some of the town's oldest houses are hidden behind modern facades. Over 150 buildings, many of them in the town centre, have been listed by English Heritage as of architectural or historic interest. Roads recently and imaginatively named provide reminders of the past, for example Blanchard Road, Colville Drive, Gunners Park, and Crickelmede whilst Houchin Street and Basingwell Street, though spelt differently, are to be found in fourteenth and fifteenth century documents. Shore Lane may be a corruption of Shard or Sward meaning 'grassy land'.

W.E. Tate's ground breaking book *The Parish Chest* was published in 1946 and 60 years later it is still in print though its title is now an anachronism. In many places, including Bishop's Waltham, the parish chest no longer exists and where it does it is empty. The Bishop's Waltham Parish Chest was described to the author by Barbara Biddell who made use of the documents which had been stored in it for centuries. It was made of oak with four panels, and measured about four feet six inches long and three feet high. It had strong locks, three keyholes and iron hinges and probably dated from the early seventeenth century. Under the Parochial Registers and Records Measure of 1978 the records which were once stored in the Parish Chest were deposited in the County Record Office at Winchester where they are safe from loss, death watch beetle or a careless incumbent or church warden. They have been transferred to microfilm or microfiche and some were transcribed and indexed for the Hampshire Geneological Society by Reg Bunyard and Bruce Tremlett in the early 1980s. The erstwhile contents of the Parish Chest constitute a major source for this book on the history of the town, church and parish of Bishop's Waltham.

1
Palace, park and ponds to 1644

THE SETTLEMENT from which the town of Waltham emerged took place at the beginning of the Anglo-Saxon colonisation of southern England, not later than 500 AD. The name Waltham comes from the Old English *wealdham* – meaning 'woodland estate' or 'settlement in the forest'. Wherever the name is found it is an indication of very early Saxon settlement.[1] When they arrived the Saxons were pagans: evidence survives in their burial sites and in the names from which four of the days of the week are derived – Tiw, Woden, Thunor and Frig were Saxon gods.[2] It was not until the second half of the seventh century that the Saxons in Sussex and Hampshire were converted to Christianity; possibly the result of St. Wilfrid preaching the gospel in the Meon valley. The Christian faith spread from top down and by 680 all the English kings had been baptised.[3]

In the years after the conversion the church was organised not in the smaller parishes with which we are familiar but in larger areas described by scholars as *parochie* (singular *parochia*) to distinguish them from the smaller parishes which came later. These minsters or mother churches were served by teams of priests operating from a central church. The distinction which we make between churches and monasteries was also blurred. A *mynster* (Old English) or *monasterium* (Latin) was a place where a number of priests and monks lived, a place of prayer and study from which they went out to preach the gospel and baptise in the surrounding countryside [4] During the reigns of the West Saxon kings Caedwalla and Ine – 685 to 726 – mother churches were founded by the West Saxon kings at Old Southampton, Titchfield and Waltham and further afield at Romsey and East Meon. The system was the result of royal policy and enhanced the kings' authority and completed the conversion of the Saxons to Christianity. [5]

The monastery or minster at Waltham was founded soon after the conversion of the Saxons perhaps by Ine the king of the West Saxons (688 to 726), in what has been described as 'the monastic boom' of the years from 670.[6] We are left to surmise what the first church looked like and where it was situated. It probably had a wooden frame with wattle and daub infill and a thatched roof and was situated on the site of the later palace within reach of the river Hamble.

An early account of the life and travels of St Willibald (701–786) says that as a

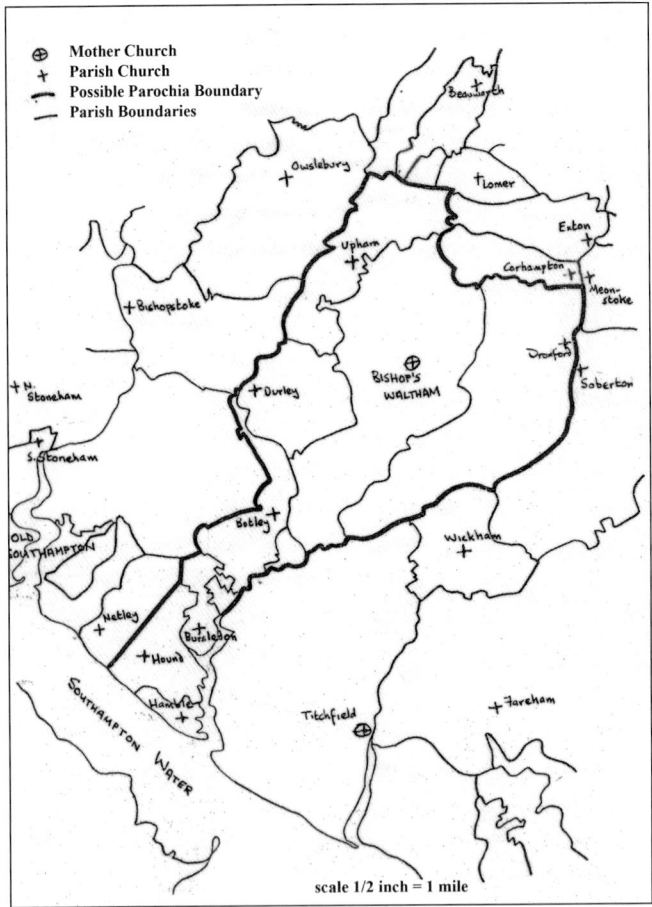

1. Bishop's Waltham Parochia.

child of five he was brought 'to the monastery which is called Waldheim'. There he was handed over to Abbot Egwald who accepted him as a novice after consulting the community. In due course he wished 'to go on pilgrimage and travel to distant foreign lands' and so, probably in 721, he set out from 'Hamblemouth, near the port of Hamwic' (Old Southampton).[7] Willibald is the first named person whom we can identify as living in Waltham.[8] He was later to become bishop of Eichstatt, near Munich in south Germany where he is buried.[9] A fragment of a Saxon cross shaft found in the garden of a house in St Peter Street dating from the eighth or ninth century is on loan to Winchester Museum. What is probably the Saxon font was also found in the garden of a house in St Peter Street in 1933 and was restored to its place in the church in 1965.

It is almost 200 years before we hear of Waltham again. In 904 Edward the Elder (reigned 901–925), the son of Alfred the Great, exchanged Waltham for the manor of Portchester, with Denewulf bishop of Winchester (879–909) because he needed it in his attempt to keep the marauding Norsemen at bay.[10] For close on a thousand years, until 1869, with two short breaks, one at the Reformation and the second during the Civil War and Commonwealth, the bishop of Winchester was lord of the manor. Waltham came in due course to be known as Bishop's Waltham, though there were alternatives: it was sometimes South Waltham (*Suthwaltham* in the Middle Ages) to distinguish it from North Waltham also in Hampshire and sometimes Waltham Episcopi – Latin for Bishop's Waltham.[11].

Nearly a century later in 1001 Waltham, according to the Anglo-Saxon Chronicle, was attacked by the Danes – though the reference is all too brief: 'And in the morning they burned down the manor at Waltham and many other estates'.[12] It has been assumed that the first church was burnt with the town, and this is probably so, but we have no written evidence. In the silent years, from 720 to 1086, we can be reasonably sure that the church at Waltham fell on hard times, was sacked, or burnt perhaps several times, but on each occasion it recovered. A priest or two would return to a half ruined building and church life would be resumed. [13]

After the Danish raid of 1001 the community came back to its burnt-out buildings and began to rebuild the town. Three generations later the Domesday entry for Waltham has been interpreted to mean that recovery was still not complete. By then the church no longer had attached to it a community of priests but neither was the transition to a parish church concluded. It was still a *parochia* or 'mother-church'. There was only one priest – Radulf – who had however two churches, St Peter's and one other which was probably at Upham.[14] He farmed 2½ hides of land, about 300 acres, a substantial holding. Many of the priests named in Domesday possessed much less which placed them on a par with villains or even the humbler bordars or cottars – perhaps about 20 acres. Radulf was a considerable landholder.[15]

In the early twelfth century Waltham was the *parochia* or mother church of the whole Hamble valley. When Bishop Henry of Blois granted the monks of Hamble permission to establish a church at Bursledon somewhere about 1160 it was at the request of the parson of Bishop's Waltham in whose *parochia* Bursledon was situated:

'Know you all that I have granted to the monks at Hamble, at the request of Walter my clerk who has obtained the parsonage of the church of St Peter at Waltham, and with the assent of Christopher my clerk who by our generosity has succeeded canonically to the aforesaid Walter in the parsonage of the same church of Waltham ... all the tithe and offerings both of the living and the dead from that hide of land which belongs to those monks ... This grant is made on condition that the ... monks shall pay to the church of St Peter at Waltham 4/- each year as a recognition payment. The parishioners ... shall pay Peter's Pence to the church of Waltham, and shall make a procession at Pentecost to the church at Waltham, and visit there on the feast of St Peter's Chains. ... They shall collect their chrism from the parson of the church at Waltham. ... The priest ... shall be presented to the parson of Waltham by the ...monks, and if the parson of Waltham wishes, he shall swear fealty to him'[16]

2. Charter of Bishop Henry of Blois undated but probably between 1153 and 1171.

It is clear that as a result of its status the church at Waltham was a centre for the collection of Peter's Pence, a church tax paid to the papacy by each diocese and a distribution point for the chrism oil consecrated by the bishop on Maundy Thursday At major festivals including St Peter's day (29th June), people from the dependent chapelries attended the processions at their mother church of Waltham.[17] It was the priest of Waltham who would induct the priest of Bursledon. As late as the eighteenth century a vestige of its status as a mother church remained: mortuary payments were made to Bishop's Waltham by Bursledon and Hamble and the rector of Bishop's Waltham had an archidiaconal jurisdiction over the two parishes.[18] By the early thirteenth century the constituent parishes of the *parochia* had probably built their own churches, had their own priests and modern parish boundaries were established.

For much of the Middle Ages the unit of government was the manor rather than the parish, which became important only in the sixteenth century. It was half a century after Domesday that the continuous recorded history of Bishop's Waltham began with the building of the Palace, the church on its present site and the lay-out of the town by Bishop Henry of Blois. The medieval bishops of Winchester were rich men, more so even than the Archbishop of Canterbury. Winchester was the richest diocese in England and after Milan the richest in northern Europe.[19] Henry of Blois was, says Dom David Knowles, 'prodigiously wealthy' whilst Christopher Brooke describes him as having 'the income of a multimillionaire'.[20] The bishops of Winchester were throughout the Middle Ages statesmen holding powerful offices under the crown. Henry of Blois (1129–1171) was the first of these bishop-statesmen.[21]

He was well connected – the grandson, brother, favourite nephew and uncle of kings – William the Conqueror, Stephen, Henry I and Henry II[22] He was a man of taste and culture, a patron of the twelfth century Renaissance, interested in and knowledgeable about architecture, sculpture and illuminated manuscripts. He was probably the patron of the Winchester Bible the greatest treasure of the medieval library at Winchester. He brought the Tournai fonts to England to adorn his cathedral and the church at East Meon.

Henry was born about 1090. His father Stephen of Blois was killed in the First Crusade in the Holy Land while Henry was still a boy and so he was sent to the great Benedictine abbey of Cluny in Burgundy to be brought up.[23] He returned to England about 1120. Six years later he was appointed Abbot of Glastonbury, the richest monastery in England. He embellished its buildings though it was a place which he rarely visited. In 1129 he was appointed Bishop of Winchester, a post which

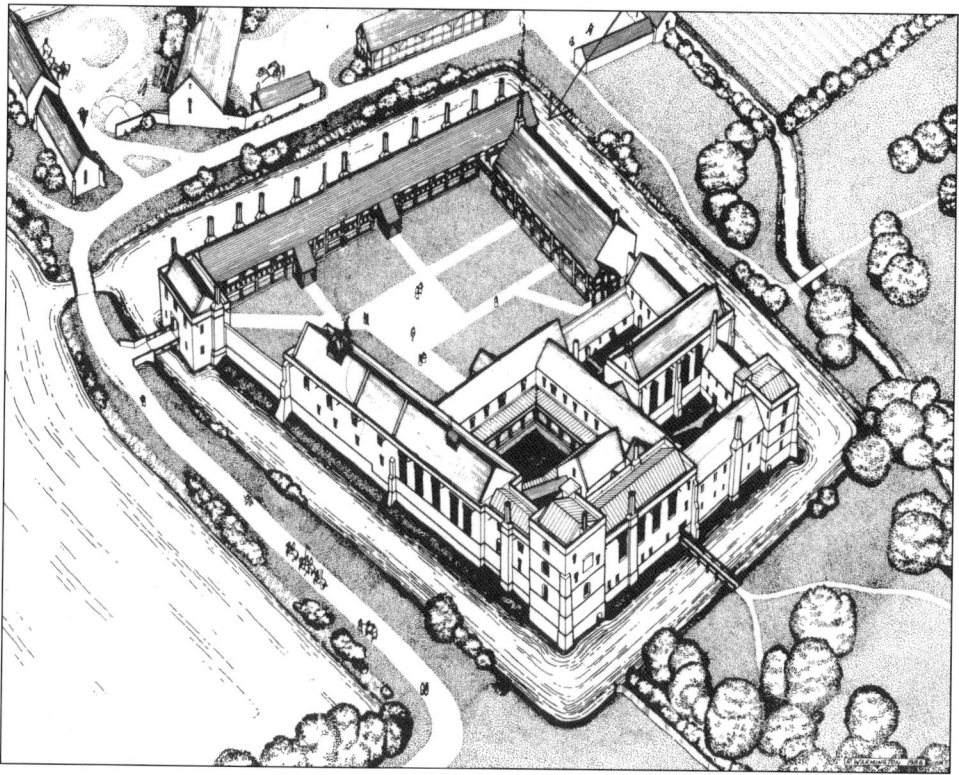

3. Reconstruction of Bishop's Waltham Palace as it may have appeared about 1450.

he retained together with the abbacy of Glastonbury for the rest of his long life. When Archbishop William of Corbeil died he was elected Archbishop of Canterbury but the pope, Innocent II, would not agree to the appointment, instead he was made papal legate, a post he held from 1139–1143, which carried precedence over the Archbishop of Canterbury but only so long as he remained legate. He supported the *coup d'etat* which made his brother Stephen king and resulted in civil war which lasted from 1135 to 1154.

Denied a voice in the government of Henry II, Bishop Henry left England in 1154 and spent the next four years at Cluny. When he returned in 1158 it was as an elder statesman and he devoted the remaining years of his life largely to the affairs of his diocese. He presided at the installation of Thomas à Becket as Archbishop of Canterbury in June 1162. He died in 1171 and is buried before the High Altar of his cathedral at Winchester.

As abbot of Glastonbury and bishop of Winchester Henry had huge estates spread over southern England.[24] In Hampshire alone these included, apart from Wolvesey Palace at Winchester itself, Alresford, Bishop's Sutton, East Meon, Highclere, Marwell, Merdon, Overton, and Bishop's Waltham. At many of these he built extensively, particularly at Wolvesey which was his main residence. In addition he was the founder of St Cross Hospital at Winchester and responsible for building its magnificent Romanesque church.

It seems likely that Bishop Henry of Blois planned the bishop's palace, the town and the church of Waltham in relation to one another. Their close connection was much clearer until the 1960s when the palace was separated from town and church by a busy main road, which in effect severed the link both visually and conceptually.

Bishop's Waltham Palace has been described as 'one of the great palaces of Medieval England' and the Middle Ages as 'the golden age of Bishop's Waltham'.[25] Living in the town must have been like living close to Blenheim or Chatsworth today, constantly aware of the comings and goings at the palace which was cheek by jowl with the town. When the bishop was in residence either for a short time or later for prolonged periods diocesan business was conducted from the palace as it was on other occasions from Wolvesey, Farnham or Southwark, or indeed wherever the bishop might be.[26]

In 1136 Henry of Blois began the Palace on its present site building an encircling bank and ditch. When he was at Cluny in the early years of Henry II's reign the palace, in common with the bishop of Winchester's other residences, was destroyed by the king so that it could not be a centre of resistance to royal authority. On his return to England in 1158 Bishop Henry rebuilt the Palace, constructing a new hall and chamber, work which may have been completed by his successor Richard of Ilchester (1174–88). It had been sufficiently rebuilt to provide a suitable venue for Henry II to hold a Council there in 1182 and for Richard I to stay at the Palace in 1194 on his way to take part in the Third Crusade.

4. Bishop's Waltham Palace: the Bakehouse & Brewhouse built by William of Wykeham, 1378-81. Upper floor added by Henry Beaufort 1439-41.

Most medieval bishops of Winchester contributed to the repair, alteration or enlargement of the Palace, for example a new kitchen and brewhouse were built in 1251 and a new chamber over the porch of the hall in 1339 and 1340. Royalty were entertained here: Henry III (1216–72) for example paid several visits in the course of his long reign. Two later medieval bishops made substantial alterations and additions: William Wykeham (1367–1404) and Henry Beaufort (1404–1447).

The Palace was the favourite residence of William Wykeham, a local boy born at nearby Wickham in 1324, who contributed more to the building of the Palace than any other bishop, so much so that he can be regarded as its second founder. He was also responsible for the rebuilding of Windsor Castle for Edward III as well as beginning the rebuilding of the nave of Winchester Cathedral and founding Winchester College (opened 1394) and New College, Oxford (opened 1386). He was twice Chancellor of England, from 1367–71 under Edward III and again under Richard II from 1389–91. When he ceased to be Chancellor he spent his remaining years at the Palace and here he died. His body was carried to Winchester for burial in front of the high altar.

William of Wykeham kept the shell but rebuilt the Palace on a larger scale giving it a new order and unity. Building continued for most of his life but can be divided roughly into four phases beginning in 1378. In the years 1379–81 he rebuilt the Hall and provided new brewhouse and bakehouse. Between 1387 and 1393 he added a new kitchen and larder with a chamber above them and the kitchen was heightened, enlarged and reroofed. In the third phase of building, 1394–96, he constructed a new Great Chamber and remodelled the chambers in the west tower. Finally in 1401 he built the Long Chamber in the inner court as well as a new gatehouse.

Wykeham used some of the foremost craftsmen of the day. William Wynford was his chief architect; Henry Yevele was largely responsible for the Great Hall in 1380 and 81; Hugh Herland worked at Waltham from 1388 though he is best known for the roof of Westminster Hall. Thomas the Glayser also made the glass for Winchester College and New College Oxford. The stone came from Beer in Devon and from the Isle of Wight, but local materials were also used – clay tiles made at Waltham and elsewhere in Hampshire and local wood and flints replaced the wooden shingles and grey-blue slate from Devon and Cornwall. The ruins we see today are largely those of buildings constructed during the episcopate of William of Wykeham.

If William of Wykeham came from humble origins his successor Henry Beaufort (1404–47) certainly did not. He was the half brother of Henry IV (1399–1413), the son of John of Gaunt by his mistress Katharine Swynford, later legitimised. He held important posts in the government of Henry V (1399–1413) and during the minority of Henry VI (reigned 1422–61) whom he crowned in Paris. He was made a Cardinal in 1427. By the time of his appointment the Palace had been substantially rebuilt by his predecessor. He nonetheless carried out further work, included heightening the West Tower in 1404, constructing a new chapel begun in 1409 but not completed until 1427 and building a new gatehouse. By now visitors expected greater privacy than had been the custom in the early Middle Ages and so Beaufort built the lodging range between 1438 and 1443. It consisted of a timber framed building on a stone foundation with brick chimney stacks. Part of this survives in the building where English Heritage has its offices and display, of the remainder only foundations survive.

Margaret of Anjou, the wife whom Henry VI married in 1445 stayed at the Palace and when Bishop Beaufort died in 1447 he left her his 'blue bed of gold and damask …in the room where the Queen lay when she was at the Palace and three suits of arras hangings in the same room'.

The building of the Palace was complete. It was separated from the town by a wall built in 1490. Though it continued to be one of their chief residences, later bishops made only minor alterations and embellishments. William Wayneflete (1447–86) the third successive bishop to hold the see for close on 40 years entertained Henry VI here in 1450 and Edward IV in 1476. He spent much time at the Palace, made his will at Waltham and died there.

Bishop Thomas Langton (1493–1501) was the last bishop to contribute substantially to the building of the Palace. He refaced timber buildings with brick, rebuilt the gatehouse and constructed the brick wall and corner turrets on the south and east

5. Bishop's Waltham Palace: the West Tower built late 12th century, altered by William of Wykeham and fourth storey added by Henry Beaufort. The bishop's private apartments.

of the Palace. His rebus and coat of arms and those of the bishopric of Winchester were found among the rubble of the inner gatehouse after the destruction of the Palace and are now on the west wall of the nave of St Peter's church. In 1501 he was appointed Archbishop of Canterbury but died of the plague before he could be enthroned.

What was perhaps the Palace's moment of greatest glory came in 1522 when Henry VIII entertained the Holy Roman Emperor, Charles V, there and concluded with him the Treaty of Waltham when they agreed to wage war together on Francis I of France. It was in the later years of the reign of Henry VIII that John Leland visited Bishop's Waltham in the course of his antiquarian tour of England undertaken at the behest of the king. He described Waltham as 'A praty tounlet…Here the Bishop of Winchester hath a right ample and goodly maner place motid aboute and a praty brooke renning hard by it. This maner place hath been by many bisshops building. Most of the three partes of the base court was builded of brike and timbre of the late days of Bisshop Langton. The residew of the inner of the house is al of stone'.[27]

In 1552 the 15 year old Edward VI visited the Palace and described it in a letter as 'a faire great old house'. Two years later Queen Mary spent nine days at the Palace (12th-21st July 1554) while she was waiting for the arrival of Philip of Spain. They were married in Winchester Cathedral on 25th July.[28]

The last reigning monarch to visit the Palace was Elizabeth I. She wrote to a court favourite, George Clifford, third Earl of Cumberland who was at sea on one of the many privateering expeditions in which he was involved. The Queen, she wrote, would not normally 'trouble our thoughts with any care for any person of rogueish condition', but she wanted to make an exception in his case and assured him 'of our most princely care for your safety and daily wishes of your safe return.'. The letter was dated 'At our court at Bishop's Waltham whither we are returned from our progress where we have spent some part of this summer in viewing our fortifications at Portsmouth…Your very loving sovereign. Elizabeth R.'[29]

Meanwhile in 1551 the first Protestant Bishop of Winchester, John Poynet (1551-53) surrendered the Palace to Edward VI in return for a fixed annual payment and it was granted to William Paulet, Earl of Wiltshire. In 1558 it was returned to the bishops of Winchester by Queen Mary. Later Tudor and early Stuart bishops continued to use the Palace as their chief residence until the Civil War. The end came suddenly and dramatically. In 1644 the Palace was besieged by parliamentary troops, abandoned by the garrison and the bishop, and set on fire by the parliamentary army. (see below) It was never again a home of the bishop nor a centre of episcopal administration. The second era in the history of Bishop's Waltham came to an abrupt end.

What we see today at the Palace is a stately ruin. When it was destroyed and subsequently abandoned by the bishops of Winchester it had over 500 years of momentous history behind it. If we want to visualise the splendour of its late medieval flourishing we have to imagine it roofed, and enriched with tapestries and bed hangings, glass and heraldic devices and equipped with all the luxuries money could then buy. It was for 500 years without question the largest, most prominent and most significant building in Bishop's Waltham.

Associated with the Palace were two other features inseparable from aristocratic life in the Middle Ages: the deer park and the Great Pond. Both are still to be found in twenty first century Bishop's Waltham though, like the Palace, they are pale shadows of their past greatness. The Great Pond is now divided into two only one of which

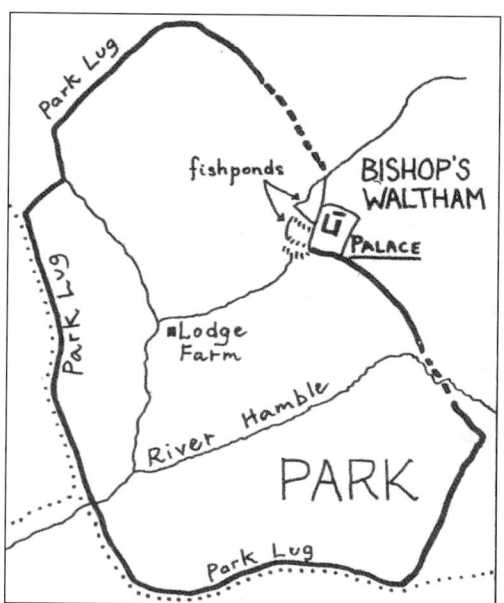

6. Plan of the Bishop's Park.

7. Park Lug near Tangier Farm (2006)

holds water throughout the year. It is reduced to a fraction of the size it once occupied and the deer park is recognisable only by the remnants of the bank and ditch which marked its boundary or *lug*.[30]

A deer park was an essential possession of the large estates of the king and his most important subjects in the early Middle Ages. Not surprisingly by 1250 all the Bishop of Winchester's residences in Hampshire except Wolvesey Palace at Winchester had a deer park and by the time of William of Wykeham, rather more than a century later, the parks had reached their greatest extent, somewhere about 8,500 acres in total. The park at Waltham was one of the earliest. There was probably already an episcopal park in late Saxon times. The Domesday Survey of 1086 refers to 'a park for beasts of the chase' (a better translation of *parcus bestiarum* than the usual 'park for wild beasts') but it was probably in the time of Henry of Blois that the 1,000 acre park was laid out.

The Park ran in a rough circle on the west side of the road or track south of Waltham and although it was disparked in the seventeenth century its boundary, the so called 'Park Lug', is still a feature of the landscape. In the middle ages the bank would have been much higher and surmounted by a substantial oak fence capable of keeping deer in and vermin out, with gates at intervals. It needed frequent repair. The Pipe Roll of the bishopric for 1301–02 includes expenditure for: 'Making the palisade of the park anew in places and mending it elsewhere £1.8.10'.[31] The bank has been eroded over the centuries with corresponding silting of the ditch and the fence has long since disintegrated.

The bishop himself may have hunted on occasion but it was chiefly his guests and the knights of his household and professional servants who hunted. Two methods were used. Deer could be driven towards the butts and shot from a static position (rather as grouse are shot today in Yorkshire or Scotland) or alternatively the huntsman could give chase on horseback. There were three species of deer in England in the early Middle Ages. Red deer and roe deer were native, fallow deer originated in the countries bordering the Mediterranean and were brought to England by the Normans. They were less hardy and in the harsher climate of England they needed food and shelter in the winter. Nonetheless it was fallow deer which were favoured and by the fourteenth century predominated. Hunting took place at most times of the year though there was an interval in the summer months when the deer were breeding.

Waltham was the base of the bishop's chief huntsman. In 1231–32 Stephen the Huntsman was at Waltham for much of the year. For 25 years he travelled round the bishop's parks in Hampshire and Surrey. He would when necessary take live deer from one estate to stock or restock another, for example in 1251 he took deer from Waltham to the new park at Hambledon. The huntsman was not the only professional employed by the bishop. In 1248–49 Jordan the Otter hunter caught two otters at Waltham and in the early thirteenth century the bishop's greyhounds were kept at Waltham. Hunt servants were responsible for keeping vermin under control. In

1208–09 no less than 71 fox skins from Waltham were sold to a Winchester trader. The park provided sport and venison. 'It was', says Edward Roberts 'both playground and larder'. [32]

Medieval bishops of Winchester lived in a style which befitted their rank and wealth Venison and fresh fish were required to be available at any of the many residences they might occupy. In Hampshire alone the bishopric created seven fishponds. The largest were the 100 acre Frensham Great Pond on the Hampshire-Surrey border and the 30 acre pond at Alresford built to provide fish for the palace at Bishop's Sutton. The ponds were constructed between 1150 and 1208 and were almost certainly begun by Henry of Blois. At Waltham the Great Pond was constructed by Bishop Henry but the Little Pond was built over a century later on the instructions of Bishop Henry Woodlock (1305–16). It was situated below what is now Duke's Mill and occupied what were marked on the Tithe Map of 1841 as two meadows covering four acres named Penstock (meaning 'sluice') and Flowes. A small breeding pond was built in the palace grounds in 1310–11. The ponds were a medieval invention and were still being maintained in 1452.

The purpose of the ponds was quite simple – to supply fresh fish reserved for the bishop and his royal and aristocratic friends to eat during Lent and on the many fast days prescribed by the church. It was not for sport, or to feed the bishop's household. Fish might be sent from Waltham to supply the needs at another episcopal residence. In 1244 for example seven pike and 300 roach were taken from Waltham pond and sent to Bitterne for the feast to welcome Bishop William Raleigh (1244–58) from abroad. In 1268 four great pike from Waltham pond were taken for a feast at Winchester at which Henry III was present. The pond was fished to supply the banquet held in the Great Hall at Wolvesey Palace to mark the enthronement of Bishop John Sandale (1316–9). If the journey were longer than a day the fish would be kept alive wrapped in wet grass and packed in a sack so that they were fresh for eating on arrival.

Fishing was not a sport but a business. Fish were caught using a large net attached at one end to the shore and at the other to a boat which was rowed in an arc so that the fish were enclosed in a large bag. There was probably a boat yard by the pond at Waltham where boats could be made or repaired.

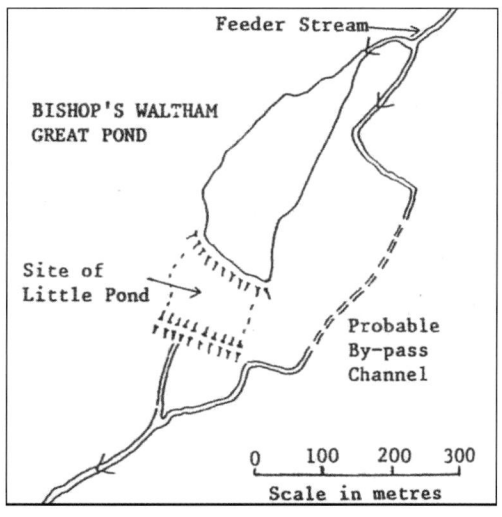

8. Plan of the Bishop's Great Pond

The making and maintenance of a successful pond was a skill and the technology was it appears brought back by the Crusaders from Muslim countries. At Bishop's Waltham a dam was constructed across the Hamble, then a substantial river. About every five years the pond was drained to keep it fresh and increase productivity, a complex operation which involved opening the sluices and placing wattle hurdles across the entrance to stop small fish escaping. Silt was then removed and the pond left fallow for several months. In 1257–58 the pond was dug with spades and barley was sown to help the cleansing process. Meanwhile the fish were netted and kept in a holding pond.

Pond management required professional expertise. Master Nicholas was responsible for all the bishop's fishponds from 1244 to 1266, travelling round the Hampshire fishponds advising on fishing, draining and restocking and providing traps for eels. Swans were to be found on the bishop's ponds. The Pipe Roll records the loss of five swans killed by foxes in 1251–52. Swans too might be moved from manor to manor in order to keep the balance.

Although the middle ages were the high point of Palace, park and ponds they were in place until the middle of the seventeenth century. The most cataclysmic event in the history of Bishop's Waltham since the town was burnt by the Danes in 1001 took place in April 1644 when the royalist garrison surrendered to the parliamentary army which two days later set the Palace on fire. Never again would Bishop's Waltham be a residence of the Bishops of Winchester.

The Civil War which began in August 1642 seemed initially to go in favour of the king but by the beginning of 1644 it was swinging in favour of parliament. The battle of Cheriton which took place on 29th March 1644 was won by a parliamentary army commanded by Sir William Waller and the Winchester garrison surrendered to parliament. Bishop's Waltham Palace, held for the king by Colonel Bennett, was now isolated. A parliamentary army under Colonel Whitehead, Member of Parliament for Southampton, laid siege to the Palace and was reinforced by the London Brigade under Major General Browne probably from a vantage point above the town on what we today call Battery Hill.

The garrison in the Palace had neither supplies nor artillery to withstand a siege and Colonel Bennett decided to surrender it to the parliamentary army rather than face the consequences of unsuccessful resistance. In return his forces were allowed to leave the Palace safely 'the Commanders and Officers …with their horses and their swords by their sides and the common souldiers (*sic*) with a rod or staffe (*sic*) in their hands' but leaving arms, ammunition and stores behind.[33]

According to Bishop's Waltham folklore the bishop, Walter Curll (1632–46) escaped in a cart under a layer of dung: Charles Walters regards this story as 'an embellishment' and Barbara Biddell uses the word 'reputedly'.[34] A likelier version of the story has the bishop disguised as a peasant accompanying a dung cart via Chalky Lane to Dundridge and thence to Soberton, Cromwell's soldiers deterred from further exploration by the strong odour of manure emanating from the cart's cargo. Two days later the Palace was set on fire in order to ensure that it could not again become a royalist stronghold. On 11th April a cavalier wrote 'Waltham House in ashes'. [35]

How much damage was done to the Palace we do not know. Two centuries later Charles Walters, who was a fervent royalist, wrote lyrically bemoaning its destruction: 'Its rifted towers, its ruined hall, once the resort of royalty, its rent and ivied walls, which have resisted the atmospherical though not the political, storms of seven centuries, speak, in affecting language, of the evils and miseries of civil discord'. [36] Bishop Curll retired to Soberton where his sister lived. He died in 1647 at his London lodgings in Paternoster Row and was brought back to Soberton for burial though oddly there is no plaque to his memory and the exact whereabouts of his grave are unknown. [37]

2
Manor, town and church to 1644

IN 1236 the hundred and manor of Bishop's Waltham included not only Waltham itself but the smaller settlements of Upham, Durley and Bursledon.[1] According to the Manor Rental of 1332 it was divided into ten tithings – Hoo, Wangfield and Mincingfield (probably Curdridge), Durley, Wintershill (part of Durley), Upham, Woodcot and Lekestede (north of Upham), Ashton and Waltham[2]. The manor was only one of the 29 manors in Hampshire belonging to the Bishop of Winchester whose estate in the Middle Ages was one of the largest and richest in the country extending over much of southern England, accumulated mostly through gifts to the bishopric made by the Saxon kings. It remained almost unaltered until the reign of Elizabeth I. In Hampshire alone by 1300 the bishop owned 28 manors and five boroughs.[3]

Detailed records of these manors are to be found in the Winchester Pipe Rolls. From 1208 to 1456 these contain a detailed account of annual income and expenditure compiled each year from the records of each manor. From 1456 to 1711 the records were kept in parchment volumes. This means that for over 500 years accounts compiled by the bishops' officials are available for study. 'The amount of information recorded in the Winchester Pipe Rolls' says Mark Page ' is vast'.[4] The accounts are so full and so detailed over such a long period that a comprehensive examination is a daunting task not likely to be completed for many years.[5] In the meantime we have to rely on the evidence which has been accumulated by scholars who have dipped into the Pipe Rolls and on the tentative conclusions they have reached. Two volumes of the Pipe Rolls, for 1301–2 and 1409–10, have been published in the Hampshire Record Series.[6] In addition Harold Barstow has translated and published the Pipe Roll for 1208–9 as well as Rentals of the Manor for 1332, 1464, 1550, 1630 and 1693, a remarkable achievement and one from which a huge amount of information can be gleaned.[7]

As feudal overlord of many manors of which Waltham was one, the bishop needed a hierarchy of officials. The senior official was the treasurer based at Winchester. Next came the steward who visited each manor twice a year and presided at the manor courts. Bailiffs, of whom there were about ten, were each responsible for a number of manors grouped geographically and had oversight particularly of ploughing and harvest. Robert of Waltham, for example – probably a native of Bishop's Waltham – was bailiff of Farnham and Bentley in the 1220s and in 1235–36 became steward.[8]

The official who mattered most to the villeins of Waltham was the reeve who might be selected by the bishop's officer or by his fellow villeins to serve for a year, though he often continued in office for longer.[9] In 1301–02 the bailiff of the group of manors of which Waltham formed part was Robert de Froyle while the reeve of the manor of Bishop's Waltham was Robert Stretthe who delivered his accounts to Geoffrey de Farham treasurer at Wolvesey.[10] He was responsible for keeping a written record of everything produced and consumed on the manor and at the end of the year rendering account to the treasurer. The post was a crucial one and the reeve needed to be able to write and probably to read. It also provided scope for a dishonest official to line his own pocket. Who for example could check the reeve's account of how many goslings or chickens had been successfully hatched and reared on the manor? Each manor also had a number of specialists, at Bishop's Waltham these included in 1301-2 swineherd, smith, hayward, shepherd of wethers, and keeper of ewes, each of whom received a reduction of their rent (a quittance) as payment for their services.[11]

The detail which can be gleaned from the Pipe Rolls is astonishing. An entry fee, described as a fine, was payable by a son when he took over his father's strips or by a father when his daughter married. The details are set out in the Pipe Roll. Fines for minor delinquencies are recorded. Thomas de Bogestok was fined 3/- for keeping the lord's wethers [castrated rams] badly; Geoffrey Frogge was fined 2/- for obstructing a former path to the nuisance of his neighbours and Thomas ate Ford was also fined 2/- for breaking the assize of ale.[12] Three halters of hemp had been bought for the plough horses at a cost of 1½d.each. A barn had been reroofed at a cost of 4/10d and its gate mended. The Great Barn had been rebuilt because it had partly collapsed through rotten timbers. This had required laths to be made costing 14/8d, large nails to fasten the rafters 3d, and slates. The palisade of the park had been renewed and in other places repaired. At harvest 347 labourers had been provided with bread and herrings.[13]

The late twelfth and much of the thirteenth century was a period of prosperity. The economy was growing – population was rising, assarts [enclosure of the waste often referred to as *purprestures*] were brought into cultivation, some only marginally economic. Prices were rising too and there was money available to the bishop's officials to spend, for example on fencing and ditching, on new barns, carts and agricultural implements. The yield of the land was increased by the use of marl to enrich the soil and by adding root vegetables like beans and peas to the crop rotation.

In 1301–2 the Pipe Rolls record a fulling mill at Waltham which was used by surrounding manors.[14] Fulling meant beating newly made cloth with fullers earth in order to scour, shrink and felt it. At first this was done manually but a fulling mill was a new invention using water power to turn a water wheel which raised and dropped heavy wooden hammers which pounded and fulled the cloth. This was the first process in the cloth industry to be mechanised.[15] At Waltham too there was a bacon curing plant for the whole estate.[16] The reign of Edward I (1272–1307) saw the grant of a market held on alternate Saturdays at Titchfield and Bishop's Waltham.[17] Bishop's Waltham never became a borough though in this period many similar places did including Alresford, Alton, Petersfield and Stockbridge.[18]

Soon after 1250 over population was becoming a problem not least in Hampshire. Half of all households in Waltham had less than 10 acres, some as few as two acres and an increasing proportion of men were landless, dependent on wages for their livelihood. The period of prosperity could only be sustained with good harvests. In wet years the marginal land would yield poorly. The early years of the fourteenth century saw a down-turn in the medieval economy. The summer of 1315 was very wet, the harvest failed and cattle disease spread. The following summers were little better. The crisis which we associate with the Black Death had begun much earlier though the events of 1348–49 deepened it.[19]

It is impossible for us to imagine the extent of the catastrophe which struck Bishop's Waltham as it did the whole of Hampshire and England in 1348–49. The Black Death – though it was not so called until after the Great Plague of 1665 – arrived in England in 1348 and Hampshire was one of its first entry points probably because of the proximity of the south coast ports. The impact was immediate: death occurred suddenly among all classes of people and on a scale never previously experienced. In the country as a whole half the population died; in the manor of Titchfield it was as high as 80%, in the manor of Bishop's Waltham 264 tenants died representing 65% of the population. When the plague returned in 1361 another 53 tenants died.[20]

Sickness and premature death were thought to be evidence of sin and the recently appointed bishop of Winchester, William Edington (1346–66) ordered the recitation of penitential psalms, additional fasting and a great Mass in the cathedral. But clergy were as likely to die as lay people. The Archbishop of Canterbury, Thomas Bradwardine, was a victim, the rector of Bishop's Waltham, John Payn (1346–66) survived. The plague had a huge effect on almost every aspect of society. There was need for less food so marginal land went out of cultivation and whole villages were deserted.[21] Sheep required less labour and flocks were increased at the expense of arable. The wool and cloth trades entered their golden era.

In the Middle Ages peasants rarely travelled. It was royalty and the court, the bishop and his entourage and feudal officials moving from manor to manor who were the main road users. Highways and tracks reflected their needs. The route from Curdridge to Waltham was along Courdriggelane, what we today call Curdridge Lane and Clewers Hill, then described as the 'royal road from Bottelie to Waltham' (The present road to Bishop's Waltham was a lane called Parkestretelane.)[22] The most frequented route was to and from Winchester. An ancient road followed what we know as Pondside Lane to Vernon Hill and so to Stephen's Castle Down and Morestead to enter Winchester at Bar End. It was this route which was followed by the cortege carrying the body of William of Wykeham for burial in Winchester Cathedral in 1404. Why we may wonder were the routes to Curdridge and Winchester apparently so round about: probably to avoid entering the bishop's Park, which was in any case surrounded by the Lug which would have provided an insurmountable obstacle.[23]

A second route to Winchester went through Upham to White Hill, Green Hill, Baybridge, Owslebury and so to Morestead. Even today stretches of this road run far below the surrounding fields suggesting centuries of wearing down by carts and coaches. Manorial officials travelling to and from Winchester may have used another ancient route through Lower Upham to Marwell.[24] The medieval road to Southampton lay not through Botley, where there was no bridge over the river Hamble until the end of the eighteenth century, but through Durley to enter Southampton at West End. The route through Hoe and Swanmore to St Clair's Farm described as the Royal Road is also an ancient one.

The manor was farmed, like all medieval manors, using the open field system in which villains had a number of strips in two or three common fields and rights in the meadow and on the common. Each tithing must have had its own open fields though we do not know exactly where they were. It was however possible for an enterprising villein to build up a considerable compact holding, perhaps through the death without issue of fellow villains. Mark Page suggests that conditions on the manor of Bishop's Waltham were favourable to this kind of accumulation. He cites William Buss who in 1332 had a holding of about 84 acres. Later holders added to this estate further land acquired by marriage and surrender until in 1409–10 William Stake had a tenement of 173 acres. The name Stakes Farm and Stakes Lane (off the Winchester Road in Lower Upham) survive in the twenty-first century as reminders of an enterprising peasant of 600 years ago.[25]

The traditional account of the lay-out of the town makes it a medieval grid-iron town with four parallel streets running south to north from St George's Square – Brook Street, High Street, Houchin Street and Basingwell Street – with French Street, now Bank Street, crossing east-west at the north end. David Lloyd, writer and lecturer on architectural topics and an authority on South Hampshire, who wrote the section on Bishop's Waltham in the Pevsner volume *Buildings of England: Hampshire* questions this traditional interpretation on the ground that the streets are too narrow and the plots of garden or land behind each house are too small. Houchin Street for example runs far too close to High Street to allow for reasonable length gardens.

He compares Bishop's Waltham with three other local 'mini-towns', Botley, Wickham and Titchfield each, like Bishop's Waltham, a market centre in the later middle ages. The other three have an open space where a market could be held.

Perhaps Bishop's Waltham was, he suggests, originally the same. If he is correct what remains of the market place is now St George's Square. Originally the central space would have extended from Brook Street to Houchin Street and from the Square to French Street used perhaps for market stalls. Basingwell Street would have been a back lane parallel to the market place. Building plots on both sides of the High Street represent later encroachments made either in the Middle Ages or as late as the seventeenth century.[26] Barbara Biddell supports David Lloyd's view suggesting that the market area was built over in the mid-seventeenth century.[27]

It has also been suggested that the area at the junction of Shore Lane, Bank Street, and Green Lane near the *White Hart* and the *Wheatsheaf* may once have been a hamlet which was engulfed by the expanding town in the eighteenth century or earlier.[28]

The medieval rentals of the Waltham manors translated by Harold Barstow contain names of places which we recognise in present day Bishop's Waltham. The rental for 1332 includes references to 'Northbrouce' and to 'Highestrete'. Robert Robmas has a cottage at Shorelane and William Giles owns a cottage and a curtilage (a piece of land of about ½ an acre attached to a dwelling house) next to the fishpond as do Roger le Carpenter and Stephen le Tanner. In 1464 there is reference to a 'messuage between two royal roads called lanes coming from the exit of Northbroke Water the…one road goes toward the town of Waltham and the other road …leads to the Butts situated at the boundary of the Frestrete of Waltham'. There is reference to ' the toft and ferling of bond land containing 10 acres' and to the cottage and garden of the rector of Waltham, Nicholas Belle (1453–87). Frenche Street leads to Church Lane. Another royal road leads to the mill of the lord called Estmylle. There are references to the common fields of Waltham – Est feld and Westfeld. Other names which we recognise include 'the Backstrete called Houchon street', 'Brokestrete', 'Basselewell Lane', 'Roverigge' (perhaps the medieval spelling of Rareridge), 'the Lord's River', 'the Great Pond of Waltham Manor' and 'the Market Place of Waltham', whilst reference to Thomas Frenshe perhaps accounts for the name of French Street.[29]

The present church of St Peter was begun by Henry of Blois in 1136 and its building was probably part of his overall plan for the town. It was laid out on a substantial scale as befitted the church close to an important episcopal residence which was also the mother church of a *parochia* which included Upham, Durley, Bursledon and perhaps Droxford. It had a large nave and a chancel rather shorter than the one we see today. The north aisle was not built until the seventeenth century. The plan survived but not the stones themselves. No part of the present building is earlier than 1200 though fragments of the original south arcade capitals were found during the restoration of 1896–7 and can be seen below the pulpit.[30]

9. *(facing page)* The Parish Registers kept from 1612. Entries for 1626 & 1627

1626. & 1627.

C. Thomas ye sonne of Richard Caut of Curdrig was baptized ye 26. of December.
C. Philipp ye sonne of John Woodman of Hoe was baptized ye first of Januarie.
C. Joane ye daughter of Robert Barfoot of Ashton was baptized ye 7. of Januarie.
C. Anne ye daughter of Richard Randall was baptized ye 14. of Januarie.
C. Thomas ye sonne of Henry Penn was baptized ye 21. of Januarie.
m. Thomas Cleverlie & Margerie Brasset were married ye 22. of Januarie.
m. John Purdeau & Elizabeth Morgan were married die supra-script.
m. Stephen Cooly widower & Mary Gale were married ye 29. of Januarie.
C. John ye sonne of Joane Danbury borne in fornicacion was baptized ye 2. of Februarie.
C. William ye sonne of William Bithil was baptized ye 4. of Februarie.
C. John ye sonne of Niat Warren was baptized ye 11. of Februarie.
B. Edward ye sonne of Ambrose Dee was buried ye 11. of Februarie.
B. William Coles of Durley was buried ye 18. of Februarie.
C. John ye sonne of Richard Trod of Ashton was baptized ye 18. of Februarie.
C. Anne ye daughter of Richard Turner was baptized ye 25. of February.
C. William ye sonne of John Woodman was baptized die supradict.
B. Alice ye wife of Richard Wiltshyre sen. was buried ye first of March.
C. Cathryn ye daughter of Henry Smith was baptized ye 4. of March.
C. John ye sonne of John Caut jun. was baptized ye 4. of March.
C. John ye sonne of William Ryues was baptized ye 10. of March.
C. Mariell ye daughter of John Skinner was baptized ye 11. of March.
B. Thomas ye sonne of Thomas Vees was buried ye 11. of March.
C. Francis ye daughter of Thomas Pepering was baptized ye 13. of March.
B. John ye sonne of William Ryues was buried ye 19. of March.
B. Alice ye daughter of Elizabeth Cleverley was buried ye 20. of March.
B. Thomas Scotcher of Curdrig widower was buried ye 21. of March.
C. Martha ye daughter of German Goldfinch was baptized ye 24. of March.

Christenings ———— 40.
Burials ———— 24.
Marriages ———— 5.

Anno Dm 1627. et regni regis Caroli Secundo

C. Andrew ye sonne of Henry Freind of Ashton was baptized martij 27°.
B. Widow Coles of Curdrig was buried ye last of March.
B. Hannah ye daughter of William Munday was buried ye 15. of April.
B. William ye sonne of John Woodman was buried ye 15. of April.
B. Alice ye daughter of Richard Freind was buried ye 17. of April.
C. Anne ye daughter of William Bound of Curdrig was baptized ye 22. of April.
C. Elizabeth ye daughter of Raphe Ring was baptized die supra-dict.
M. Raphe Hurson & Alice Grante were married ye 26. of April.
C. Mary ye daughter of Robert Knight of Curdrig was baptized Aprilis 29°.
B. Widow Bigbrook was buried die supra-dict.
C. Joane ye daughter of Richard Cosyn jun: of Hoe was baptized maij 9°.
B. A child of Richard Freinds unbaptized was buried maij 10.
m. Robert Eyles and Anne Fisher were married ye 21. of May.
B. Francis Hacket of Curdrig was buried ye 28. of May.
B. Richard Giuer of Curdrig was buried ye first of June.
B. Thomas ye sonne of Henry Penn was buried Junij 5.
C. Mary ye daughter of Henry Cleverley was baptized Junij 10.
B. Walter Bois was buried ye 23. of June.
B. John Vilson was buried ye first day of July.
C. Robert ye sonne of Thomas Woodman of Hoe was baptized ye 8. of July.
B. Thomas ye sonne of Niat Warren was buried ye 22. of July.
B. Henry Freind of Curdrig was buried ye 5. of August.
B. A child of Richard Stubbingtons jun. of Ashton unbaptized was buried die supra-dict.
C. James ye sonne of Maurice Martyn was baptized ye 5th of September.
C/B. William ye sonne of Edward Holt of Curdrig was baptized 16° Septembris. And buried ye of March foll.
M. John Haisler and Alice Prior widow were married Septembris 24°.
C. Robert ye sonne of Robert Biggs was baptized Septembris 27.
C. William ye sonne of William Cobb was baptized ye last of September. And buried 14. of
M. ...ford and Margaret Porter were married ye 8. of October.

Bishop Henry gave the advowson (the right to appoint the rector) to his foundation of the Hospital of St Cross, at Winchester and provided clues to the nature of the new building: 'The church of the Blessed Peter at Waltham which we have removed from a low lying and narrow place to a high and spacious place and have rebuilt at our own expense, we have given and granted to the House of the Hospital of the Holy Cross Winchester for the refreshment of the Poor of Christ with two hides of land lying next to the same Church.[31] The right of presentation reverted to the bishop by 1284 and it remained with him until 1927.

We know little about the church in the middle ages though there is a list of rectors from 1289 drawn from the Episcopal Registers of the Bishops of Winchester. (see Appendix A) They were priests, expected to be celibate from the decree of Archbishop Lanfranc in 1076. They farmed the glebe and collected their tithes but where they lived we do not know. They may not all have been resident and if that was the case the parish would have been served by unbeneficed curates. The Pipe Roll of 1302 includes a list of the possessions of the church, things necessary for the performance of worship – missal, alb with a hood, maniple, stole, chasuble, chalice and paten and an altar frontal of silk.[32] The main Sunday service was Mass and in the afternoon Evensong. During the week there would be daily Mass to which a few parishioners came. There may have been a clerk who helped to sing the services.

William of Wykeham bishop from 1367–1404 was a local boy and the Palace was not surprisingly his favourite residence He embellished St Peter's, lengthening the chancel and building a south porch at the west end of the church. He also provided an aumbry in the north wall of the chancel and a piscina in the south wall.[33]

After the death of William of Wykeham in 1404 silence once more descends. Over a century later, in September 1525, Gilbert Burton was appointed rector and remained so for 41 years through the later years of Henry VIII, the reigns of Edward VI and Mary and into the early years of Elizabeth I. Bishop's Waltham was a good living though not perhaps a rich one. According to the *Valor Ecclesiasticus* (a valuation of church livings made in 1535) Bishop's Waltham was worth £26.5.10½.[34] But Bishop's Waltham was not Gilbert Burton's only parish. In 1524 he had become rector of North Waltham worth £15.13.4.[35] When in 1562 Archbishop Parker asked the bishops of the southern province to provide a list of their parishes and incumbents Gilbert Burton was described as *non coniugatus* (not married), and in reply to where he lived – *ubi deget?* – the bishop's answer was – *in rectoria sua de North Waltham* – in his rectory at North Waltham. But that was not all. There was a further question – 'How many benefices has he?' To which the answer was 'four'. Burton was a pluralist on some scale. We do not know where his other two parishes were though not, it appears, in the diocese of Winchester. He was it seems tight-fisted: in 1533 his curate at Waltham wrote to Lady Lisle asking for the gown cloth which she had apparently promised him: 'You have so many whelps pertaining to you that poor Thomas Gilbert shall be forgotten'.[36] In 1541 there were curates at both Bishop's Waltham – Richard Knyght – and at North Waltham – Robert Nicholson. [37]

In Gilbert Burton Bishop's Waltham had its own Vicar of Bray – a man who continued in office whatever the ecclesiastical complexion of the day. He was not the only local priest with more than one parish: William Overton, one of the few local priests to be married, held the livings of Upham and Exton and in 1560 added that of Nursling though he appears to be living in Winchester.[38]

For lack of documentary evidence we are left to imagine the changes which must have taken place during these years. In the 1530s there would have been a holy water stoup at the entrance to the church, a rood screen and loft – bearing the figure of the crucified Christ – at the entry to the chancel, wall paintings and stained glass windows telling the story of salvation and holding out the hope of heaven and the threat of hell. Mass would have been celebrated in Latin, the priest facing the stone altar and wearing a chasuble. There would have been a multitude of feast days and catholic practices to which the priest at Waltham would instinctively adhere. Some twelve years later all that began to change.

The Bible in English was placed in all churches on the orders of Thomas Cromwell in 1538. Less than a decade later the mass vestments were replaced by surplice and stole, and on Whitsunday 1549 the first Book of Common Prayer in English was ordered to be used in place of the Latin Missal and became the only permissible service book. The accession of Edward VI in 1547 saw the Reformation go further. Stone altars and stained glass were often smashed and replaced by wooden tables and plain glass, wall paintings were lime-washed and monuments demolished or defaced.

The accession of Queen Mary in 1553 meant a return to papal allegiance and catholic worship – but only briefly. The accession of Elizabeth I five years later witnessed a final round of changes. The Prayer Book of 1559 was introduced and the rood screen if it had survived or been restored was dismantled once and for all. The wooden altar and the sanctuary rails in use today at St Peter's date from the early Elizabethan period.[39] Since the people now received both bread and wine at Holy Communion a larger chalice would be needed and bread was substituted for wafers. Perhaps scriptural texts, the Lord's Prayer and the Ten Commandments were inscribed on either side of the Holy Table which may have been placed lengthwise in the chancel. Commissioners toured the country to ensure compliance but this was scarcely needed at Bishop's Waltham with a Protestant bishop installed at the Palace.

How did the curate and people react to these changes? Did they welcome the appointment of John Poynet first Protestant bishop of Winchester (1551–1553)? Three consecutive bishops ended up in the Tower of London for opposite reasons – Stephen Gardiner in 1548 under Edward VI and John White under Elizabeth for adhering to the Catholic faith and John Poynet in 1556 under Queen Mary for being a Protestant. Were the citizens of Bishop's Waltham pleased when Queen Mary released Bishop Gardiner from the Tower of London and reinstated him as bishop of Winchester?

The Act of Uniformity passed in 1559 required everybody to attend services which used the Book of Common Prayer and prescribed a fine of 12 pence for those who did not do so. In 1581 this was increased to the enormous sum of £20 per month – not far off £1000 in modern currency. There were two categories of offender: 'recusants' who refused to attend church at all because they were convinced catholics and 'church-papists' who attended church as a legal requirement but would not receive the Holy Communion of the Church of England perhaps because bread rather than wafers was used signifying a doctrinal change from the Mass.

Robert Horne who became bishop of Winchester in February 1561 and remained in office until 1579 was a Puritan and strong anti-papist. He faced an uphill struggle and encountered particularly strong opposition from his see city of Winchester. He had been chaplain to Edward VI and spent the reign of Queen Mary in Zurich, Frankfurt and Strasburg. He wrestled with the problem of finding sufficient suitable clergy to fill the places of those deprived for their catholic sympathies in the 1560s. Many of his ordinations were held in the chapel of Waltham Palace.[40]

Bishop Horne made determined efforts to remove all trace of Roman Catholicism from his diocese. He objected to a vicar who brought 'corpses to church with candles and tapers'. He ordered a rector to 'preach against auricular, idolatrous confession'. In April 1569 the rectors of Meonstoke, John Brereton (who had been a Marian priest) and Droxford, John Williams, were ordered to preach against 'papistical depravity, the usurped jurisdiction of the Pope and the private Mass.'[41]

It seems likely that Bishop's Waltham toed the Protestant line not least because the bishop lived much of the time in Bishop's Waltham Palace and his wife – he was the first married bishop of Winchester – may have worshipped at St Peter's. She was certainly buried on the south side of the sanctuary when she died in 1575. The inscription, now illegible, read *'Margeria hic recubat, conjux quae praesulis Horni. Una exul Christi, vera Tabitha fuit'*. ('Here lies Margery, the wife of Bishop Horne. Once an exile for Christ, she was a true Tabitha' – a reference to Acts chapter 9)[42] When the Bishop himself died four years later he was buried in Winchester Cathedral and is also described on his tomb as 'Formerly an exile for the sake of Christ'.

Gilbert Burton's successor as rector of Bishop's Waltham was John Bridges the only rector of Bishop's Waltham to become a diocesan bishop and also the first to be married – to Jane Davey; they were married in October 1592. He was born about 1535, became a Fellow of Pembroke Hall, Cambridge and a Doctor of Divinity in 1575. He held a number of parish appointments in Kent, Berkshire and Hampshire including Cheriton which was worth £66.2.4½ as well as Bishop's Waltham where he was rector from 1566–76 He made his name as a prolific pamphleteer attacking both Catholics and Calvinists. He has a long entry in the Dictionary of National Biography but Bishop's Waltham is not mentioned. He was probably another non-resident rector. He became Dean of Salisbury in 1577 and was Bishop of Oxford from 1604, and unlike his predecessors lived in his diocese, until his death 'at a great age' in 1618.[43]

His successor at Bishop's Waltham was William Singleton who had been ordained by Bishop Horne in the Palace chapel in October 1569. He too held a number of livings but was probably the first resident rector for half a century. His burial is recorded in the first Parish Register: 'Mr William Singleton person [parson]was buried 2 December 1619'.

About the attitude of Bishop's Waltham laity to the changes taking place in their church during the Reformation we know little. In 1574 according to episcopal records there were 47 non-communicants in the parish – a relatively high number though most of them probably attended church but refused Holy Communion.[44] By the end of the century there were only three recusants at Bishop's Waltham, comparable with the number in most local parishes except Hambledon where there were 17.[45] It appears that by the end of the reign of Elizabeth the great majority conformed at least outwardly to the Church of England. How many still had private reservations we have no means of knowing.

It was that arch-bureaucrat of the reign of Henry VIII, Thomas Cromwell, who in 1538 ordered 'every parson, vicar or curate of every Church to kepe one boke or register wherein ye shall write the day and yere of every wedding, christening and burying made within yowr parish for yowr time and so every man succedyng you likewise'. (Spellings original) To store the registers the parish must provide 'a sure coffer' with two locks, one to be held by the parson and the other by the churchwardens. Entries were to be made each Sunday after service in the presence of the churchwardens. In the early years records were often kept on loose sheets which were easily lost or mislaid so in 1598 the government of Elizabeth I ordered the records to be copied on parchment into a book. Like the earlier instruction it was not always carried out.[46]

At St Peter's there are no surviving registers before 1612.[47] They were either not kept or have been lost. From 1612 they have been kept without a break. The first register contains a record of christenings, marriages and burials in date order (usually) but not divided by category, each identifiable only by the letters C, M or B before the entry. The heading on the first page reads 'The names and forenames of all such as have been Christened, Married or Buried since the 25 of March 1612 within the parish of B.Waltham in the county of South.'[48] Parchment was expensive and so in the early years the writing is very small, sometimes so small that you wonder how the clerk could write in so minute a hand. The maximum number of entries is crammed on each page – sometimes over 60 lines. The Registers of St Peter's were from the beginning kept in English in contrast for example with the registers of Durley which were kept in Latin until 1748.[49]

Although the registers do not begin until 1612 there is a summary at the end of the first volume, now scarcely legible, of important events in the history of the church from 1582 to 1669. It is repeated in the second and third registers under the heading 'Remarkable occurrences', a reminder that contemporaries realised that the registers kept in the parish chest were the surest way of informing posterity of significant happenings. The number of christenings, marriages and burials is totalled each year, christenings easily outnumbering burials which suggests that the population must have been growing steadily in this period.

The first event listed in the back cover of the first register reads: 'The Steeple and Tower of ye Church fell down ye last Day of December 1582. And began to be re-edified in 1584. And was finished 1589'. Why did the tower collapse and was its fall foreseen? Was anyone hurt? St Peter's has a peal of eight bells but only two were placed in the tower immediately after the rebuilding. The tenor bell is inscribed '*O Laude the Lord. J.W. 1597*' and the seventh bell '*Prayse the Lord. J.W. 1599*'.[50] Change ringing must have been a later development in the parish.

From 1619 to 1626 the Bishop of Winchester was Lancelot Andrewes one of the seminal figures in the early history of the Church of England, notable as preacher, saint and scholar and known to posterity for his *Preces Privatae* (Private Prayers).He was also a high churchman who, according to the Puritan pamphleteer William Prynne, adorned his chapels at the Palace and elsewhere with 'Popish Furniture' – silver candlesticks, censer and incense boat, cruets for water as well as wine,and bason and ewer for the priest's ablutions before the consecration.[51] During his short episcopate he was responsible for presenting two men of academic distinction to the living of Bishop's Waltham.

Andrewes' first appointment to Bishop's Waltham was Nicholas Fuller (1619–22) an outstanding Hebrew scholar, at that time a rare accomplishment. Born in Southampton in 1557 he became at an early age secretary to Bishop Horne. He took his degree at Oxford and then held the living of Allington in Wiltshire and became a canon of Salisbury Cathedral. He died at Allington in February 1622. During the three years he was rector of Bishop's Waltham it is unlikely that he lived in the parish – another non-resident parish priest.

The next rector was also a considerable scholar. Dr. Robert Ward had been the bishop's tutor at Pembroke College, Cambridge and it was thorough him according to Charles Walters that Andrewes was 'bred to learning'.[52] Lancelot Andrewes, was one of the translators of the King James Bible, Director of the First Westminster Company responsible for the early books of the Old Testament. Robert Ward was a member of the Second Cambridge Company which undertook the initial translation of the Apocrypha. When Andrewes was bishop of Chichester he made Ward a prebendary of Chichester Cathedral and when he came to Winchester rector of Bishop's Waltham (1623–29).

In the year before he died Lancelot Andrewes gave to Robert Ward the handsome pulpit which is the single most distinguished item of furniture in St Peter's.[53] Robert Ward was buried on the south side of the sanctuary alongside the wife of Bishop Horne. As Charles Walters comments, 'The Church of Waltham …contains what only 47 others in England can possess, the remains of a translator of the Bible'.[54]

Lancelot Andrewes died at Winchester House in Southwark, which belonged to the Bishops of Winchester and was buried in St Saviour's church, now Southwark Cathedral in 1626.

Andrewes' successor, although only briefly, was Richard Neile (1628–32) who had the unique distinction of holding successively no less than five bishoprics. He was bishop of Lichfield, Lincoln and Durham before he came to Winchester and in 1632 he left Winchester to become Archbishop of York. He no doubt owed his promotions to being 'a strenuous partisan of Archbishop Laud'. While he was bishop of Winchester he presented his son Richard to two of the richest livings in his diocese – Droxford in 1628 and Hambledon in 1629.

It was soon after Walter Curll became bishop of Winchester and Benjamin Lang was rector that a further alteration was made to St Peter's. 'The North Isle of ye Church was built to enlarge ye Church 1637', reads the entry in the Parish Register. It is believed that stone from the now disused chapel attached to the house at Ashton belonging to the Master of St Cross Hospital in Winchester was used in the building. In addition to stone and tiles a fine coloured alabaster monument to Thomas Ashton who had died in 1629 was brought to St Peter's and is now high on the north wall of the north aisle. It reads:

Thomas Ashton

Who	*Anne*
After he had lived	*His desolate and disconsolate relict*
57 years providentlie	*Hath erected this monument*
Born his sickness patientlie	*Of his dissolution the 7 of August 1629*
Disposed of his estate Charitablie	*Of her resolution to wayte*
Ended his life christianlie	*All the days of her appointed time*
Lieth heer interred decentlie	*Until her change shall come.*

Thomas Ashton asked to be buried in the 'Church of Waltham', and left 20 marks for a 'monument of brass with such an epitaph as Robert Moore, Doctor of Divinity shall think fit'. Anne Ashton commemorated her husband not with a brass monument but with a more expensive one made of alabaster with the inscription presumably composed by his friend Robert Moore, a prebendary of Winchester cathedral. Thomas Ashton was buried in St Peter's on 16th August 1629 which suggests that the monument must have been here before the north aisle was built. Was the aisle perhaps named after Thomas Ashton rather than after the chapel from which the building material came? [55]

There is a further mystery about the Ashton aisle. At its west end is a gallery which was built at the same time as the aisle. It can be reached not only by an internal staircase but by an external one in a projecting buttress over which is the date '1637'. Why was the room added and why did it have an external entrance? It is usually said that it was to provide access for a school which met there but the grammar school which might have used it was not endowed until 1679 over 40 years later [56] Perhaps there was an earlier school?

3
After the Palace 1644–1759

BISHOP'S WALTHAM had no Samuel Pepys to provide an eye-witness account of the state of shock experienced by its citizens following the burning of the Bishop's Palace and the escape of Bishop Walter Curll. From being the centre of affairs with an episcopal residence dominating the town and visits of notabilities from time to time Bishop's Waltham became a small Hampshire market town different from others only in that it had a distinguished past. When Bishop Walter Curll died in 1647 there was no longer even a bishop of Winchester in exile. The sack of the palace and the death of the bishop were not the last shocks for the people of Bishop's Waltham. In January 1645 parliament replaced the Book of Common Prayer with the Presbyterian Directory of Public Worship, in October 1646 episcopacy was abolished and on 30th January 1649 the king was executed.

'The history of Waltham,' wrote Charles Walters two centuries later, 'is that of the great, the wise and the good; of kings, potentates, prelates, the brave in fight, the wise in council, the patrons of learning, the encouragers of the arts, the benefactors of the human race…' but it cannot have felt like that in the 1640s.[1] By the end of the decade the old landmarks had all gone: monarchy, House of Lords and the Church of England. If you were a royalist as was Dr Joseph Goulston, rector of Bishop's Waltham, and most of his parishioners you kept your head down and hoped for better times.[2]

Joseph Goulston became rector in January 1642 just before the outbreak of the Civil War and must therefore have been a witness to the sack of the Palace. He survived through the bewildering changes of the next quarter of a century into the reign of Charles II. But it was a close run thing. He was suspect as a convinced royalist and was summoned to appear before the Committee of Plundered Ministers in April 1646 but kept his living. Two years later he journeyed to Newport Isle of Wight to preach before the king. In 1655 he was still on the Major Generals' list of suspects and was fortunate not to have his living sequestered. In the nearby parish of Upham the rector, Myrth Wayferer, lost his living in 1658 and Matthew Stocke was intruded for the duration of the Commonwealth.[3]

If William Singleton is the first rector whose burial appears in the Parish Registers

Joseph Goulston is the first whose children were christened and buried at St Peter's. Between 1645 and 1655 the rector and his wife had eight children, three of whom died in infancy – Clemence, Joseph and John and there is a memorial to them on the north wall of the chancel at St Peter's. When sometime after Clemence's death another girl was born she too was named Clemence. Parents often named a child after a sibling who had died. In some parishes baptism ceased altogether during the Commonwealth in protest at the abolition of the Prayer Book service. At Bishop's Waltham the registers were kept without interruption and the number of baptisms does not fluctuate from the period before and afterwards, which may suggest that the rector continued – illegally – to use the Prayer Book during the Commonwealth.

Dr Goulston – he was made Doctor of Divinity at Oxford in 1643 – was rewarded for his loyalty when Charles II returned. He was made a canon of Winchester Cathedral by Bishop Brian Duppa and in 1663 was appointed Precentor and Dean of Chichester cathedral though remaining rector of Bishop's Waltham. Whether he resided in the parish and how he combined his several posts we do not know. In 1668 he resigned from Bishop's Waltham on being appointed rector of Felpham near Chichester but died the following year.[4]

During the Commonwealth parliament confiscated the possessions of the bishops and the manor of Bishop's Waltham which had belonged to the bishops of Winchester since 904 was bought by Robert Reynolds for £7,999. Meanwhile the churchwardens took advantage of the derelict state of the Palace to undertake work on the fabric of St Peter's. The first Parish Register lists three embellishments to the building which took place during the next few years. In 1651 'the three small Bells were new cast and ye ring made tuneable'; perhaps the bell metal came from the Palace. The following year 'The South isle of ye Church was taken down and new built and enlarged', probably with stone from the Palace. Finally in 1669 'The roof of ye middle Isle was made new and ceiled ...'. This presumably means that the timbers were renewed but were not visible until the ceiling was removed in 1869.[5] Finally, though not mentioned in the register, it was at this time that St Peter's acquired the handsome fourteenth century clock, also from the Palace, which is still a feature of the church.

The restoration of Charles II in 1660 was seen by the Church of England as a deliverance and was duly commemorated in the Book of Common Prayer by a form of service which was in use yearly from 1662 until 1859. It was ponderously entitled 'A Form of Prayer with Thanksgiving to Almighty God for having put an end to the Great Rebellion, by the Restoration of the Government after many years Interruption; which unspeakable mercies were wonderfully completed upon the Twenty-ninth day of May, in the Year 1660.'[6] Churches were required to erect the royal arms and St Peter's was no exception – the arms of Charles II are still in the church though relegated to a wall over the school gallery and not often noticed,

Those appointed to the more prestigious bishoprics after the Restoration were naturally enough men who had been conspicuously loyal to the Stuarts. Brian Duppa bishop of Salisbury spent the years from 1653 at the court of the exiled Stuarts and was rewarded by translation to the richer and more prestigious bishopric of Winchester in 1660. He may have intended to restore Bishop's Waltham Palace as the residence of the bishop. He was however already 72 in 1660 and died after only 18 months in office. His successor George Morley, who had preached the Coronation Sermon for Charles II in April 1661, had other ideas. Bishop's Waltham Palace was in his view beyond recovery and Southwark House the Bishop's London residence had also sustained damage in the recent troubles.

He embarked instead on the restoration of Wolvesey and Farnham Castles and the latter became the main residence of the bishops of Winchester and remained so until the division of the diocese in 1927. He also bought for £4000 a new brick house in the manor of Chelsea stipulating that it was not to be subject to the jurisdiction of the bishop of London or of the dean and chapter of Westminster Abbey.[7] Bishop's Waltham Palace remained a ruin. It became a source of building stone for the rebuilding of the bishop's other residences and plunder for local people though remaining the property of the bishop down to 1869.

The park which had belonged to the bishop for at least 500 years ceased to exist. It was split up and leased for periods of 21 years to tenant farmers. One hundred acres were given to the rector of Bishop's Waltham tithe free and remained part of his emoluments until 1909. Cookes Farm, Lodge Farm, Russells Farm and Tangier Farm were among the farms which came into existence at this time. Tangier Farm owes its name to the port of Tangier in Morocco which was part of the dowry of Catherine of Braganza when she married Charles II in 1662 [8]

When in 1664 the bishop leased Cookes Farm he reserved the right 'to cut dig or make Drains Dykes Watercourses Trenches sewers canals and Receptacles for water through any parte of the land meadow and pasture ground…' to make possible the carriage of goods ' from the towne of Bishopps Waltham …to and from the Sea at or neere Botley'. *(original spelling)*

The following year saw an Act of Parliament 'for making divers rivers navigable'[9] The 'divers rivers', included in Hampshire the Itchen, the Test and the Hamble. Only one canal was ever constructed, the Itchen Navigation from Southampton to Winchester.[10] The proposed Hamble Navigation never materialised. It is likely that the practicalities of building were not considered either before or after the passing of the Act. As David Chunn writes 'It was … only one of a seeming rag bag of southern rivers dealt with by the statute… and the reservation of rights in the 1664 lease signifies nothing more than an episcopal pipe-dream'.[11]

When Charles II was restored in 1660 parliament reckoned that he needed £1,200,000 for peacetime expenditure. The financial settlement failed however to generate sufficient and so after long debate parliament hit on the idea of the hearth tax. The occupier would pay a levy of 2/- on each hearth or stove in his house in two six monthly instalments. Those who did not pay poor rate or church rate and some others were exempt. It was intended as a temporary expedient but despite its unpopularity it was not abolished until 1689.

Apart from being one of the oddest means of raising taxes – and one never previously tried in England nor repeated – its interest lies in the information which the records provide – a directory of all householders in the parish in the mid-1660s. Everybody who paid the tax was listed as well as those exempted and alongside each name was the number of hearths which the house contained. Unfortunately there is not much more information – houses are not identified, street names are not listed nor occupations included. Occasionally there is an indication of status – Mr., esquire, widow, gentleman, for example.

Hearth tax returns are often used to estimate population. But what multiplier should be applied to convert number of households into number of people? The accepted figure is 4.5. Applied to the tithings of Bishop's Waltham this gives a population of 1300, close to the figure for the same period derived from other sources.(see Appendix B). The number of hearths is also an indicator of poverty and affluence. About one third of all houses in the parish are recorded as having one hearth. This probably means a single combined kitchen and living room. Rather under a further third had two hearths. This means that approaching two thirds of all households were living below the poverty line and many of them were exempt from paying the hearth tax.

At the other end of the scale was 'Mr Peter Browne' with nine hearths. The rector Dr Goulston had seven hearths and he was also assessed for hearth tax on the ten hearths in his substantial house in the Close at Winchester. His neighbour the rector of Upham was even better off. In addition to seven hearths in his rectory he had no less than thirteen hearths in his house in the Close. The returns list surnames many of which go through centuries of the town's life – Cleverly, Barfoot, Dipnell, Penford, Prowting, Trodd, Peperinge, Stubbington – for example.[12]

Dr.Goulston was followed as rector by Robert Sharrock (1669–1684). On the north side of the sanctuary of St Peter's are memorials to members of his family, eminently readable and composed in English rather than the Latin which had up to this time been more usual for funerary inscriptions. Robert Sharrock was the friend of Robert Boyle, one of the founders of the Royal Society and in 1663 he edited Boyle's *Usefulness of Natural Philosophy* [13] His burial is recorded in the Parish Register on 13th July 1684.

Francis Morley, who succeeded Robert Sharrock, was a nephew of Bishop George Morley. Born in 1657 he was educated at Christ Church, Oxford, was rector of Wroughton, Wiltshire and Meonstoke before he came to Bishop's Waltham in 1684. In the same year he was appointed a canon of Winchester.

There is a curious entry in the Poor Rate book dated 9th November 1684. 'It is agreed between Francis Morley, Rector of Bp.'s Waltham and the inhabitants thereof, that whereas there was an anhint (*sic 'ancient'*) custom that the Rector should

10. Extract from Poor Rate Book 1656 containing signatures of Joseph Goulston, Rector, John Woodman and James Hampton, Churchwardens.

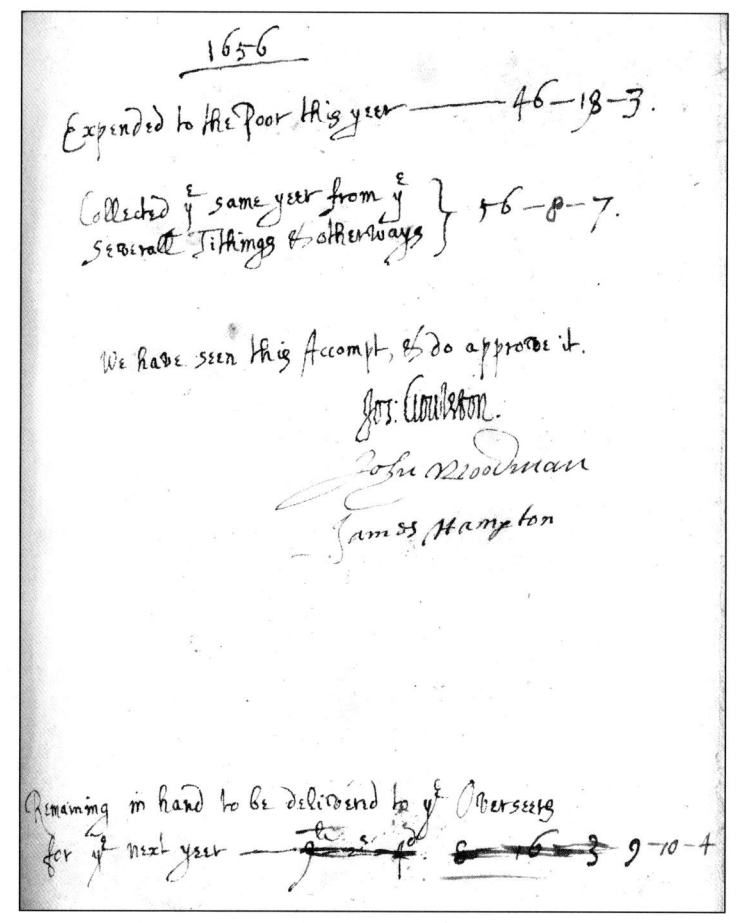

give an hogshead of beer to the parishioners upon Christmas day yearly, now in lieu of that the Rector is obliged to give forty shillings p. annum to the poor to be distributed according to the dicishon *(sic)* of the churchwardens and overseers. In confirmation whereof we have set our hands'. There follow the signatures of 'Fran. Morley, Rector' and eleven parishioners of whom three make their mark. The custom of the rector presenting the parish with a hogshead of beer probably dated from the days of church ales by now frowned upon.

Four years later there was a crisis in the affairs of the parish. The sexton and one of the churchwardens were excommunicated by the bishop, Peter Mews (1684–1706) for some offence which is not specified. They continued however to hold the keys to the church so that neither the rector nor parishioners could gain entry. In a letter to the rector Francis Morley the bishop instructs him to call a parish meeting and demand the return of the keys. Should they not be handed over he and the remaining churchwardens are authorised to bring the delinquents before a magistrate and in the meantime to fit a new lock on the church door so that services could be held and the

11. List of Churchwardens, Overseers of the Poor and Surveyors (incomplete) 1709–1713 from Poor Rate Book.

12. 'The New Key' made on the instructions of the Bishop of Winchester 1688.

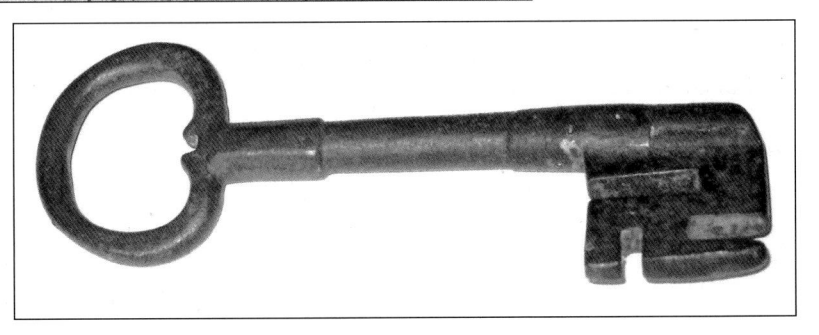

church plate kept in safety. In future the bishop decrees that the posts of parish clerk, sexton and gravedigger should be combined. Finally he requires this letter to be kept 'in the publick chest or Repository where the ancient Writings and Records relating to the said Parish are preserved' – which no doubt explains why these two documents were copied into the new Register. The new lock can be seen in the large south door of the church and the key is among the treasures of St Peter's.[14]

Between the beginning of the eighteenth century and the middle of the nineteenth many churches built galleries. They rarely enhanced the beauty of the building and were frequently dismantled as part of Victorian restoration. St Peter's had two galleries built 60 years apart, one in 1733 which survives and the second in 1797 which was demolished a century later. Both caused considerable trouble.

What is usually called 'the Faculty Gallery' was erected at the west end of the church at the request of 'William Horner, Peter Newlyn, John Nash, Richard Biggs and Harry Willis…Inhabitants of the said parish who are desirous to have Seat Room in the Church there to sitt (*sic*) together to sing Psalms'. They proposed 'to erect and set up at their own proper Costs and Charges a Gallery in a void place at the West End of the said church to be divided into eight seats or Pews … also for the Singers to Stand, Sit and kneel therein at the time of Divine Service'. Pews 1,2 and 3 were for the singers, 4,5,6,7, and 8 for initiators of the scheme and the future owners of the houses in which they lived – Northbrook House, St George's House (now Barclays Bank), Vernon Hill House, Mill House and a house in Lower Basingwell Street which is now divided into three.[15]

The gallery was built and the following year Mr William Horner obtained a Father Smith organ from Southwick House and an organ loft was erected above the new gallery. Bishop's Waltham must have been one of the first parish churches in Hampshire to have an organ to accompany the metrical Psalms at Morning and Evening Prayer – no hymns were yet permitted in Anglican worship. A village band, a barrel organ or a pitch pipe were more usual. Bernard Smith was a famous seventeenth century organ builder and a local man; his wife was buried in Upham churchyard in September 1689 at the age of 63. Her tombstone says more about her husband than it does about her, describing him as 'chief of all that this nation has known in the art of organ making'.[16] The organist was Ezekiel Donniger, the first of three generations of Donnigers all called Ezekiel who played the organ at St Peter's over the course of the next century. The name Donniger is still attached to a house and land once owned by the family, now in the parish of Swanmore but then in Bishop's Waltham though the name is now spelt Doniger.

Because of its proximity to Portsmouth, one of the country's leading naval bases, Bishop's Waltham has over many years been the home of senior naval officers. The first of these was Admiral Edward Vernon who lived at the eponymous Vernon Hill House. He was born in 1684, the son of James Vernon, Secretary of State during the reign of William III (1698–1702). He joined the navy at the age of 16 and served in the Mediterranean, the West Indies and the Baltic and became Member of Parliament for the Cornish borough of Penrhyn in 1722. He probably lived at Bishop's Waltham during the 1730s whenever he was not at sea.[17] Vernon returned to sea in the late 1730s and in the War of Jenkins' Ear against Spain was credited with an important victory when he took Porto Bello in the Caribbean, a fame he did not deserve since the Porto Bello garrison surrendered without a fight. He subsequently failed at Cartagena, Santiago in Cuba and Panama.

Admiral Vernon is remembered in the navy for a more mundane achievement: and not a popular one. Concerned at the amount of drunkenness amongst sailors he ordered that the customary rum ration should be diluted with water – half a pint of rum to a quart of water. His nickname in the navy was 'Old Grog' after the grogram cloak he often wore and so the diluted rum ration quickly became 'grog'. Vernon left Bishop's Waltham in the early 1740s to live at Nacton in Suffolk, since he had by then become Member of Parliament for Ipswich, and there built a house named Orwell Park. He died in 1757.[18]

Vernon Hill House, though not with that name, was a small Jacobean manor house. The front of the house was originally on the north side reached through a cobbled yard from the approach road and the windows with small panes and the porch survive from the seventeenth century house. Admiral Vernon made substantial alterations, in particular moving the front of the house from north to south. The

13. Vernon Hill House rear garden (2007)

windows on the south side were replaced by sash window, then fashionable. He built the Georgian entrance porch, erected the balustrades, put in the impressive staircase and the cornice in the drawing room. The original hall with its stone floor and open fireplace is now at the back of the house.

Little is known about the house until it was bought by Arthur Helps in 1847. He added the east wing and built the cottage next to the house for servants. He was a friend of George Lewes the long time partner of George Eliot the author of *Middlemarch* and other novels. She was however never permitted to come to Vernon Hill House on account of the irregular relationship with Lewes which Arthur Helps could not afford to condone on account of his royal connections. [19]

When Arthur Helps died of pleurisy in 1875 the house, which had already been rented, was sold and since then it has not been occupied for long by any one family. Major General Frederick Robert Elkington who had fought in the Crimean War bought it in 1875 and lived there until 1919. In 1939 Brigadier General Bryan James was living at Vernon Hill. In 1948 it was bought from General Curling by Peter and Felicity Legh who brought up their family there. Peter Legh became Member of Parliament for Petersfield in 1951 and remained so until 1960 when – reluctantly – he entered the House of Lords on the death of his father Lord Newton. Vernon Hill was one of the houses whose owners are entitled in perpetuity to a pew in the west gallery of St Peter's. The last occupants of the family pew were Lady Newton and her children in the 1950s (Lord Newton sang in the church choir) [20]

The Waltham Blacks are part of the folklore of Bishop's Waltham though their long-term significance was national rather than local. They were masked men who blacked their faces, wore fur caps and deer skin coats and in the early 1720s terrorised the neighbourhood, burning hayricks and poaching deer, feared in part because nobody was quite sure who they were or what they wanted. Their anonymous leader was 'King John'. Waltham Chase or Horderswood where they operated, was a huge area, some 2000 acres, south and east of Bishop's Waltham largely in the southern part of the parish of Droxford, much of it heavily wooded, criss-crossed by streams and with substantial areas of bog, not unlike parts of the Moors Nature Reserve today but stretching for miles to join Bere Forest. There were rumours that the Waltham Blacks were Jacobites plotting to put James, the Old Pretender, on the throne in place of George I. In March 1723 'King John' and some of his followers announced that they would appear at *The Chase Inn* (now *The Fountain*) A crowd of 300 assembled to meet them and heard 'King John' swear his loyalty to the Hanoverian king George I and publicly disband the Waltham Blacks though they took nine deer while the crowd looked on.

The authorities took the Waltham Blacks seriously enough as a threat to law and order or perhaps a cover for a Jacobite plot to pass the Waltham Black Act (9 George I c.22). It prescribed over 200 offences for which the perpetrator could be hanged. They included burning a house, poaching a rabbit, breaking down the head of a fish pond, and appearing on a high road in disguise, though poaching deer was the commonest capital offence under the Act. It was not until the 1820s that most of the offences specified in the Waltham Black Act were repealed.

The first edition of the Ordnance Survey map of the area dated 1810 shows a gibbet close to *The Chase Inn* which seems likely to have been placed there at the beginning of the eighteenth century. In 1726 Benjamin Rivers was tried at Winchester Assizes, convicted under the act and hanged on the Chase.[21]

The aspect of life in the country in the Middle Ages which we find most strange is the open field system in which land, though owned by the lord of the manor, was held by those who farmed it communally. It was a system which in many places lasted until the eighteenth or even the nineteenth century. 'In 1700' wrote Chapman and Seeliger, 'a large part of Hampshire's arable land still lay in great open fields with each individual's lands scattered in a multitude of tiny unfenced strips'[22] In the middle ages the manor of Bishop's Waltham was divided into ten tithings but we do not know whether each had its own field system and if it did whether there were two or three fields in each system. By the sixteenth century there were four tithings in the parish of Bishop's Waltham and there were open fields in at least three of them – Ashton, Curdridge and Bishop's Waltham. Each probably had two open fields which can be located approximately. Each tithing also had meadow and common land belonging not to individuals but to the community.

Enclosure is the name given to the process by which land held communally came to be held individually (or severally) and the term is applied equally to pasture, meadow and common as well as to arable land. It was a long slow process taking place over hundreds of years and by a variety of means. In many places no record survives. Open fields could be enclosed informally by an arrangement made between the lord of the manor and the other landholders or by formal agreement. In Hampshire about two thirds of the land was enclosed in these ways. The means of enclosure which is best known however is parliamentary enclosure. Until 1836 each scheme required a separate act of parliament – costly and time consuming. When the General Enclosure Act was passed enclosure could take place provided that holders of two thirds of the land agreed. Abuse was possible and from 1845 parliament regained a degree of control through the Inclosure Commission which scrutinised each scheme, (official documents describe the process as Inclosure, spelt with an I)

Much of Hampshire remained in common fields in the sixteenth century. Leland travelling through the county in the 1530s described what he saw: 'From Wickham to Waltham, a pratty towne 3 miles by enclosed ground, good pasture, woods and corne. From Waltham to Winchester 7 miles, 3 by enclosed and woddy grounds and 4 by chaumpaign' [unenclosed land] By 1675 about 30% of land in Hampshire remained in common fields.[23] About 160 parliamentary enclosure acts were passed which concerned land in Hampshire the first at Ropley in 1709 and the last at Alverstoke in 1887.

14. Title page of the Act of Parliament for enclosing arable fields at Ashton 1759

An ACT *for Dividing and Inclosing certain open Arable Fields in the Manor of* Bishops Waltham, *in the County of* Southampton.

Whereas there are in the Manor of *Bishops Waltham*, in the County of *Southampton*, several open arable Common Fields, called *Ashton Field*, *Pilard Field*, and *Oat Field*, containing, by Estimation, Two hundred and Five Acres, or thereabouts: Preamble.

And whereas the Right Reverend Father in God *Benjamin* Lord Bishop of *Winchester*, in Right of his Church and See of *Winchester*, is Lord of the said Manor of *Bishops Waltham*, in the said County of *Southampton*:

And whereas *Daniel Brown*, *Richard Trod*, *Walter Barefoot*, *Richard Eyles*, *David Prowting*, *Thomas Dipnal*, *William Horner*, *William Aylen*, *Catharine Friend*, and others, are the Owners and Proprietors of the Lands and Grounds in the said open arable Common Fields, and have a Right of Common thereon:

And whereas the Lands and Grounds belonging to the several Proprietors in the said Fields, lie intermixed and dispersed, and it would be advantageous to the several Proprietors of, and the Persons intitled to Right of Common in and upon, the said Fields, to have the same divided and inclosed, and a specifick Share allotted to each Proprietor, according to his or her respective Interest therein: But as such Division and Inclosure cannot be effectually made and established, without the Authority of Parliament;

A May

In the parish of Bishop's Waltham there was an act to enclose three fields in Ashton in 1759 – Ashton Field, Pilard Field and Oat Field – arable common fields containing a total of 205 acres. The Act names the eight men and one woman who are among the 'Owners and Proprietors of the land and have Rights of Common', who have sponsored the act. The lands are 'intermixed and dispersed' and it is intended to divide and enclose them 'allotting to each of the named proprietors a share'. A commission would be appointed charged with 'setting out, dividing, allotting and inclosing the said fields' and was 'to show no undue preference for any party'. Notice of meetings would be given in church. The scheme would include making 'the necessary roads, ditches, fences, drains, bridges, gates and stiles'. The new public roads would be 40 feet wide and former roads and tracks, probably

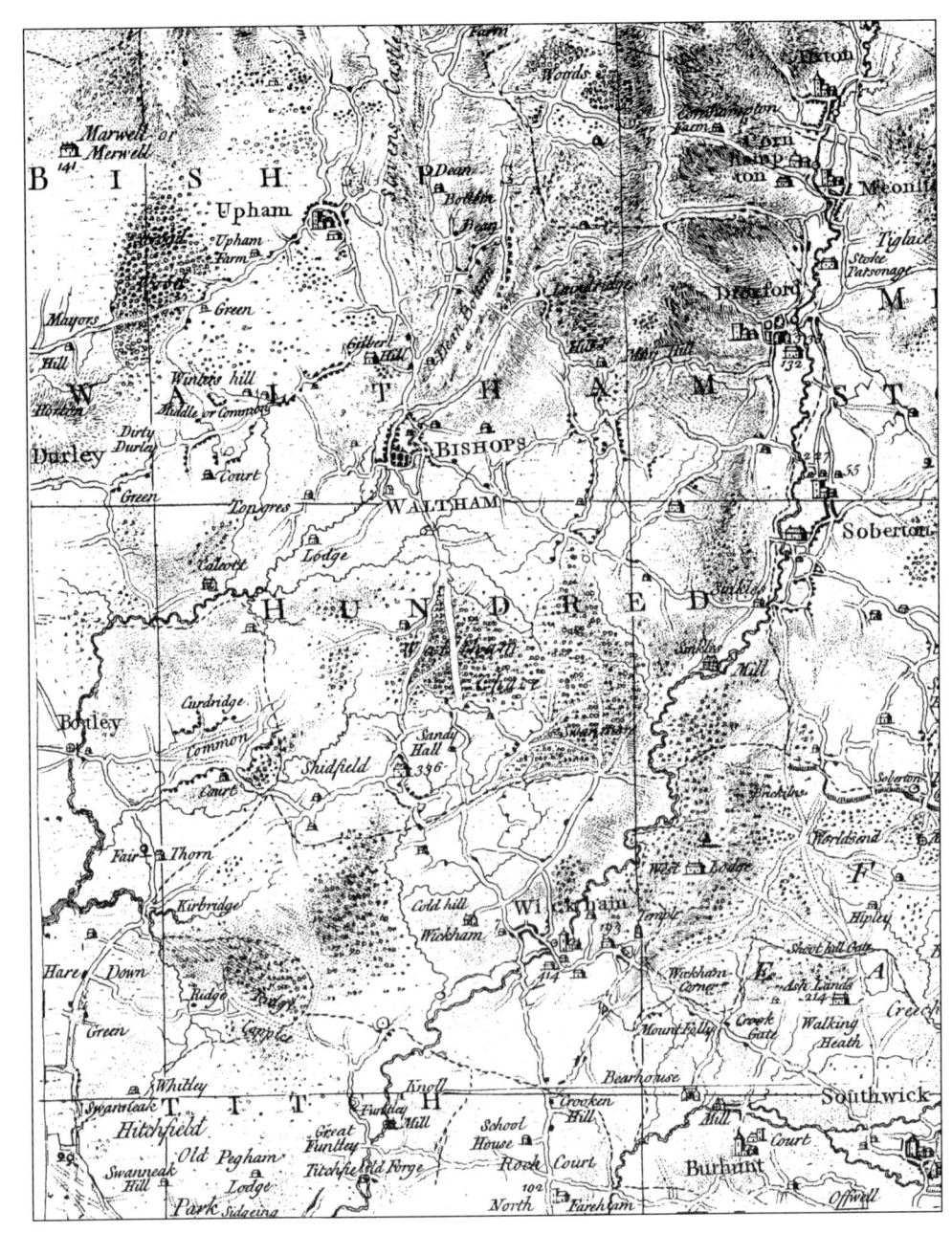

15. Map of Hampshire Taylor, 1759 Sheet 11

leading to individual strips in the open fields, would be extinguished. Land was allotted to 19 people of whom four received more than 10% – Richard Trodd 30 acres, Richard Eyles 29 acres and Walter Barfoot and Daniel Brown who each received 26 acres. [For later enclosures in Bishop's Waltham see p.152]

4

Poverty, pestilence and fire 1644–1840

WHEN in the seventeenth and eighteenth century citizens of Bishop's Waltham spoke of government they meant the parish vestry and the overseers of the poor, supervised by the Justices of the Peace in Quarter Sessions. Central government and parliament were infinitely remote. The great bulk of legislation passed by eighteenth century parliaments consisted of local acts on such matters as authorisation of turnpike trusts or the enclosure of commons or open fields. England would not be a welfare state for another two centuries but in Bishop's Waltham in common with other towns and villages welfare was organised, administered and paid for by the parish. Nobody reading the records can fail to be impressed by the extent of the problems faced by churchwardens and overseers of the poor and the thoroughness with which they were tackled. Poverty, orphaned children, old age, illegitimacy, infectious diseases, and fire were all matters which a largely self-contained community was left to face alone; free from government interference but also denied government support. Not until the 1830s did government begin to impose central control and curtail the initiative of the parish.

It was in the reign of Elizabeth I that the parish replaced the manor as the unit of local government and an increasing number of duties was laid on its officials by Tudor and Stuart legislation. The parish priest has been described as 'the nucleus round which the parish organisation developed.'[1] He became by common law the chairman of the parish vestry, a meeting which all parishioners were entitled to attend though few did. It was the vestry which annually nominated the four principal lay officers: churchwardens, overseers of the poor, surveyor of the highways and the constable.

The office of churchwarden originated, in some places as early as the fourteenth century, in the need for the maintenance and repair of the parish church. The churchwardens collected church rate and were also responsible for the morals of the parish. It was to the parish priest and the churchwardens that Thomas Cromwell in 1538 naturally gave responsibility for recording christenings, weddings and burials.

The overseers of the poor were established by an act of parliament in 1572 and were charged with collecting a poor rate and responsibility for relieving poverty. The constable, the third ancient parish officer, was responsible for maintaining law and order and dealing with outbreaks of fire with the assistance of a tithingman from each tithing or sub-division of the parish.

The quartet of parish officials was completed by the surveyor of the highways, responsible for inspecting the condition of the roads of the parish and for organising their maintenance, using the statute labour which was compulsory until 1835 or collecting the rate which parishioners paid in lieu of performing the service in person. All four offices were unpaid, compulsory, annual appointments which all citizens might be required to undertake or to appoint a deputy.[2] Churchwardens were chosen by the incumbent and the vestry and the remaining officers by the Justices of the Peace for the county from a list of qualified men supplied by the vestry.

Bishop's Waltham was a large parish divided into four tithings – Hoe, Bishop's Waltham, Ashton and Curdridge – each of which had its complement of four parish officers. The names of some of the churchwardens and overseers and sometimes the surveyors of the highways for each tithing are recorded in the opening pages of the first Poor Rate Book and cover the years from 1633 to 1737 with a few later entries for the 1760s and 1770s.[3] (see page 36)

Accounts kept by the overseers of the poor in Bishop's Waltham have survived from 1650 to 1833. They were kept meticulously, copied up at intervals, signed by churchwardens and overseers, approved by Justices of the Peace, all of which suggests a considerable degree of literacy. In the eighteenth century perhaps these records were kept by men who as boys had attended Bishop Morley's Grammar School founded in 1679 The records were stored in the Parish Chest and were pored over by Barbara Biddell who put the information they contained alongside records of baptisms, marriages and burials recorded in the Parish Registers. She used the information gleaned from both records in the chapters in her history of the town devoted to the welfare system.[4]

The Poor Rate books are now preserved in the Hampshire Record Office bound in nine volumes in which are listed the poor rate paid by eligible citizens and in some volumes the 'disbursements'.[5] The rate was collected whenever it was required, sometimes twice a year but frequently more often. In 1652 the person who paid most in poor rate was Robert Reynolds who owned the bishop's lands during the Commonwealth and paid £2–5–0 in poor rate. The second highest payer was the rector 'Doctor Goulston' who paid poor rate in all four tithings – 5/- in Bishop's Waltham, 1/6 in Hoe, 5/6 in Ashton and 4/- in Curdridge, because as rector he owned glebe land in all four.[6] The post of overseer was an onerous one and some of the work was delegated to a paid assistant overseer. The overseers were the key people in caring for the poor of the parish down to the 1830s and they survived, though with much reduced responsibilities, until 1925.

From 1722 the disbursements contain a great deal of information, sometimes detailing the amount of money given in poor relief, sometimes the sort of relief provided to meet every kind of need: widows who had no support, children orphaned by the death of parents, illegitimate children, the unemployed as well as the old who could no longer work, the sick who needed medical care, and the dead who had nobody to provide a decent burial. The relief is sometimes a single payment, sometimes it lasts over months or years.

In 1725 a blind man named Knight died in Bishop's Waltham. Items recorded include:

Relief to the old blind man at Knights	3/-
Pd. The Widow Knight for his sickness	5/-
Pd for laying him out and carrying him to church	6/-
For ringing his knell and digging his grave	2/-
Pd.John Earwaker for his coffin	2/-

In 1726 'Old Eames' who lived in Hoe tithing was given poor relief::

Pd. for two shirts for Old Eames	5/8
Pd. for a pair of stockings for him	1/3
Old Eames	4/-
Mary Eames	6/-
Pd for a coat for Old Eames and making	£1.1.7

Perusal of the overseers' accounts is fascinating and brings alive many facets of life in the town and surrounding countryside in the two centuries after the Palace ceased to be the home of successive bishops and the source of relief. The following are extracts from the disbursements for the year 1761 for the tithing of Waltham.

For John Matthew for tipping of Shoes	4/5
To Robert Colebon's Bill for Shoes	18/11
Relief to Harry Kervill	1/-
To Mary Parsons to pay for her lodging	2/4
To Mary Parsons @ 4d per week	1/8
Relief to Wm.Levelle the Frenchman	1/-
Paid for small necessaries for the soldier's wife that lay in at Coleborns (Wid. Coleborn's)	5/-
Paid on account of carrying a Sholdier (?) in the Small Pox viz the Shroud 3/6: two men assisting 5d: Cart 2/6:to bring him to Master Stubington For his Knell and Grave.	11/-
To Mr Fox for a Fatt Hogg wt.17.2lb	£4 -4- 6

An Act of Parliament passed in 1723 allowed a parish, instead of providing what was called 'outdoor relief' – a financial payment – for the poor, to rent or build a workhouse. From the late 1720s Bishop's Waltham took advantage of this permission

16. Accounts prepared by William Ledwell, Master of the Workhouse 1756–57.

Bishops Waltham Parish

The State of the Acc.ᵗ between the Parish and W.ᵐ Ledwell the Master of the Workhouse from the 5.ᵗʰ of May 1756 to the 5.ᵗʰ May 1757.

	£	S	D
The Charge			
The Masters Salary	290	0	0
More on Account of y.ᵉ Smallpox as agreed	20	0	0
More being Money by him paid on the Parish's Acc.ᵗ towards Old Arrears as settled in Vestry	17	11	3
More by him paid for the Parish to M.ʳ Whitear for Rent for y.ᵉ Use of M.ʳ Pink	2	5	0
More by him paid for the Parish to M.ʳ Horner for y.ᵉ Rent of the Alms House	3	0	0
The Whole Charge £	332	16	3

The Discharge

	£	S	D
Paid him by 1.ˢᵗ & 2.ᵈ Rates collected himself in Waltham Tything at £32..9..11 each Rate	64	19	10
By M.ʳ Harris Overseer of Waltham in Part of the 3.ᵈ & 4.ᵗʰ Rates	30	0	0
By the 5.ᵗʰ & 6.ᵗʰ Rates collected himself in Waltham Tything	64	19	10
By the 1.ˢᵗ Rate collected himself in Ashton Tything	19	7	0
Paid him by M.ʳ Rob.ᵗ Barefoot Overseer of Ashton at several times being part of the 2.ᵈ: 3.ᵈ: 4.ᵗʰ: 5.ᵗʰ & 6.ᵗʰ Rates collected in Ashton	48	3	0
By all the Six Rates collected himself in Curdridge Tything at 16..17..6 each Rate	101	5	0
By the 1.ˢᵗ 2.ᵈ 3.ᵈ & 4.ᵗʰ Rates collected			

and rented a house on the Chase. We know of the existence of the first Bishop's Waltham workhouse because in 1729 it was from the workhouse that William Fisher, one of its inmates was buried. The workhouse does not seem to have been a healthy place. Between 1740 and 1745 no less than three of its masters died and in September and October 1740 there were 11 burials from the workhouse including Elizabeth Wright the wife of the master.[7]

In 1756 the overseers appointed William Ledwell master of the workhouse. He was in effect a professional employee whom the overseers expected to supervise the pest house as well as the workhouse. He both received and paid out the poor rate, ordered food for the workhouse and dealt with such matters as settlements in the parish, for all of which he received almost the whole of the poor rate which in 1757 came to £322. Unfortunately the overseers arrangement with Ledwell did not last long. In 1759 he was accused of fathering a child by Eleanor Hackett an inmate of the workhouse. Eleanor was brought before the magistrates at Fareham, the baby boy William died when he was only a month old and William Ledwell was fined at Winchester Assizes and dismissed by the overseers.

For the next few months the overseers ran the workhouse themselves, a good deal more cheaply than William Ledwell had done, and conditions for the inmates improved too. Beef, bacon and cheese were included in the diet, and malt and hops were bought for brewing beer. The garden was planted and pigs bought to be fattened. The chimney was swept and the spinning wheel refurbished so that inmates could earn money from spinning. 'The Poor People' were given 4/- 'as an Encouragement'.[8] But delegation was preferred by the overseers so in 1767 they reappointed William Ledwell and he remained master until his death in November 1771.

In the meantime the workhouse on the Chase was proving inadequate and so in June 1762 the vestry resolved to replace it and to lease 'a House of Mr William Lacy …for the Lodging maintaining and imploying all such poor of the said parish as shall desire Relief viz a convenient part of his Hop Kilns situate in the Town of Bishop's Waltham …for the term of Eleven Years. And moreover we do consent and agree to take away from the present Workhouse the Pump, Furnace … and other Materials as shall be thought proper and necessary for the benefit of the parish.'[9] The new workhouse was probably part of what later became *The Barleycorn* in what we know as Basingwell Street but was for a time called Workhouse Street.

But this workhouse too proved inadequate and in 1808 the vestry made the curious decision to build an extension adjoining the pest house to provide the extra places it needed – curious because the point of the pest house was to isolate the victims of smallpox. The rector, James Ogle, agreed to ask the bishop – his father-in-law – for the land and timber to build a poor house to measure 20 feet by 45 feet.[10]

The early years of the nineteenth century saw a nationwide crisis in provision for the poor. The Revolutionary and Napoleonic Wars, which lasted with a brief interval for over 20 years from 1793 to 1815, saw a dramatic rise in the price of corn due in part to increase of population and in part to Napoleon's successful blockade. The years

17. The Barleycorn Inn, Basingwell Street c.1895 – the parish workhouse from 1762.

after the war ended in 1815 were difficult too since the Corn Laws remained in place restricting the import of grain in the interest of the landed class. There was widespread suffering, considerable unemployment and unrest and the poor rate grew astronomically in Bishop's Waltham as elsewhere. In 1812 it reached £1869.3.3¼ made up of monthly payments of £570.19.0 and occasional payments of £1298.4.3¼. The Poor Rate book lists payments to meet every possible contingency. Although there is a list of payments only occasionally is there an indication of why they were made.

In 1787 there is an entry showing an endearing sign of fallibility: 'Person unknown or forgot 3/-'. There was a different overseer for each tithing and for each year. How far were they consistent in what must have been an exacting and time consuming task? The Justices countersigned the accounts each year but cannot have had time to scrutinise the reasons for each payment. In 1810 7/0 was paid to 'Jas. Hammond having the misfortune to lose a cow', 2/6 for medicines, 7/- for repair of boy's shoes. There are payments too for 'sparrow heads 6d, hedgehogs at 4d. each'.[11]

In the early years of the nineteenth century the Vestry, under the chairmanship successively of James Ogle and William Brock, was concerned both by the growth in the poor rate and in the misery of many poorer people. In the years after 1815 in particular the number of paupers, many of them the victims of unemployment, grew and so did the poor rate. The Vestry led by the James Ogle and Charles Walters, rector and curate, petitioned the House of Commons, expressing 'Feelings of most acute Distress' that the 'unexampled Difficulties of the Agricultural Interest are become so great that it will be impossible for the Occupiers of Land to continue to cultivate the same under the existing Distress and unless some speedy Relief be afforded not only the whole of the Yeomanry of this Kingdom but the labouring and industrious Classes dependent on them for Employment and Support must be reduced to utter Ruin.' There is no date attached to this *crie de coeur* but it is probably between 1816 and 1820 when rural distress was at its worst.[12]

The parish adopted what was called the roundsman system. Pauper children living in the Poor House were allocated to payers of the poor rate who took them into their own homes and provided keep and employment. The poor rate of those who took the pauper children was reduced. For several years there was an annuual ballot for the pauper children. In 1809 there were 9 children, in 1816 there were 13 children between the ages of 10 and 15 and in 1817 no less than 20 children [13]. Alternatively the children could become domestic servants or apprentices and a weekly allowance was paid to the employer dependent on the age of the child.[14] A scheme of this sort seems to have lasted until about 1830.

Paupers were to be employed in their own tithing so that they did not have too far to travel. The people for whom they worked were to provide them with a ticket detailing the time they had worked and the paupers would only receive poor rate on producing evidence of employment. Many paupers came from large families and space in the Poor House was limited. In 1828 vestry proposed to build cottages on land attached to the Pest House or to build a new Poor House.

The next suggestion was to employ the poor of the parish to reduce the gradient of Coppice Hill, a scheme which was not however implemented. In 1833 the vestry proposed to rent land in each tithing and allocate five acres to any unemployed labourer on condition that he did not apply for the poor rate. Every family with more than three children would be allocated an additional ¼ acre for each child. This was called the Labour Allotment Scheme. The vestry minutes list 13 men with between three and nine children each. What comes across powerfully is the seriousness and vigour with which the Bishop's Waltham vestry tackled the acute problems of the countryside in the first 30 years of the nineteenth century.

The Whig government which took office under Lord Grey in 1830 was the first reforming government in British history. One of its priorities was the poor law. Following a commission of enquiry set up in 1832 parliament passed the Poor Law Amendment Act in 1834 which changed radically the organisation of poor relief. It was taken out of the hands of the parish vestry and the overseers and became the responsibility of the Poor Law Commissioners based in Somerset House, London with a paid secretary of whom the first was Edwin Chadwick. The act was based on two principles. First, unions of parishes were to be set up to build and administer a workhouse for the area they served. Second, outdoor relief for the able bodied was abolished. In future the poor who were able to work would be obliged to seek relief in workhouses organised on the principle of 'less eligibility' – conditions in the workhouse must be less favourable than they could possibly be outside – so as to provide a strong incentive to stay out of the workhouse.

At its meeting in January 1835 the Bishop's Waltham Vestry decided that it would not adopt the new act. If there were to be a union of parishes then they would prefer to join with Upham and Durley and would build a new workhouse at Bishop's Waltham.[15] They soon learnt that they had no option, that the union of parishes would be far wider than they envisaged and that the new workhouse was to be built at Droxford. In future the parish would elect two poor law guardians who would form part of a larger body charged with organising poor relief for the Droxford Union – Bishop's Waltham and ten adjoining parishes – Corhampton, Droxford, Durley, Exton, Hambledon, Meonstoke, Soberton, Warnford, West Meon and Upham. The union workhouse was opened after some delay at Droxford in 1837.

The first Minute Book of the Droxford Union provides a vivid and compelling, if at times harrowing, picture of the institution which the Guardians were required to set up. It covers the period from their first meeting on 24th December 1835 to 3rd October 1837.[16] The Guardians met weekly at *The White Horse* at Droxford under the chairmanship of Robert Hatch Stares. They faced a huge task. Not only had they to provide for the poor of eleven parishes but there were currently four parish poor houses- at Hambledon, Droxford, Soberton and Bishop's Waltham – which they had to use until the union workhouse could be built and then to close. There were 176 paupers of whom the largest number came from three parishes – Bishop's Waltham with 58, Droxford 41 and Hambledon 30 whilst West Meon, Durley and Corhampton had one each.

They had already found a site for the Union Workhouse – Gibbs Croft at Droxford – owned by the Marquess of Winchester and leased to Louis James Lovekin of Bishop's Waltham who was the Medical Officer of Health. He was prepared to relinquish the lease for £100. There were delays in borrowing the necessary money and in obtaining a sufficient supply of bricks. As a result the Guardians were obliged to make temporary arrangements. They provided accommodation for children under 13 in the Bishop's Waltham Poor House; for the over 60s and the 'partly Idiots' at the Droxford Poor House whilst the able bodied would go to Hambledon.

In the meantime the Guardians had absorbed the principle of economy on which the new poor law was based. When inmates died they would provide only coffin and burial fee – no frills such as a pall over the coffin or bells to mark a passing. The cost of coffins was graded – 5/- for an infant, 10/-for a child aged 6–10, 12/- for a child of 11–15 and 16/- for an adult. For the living dress would be uniform. They ordered 25 suits of grey cloth for the men costing 18/6 each, 20 boys' suits at 13/6 each, 100 pairs of half-boots of different sizes at 5/- per pair and for women 100 yards of grogram (SOED spelling, the person who wrote the Minutes had difficulty with the word which he spelt in several different ways!) at 7½ d per square yard to be made up into dresses. Workhouse inmates would of course sleep in dormitories and the women and children would share beds with each other, so they ordered 70 cast iron beds, 15 double beds for women, 15 double beds for children and 40 single beds for men each with mattresses of specified length with bolsters marked D U for Droxford Union to discourage theft.[17] It cannot be surprising that several inmates of the workhouse absconded sometimes with workhouse property and when caught were brought before the magistrates.

As a further interim measure the Guardians arranged for some of the paupers from parishes in the Droxford Union to go to the new workhouse at Fareham which had surplus places. It was from this arrangement that a particularly shameful incident arose. Three small boys Robert Withers, Jonathan Cook and William Warren, all aged four or five years old, were sent to Fareham workhouse on 17th January 1837. The boys were orphans, they were physically weak and mentally retarded and in addition incontinent. They remained at Fareham for about two months and were then sent back because the authorities found their presence intolerable. They returned to Bishop's Waltham Poor House 'faint and exhausted, in a very debilitated condition'.

The Guardians initiated an enquiry, a summary of which occupies six foolscap pages of the minute book and constitutes a damning indictment of the Fareham workhouse at every level. The Master had exceeded his authority and neglected his duty, the Medical Officer had been negligent. The boys had been sent to school where the mistress had placed them in the stocks, a punishment of her own devising which was physically dangerous for children of this age and inhumane treatment for children of any age. The medical officer at Bishop's Waltham, Louis James Lovekin thought they had been beaten and half starved.[18] The resulting scandal provoked a debate in parliament and a piece in *The Times*.[19] It was comparable with the scandal of the Andover Workhouse in 1845–6 where the inmates had been kept so hungry that they had resorted to eating scraps of meat and gristle from the bones of dogs and horses which they had been set to crush.[20]

Although after more than 200 years the parish was no longer responsible for its poor the Vestry continued to show concern and the minutes of a meeting of parishioners on 3rd January 1839 give some idea of how desperate was the plight of many of the poor. Vestry seems to have tried at all costs to keep the poor out of the workhouse. It was decided to collect subscriptions in order to distribute food and fuel to the poor. Soup would be available every week which the poor could purchase at the rate of one pint per person not exceeding four quarts for one family. They would be able to buy coal at 6d. per hundredweight per fortnight. The committee was authorised to provide clothing 'under circumstances of peculiar necessity'. A committee appointed to manage the distribution of soup and coals was to include the district visitors and would meet 'two days hence' on Saturday 5th January in the National School room at 12 o'clock. Finally 'Persons of notoriously idle and disorderly habits to be excluded from this charity'.[21]

After the Fareham workhouse scandal William Brock, the rector, offered to take children of the poor into the parish school. Mr Harrison the master of the Bishop's

Waltham poor house was asked to send notice of the death of any pauper to the rector so that the bell could be tolled whilst the guardians had in mind the provision of a pall for use in the Union. Mr Harrison reported too his belief that the ½lb of potatoes per week specified in the Diet Scale was insufficient and with the agreement of the Poor Law Commissioners it was doubled to 1 lb.[22]

The early years of the workhouse were the worst. The government had succeeded in its aim of reducing the poor rate but at the price of pauperising people whose poverty was not their fault but that of economic conditions. The system was worst for the old, who feared the stigma of the workhouse, and for children. Bishop's Waltham provides brief and vivid cameos of a harsh system at work in its early years.

Smallpox was the scourge most feared and the disease from which most people died in the countryside in the eighteenth century. The first recorded death of small pox in the Parish Register was that of Ann Cleverley of Curdridge in 1684. There were epidemics in 1723–4, in 1740–1 and most serious of all in 1773–5. Inoculation which meant giving the patient a mild dose of the disease was an uncertain remedy but the only one as yet available. Written across the page of the Burial Register for 1774 when there were 58 deaths, 14 of them infants, are the words 'this year there was a general inoculation in the town'. The following year the number of recorded burials had fallen to 27 of whom only three were infants, and in the two following years 31 and 24.[23] It was not until Dr Edward Jenner a Gloucestershire doctor developed vaccination, which involved giving patients a dose of the harmless cowpox, in 1791 that a more effective remedy became available.

The first victims of the 1723–4 outbreak were William Trodd and his mother Widow Trodd. After that the parish stumbled on the device of isolation: from April 1724 sufferers were cared for in a house belonging to Mary Bassett. The poor rate book records payments to 'Goody Allingham for her assistance for carrying away Goody Sparrow in the small pox' and to John Reeves for his 'trouble and assistance' in carrying Goody Sparrow and others 'to the fforest'[24] In October he went again to the Chase and brought back 'ye small pox people'[25] The fear of a recurrence of smallpox is well illustrated by the entry in the poor book in June 1726 when the overseers at a total cost of 2/6, 'Gave some travellers who had the small pox upon them 2d and 6d' provided 'they should pass without begging about the town'.[26]

In the 1740–1 outbreak many of those who died were from the workhouse, particularly in the months of September and October including Thomas Prior the master of the workhouse who was buried on 12th September. [27]After this the parish built its own isolation hospital, the pest house on the Chase, and employed a master and mistress to nurse sufferers. Not all appear to have accepted isolation, some remained at home or in the workhouse and as a result more probably died in later outbreaks than need have done. In the late 1760s William Ledwell was appointed master of the pest house as well as the workhouse.

In the smallpox epidemic of 1773–5 no less than 109 people in the parish died of the disease, many of them inmates of either the pest house or the workhouse. Inoculation was introduced in 1775 and the death toll fell, though by then the epidemic may have spent itself. Smallpox remained an ever present fear, breaking out in the tithings of Hoe and Curdridge in 1794, though never again would there be an outbreak in Bishop's Waltham on the scale of 1773-5.

In April 1818 the vestry decided that all those who received parish relief must be vaccinated. If anybody who had not been vaccinated caught smallpox 'either by infection or inoculation' they would not receive poor relief.[28] Perhaps smallpox was no longer the scourge it had been. In 1828 the vestry was planning to enlarge the pest house on the Chase to 'place several paupers with large families'.[29] When the Union workhouse was opened at Droxford in 1837 the parish pest house was no longer needed. It was sold in 1842 and became a private house. It was demolished in 1964.

The great scourge of the early nineteenth century was cholera and in 1831 the vestry adopted preventive measures. They passed a resolution which conveys much about the state of the centre of town as well as about the degree of regulation which the vestry could impose. It reads:

> 'To prevent contagion of Indian cholera or any other contagious disease the following regulations were agreed and recommended for adults in the parish;
> 1. Parochial authorities will visit the houses of the poor and point out the necessity of keeping houses clean of filth and offensive matter and of promoting ventilation.
> 2. Owners of all houses in which the poor reside are requested to whitewash if necessary the same.
> 3. All houses in which the poor reside to be forthwith whitewashed according to instructions to be given by the churchwardens and the overseers.
> 4. All persons to be required to remove dung heaps and other accumulations of dirt and filth from the streets and other confined situations.
> Recommended that the parish officers assist the constable and beadle in clearing the parish of vagrants.'[30]

The constable was the parish officer responsible for maintaining law and order and for ensuring that the parish had adequate protection from fire. He had available a variety of minor punishments. He could place malefactors in the stocks which were maintained in each tithing or sentence people to a short term of imprisonment in the cage under the market house in the Square. In 1770 Grace Sparrow was sentenced to be publicly whipped in the square at Bishop's Waltham, a sentence carried out on 8th May under the direction of the constable. He also tried to keep the town free from vagrants who might otherwise carry infectious diseases from place to place. During the Napoleonic Wars the constable and tithingmen were urged to obtain recruits for the navy or the militia and they were paid £2-2-0 from the poor rate.[31]

18 The eighteenth century fire engine in use until 1910 on an occasion when it was brought out as a curiosity.

Fire was a serious hazard at a time when wood was a major component of many buildings. An Act of Parliament of 1706 required each parish to equip itself with a fire engine and Bishop's Waltham soon did so.[32] Until 1841 fire fighting equipment was kept in the market house in the Square and it was its dilapidated state and imminent demolition which led to a town meeting at *The Crown* with the rector in the chair to discuss how in future to protect the town from fire. The meeting resolved 'That the Fire Engines of the parish (and particularly the one called the Old Engine) are in a bad and ineffective condition'. The meeting set up a committee which appointed Mr Stoneage principal fireman with a salary of £2 per year. Subscriptions were to be solicited at 1d in the £ from all who paid the poor rate. Anybody who did not subscribe and was the victim of a fire would have to pay £5 for the services of the fire engine. The poor were of course exempt from payment. The meeting further resolved to ask Captain Robbins of the police force to send police to Bishop's Waltham on 5th November to point out the danger of making bonfires and throwing fireworks on Guy Fawkes Day. The committee subsequently built an Engine House in what would later be called Station Road.[33]

5
The Turnpike Roads

UNTIL THE middle of the eighteenth century the roads round Bishop's Waltham were in the same appalling state as those of the rest of the country. As traffic increased from 1650 onwards so roads deteriorated and travel became slower and more hazardous. Under an act of parliament of 1555 each parish was responsible for the upkeep of its own roads. A surveyor of highways was appointed and parishioners were obliged to provide materials, implements, horses and labour at the rate of four days each year. Though the arrangement remained in force until 1835 in most places it never worked satisfactorily and the state of roads remained deplorable.

Significant improvement only began with the introduction from the early eighteenth century of a form of private enterprise: turnpike trusts. The idea was simple. An act of parliament authorised a group of local people to form a trust, sell shares, invest the money to build and maintain a road and in return charge a toll for its use. Until 1835 they could call on statute labour though this was often commuted to a money payment. Exemption from paying tolls was granted to specific categories of people for example to pedestrians, soldiers, and people going to church on Sundays. The result was a network of more or less satisfactory roads for the first time since the Romans left Britain. Until the building of the motorways during the second half of the twentieth century the turnpike roads formed the basis of the main roads which we use today.

By 1837 Hampshire had 36 trusts covering 627 miles of road with an average length of 17.4 miles whilst nationally there were approaching 1000 trusts with over 20,000 miles of road and about £1½ m. in toll receipts collected annually.[1] The period from 1751 – 1772 has been described as the era of 'turnpike mania'.[2] Some turnpike roads were new, following routes where there had not previously been a road, but most were not. Some joined up old roads with new sections; others widened, resurfaced and straightened existing roads and long established tracks. There were examples of all three close to Bishop's Waltham. Turnpikes were not generally popular. People who had all their lives used the roads free resented paying toll. There were riots as well as attempts to bypass tollhouses to avoid paying tolls. Trustees retaliated by having them blocked by a ditch or bank; again there are examples in the parish of Bishop's Waltham.

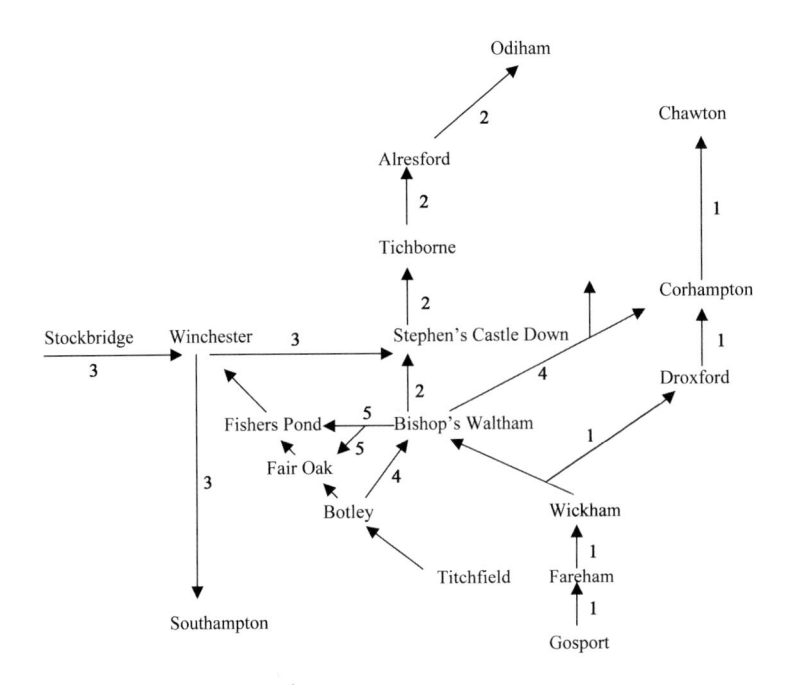

Diagram to show network of Turnpike roads round Bishop's Waltham – not to scale (based on W.Albert Appendix B)

		Act of Parliament
1.	Gosport to Chawton – branch from Wickham to Bishop's Waltham	1758
2.	Bishop's Waltham to Alresford to Odiham	1758
3.	Stockbridge to Winchester; Winchester to Stephen's Castle Down; Winchester to Southampton	1758
4.	Curdridge Common to Corhampton (part of Southampton to London)	1801
	[Titchfield to Twyford via Botley – 'Cobbett's Road']	1810
5.	Bishop's Waltham to Fishers Pond (branch to Fair Oak)	1833

19. Diagram to show turnpike roads round Bishop's Waltham.

The first turnpike road in Hampshire was from Portsmouth to Petersfield, part of the present A3, authorised in 1710 (9 Anne c.33). In 1758 parliament authorised three turnpikes which came through or close to Bishop's Waltham – Gosport to Chawton (31 George II c.73), Bishop's Waltham to Alresford to Odiham (31 George II c.74) and the three pronged road from Stockbridge to Winchester, Winchester to Southampton and Winchester to Stephen's Castle Down, (31 George II c.75).[3] Roads were often not made for some years after they had been authorised. Delays were

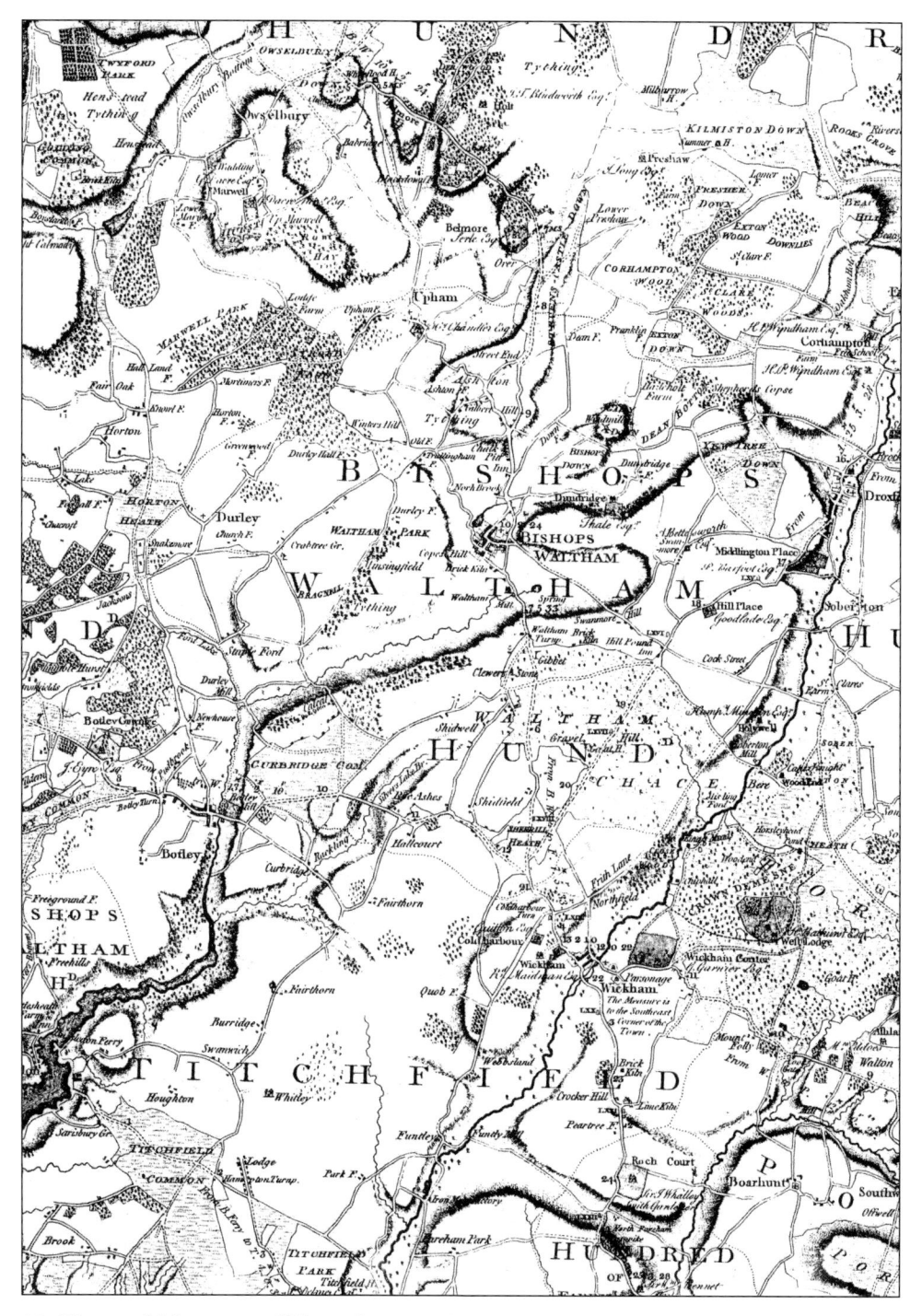

20 Thomas Milner map of Hampshire 1791 sheet 17 showing the Coldharbour and Waltham turnpike gates, the Gibbet on the Chase, Coppice Hill brickyard, the Mill on the Chase, Curdridge Lane as the main road from Curdridge to Bishop's Waltham and Green Lane continued to join the Gosport road.

inevitable; trustees had to meet, surveyors must negotiate the route and buy the land and money had to be raised before construction could begin. Sometimes only part of the approved road was built and a further section opened later.

The Gosport to Chawton turnpike came through Fareham and divided north of Wickham with one branch to Bishop's Waltham and one via Shirrell Heath, Swanmore and Droxford to Chawton. (The section of the present A32 from Droxford to Wickham was not built until 1860). There were toll gates at Brockhurst, Fareham, Cold Harbour (later renamed Wickham), Waltham (opposite Paradise Lane), Warnford and Rotherfield. The treasurer was James Bedford and the record of his disbursements provides a valuable insight into the expenses of turnpike trustees. In 1784 he paid for 52 days cartage of gravel, for iron work on the gates at Brockhurst, for window shutters on the toll house and for repairing the gate, whilst one day's work was needed 'to remove snow'. In the early years the Gosport turnpike was profitable. At the Bishop's Waltham gate there was a surplus of about £5 to £6 per month after the gate keeper's salary of £1.5.0 per month had been paid. He was also entitled to fire and candles which cost £2.10.0 for the year.[4]

The turnpike road from Bishop's Waltham to Alresford and Odiham had no less than 185 trustees including the leading aristocrats, landowners and clergy of Hampshire, among them James Cutler the rector of Droxford and Bishop's Waltham. The Act passed in 1758 was 'for Repairing and Widening the Roads from the Town of Bishop's Waltham … over the Top of the Down called Steven's Castle Down (*sic*) and through Salt Lane and Tichborne to the Town of New Alresford; and from the Market-house in the said Town of New Alresford through Old Alresford, Bradley Lane and over Herriard Common to the Town of Odiham.' The present roads were 'in a ruinous condition, narrow in many Places and dangerous to Travellers and the same cannot be effectually repaired and widened without the Aid of Parliament'. The surveyor of the new road was authorised to cut, dig, gather, take and carry away… Furze, Heath, Stones, Gravel, Chalk, Sand, Flints out of the waste for repairing roads. He could make 'Causeways, Bridges, Drains and Watercourses'. There were to be three or more gates at which tolls specified in the Act might be collected.

Five trustees were appointed to decide the line of the road and they were authorised to sell the obsolete road. The trustees might also erect side gates across any lane leading into or out of the turnpike road 'to prevent Persons evading the Payment of the Tolls'. There were to be no gates nearer to the town of Bishop's Waltham than three miles. Nobody was to be required to pay at more than two gates between Odiham and New Alresford nor at more than one gate between New Alresford and Bishop's Waltham. You qualified for free travel if you fell into one of a number of named categories: if you were repairing the road, carrying manure for use on your own land, if you were travelling to elect a knight of the shire or if you were in a vehicle carrying mail. Soldiers on the march did not pay nor did those travelling with vagrants. The trustees might use statute labour and were to erect signposts and milestones.[5]

21 The Waltham Turnpike House on the Gosport turnpike.

The Stockbridge, Winchester and Southampton turnpike had three branches – from Stockbridge to Winchester (8 miles), Winchester to Stephen's Castle Down via Bar End and Belmore Lane (8 miles) where it would join the Alresford Turnpike, and from Winchester to the Bargate, Southampton via Otterbourne (5 miles). It was in effect three turnpikes operating under one set of trustees. Its purpose was ' the repairing, widening and improving' of existing roads rather than constructing new ones. The trustees were a highly professional body who met monthly, at the *White Hart* or elsewhere in Winchester.

The minute books of the trust survive in four large volumes for the whole of its life from 1758 to 1875 and record the details of the work which they undertook for example: reface the milestones on the Bishop's Waltham road and erect a new one at Twyford Down, erect a post and rail fence at Morestead Pond, paint all the toll gates, cover flints with gravel or gravel and chalk, lop the trees which lay over the turnpike road. In 1828 they resolved to erect a toll house on the road which led from Morestead to Twyford presumably because travellers had been leaving the turnpike at Twyford in order to avoid paying toll at Bar End. They held their last meeting on 11th December 1875 and agreed to distribute the balance of £110/7/-. The last toll gates at St Cross and on the Waltham road had already been removed and sold at auction.

22. Milestones on the Gosport turnpike and the London to Southampton turnpike

The surveyor was paid £105 and the clerk £54 in lieu of three years salary. From 1st November 1875 the use of the roads was free: the turnpike era was over.[6]

At the beginning of the nineteenth century a fourth turnpike was authorised affecting Bishop's Waltham. It was described in the Act (41 George III c.8) as Curdridge Common to Corhampton but it was intended to form part of the turnpike from Southampton to London linking Botley with West Meon, with a spur to Corhampton Down. It replaced the earlier road from Curdridge to Bishop's Waltham which had followed Curdridge Lane and what later became known as Clewer's Hill. William Gunner was its clerk and there were tollgates at Curdridge Common and Northbrook.

Local people took considerable pains to avoid paying tolls at Northbrook and the trustees in preventing this by stopping up the lanes – Chalky Lane, Windmill Lane, Watery Lane and Limekiln Lane and the road over Galley Down – all of which could be used to get round the gate.[7] The battle was one which the trustees lost, the Northbrook toll gate never made a profit and the turnpike house was sold a full 20 years before the turnpike itself ended. The eventual closure of 'the London to Southampton turnpike through Bishop's Waltham' was announced in *The Times* to take place on 1st November 1874.[8]

William Cobbett was the driving force behind a turnpike road from Titchfield to Twyford via Botley and Fair Oak authorised by an Act of Parliament passed in 1810

(50 Geo.III c.22). The first reaction of Bishop's Waltham people was hostility. It would detract from the profitability of roads in the parish and its upkeep would be the responsibility of the parishes through which it passed which included Bishop's Waltham.[9] It is ironical therefore that the last and in some ways the most important turnpike in Bishop's Waltham should have been a link between the town and Cobbett's road at Fishers Pond.

In February 1833 a group of men met at *The Crown* to discuss the project for a new road from Bishop's Waltham to Winchester (authorised by 3 William IV c.17). They pointed out that 'The present road …is ten miles in length in which are seven very Steep Hills and not one mile of Level Road, whereas the proposed new Line of Road is level throughout and the distance somewhat less'. The new road ' will afford the nearest communication between the great and populous Towns of Portsmouth, Portsea, Gosport, Havant and Fareham and other places in Hampshire as well as parts of the county of Sussex and the City of Winchester'.[10] They wasted no time. The first meeting of the trustees was held on 19th April 1833 and by July they were seeking tenders for the new road divided into three sections – the Market House at Bishop's Waltham to the road from Ashton to Wintershill, from thence to Lower Upham including the proposed branch to Fair Oak and finally for the section from Lower Upham to Fishers Pond. Mr. Gunner's salary as clerk was fixed at £25 per year. There were to be tollgates at Park Lane and at Fishers Pond. The number of days statute labour was assessed for each category of ratepayer and then commuted to a money payment.

Where possible the road followed the existing highway interspersed with sections of new road. It began with a stretch of new road from the town as far as Park Lane, where it joined an existing road, then came another new stretch as far as Stakes Lane. From there the turnpike followed the old road to Lower Upham. From Old Streets Gate at Lower Upham there was another new section to Deeps Lane (now Popes Lane). Finally there were two miles of new road to bring the toll road to Fishers Pond. [11] An order was made stopping up Park Lane and Old Streets Lane which were no longer needed and were likely to be used to avoid tolls at Park Gate.

By 1839 turnpikes were already falling victim to the railways. The days of coach travel were numbered. Only the faint hearted it was claimed now travelled by coach the intrepid braved the new and faster trains. As a result turnpikes were no longer profitable; either repair of the roads was neglected or the trusts were obliged to stop paying dividends to their shareholders. Not until the advent of bicycles and motor cars at the end of the century was interest in roads revived.

The archaeology of turnpikes includes surviving toll houses and milestones. Both were placed close to the road and so were often victims of later road widening. Toll houses can usually be identified by closeness to the road, sometimes with a window set at an angle to enable the toll keeper to see traffic coming in both directions.[12] In Bishop's Waltham there were four tollhouses, two of which have disappeared altogether – opposite the end of Calcot Lane in Curdridge and at Northbrook, on the

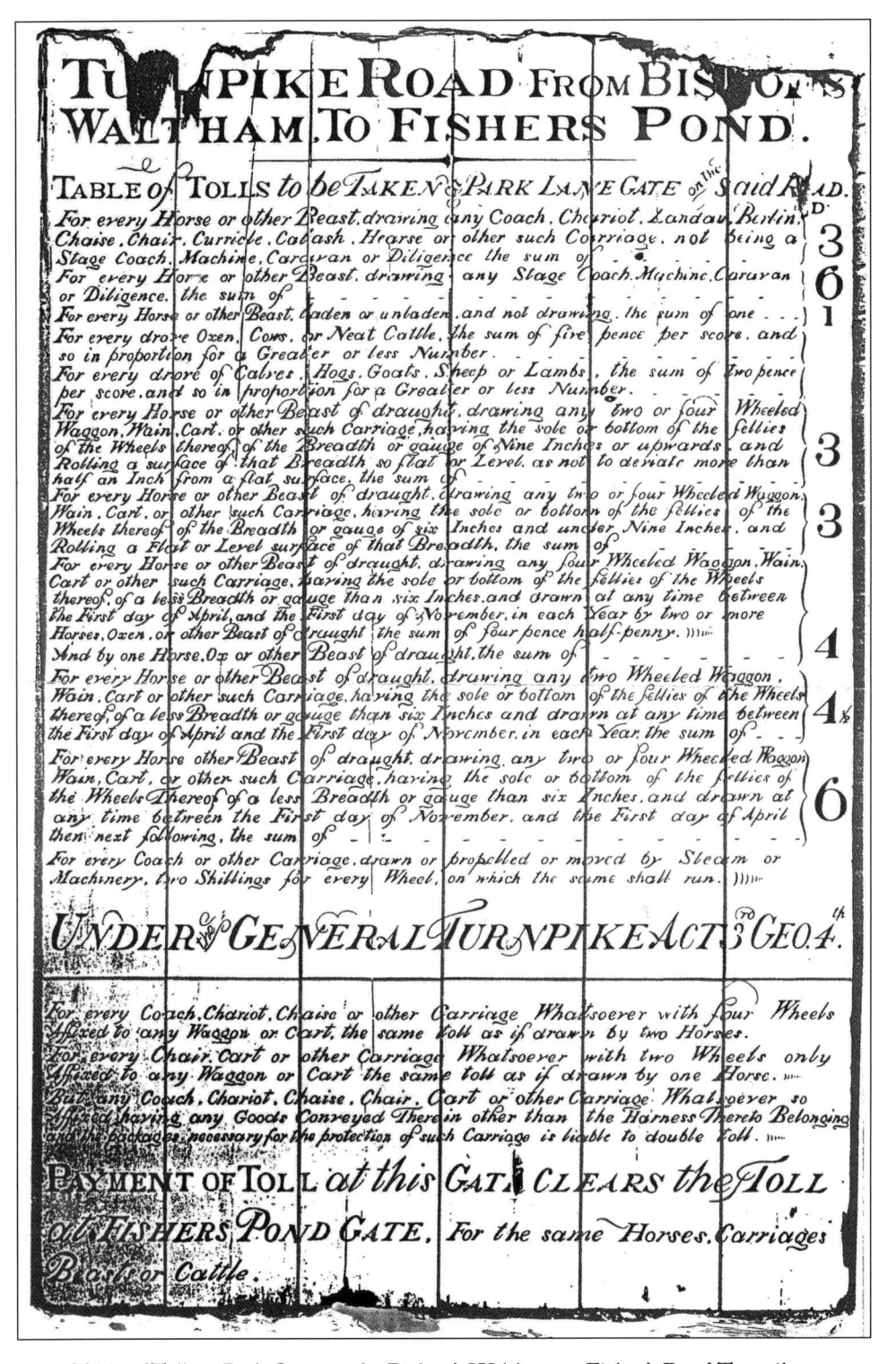

TURNPIKE ROAD FROM BISHOPS WALTHAM, TO FISHERS POND.

TABLE OF TOLLS to be TAKEN at PARK LANE GATE on the said Road.

	D
For every Horse or other Beast, drawing any Coach, Chariot, Landau, Berlin, Chaise, Chair, Curricle, Calash, Hearse or other such Carriage, not being a Stage Coach, Machine, Caravan or Diligence the sum of	3
For every Horse or other Beast, drawing any Stage Coach, Machine, Caravan or Diligence, the sum of	6
For every Horse or other Beast, laden or unladen, and not drawing, the sum of one	1
For every drove of Oxen, Cows, or Neat Cattle, the sum of five pence per score, and so in proportion for a Greater or less Number.	
For every drove of Calves, Hogs, Goats, Sheep or Lambs, the sum of two pence per score, and so in proportion for a Greater or less Number.	
For every Horse or other Beast of draught, drawing any two or four Wheeled Waggon, Wain, Cart, or other such Carriage, having the sole or bottom of the fellies of the Wheels thereof, of the Breadth or gauge of Nine Inches or upwards, and Rolling a surface of that Breadth so flat or Level, as not to deviate more than half an Inch from a flat surface, the sum of	3
For every Horse or other Beast of draught, drawing any two or four Wheeled Waggon, Wain, Cart, or other such Carriage, having the sole or bottom of the Wheels thereof, of the Breadth or gauge of six Inches and under Nine Inches, and Rolling a Flat or Level surface of that Breadth, the sum of	3
For every Horse or other Beast of draught, drawing any four Wheeled Waggon, Wain, Cart or other such Carriage, having the sole or bottom of the fellies of the Wheels thereof, of a less Breadth or gauge than six Inches, and drawn at any time between the First day of April, and the First day of November, in each Year by two or more Horses, Oxen, or other Beast of draught the sum of four pence half-penny. And by one Horse, Ox or other Beast of draught, the sum of	4
For every Horse or other Beast of draught, drawing any two Wheeled Waggon, Wain, Cart or other such Carriage, having the sole or bottom of the fellies of the Wheels thereof, of a less Breadth or gauge than six Inches and drawn at any time between the First day of April and the First day of November, in each Year, the sum of	4½
For every Horse or other Beast of draught, drawing any two or four Wheeled Waggon, Wain, Cart, or other such Carriage, having the sole or bottom of the fellies of the Wheels thereof of a less Breadth or gauge than six Inches, and drawn at any time between the First day of November, and the First day of April then next following, the sum of	6
For every Coach or other Carriage, drawn or propelled or moved by Steam or Machinery, two Shillings for every Wheel, on which the same shall run.	

UNDER the GENERAL TURNPIKE ACT 3rd GEO. 4th

For every Coach, Chariot, Chaise or other Carriage Whatsoever with four Wheels affixed to any Waggon or Cart, the same toll as if drawn by two Horses.

For every Chair, Cart or other Carriage Whatsoever with two Wheels only affixed to any Waggon or Cart the same toll as if drawn by one Horse.

But any Coach, Chariot, Chaise, Chair, Cart or other Carriage Whatsoever so affixed having any Goods Conveyed Therein other than the Harness Thereto Belonging and the packages necessary for the protection of such Carriage is liable to double toll.

PAYMENT OF TOLL at this GATE CLEARS the TOLL at FISHERS POND GATE. For the same Horses, Carriages, Beasts or Cattle.

23. Table of Tolls at Park Gate on the Bishop's Waltham to Fisher's Pond Turnpike, 1834.

north east side of the road leading to Beeches Hill both on the Southampton to London turnpike. Two remain though one, at Park Gate on the Bishop's Waltham to Fishers Pond turnpike, is in an advanced state of decay and will need to be rescued quickly if it is to survive. The table of tolls has however been rescued and is in the Bishop's Waltham Museum. The second tollhouse in the parish, serving the Gosport to Bishop's Waltham turnpike, is opposite the end of Paradise Lane and has recently been restored.

The toll house at Northbrook was of brick and tile construction with a garden. Downstairs was a sitting room and a small back room and upstairs a bedroom. At the side was a 'skilling' room (outhouse) and a wood shed. At the sale at *The Crown* in November 1852 it was bought by John Apps for £71.[13] The Curdridge toll house also on the London to Southampton turnpike was sold in 1874 for £92.10.00 and the gate and post for a further £1.15.00. By then the turnpike era had ended

Many turnpike trusts erected milestones and after 1776 were required to do so. They too have fallen victim to road widening but also to removal at the beginning of the Second World War when it was thought that they might assist an enemy landing from the air. Some were replaced but not all. There are several on the roads around Bishop's Waltham, their location indicated on Ordnance Survey maps.

Until the Highways Act of 1835 ended statute labour citizens were obliged to pay a highway rate and in turn those who laboured on the roads including the new turnpikes were paid for their work. The Highway Rate book for the early 1830s records both the payment of the highway rate and the disbursements of the surveyors, all kept in meticulous detail in beautiful copper plate handwriting. Payments depended on the amount of land owned or occupied. Disbursements were for a variety of services and included money paid to boys – and girls – for 'picking loads of stones', 'carriage of timber', 'two days stonebreaking, Lock's boy 1/-' 'delivering 32 loads of stones 16/3', 'watching for 3 nights', 'beer for the bricklayers', 'Newlyn – picking 17 loads of stones 8/6', 'Woodhatch, 11 loads of stones 5/6'.[14] The standard rate for a day's work was 1/-, gathering a load of stones brought in 6d.

An Act of Parliament of 1863 provided for the setting up of Highway Boards. The Droxford Highway Board came into existence in 1873 covering the same eleven parishes which constituted the Poor Law Union and met in the Board Room at the workhouse. Its first chairman was Bettesworth Pitt Shearer of Swanmore Park. It seems to have been concerned with the same trivia which had exercised the turnpike trustees: impounding straying cattle, manure deposits on the roads and the safety of the pond, boathouse and causeway at Bishop's Waltham.[15]

6

From the French wars to the Census of 1851

FOR MUCH of the eighteenth century Great Britain was at war with France. Recruits for both army and navy were needed at a time when service in the forces was not an attractive proposition. Parishes were expected to provide recruits and could pay a bounty from the poor rate. In February 1784 the overseer of the poor at Bishop's Waltham ' Paid Ts.[Thomas] Flack drafted for a Militia Man £2.10.0'. Several similar payments are recorded. But once the French Revolutionary War began in 1793 the bounty was raised: 'Paid to Wm. Chip by order of the Justices being drawn for the Militia £5.0.0'. Service in the navy was even more unpopular than in the army since life was harder and involved absence from home for longer. Each county had to provide 'quota men', parishes cooperated to raise recruits and the bounty was higher: in 1795, 'Paid for 2 Men raised for the Navy between this Parish and the Parish of Warnford £40.0.0.' The contribution of Warnford, a small parish was only £5.[1]

French prisoners were to be found in Bishop's Waltham earlier in the eighteenth century but were a prominent feature in the town during the French Revolutionary and Napoleonic wars which lasted with a short break for more than 20 years, from 1793 to 1815. During these years, when a considerable number of French and Spanish prisoners were held in the towns of the south of England, the government was fearful that they might spread revolutionary ideas among disaffected citizens. The 160 prisoners at Waltham in June 1793 were for example 'strongly against monarchy' and might, it was believed, contaminate citizens with republican sentiment.[2] It was a not unreasonable fear. In 1789 the infant United States of America had chosen a republican form of government and installed its first President, George Washington, whilst even more recently France had abolished the monarchy and in January 1793 executed its king Louis XVI.

From the beginning of the war in 1793 Bishop's Waltham was one of 93 towns to which prisoners were parolled and to which a constantly changing population of captured officers, mostly French, were sent.[3] John Penny who lived at Palace House was appointed the government's agent in the town answerable to the Transport

Board in London. His duties included collecting and storing the prisoners' swords and returning them when they left Bishop's Waltham, paying them a daily allowance of 1/6 and finding and supervising their billets. It was an arduous and thankless task involving almost daily contact with the authorities as well as blame when the prisoners escaped. Only officers were parolled but they were allowed to bring their servants with them. Sailors and other ranks were kept at Portchester Castle or in hulks moored in the Solent.

There were probably between 160 and 200 in the town at any one time so they must have been a presence which nobody could ignore. Many places in the town provided billets particularly houses in Basingwell Street and Houchin Street as well as the cellars of the Rectory and *The Crown* and other public houses. The prisoners were required to be indoors between sunset and 6am. At other times they were allowed to walk one mile from the town provided they kept to roads. Frenchmens Bridge on the Botley Road represented the permitted limit in that direction hence its name.[4]

Bishop's Waltham provided accommodation for several high ranking prisoners but none was more renowned than Admiral Pierre-Charles Villeneuve, the commander of the combined French and Spanish fleet defeated by Nelson at the Battle of Trafalgar on 21st October 1805. He was however in the town for less than a month. He reached Bishop's Waltham attended by ten officers and men on 1st December 1805. He was at first accommodated at *The Crown* but within a short time was moved to Vernon Hill House. He asked to be billeted closer to London and so on 26th December was sent to Reading. It was from there that he travelled to London on 9th January to attend the funeral in St Paul's Cathedral of his famous adversary Horatio Nelson. Three months later he was exchanged for four British naval captains and returned to France. He stayed overnight at Rennes and the following morning was found dead with five stab wounds in his chest. The suicide note left close to him could not disguise the fact that he had been murdered, probably on the instructions of Napoleon who blamed him for defeat at Trafalgar.[5]

Apart from Admiral Villeneuve the best known alleged parole prisoner in Bishop's Waltham was the painter of sea scapes Amboise-Louis Garneray. He wrote an account of his life entitled *Mes Pontons* including time in the hulks off Portsmouth, parole to Bishop's Waltham, escape and subsequent recapture by the British navy. The book was not however published until 1851 nor known in England for a century after that. A recent writer, Richard Rose, has studied his account in detail and concluded that it is largely invention and that Garneray never came to Bishop's Waltham. In Barbara Biddell's latest book she sets out the case for the substantial truth of Garneray's own account and invites readers to decide for themselves.[6] In Bishop's Waltham Garneray has been credited with two paintings on the wall of an attic room in Hope House in St Peter Street. They were seen as recently as the early 1960s but have disappeared, perhaps painted over by a new owner unaware of their historic interest.[7]

French prisoners might be exchanged for British prisoners in France but would not seek to escape. By 1810 that understanding had broken down and a large scale break out was feared. There was 'a well organised escape network' and even a collaborator in Bishop's Waltham.[8] The authorities decided to move all parole prisoners from towns close to the south coast to Wales, Scotland or Shropshire where escape would be more difficult. John Penny was informed in December 1811 that Bishop's Waltham would no longer be a parole town and by the following June almost all prisoners had left the town.

The Register of St Peter's records the burial of seven French and one Spanish prisoner while they were in the town, and folklore has it that they lie in two communal graves one on either side of the door on the south side of the chancel.[9] They include Peter Druett (buried 6th September 1795), Pierre Jouant (31st May 1796), Peter Combes (1st July 1796), Francois Doyhan of the parish of Marigot, Martinique (10th March 1797) Pedro de Ybarsa (Spanish, 4th February 1807) and Sebastian Nicolas Godard (21st August 1810) who are all described in the Register as 'French/Spanish prisoner of war on parole'[10]

Northbrook House was built in the late eighteenth century by Robert Barton on the site of an earlier house. It lay in some four acres of garden and landscaped grounds, bounded by the Rectory, Free Street and Lower Lane and was a substantial gentlemen's residence. There were four reception rooms, seven bedrooms with accompanying dressing rooms and ample accommodation for a large staff of servants. Outside was stabling for eleven horses, coach house, harness room and a further five staff bedrooms. There was a walled garden, vinery, greenhouses for apricots, peaches and grapes as well as a forcing pit. The gardens were substantial with lawns, shrubbery walks, and ornamental vistas. [11]

Sir Edward Griffith-Colpoys bought the house in 1821. The Colpoys family were of Huguenot extraction. George Colpoys left France shortly after the Revocation of the Edict of Nantes in 1685 when many French Protestant families departed and settled in County Clare in Ireland. Four generations later a descendant, Sir John Colpoys, was an admiral in the British navy. Born about 1742 he entered the navy in 1756 and served in a variety of stations before becoming a rear admiral in 1794. He found himself on board the *London* at the time of the naval mutiny at Spithead in 1797 and was ordered by the Admiralty to submit to the mutineers. He became a full admiral in 1801, commander in chief at Plymouth in 1803 and ended his naval career as Governor of Greenwich Hospital. He died in 1821. In the Spithead mutiny Sir John had been accompanied by his nephew, Captain Edward Griffith, the son of Sir John's sister Anne. After his uncle's death Edward Griffith bought Northbrook House and changed his name to Griffith-Colpoys. His eldest son who was born in 1800 was named James Adair Griffith Colpoys and became Rector of Droxford in 1830. He married Ann the daughter of J.B.Sumner who was Archbishop of Canterbury from 1848 to 1862.[12]

Northbrook House like so many other houses in Bishop's Waltham has never been owned or occupied by a single family for long. It has instead been the home of a series of people distinguished in service or secular life. In the 1830s it was occupied but not owned by Sir William Parry (1790–1855) a naval officer who is best known for feats of Arctic exploration. He commanded expeditions searching for the North West Passage between 1819 and 1825 and attempted to reach the North Pole from Spitzbergen in 1827 but was forced to turn back. He was knighted in 1829 and in 1847 became Governor of the Royal Naval Hospital at Haslar. When he retired from Haslar in 1852 he returned to Bishop's Waltham to live at Northbrook House. He died at Ems near Coblenz in 1855.[13]

There are few records relating to the Palace House. It was built in the grounds of the Bishops' Palace probably during the seventeenth century but there have been many subsequent additions and alterations. [14] Originally about half the size of the present house, it faced towards the Palace. When it was extended it was turned through ninety degrees so that front door and porch now face north and the original drawing room became a spacious entrance hall. [15] The so called 'river of the lord' ran from the pond under the road through the palace grounds and The Palace House garden to join the river Hamble, passing under the remains of a turret built by Bishop Langton about 1500. Close by, in the walled garden, is a Victorian greenhouse, which has been

24. The Palace ruins across the pond, 1784.

renovated by the present owner, and a pear tree reputed to have been planted by William of Wykham. It has been grafted since but still bears fruit. As long ago as 1784 Francis Grose wrote in his *Antiquities of England*, 'Against a wall near the ruins is shewn an ancient pear tree, said to have been planted by William of Wykeham, it has lately been grafted, and anno 1780, produced burgamy pears, mostly of two pounds weight, and some few weighing thirty-seven ounces' [16]

The Palace grounds including Palace House were still owned by the bishop who leased it on several occasions in the nineteenth century usually for a term of 21 years. At the beginning of the century the lessee was John Penny, who was appointed to the time consuming and thankless task of government agent for paroled prisoners in Bishop's Waltham during the Napoleonic wars (see above). Later the Palace House was leased by Richard Clark, gent. (1831) and Lieutenant William Barr (1844). In 1863 Arthur Helps leased the Palace House though he did not live in it.

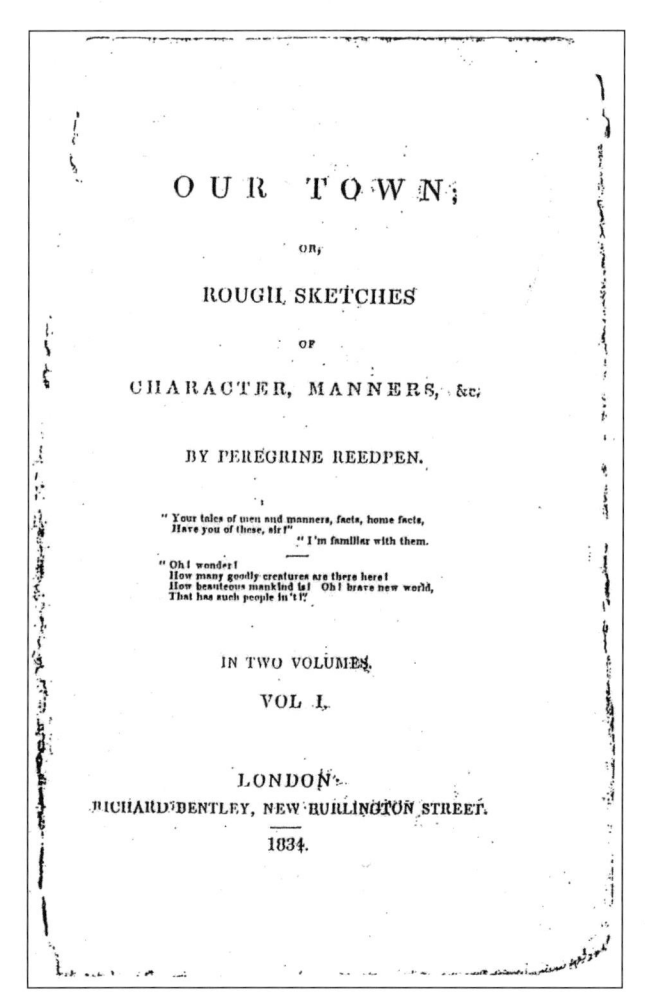

25. Title page of *Our Town* Volume I by Peregrine Reedpen, 1834.

In the 1830s there occurred one of the most bizarre episodes in the history of Bishop's Waltham, the publication of a book entitled *Our Town*, a ferocious caricature of the town and some of its leading personalities, written by Charles FitzAdderley who lived in Basingwell Street and wrote under the pen name Peregrine Reedpen. His title was deliberately reminiscent of Mary Russell Mitford's *Our Village, Sketches of Rural Life, Character and Scenery* published in 1832 and based on life in the village of Three Mile Cross near Reading. She had originally intended to call her later book drawn from life in Reading, *Our Town*, but changed her mind and called it instead *Belford Regis* when she learned of the already notorious book entitled *Our Town*. [17]

Charles FitzAdderley subtitled his work *Rough Sketches of Character, Manners etc.* It was published in two volumes – some 700 pages – by Richard Bentley of New Burlington Street, London, a well known publisher responsible for some of the works of Charles Dickens. It retailed at the substantial sum of one guinea. Bishop's Waltham was named neither in the title nor the text. 'There may', wrote the author 'be some who will fancy their own town is meant and there may be others who will fancy they know the places and persons intended to be described but for this let not the Author be blamed.' [18] Yet almost at once the guise of anonymity slips: 'We lie in a delightful hollow ... we are now standing at the door of the head inn, posting house and post office, called *The Crown*... Opposite is *The King's Head* ... On our left stands an indescribable sort of erection, called The Market House ... It now serves as a rendezvous for all the ragged and idle boys in the place, where they learn to swear and gamble'. Anybody who knew Bishop's Waltham would recognise it at once. [19]

Volume II opens with a description of The Poacher. Old Lot earns his daytime living as a tailor: 'diligently plying his needle with all the seeming industry of a man who gets his subsistence by his daily employment'. Old Lot is however in imagination 'sniggling a hare'. His features are 'long, thin, sharp, shrewd and cunning. ... His deep set eyes and overhanging brows denote sagacity and determination'. He is 70 years old: 'How he contrives to work as he does all day and to be out rambling all night, nobody can tell'.[20]

The feature of the book which gained it notoriety is the scurrilous pen portraits it contained of some of the town's leading citizens. Peregrine Reedpan's victims included Thomas Scard, curate of Durley and headmaster of the grammar school, who appears as 'the Bishop of Burley', George and Maria Clark as 'Mr and Mrs Thrivewell', and George Clark their son as 'the fox hunter'. His main targets however were three – Thomas Goolding Seymour, one of the town's doctors ('Dr. Slaymore'), William Gunner, solicitor and banker ('Shooter') and Miss Rosewell who ran a school at Hope House in Church Lane ('Miss Rosebell at the Temple of Hope'). What he has to say about them was libellous.

About Dr Slaymore he writes 'When a patient did happen to recover he [Dr Slaymore] was universally acknowledged to be 'a clever man', an assertion which he never denied. He is a bit of a gourmand, and has an abominable zest for hot suppers.... He hates children ... Let him catch one on his own premises he will chase him as he would a pole-cat. If the doctor could have things his own way he would be a second Herod.'[21]

Of Shooter he writes '…he is pompous in his manner and gait. The latter is that of an old bantam-cock. His features are harsh. He has never uttered a civil word to a man poorer than himself since [events described above] and never will. He rides on the top of a tall horse, or shuts himself up in his great coat in his lumbering phaeton, like a small oyster in a huge shell and looks proudly and disdainfully at everybody but those he hopes to profit by'. There follows an account of a party held by Shooter to celebrate the completion of an extension to his house – presumably Holm Oak – with its 'new drawing room, dining room and chamber above'.[22]

About Ambrosiana Rosebell he is equally scurrilous. 'A worm could not pop its head above ground to enjoy a mouthful of fresh air or a passing shower, but this lady would see and report its movements. …[She] has the vilest temper and breath of any in creation; and the anacondra itself with all its pestilential vapours, could scarcely be a more dreadful object to approach than this tall spinster.' Miss Rosebell was now 'absolute empress of some two dozen miserable little girls over whom she ruled with a rod of – birch…. Rewards were scarce, punishment or as the lady herself would term it, *poon*ishment, abounded.'[23]

Apart from the curiosity of such an odd episode in the life of the town, the interest of the book to the present day historian of Bishop's Waltham is the picture it incidentally conveys through caricature of some aspects of small town life in the 1830s. Not surprisingly the author does not appear in the 1841 census: he had presumably wisely withdrawn from Bishop's Waltham soon after the publication of his book. In Pigot's Directory, 1831 there appears the name of Sarah FitzAdderly, the author's wife, living in Basingwell Street and running a 'Ladies Boarding School' but by the time of the 1841 Census she too has disappeared. Why did he write; what did the town think of its chronicler; did Shooter or any of his other victims sue or threaten to sue?

By 1841 only one of the characters who figure most prominently in *Our Town* were still to be found in Bishop's Waltham. John Goolding Seymour ('Dr Slaymore') had died in 1840 and is commemorated on a handsome marble plaque in the chancel of St Peter's. Of Miss Rosewell's school there is no sign, and neither Charles nor Sarah FitzAdderly was living in Bishop's Waltham. William Gunner, banker and solicitor alone survived.

The first census of population was taken in 1801 but not until 1841 were names recorded. From the census of 1851 much more information of use to family and local historians is included. Although names are not found in the 1831 census it does tell us that there were 447 families in the parish with a total population of 2181. The average family size was therefore 4.87. The 1831 census also provides figures for families which are 'chiefly employed in agriculture' – 198, those chiefly employed in trade or manufacture –134 and others –115. Bishop's Waltham was predominantly an agricultural community.

The census of 1841 taken on the night of 6th –7th June contains the names and ages of all who lived in the parish and together with Pigot's Directory of 1844 provides a reliable snapshot of the town – its people and occupations as well as where they lived.[24] Exact ages were required for children up to the age 14, after that you could provide your age in five-year groups rounded down to the nearest multiple of five, so that anybody for example between the ages of 15 and 19 could give their age as 15, anybody between 21 and 24 could give their age as 20. In Bishop's Waltham about one third of those aged 15 and over gave their exact age. Heads of households were required to list their trade or occupation. Some others also did so particularly agricultural labourers – abbreviated Ag. Lab, and male and female servants – abbreviated MS and FS. This census did not list 'Scholar'.

The overall population of Bishop's Waltham was growing slowly. In the twenty years from 1821 to 1841 it increased only from 2126 to 2193. Not until the 1860s was there any significant growth (see Appendix B). There was an obvious distinction between the town where shopkeepers, craftsmen, medical practitioners and solicitors lived and where the schools were to be found and the outlying parts of the parish which consisted almost entirely of farms and the cottages of labourers and their families. Farming was a labour intensive business. The census lists 22 farms and just over 300 agricultural labourers.

Children and young people predominated and did so for the rest of the century. The median age was about 20. The number of people by age in successive decades formed a pyramid. There were 485 children under the age of ten; about 200 people in their forties and about 140 men and women in their fifties. Families were large, many between six and ten children living at home at the same time. In the cottages of agricultural labourers there must have been gross overcrowding and little privacy. There was no reliable form of birth control so many women were pregnant for much of their child bearing years. The census does not of course identify where children have died; in some cases they were born and died between censuses and so can only be found from birth or baptism records, though a gap of several years between consecutive children in a family often means the death of a child or children.

At Ashton Farm lived Stephen Steele (55) and his wife Amelia (50) with their six children – Mary (24), Stephen (23), Richard (21), Marion (17), Jane (12), Frances (5), and Margaret (2). Over the course of 24 years Amelia had at least six children and probably more – there are two gaps of five years between recorded births. Close by also at Ashton but in a labourer's cottage lived John Coffin (35) and his wife Elizabeth (35). They already had seven children – Henry (13), Charles (12), James (11), Caroline (9), John (5), Elizabeth (4) and George (1). At Dundridge lived George and Rebecca Gibson. George was also an agricultural labourer and he and his wife had eight children all still at home – daughters of 19, 17,15, 13, 11 and 8 and sons of 3 and 1. As soon as they were old enough sons would become like father, labourers on the farm, and daughters would help mother with the household chores and look after younger children or perhaps become a living-in servant in a more affluent household.

Large families crossed every class divide. The rector William Brock had a total of 13 children by two wives over a period of 26 years(see below p. 133)

Fairthorn was then in the parish of Bishop's Waltham. William Tovey (55) land surveyor lived there and had nine children ranging in age from Helen who was 20 to 'a female infant'. What tragedy lies behind these stark facts? It seems quite likely that his wife had died recently perhaps in child birth leaving him distraught and with an as yet unnamed infant daughter.

In the outlying parts of the parish – Dean, Dundridge, Ashton, Curdridge and the tithing of Hoe – farms large and small were adjacent to one another and the only possible occupation was farm labourer. For girls the normal employment was 'servant'. It was not only the big houses which employed one or more living-in servants, the larger farms did so too. Sons were often apprenticed to their fathers. George Haslar (20) who lived on Curdridge Common was an apprentice hoopmaker to his father James (60); at Wintershill Thomas Smith (17) and Adolphus Dawe (14) were apprenticed to James Heath (40) a wheelwright. Other examples include apprentice shoemaker, saddler and blacksmith.

Relatively few women had named employment. The census of 1841 lists about 80 girls as female servants. Apart from school mistresses there was one nurse, three dressmakers, a laundress and a staymaker. More surprising however was Elizabeth Prowting (55) who lived at Bishopsdown Farm and is described in the census as 'farmer'. She does not appear to have husband or family. She employed seven men aged between 50 and 14 presumably as farm labourers and two female servants aged 20 and 14.

The town was self sufficient. It is hard to think of any occupation not represented among its workforce. Bakers, blacksmiths, boot and shoe makers, butchers, fishmonger, grocers, green grocers, hair dressers, harness makers, leather cutters, saddlers, tailors and wheelwrights – all are to be found listed in the census and in Pigot's Directory. Among less familiar crafts were straw hat maker, tanner, cooper, hoop maker (several), horsebreaker, chandler, wool carder, sieve and basket maker, maltster, brush maker and breeches maker.

Three other crafts were well represented. There were six paper makers all living on Curdridge Common which had not then been enclosed and five maltsters in the town. At Coppice Hill brickmaking had been carried on since the fourteenth century and in 1841 eight men are listed as 'bricklayers', a term used for a variety of crafts related to brickmaking. They included three members of the Dowse family John (65), George (29) and a younger John (20).

If you needed professional services then the town could supply these too. There were accountants, attorneys and banker. Mary Ellyett of High Street was bookseller and printer, James Robert Knight (55) of Great Houchin Street was parish clerk. There were three 'surgeons': Louis James Lovekin (30 – but probably 34) of French Street who combined medical practice with being Registrar of births, marriages and deaths, a post introduced in 1837 when secular registration was made obligatory. The other 'surgeons' were James Colson (43) who also lived in French Street and Frederick Josiah Burgess (36) who lived in Basingwell Street. The Post Office was in St Peter Street and the postmaster was John Maunsell.[25]

Bishop's Waltham offered a wide choice of places to drink alcohol variously described in the trade directories as inns, taverns and public houses. No less than nine are named most within a short distance of each other. *The Crown* and *The King's Head* were both in St George's Square, a few yards away was *The Dolphin* in High Street. *The Bunch of Grapes* was in St Peter Street and *The White Swan* almost opposite in Bank Street. At the end of Bank Street were *The White Hart* and *The Wheatsheaf*. Outside the town centre were *The White Horse* in Beeches Hill and *The Fountain* on the road to Fareham.

Should you need to travel further afield, perhaps to visit relations, you could now go by road or rail though if you used the train you had to travel by road to the recently opened station at Botley. The coaches listed in the Directory of 1831 no longer ran but Pigot's Directory of 1844 included means of reaching Botley – Henry Ford (29) ran a daily service from his house in French Street. On Monday or Thursday you could go to London or Gosport taking William Bennett's Fly Wagon from John Woodman's house in High Street. There was similar provision for reaching Alresford, Portsmouth, Southampton or Winchester and thanks to the turnpikes the roads were by now much less hazardous than they had been earlier. Finally Pigot's Directory informs us that Market Day was Friday and that there were three annual fairs – on the second Friday in May, 30th July and 'the first Friday after Old Michaelmas Day'.[26] By the 1880s the weekly market and the three fairs once so important a part of the scene were no longer held.[27]

The census of 1851 provides information about the relationship of each named person to the head of the household – wife, son, daughter, servant, visitor etc. It also tells us whether they were married, single, widow or widower, their occupation and where they were born. The leading families do not appear to patronise the National School but instead made their own arrangements for the education of their children. At the Parsonage House (so named in the census) William Brock employed a living in teacher for his three daughters and a son who are described as 'scholar at home'. Next door at Northbrook House Hugh Vaughan's seven children had a governess whilst at Frogmore House Arthur Coles' eldest daughter, only 15 herself, was governess to her five younger sisters and two nieces.

Some of the road names which appear in the census are strange to us. Until the 1880s Lower Lane appears as Frogmore Lane (1841 & 61) or Frog Lane (1851) named probably after Frogmore House. There is no Free Street; instead it appears as White Hart Road at one end, Maypole Corner with six cottages in the middle and Northbrook at the northern end. Free Street does not appear until the end of the century. Basonwell Street is recognisable even if its spelling in 1851 and 1861 is strange to us. Hoe Road is Hoe Lane.

There were two lodging houses in the town, one in Bank Street and one in Basonwell Street. Those living in Bank Street varied in age from 19 to 63, and included agricultural labourers, a Chelsea pensioner, a tanner and a watchmaker. No less than six lodgers were born in Ireland and the remainder came from as far afield as Kent, Cornwall and Manchester. The house in Basonwell Street catered for 22 also mostly men and all described as 'traveller', coming from a variety of places with varying occupations though many were agricultural labourers.

The census names 26 farms varying in size from Ashton Farm where Charles Stubbs farmed 630 acres and employed 25 labourers to smallholdings where a man on his own farmed as little as six acres sometimes combining this with another occupation. Other large farms were Stakes Farm where William Carver had 540 acres and employed 18 men and Lodge Farm where Edward Wyatt farmed 483 acres and employed 17 labourers. In total the census lists almost 4000 acres of farms excluding the tithing of Curdridge whose census returns are illegible.

One family well known to many in Bishop's Waltham is not to be found in the census. Its contemporary representative, the younger Charles Walters who had been curate at St Peter's from 1812 to 1831, was now rector of Bramdean. In 1844 he gave a lecture to the Literary Institution of Bishop's Waltham entitled *The History of the Town, Church and Episcopal Palace of Bishop's Waltham from the earliest period to the present time.* It was printed 'at the special request of those who were present at its delivery'.[28] It is a work of considerable erudition peppered with Latin and Greek quotations.

Charles Walters was a representative Anglican priest of the mid- Victorian years, sympathetic neither to Rome nor to Protestant dissent. He describes Queen Mary as 'that evil genius', and Bishop Stephen Gardiner of Winchester as 'crafty, designing, unprincipled, faithless, a very image of Popery incarnate'. The reformers who returned to England from exile on the death of Queen Mary also get short shrift, they 'brought with them …the seeds of dissent and schism which have since sprung up throughout the realm and produced such baneful fruits'.[29]

Walters was according to his son a man with encyclopaedic knowledge and an accomplished conversationalist. '… he always had at hand a suitable remark, an apposite anecdote, a fitting sentiment, a courteous word, a sensible saying and was especially ready in classical, astronomical and theological subjects'.[30]

From at least the eighth century laity were required to pay tithe for the upkeep of church and clergy. It was usually paid in kind – one tenth of all that was produced. Gradually a money payment came to be a more convenient way to pay though some tithe was paid in kind right down to the eighteenth century. By the late eighteenth century it was greatly resented by many landowners.[31] A series of Tithe Commutation Acts passed in the 1830s regularised the payment which in future would be a money payment based on the average price of wheat, barley and oats during the previous seven years. In order to assess liability for tithe each parish needed to be surveyed with great accuracy. Every field was named or described, and measured, its owner and occupier were named, and its use – arable, wood, meadow, pasture or premises – recorded. The result is a description of the countryside unparalleled since the Domesday Survey made in 1086 and one which has been used to identify property ever since. The tithe map was accompanied by the award, hand written on large parchment sheets which listed the owners and occupiers of land by name together with their property numbered according to the map and attached to it.

At Bishop's Waltham the Parish Vestry invited tenders for surveying the parish and preparing the map in December 1837.[32] They were not however satisfied with the valuation they received and there was considerable delay before agreement was reached. The valuer was George Habin Appleby of Swanmore. The rent charge payable to the rector was £1265 and the award was sealed on 29th September 1841.[33] The Tithe map of the parish is a huge and unwieldy document, measuring 9 feet 8 inches by 12 feet 7 inches and the award attached to the map though smaller is not easy to use either. The two documents contain a vast amount of invaluable information. Three copies were made and in the case of Bishop's Waltham all are still in existence. One was the property of the Tithe Commissioners and is now in the Public Record Office at Kew, the diocese of Winchester held one and the parish copy was kept in the Parish Chest. These two are now in the Record Office in Winchester.

Because the scale of the map is so large it is of great value in establishing the topography of the town in 1841. The Palace ruins are prominent with the farm yard close by and the barn in which royalty were to be entertained in 1865 when the Royal Albert Infirmary was opened. The pond is already smaller than it had been during the middle ages but it had not yet shrunk to the proportions it has today. The turnpike roads appear on the map and so do the four tollhouses in the parish. The Coppice Hill brickworks are shown. The Market House is still a prominent landmark in St George's Square but only just: it was demolished soon afterwards. No railway had yet reached Botley still less Bishop's Waltham, whilst Curdridge Common and Waltham Chase had not yet been enclosed.

St George's Square with *The Crown Inn* leading into High Street has always been the centre of the town. Writing in 1892 William Houghton of Locks Farm recalled the town in the early years of the century. 'It was' he said 'a great place for cock fighting which took place in a barn near *The Crown Inn* on a very large scale and brought many sporting men to town'.[34] At the entrance to St George's Square stood the stocks. Until about 1870 there was a Maypole on the plot of grass outside the Rectory though it had not been used for dancing for many years [35]

The year 1841 saw the demolition of the Market House in the Square built soon after the destruction of the Palace to provide the town with facilities which the bishopric could no longer offer. It was constructed with cloisters at ground level, a room at first floor level and included a fire hose with long handle to pull burning thatch from a roof as well as a cage or lock up. The Vestry Minutes for 26th November 1841 read: 'The Market House including the Cage for Prisoners being rendered useless and in a very dilapidated state it is expedient that the same should be taken down and the cages rebuilt with the same material in another place together with a building for an Engine House under the same roof.' [36]

7

Registers and rectors 1737–1833

THE SECOND parish register of St Peter's runs from 1669 to 1736 and follows the same format as the first one with christenings, marriages and burials listed together. From about 1730 the name of the mother as well as the father of the child is included in the notice of christening. The register ends in 1736 even though it is less than half used. The reason appears to be that paper would no longer suffice; the register must consist of sheets of parchment. There are instructions for overcoming the difficulties in writing on parchment: 'If the Parchment in any Part of this Book should not take the Ink well, rub it with a little Pounce, and let no Sand be used at all, but Sinking Blotting Paper'.[1] The new Register includes christenings and burials over a period of three quarters of a century from 1737 to 1812 but marriages only from 1737–1754.

Infant baptism according to the Prayer Book was almost universal so the register is in practice if not in theory a record of births, the only one available until secular registration was introduced in 1837. There are a number of illegitimate births. They are no longer described as they had sometimes been in the previous century as 'born in fornication', the more usual term now is 'baseborn' or 'bastard child of…'. Sometimes the only indication of illegitimacy is the absence of the name of father or mother or even both. On 8th January 1737 James Lake, 'son of a stranger' was baptised. On 25th February 1738 'a child left in the night at Dean farm on 14th February' was baptised – 'Valentine Dean'. Children born in the workhouse were often 'baseborn'. Soldiers passing through or stationed in the town were sometimes named as the father – Lord Coventry's Regiment, the Welsh Fusiliers, Colonel Harrison's Regiment among them.

Place of residence in the parish is sometimes included – Curdridge (including 'at the paper mill'), Swanmore, Ashton, Dean and oddly 'Shidville'. (Was this a variant for Shidfield, itself the usual spelling of the village we call Shedfield?) Biblical Christian names were preferred; for girls Mary is easily the most popular followed by Elizabeth, Ann or Hannah, Sara and Martha; for boys William, John, Thomas, Peter, James and Richard all occur frequently.

In 1754 parliament passed Hardwicke's Marriage Act 'for the better preventing clandestine marriages'. In future records of the calling of banns of marriage and of

Christenings 1758

- James Son of James & Elizabeth Smith.
- Mary Daughter of John & Martha Houghton.
- Thomas Son of William & Elizabeth Sargent.
- Dinah Daughter of Robert & Ann Earnaker.
- 3. Elizabeth Daughter of Richard & Mary Hartly.
- 15. Mary Daughter of Samuel & Martha Jennings.
- 24. John the Son of John & Elizabeth Dipnall.
- 10. Edward base-born Son of Mary Mayor & Michael Herriot (a Frenchman)
- Kezia Daughter of Peter & Sarah Binsted — Curdridge.
- 12. Anna Daughter of John & Jane Mathews.
- 29. Sarah Daughter of Richard & Sarah Veal.
- 14. Mary Daughter of Thomas & Sarah Wilkins.
- 1. James Son of Felix & Hannah Miller.
- James Son of Thomas & Mary Jackson. Curdridge.
- 16. Hannah Daughter of Thomas & Mary Jackson.
- 19. William Son of William & Ann Steel.
- 28. James base-born Son of Elizabeth Brown Widow.
- 10. John Son of William & Ann Nash.
- 14. Mary Daughter of John & Mary Seagrave.
- James Son of James & Mary Budd.
- 16. Michael & William Twin Sons of Robert & Ann Baynes.
- 19. Joseph Son of Roger & Mary Edmunds.
- Frances Daughter of Robert & Mary Barfoot. Ashton.
- 7. Luke Son of Peter & Grace Dowling.
- 21. Richard Son of James & Mary Galyer.
- 25. Mary Daughter of Elizabeth & Charles Mitchell. Swanmore.
- 16. Jane Daughter of John & Jane Parkley.
- 23. Leah Daughter of James & Ann Bernard.
- 12. Mary Daughter of Richard & Mary Palmer.
- 28. Vincent Son of Vincent & Christian Mist. Shidville.
- 30. William Son of James & Hannah Emmet. Winterhill.
- 25. James Son of Francis & Elizabeth Martin.
- 30. Elizabeth Daughter of William & Mary Wilton.
- 3. Cuthbert Son of Cuthbert & Elizabeth Dowse.
- 6. John Son of Edward & Mary Wyatt.
- 15. Mary Daughter of James & Amy Knight.
- 20. Harry Son of Edward & Ann Smith. Raglington.
- 27. Sarah Daughter of James & Hannah Rider.
- John Son of Charles & Rebecca Partridge.
- Mary Daughter of William & Mary Rood.
- 4. William base-born Son of Ann Stickett.
- 1. Andrew Son of Jane & Richard Mear.
- 7. Elizabeth Daughter of Thomas & Elizabeth Privet. Hoe.
- 26. Mary Daughter of James & Sarah Elcock.
- 9. Martha Daughter of Richard & Mary Mills.
- 15. Mary Daughter of John & Joanna Dee. Hannah
- William Son of John & Martha Wyatt.
- 29. Hannah Daughter of Abraham & Hannah Sanson.

26. Parish Register – christenings for the year 1758 signed by
Joseph Challoner Bale, Curate.

(The Year 1767)	Page 37

No 144

Thomas Knight — of [th]
and Mary Smith Both of [this]
Parish were
Married in this [Church] by [Banns]
this twenty second Day of December — in the Year One Thousand seven Hundred
and sixty seven by me Jos: Th: Bale [Curate]
This Marriage was { The mark of
solemnized between Us { Thomas + Knight
Mary Smith
In the { A H Bale
Presence of { James Cole

1768	No 145

Edward Garrett — of [th]
and Susanna Edmunts both of [this]
Parish were
Married in this [Church] by [Licence]
this Third Day of February in the Year One Thousand seven Hundred
and Sixty Eight by me Wm Ralfe [Curate]
This Marriage was { The mark of Edward + Garrett
solemnized between Us { The mark of Susanna + Edmunts
In the { Ths Webb
Presence of { John Stubington

No 146

William Bridges of [th]
and Ann Parker both — of [this]
were
Married in this [Church] by [Banns]
this 7th — — Day of February in the Year One Thousand Hundred
and 68 — — by me Ri: Richards — [Curate]
This Marriage was { The mark of Wm + Bridges
solemnized between Us { The mark of Ann + Parker
In the { John Parker
Presence of { Thomas Cole

No 147

Peter Memit — of [th]
and Olivia Taylor Both of [this]
Parish were
Married in this [Church] by [Licence]
this sixteenth Day of February in the Year One Thousand seven Hundred
and Sixty eight by me Jos: Th: Bale [Curate]
This Marriage was { The mark of Peter + Memit
solemnized between Us { Olivia + Taylor
In the { Bentord
Presence of { John Parker

27. Parish Marriage Register for 1767 – bride and groom often make their mark.

the ceremony itself were to be kept in a book which contained printed forms for both. The result is a more thorough and consistent record from which much information can be gleaned. Banns called in the parish and marriages celebrated in St Peter's were kept in this way from 1754 and can thus be analysed. The numbered forms in the register of marriages required the bride and groom to sign their name or to make their mark – a cross endorsed by a witness. This provides an index of literacy. If you couldn't write your name it was unlikely that you could write anything else or that you could read. The signature of some of those who signed their name rather than making their mark suggests that writing was not an accomplishment they often used or did so with any facility. The proportion making their mark shows little change between 1754 and 1788. About 60% of men and about 40% of women signed their name whilst in about one third of marriages neither partner signed their name.[2]

The parish was a closed community. You rarely went far afield and naturally found friends and in due course marriage partners from the neighbourhood. Between 1790 and 1805 the banns were called for one hundred intended marriages. The prescribed form required the minister – usually the curate – who called the banns, to enter the place of residence of the partners. Not one single person found an intended husband outside Hampshire and 70% of couples came from Bishop's Waltham. Of those whose husbands came from further afield most were from adjoining parishes – six from Upham, six from Wickham, five from Droxford, which then included Swanmore and Shedfield with the odd one or two from Titchfield, Corhampton or Fareham. The furthest anybody ventured to find a husband was Stoke Charity, Bedhampton, Portsmouth, Widley and Portchester. Several entries read 'Resident in this parish' – probably servants whose home was elsewhere but who had met their bride while working at one of the big houses.[3]

The last eighteenth century rector who lived in the Rectory at Bishop's Waltham was probably Robert Ashe, 1750–1753, whose wife gave birth to their son Benjamin on 8th June 1752. He was baptised in St Peter's on 3rd July. In 1753 Robert Ashe accepted the living of Cheriton where, he informed the bishop, he resided for the seven summer months moving in the winter to Winchester where 'I reside upon my prebend'. 'There is a curate constantly in attendance' he added.[4] It may be that when he was rector of Bishop's Waltham he likewise preferred Winchester to Bishop's Waltham as his winter residence.

The next four rectors were non-resident pluralists: they did not live in the parish, paid only occasional visits to Bishop's Waltham and enjoyed its emoluments as well as those of one or more other parishes. Nor was this state of affairs exceptional or even unusual. Pluralism does not seem to have been regarded as any more reprehensible than multi- directorships are today. The eighteenth century Church of England was short of clergy, many clergy houses had fallen into disrepair and clerical stipends were low. The cure of souls in the parish was entrusted to curates who were paid a meagre stipend whilst the non-resident rector collected the income, sometimes

(The Year 1786)   Page 55

Nº 271

Banns of Marriage between Wm Harfield,
and Ann Munday, both of this Parish
were published on the three Sundays underwritten:
That is to say, On Sunday, the 16th ⎫
   On Sunday, the 23d   ⎬ of July, 1786, by me Cha Walters, Curate
   On Sunday, the 30th ⎭

Nº 272

Banns of Marriage between James Evans, residing in this parish
and Mary Wilkins, of this parish, Widow
were published on the three Sundays underwritten:
That is to say, On Sunday, the 3d ⎫
   On Sunday, the 10th ⎬ of Septr 1786, by me Cha Walters, Curate
   On Sunday, the 17th ⎭

Nº 273

Banns of Marriage between William Lambert of this Parish
and Ann Hellyet of the parish of Botley
were published on the three Sundays underwritten:
That is to say, On Sunday, the 10th ⎫
   On Sunday, the 17th ⎬ of Decr 1786, by me Cha Walters, Curate
   On Sunday, the 24th ⎭

1787.

Nº 274

Banns of Marriage between Thomas Dowse, residing in this Parish
and Ann Whytingham of the parish of Droxford
were published on the three Sundays underwritten:
That is to say, On Sunday, the 19th of August ⎫
   On Sunday, the 26th ⎬ 1787, by me Cha Walters, Curate
   On Sunday, the 2d of Septr ⎭

Nº 275

Banns of Marriage between Thos Cotton residing in this parish
and Ann Doves, widow, of this parish
were published on the three Sundays underwritten:
That is to say, On Sunday, the 26th of August ⎫
   On Sunday, the 2d of Septr ⎬ 1787, by me Cha Walters, Curate
   On Sunday, the 9 ⎭

28. Parish Banns Register for 1786 – banns signed by Charles Walters, Curate 1785–1811.

substantial, of the benefice derived from tithe and glebe. The word curate signified not an assistant priest who shared the cure of souls with the rector but a priest who took services, baptised, married and buried in the absence of the rector sometimes licensed by the bishop but without the security of the freehold. From the 1750s we know the names of the curates – Ambrose Kent, Joseph Challoner Bale and Charles Walters I all served for a considerable period.[5]

When Dr James Cutler was appointed rector in 1753 he had been rector of Droxford since 1746 when he was aged 29. The bishop justified presentation to Bishop's Waltham on the grounds of the 'Value of the Livings (Droxford £300, Bishop's Waltham £352) and Distance' – presumably he thought that £300 was not sufficient and that two adjoining parishes could be placed in the care of one person.[6] James Cutler remained rector of both Droxford and Bishop's Waltham until his death in 1782, living in the newly built early Georgian rectory next to Droxford church and was buried in the south aisle there.[7] From September 1753 until May 1755 Gilbert White, later famous as the author of *The Natural History of Selborne*, was curate of Durley but lived in the rectory of Bishop's Waltham.

In his history of Bishop's Waltham published in 1844 Charles Walters II refers to Dr Henry Ford, Cutler's successor and rector from 1782 to 1794 as 'another learned rector of Waltham.' He does not add that St Peter's saw little of its learned rector who he tells us 'was said to have been acquainted with 22 languages and dialects classical, Oriental and European'.[8] Dr Ford was at the same time also Principal of Magdalene Hall and Professor of Arabic in the University of Oxford.

From 1780 the bishop of Winchester was Brownlow North who was one of the most spectacular exponents of pluralism, non-residence and nepotism in the eighteenth century Church of England. He was the brother of the Lord North who became First Lord of the Treasury (Prime Minister) at the age of 36 in 1770 and to whom is attributed the loss of the American colonies. Brownlow North moved steadily up the episcopal ladder, each diocese which he occupied worth more than the previous one – Coventry and Lichfield 1771 when he was aged 30; Worcester 1774, Winchester 1781. Here he stayed for almost 40 year until his death in 1820. Bishop North's relations, close and remote alike, benefited from presentations to some of the most lucrative appointments in the diocese. His sons occupied the richest livings and so did the men whom his daughters married. Francis North, the bishop's eldest son turned his seventeenth century rectory at Old Alresford into a sixteen bedroom mansion, so large that it allegedly took one of the servants a whole morning just to trim the wicks on the oil lamps.[9]

Bishop North's relations were to be found in the parishes round Bishop's Waltham. His eldest daughter Harriet married William Garnier who was rector successively of Upham with Durley and Droxford as well as a prebendary of Winchester Cathedral. His successor at Upham and Durley in 1814 was John Haygarth who was married to Sophia the fourth daughter of Edmund Poulter the bishop's brother-in-law. When Bishop North died at Winchester House, Chelsea on

29. Brownlow North, Bishop of Winchester, 1781–1820.

12th July 1820, of the twelve prebendaries who acted as pall-bearers at his funeral eight were his relations [10]

Edmund Poulter was himself rector of Bishop's Waltham from 1794–1797. He was born Edmund Sayer but assumed the name Poulter when he was called to the bar in 1778. On marrying the bishop's sister-in-law he concluded, no doubt rightly, that his prospects in the church were decidedly better than in the law and so he was ordained in 1788 by Bishop North and at once given the living of Crawley. This was followed by Meonstoke where he was rector from 1791 to 1832. When he was appointed to Bishop's Waltham Bishop North provided 'A Certificate of Value and Distance'. Each parish – Meonstoke and Bishop's Waltham was now worth £600 and the distance between them was 'not exceeding 4 miles'. Edmund Poulter was also appointed to a prebendal stall in Winchester Cathedral with a house at No.1 The Close. In due course he added a further selection of livings – Calbourne in the Isle of Wight, Buriton and Petersfield, Alton and its associated parishes – Selborne, Binstead and Kingsley – for example. He was also like many clergy in the eighteenth century a Justice of the Peace dealing with malefactors and on occasion sentencing them to transportation for a term of years.

Frances Collins the historian of Meonstoke describes Edmund Poulter: 'It seems that he and his wife aroused feelings of strong dislike, but perhaps that is a reflection of the general opinion of the Norths…he was a place seeker with both eyes on every chance of promotion. … From No. 1 The Close with periods of residence in his various rectories, he entertained, hunted, shot, played cricket, and sat on the Bench (where he sometimes fell asleep) and cultivated the acquaintance of the County'. Edmund Poulter died in January 1832 and was followed at Meonstoke by Charles John Hume who served for the remarkable period of 61 years.[11]

By now the people of Bishop's Waltham can scarcely have expected their rector to reside and in this their next incumbent did not disappoint. Edward Salter (c.1742–1812) had been presented to the rectory of Stratfield Turgis in 1775 and added Stratfield Saye in 1795 where he chose to live. He had since 1784 also been a prebend of York and added a canonry of Winchester in 1807.[12] His visits to Bishop's Waltham were few and far between.

Church life went on despite the absence of the rector. Services including baptisms, marriages and burials were taken by a curate paid a pittance by the non-resident rector. The parish clerk lined out the psalms and said the responses on behalf of a congregation which attended out of duty. In the tower there is a reminder that the bellringers were active. On the wall is a doggerel verse not unlike that to be found in other belfries and dated 1766:

> *You ringers that use this belfry,*
> *Your hats throw off, your gloves lay by.*
> *The stewards' fee you can't deny,*
> *You must pay twopence ere you go.*
> *And if you take God's name in vain*
> *You shall pay sixpence for your pain;*
> *And if you shall a wager lay*
> *Or such a thing presume to say,*
> *And when you go the bells to ring*
> *Drink soberly, God save the King.*

The last years of the eighteenth century saw the building of a second gallery at St Peter's, over the whole of the south aisle, it was aesthetically unpleasing and structurally disastrous. It was the result of a petition from 30 parishioners. The south arcade of the nave was dismantled and the new gallery was supported on wooden columns with a staircase built to reach it. At the same time the chancel arch was distorted in order to provide visibility for those sitting in the gallery. Light was provided by three dormer windows inserted into the sloping roof; their location still visible from outside the building by the different colour stone used to replace them in 1897.

Bishop's Waltham's first incumbent in the nineteenth century was at the age of 25 the youngest person to hold the living and likely to remain so. More significant he was the first to reside at the rectory for half a century. James Ogle was the son of Rear Admiral Sir Chaloner and Lady Hester Ogle, of Martyr Worthy in the Itchen valley. Sir Chaloner was the father of an illegitimate son born to Grace Knight, a Bishop's Waltham girl in 1778.[13] The presentation to the living was no doubt the result of his relationship to his bishop. James Ogle was twice related to Bishop North: his mother was the bishop's youngest daughter and his wife was Elizabeth the daughter of Edmund Poulter.[14]

James Ogle took his degree at Merton College Oxford in 1798 and three years later was ordained by Bishop North; deacon in September and priest in December of the same year. He came to St Peter's in 1802 and at once enlarged the seventeenth century rectory, building on rooms on the south and west, in particular the west facing dining room, to make a house fit for a gentleman. Pluralism was increasingly frowned upon but that did not prevent the Master and Brethren of St Cross Hospital presenting James Ogle to the vicarage of Crondall near Basingstoke in 1811, a post he held for the rest of his life, in addition to Bishop's Waltham. The vicarage at Crondall was in such a dilapidated state that even the curate whom James Ogle installed there was obliged to live in lodgings.[15] He was however Bishop's Waltham's last pluralist rector. Things began to change – even in the diocese of Winchester – but it was far into the nineteenth century before pluralism and non-residence were eliminated. In 1827 of 10,533 Church of England benefices the incumbents of only 4,413 were resident.[16]

The Old Rectory as it is now called was probably originally built in the seventeenth century though some of the timbers in the cellar had been reused and have been dated to the eleventh century. The house was a substantial one and the rector lived in some style. On the ground floor were drawing room, dining room, lounge and study as well as kitchen, scullery, larder and pantry. There was also a room for parish use. On the first floor were six bedrooms three of them with dressing rooms as well as maid's bedroom and a bathroom and on the second floor a further six staff bedrooms. In the basement were two storerooms and a wine cellar.[17] There was a huge key to the front door.

Outside were brew house with pump, wood store, and washhouse with built-in brick boiler. These remained until the space they occupied became the site of Church House built in 1992. The grounds which included rockery and woodland walk were substantial, in total about four acres fronting on to Lower Lane.[18] The carriage way to the house cut across the green where the Maypole had stood in the seventeenth century, and entered the Rectory grounds to the right of the present entrance which came into use only when the new Rectory was occupied in 1964. It led to the front of the house then round to three coach houses, tack room, stables and loose box. The rector could reach the west end of the church through the gate in the churchyard wall which also gave ready access for parishioners who wished to call on the rector.[19]

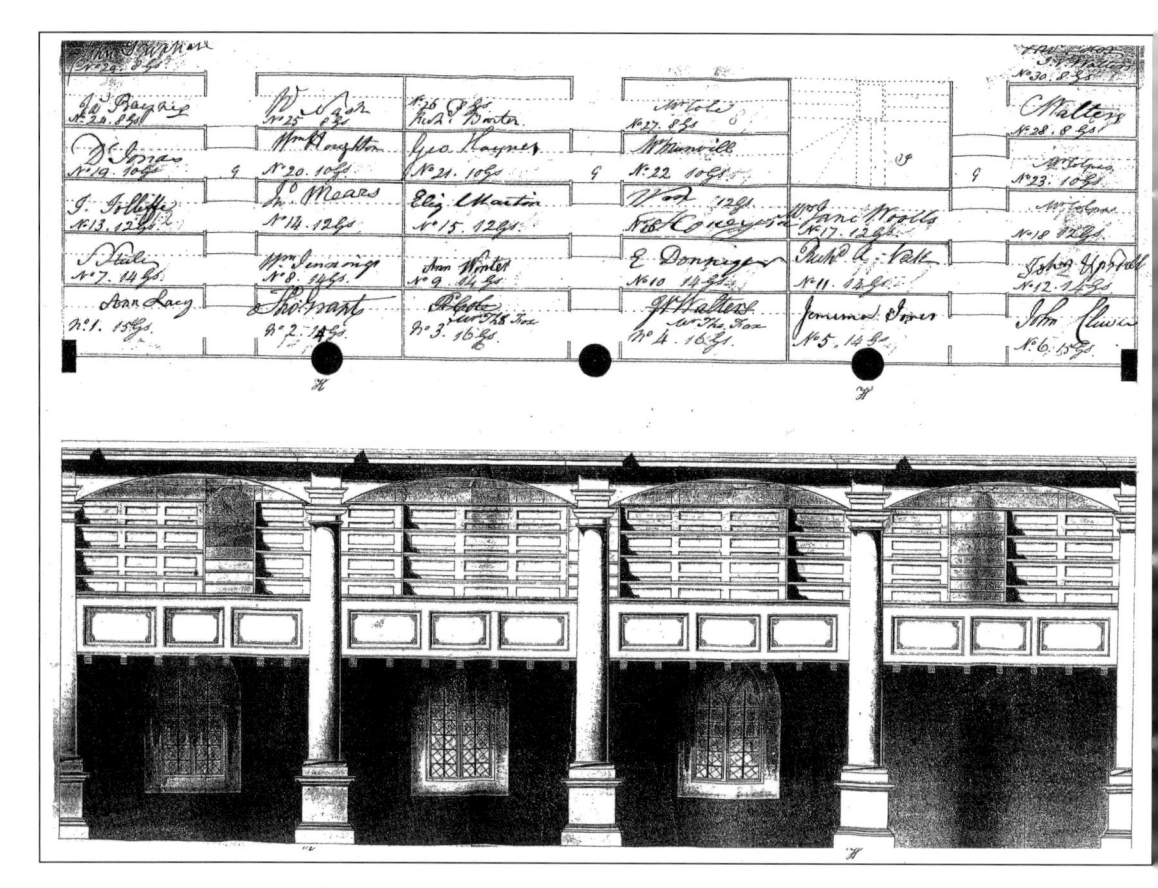

30. Plan of the South Gallery erected in St Peter's Church 1797.
Names of pew holders include No.5 Jemima Jones (girls' school in Church Lane),
No.10 Ezekiel Donniger, organist, No.29 the Revd Charles Walters curate,
No 30 the Revd John Vodin Walters. The amount each occupant paid annually in pew
rent is also shown.

The south gallery had stood for little over 20 years before its state caused concern. The wooden supports had decayed and at a vestry meeting in January 1822 it was decided that they must be stripped and their condition examined by a surveyor who would also be asked to recommend how the repair should be carried out. One suggestion was that the gallery should be supported on square brick piers with no ornament, a proposal dismissed as 'fitter for a brick kiln than a church'. The two surveyors agreed that the church needed immediate repair since in its present state it was not safe It was decided 'to prop up the church in a secure manner' at once. [20]

Eventually columns of Portland stone were erected, paid for by a church rate and they remained in place until the much more ambitious restoration carried out in 1896–7.

8

From the Grammar School to the Educational Institute

THE LAST years of the eighteenth century saw the growth of private day and boarding schools and academies to provide for what contemporaries described as 'the middling sort' – the children of farmers and tradesmen of whom there were many in Bishop's Waltham – a practical but genteel education for those willing to pay for it. According to a Hampshire Directory of 1793 'the place [Bishop's Waltham] may be called a little university as it has ever been famous for its schools; among them one for female education has been peculiarly successful'.[1] Most of them were single sex and more for boys than for girls. No qualification was necessary to open a school nor was there any regulation. Not surprisingly many did not last long.

In the 1780s there were three private schools in Bishop's Waltham. The Revd Charles Walters, headmaster of the grammar school and William Jennings, bookseller and stationer, each ran a boarding school 'for young gentlemen'. There was also a school for girls. 'The Bishop's Waltham School for Young Ladies' was opened by

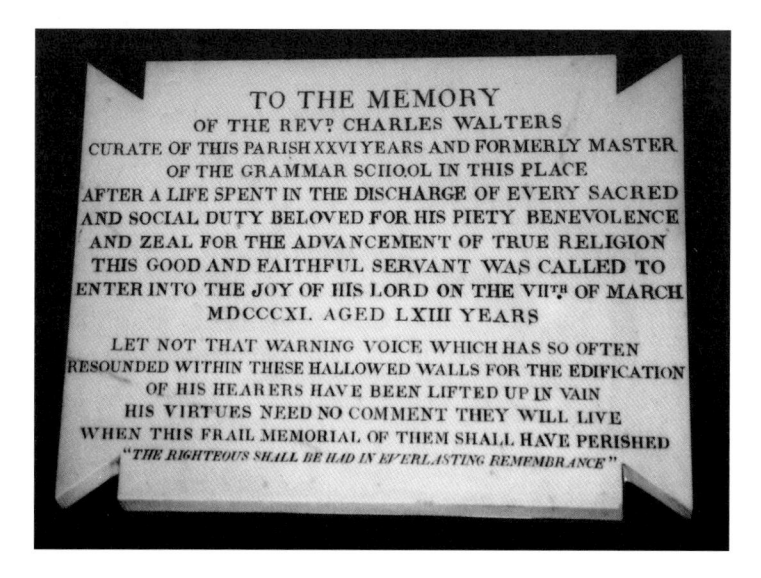

31. Tablet in the chancel of St Peter's church erected in memory of the Revd Charles Walters.

Mrs Wyatt and taken over by Jemima Jones in 1771.[2] It was this school which 'came to grief through a love affair between one of the girls and a French officer imprisoned in Bishop's Waltham during the Napoleonic Wars'. The love-lorn officer apparently threw a letter intended for the young lady over the wall of the school at Hope House in Church Lane (later St Peter Street). It was picked up by a servant. The incident which took place in 1807 came to the ears of Jemima Jones who at once packed the girl off home and dismissed the servant – both actions which seem extreme – but according to James Padbury, writing much later, Miss Jones' prompt action 'failed to save the school'.[3]

By 1831 educational provision for 'the middling sort' was even wider. Charles Robinson had a 'gentlemen's' boarding school in Northbrook Road (probably Lower Lane). There were two ladies' boarding schools, one in Basingwell Street run by Sarah FitzAdderley and one at Hope House now managed by Maria Rosewell. According to the census of 1841 Hope House was no longer a school but Sarah Battershell a young woman of 24 ran a school at another house in the same street where she had ten girl boarders.

Newcomers to Bishop's Waltham are surprised to discover that for two hundred years, from the late seventeenth to the late nineteenth century, Bishop's Waltham had a grammar school. Almost nothing now remains. Until 1962, when it was demolished to make way for a car park, there was a building in Portland Square (at the end of Brook Street) known as the Old Grammar School. There are tablets on the north wall of the chancel of St Peter's church to two early nineteenth century grammar school masters – Charles Walters and his brother John Vodin Walters – and an obelisk in the church yard erected by school boys to the memory of a fellow pupil, Samuel Jefferys, who died in 1833, by then an undergraduate at Magdalen Hall, Oxford. Why and when did the grammar school disappear? The key to its failure lies in the inadequacy of the original endowment. There were insufficient funds to provide either a school building or a house for the master and hence ensure its continuation. No trustees' minutes have survived before 1877, and we know little about schoolmasters, teachers or scholars or about its curriculum and sporting activities. Its history has to be pieced together from meagre and scattered evidence. The grammar school closed in the early 1880s and attempts to refound it failed. The endowments were used for the Educational Institute which opened in 1899 and in turn lasted for almost exactly a century before it too closed.

Between the sixteenth and the eighteenth centuries most towns in Hampshire and elsewhere acquired a grammar school, often endowed and established by a local worthy. Grammar schools founded before the late nineteenth century were rarely selective academically. They were intended for anybody likely to enter a profession or to become a clerk needing to read and write English and probably Latin too. Until the eighteenth century Latin was the language of the professions used by lawyers, the universities, clergy, schoolmasters and professional men generally.

In Hampshire Eggar's School at Alton was founded in 1638, Robert May endowed a school at Odiham in 1694, Richard Churcher at Petersfield in 1722 and Richard Taunton at Southampton in 1752.[4] Bishop's Waltham was no exception. In 1679 Bishop George Morley (1662–84) founded and endowed the grammar school with land which had previously belonged to Mottisfont Abbey. He left an annuity of £10 for the schoolmaster who was to be appointed by the rector and churchwardens and licensed by the bishop. He was 'to teach the children of the poorer sort to read English and to write without being paid by such children, their parents or guardians'. The rector and churchwardens were to have oversight of the school and could if they thought fit remove the schoolmaster and elect another.[5]

Robert Kerby and Mary Bone later added to the endowment. Robert Kerby died in 1721 leaving £400 to be invested in land, the income to be divided, £3 for the poor and £13 for the education of six poor boys who were to be known as 'Kerby's Scholars'. His bequest was used to buy land on the north side of Curdridge Lane which became known as the Poor's Bargain. In 1732 Mary Bone died leaving £20 per year for the education of ten poor boys between the ages of eight and fifteen in reading, writing, Latin, arithmetic and Church Catechism. The land she bequeathed to the school was in the village of Lomer, deserted when it was enclosed for sheep in the sixteenth century.[6]

At first the school seems to have made use of the school room in the parish church which had its own external entrance but later moved to more commodious premises in the town and took boarders. The rector appointed the schoolmaster who was a priest licensed by the bishop who usually held another post, often curate to the absentee rector. He sometimes engaged an assistant who taught the pupils. In February 1745 for example Bishop Benjamin Hoadly (1734–61) licensed the Revd James Gibson 'to perform the office of schoolmaster in teaching Bishop Morley's scholars and others in the town and parish of Bishop's Waltham'.[7] He appears to have remained headmaster for 30 years resigning on 19th December 1775. His successor was the Revd John Evans licensed by Bishop John Thomas (1761–81). There was then a disagreement between the trustees and the rector which the rector won and his nominee, the Revd Charles Walters, became headmaster and taught Latin whilst the trustees' nominee taught English.[8]

The grammar school reached its zenith in the late eighteenth century and the first half of the nineteenth century. Trade directories of the time describe it as 'in a very prosperous state, and conducted with great propriety'. Charles Walters remained headmaster until his death and from about 1785 was also curate of the parish church. He was assisted in the grammar school by his brother the Revd. John Vodin Walters who was curate of Meonstoke. When they died within a year or so of each other in 1811 and 1812, eloquent memorials were placed in St Peter's church. According to a local paper Charles Walters' funeral was attended by 1700 people.[9] He had managed also to run a private school in the town advertising in *The Hampshire Chronicle* his 'boarding school for young gentlemen'.[10]

Charles Walters' son, another Charles, born in 1784 took over both the headship of the grammar school and the curacy of the parish on his father's death. He received £32 for the headship and increased the pay of the assistant master to £25. He seems also to have continued his father's private boarding school. Here his most distinguished pupil was Frederick Madden (1801–73), a Portsmouth boy who became one of the outstanding palaeographers of the period, Fellow of the Royal Society before he was 30, knighted at the age of 32 and head of the Manuscripts Department of the British Museum from 1837.[11]

In 1822 Charles Walters II in turn relinquished the headship of the grammar school though remaining curate until 1831 when he became Rector of Bramdean. He later moved to a parish in Winchester and died there on 7th June 1869 aged 85.[12] The new master of the grammar school was Thomas Scard who was also curate of the parish of Durley. He ran a highly successful school in Brook Street with the help of a series of assistants for close on 20 years. According to the census of 1841 Thomas Scard and his wife Eliza had no less than 52 male boarders mostly between the ages of 11 and 15 though Ivan Fernandez was 17 and Henry Simonds only seven.

Only tantalising glimpses of the life of the school and its pupils have survived. Two handwriting books belonging to a pupil, Richard Parsons, dated 1808 and 1810 are in the Hampshire Record Office. The curriculum included learning a copperplate hand so Richard practised by copying out exemplary sentiments such as 'Writing is an elegant and useful accomplishment', 'Cleanliness promotes health of body and delicacy of mind'.[13]

Each year the grammar school celebrated 29th May – Royal Oak Day (sometimes called Oak Apple Day), the birthday of Charles II and the day on which he had entered London on his return as king in 1660, when the boys competed for a prize poem. The winning entry was printed and a file of these composed between 1828 and 1845 has also been deposited in Hampshire Record Office. They are lengthy, conform to classical models and are full of conventional poetic diction. The subjects are historical, classical or religious – *The Druids* (1829), *Hannibal Crossing the Alps* (1832), *The Mutiny on the Bounty* (1834), *The Prophet Elijah and his Ascension* (1836). In 1839 John Gorham won the prize with a poem of some 175 lines on *The Remains of the Episcopal Palace and Castle, Bishop's Waltham, Hants*.[14] It includes these lines:

> Decay's sad impress stamp'd upon the scene,
> The wild flow'r's bloom, the ivy's mantling green,
> The brown moss gathe'ring on each tottering stone,
> The moat half choked, the grim portcullis gone…
>
> Now, in the hall a monarch's presence grac'd,
> The gloomy owl her nest has plac'd,
> And where the royal banquet once was spread,
> Rude cattle graze – the grass-grown floor their bed.
> Whence came sad ruin? …

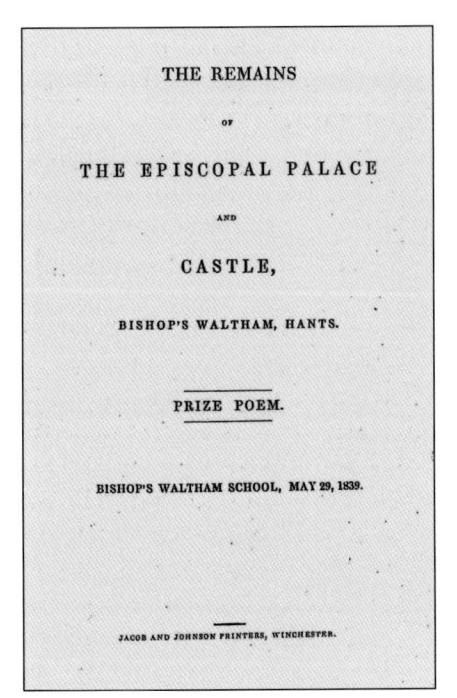

Two further glimpses of the grammar school survive. On Saturdays a dancing master came over from Winchester and joint classes were held with the private girls school in St Peter's Street. 'Saturday was looked on as a golden afternoon' wrote a former pupil many years later. The two schools enjoyed an 'enviable reputation' in the county it appears. Each year Domum Day was celebrated when former pupils organised a feast at which it was customary for one of them to present a whole lamb to be roasted and placed on the table as one of 'the delicacies' which formed the main course of the celebratory dinner.[15]

According to the 1851 census there was a boarding school in Brook Street run by the Revd William Allen. He describes himself as 'Clergyman of the Church of England without parochial charge. Master of a Private

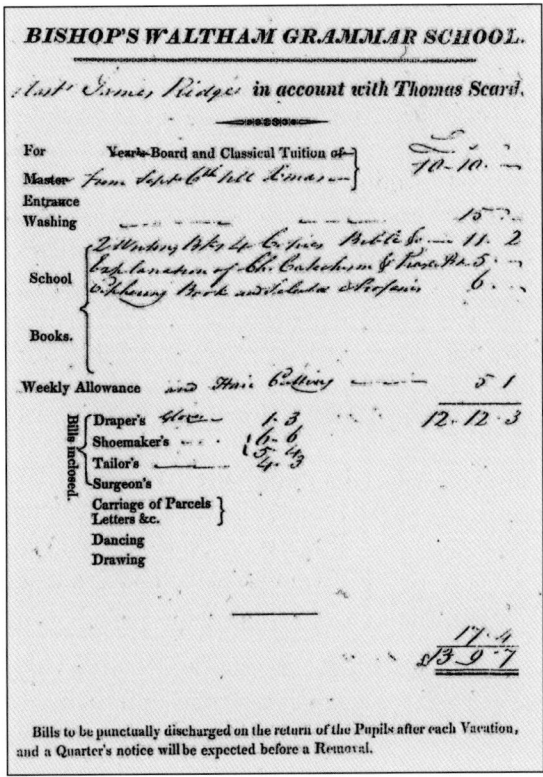

32. Cover of printed prize poem entitled *The Remains of the Episcopal Palace* dated 29th May 1839.

33. Termly account for Master James Ridge a boarder at the Grammar School, payable to the Revd. Thomas Scard, c.1840.

34. The Old Grammar School on the corner of Lower Lane and Brook Street, shortly before demolition in 1962.

School and Chaplain of Droxford Union.' He was assisted by 18 year old Charles Tompkins and the school had 26 boarders, boys between 9 and 15, from solid middle class families some local and some from further afield.[16] It seems unlikely that this was the grammar school which by now had probably ceased to take boarders.

According to White's Directory of Hampshire 1859 F.W.Richardson was Master of the Grammar School but though the School House 'adjoining the church' had room for 40 boarders and there were two acres of land the 1861 census contains no reference to a boarding school. By 1871 the Master of the Endowed Grammar School was Peter Flynn.

But Bishop Morley's Grammar School was in trouble. Peter Flynn was succeeded by Mr Evans and when he resigned in October 1874 the rector was unable to find a suitable replacement and, high-handedly, it appears closed the school. What had happened to the trustees whose agreement to closure would presumably have been required or who would have felt responsible for ensuring its survival?

The town was dismayed and the Charity Commissioners investigated. They believed that a purpose built school should be provided, the curriculum reformed and fees specified. The master should receive £65 per year plus capitation fees – then usual as an incentive to increase recruitment. The Commissioners might recommend but could not will the means to the achievement of their proposals. The Royal Albert Infirmary had been empty since its 'opening' in 1865 and would it was thought provide an acceptable temporary school building provided it could be secured cheaply. In 1875, however, its owner Sir Arthur Helps died, the Infirmary was deemed to be part of his estate and was sold to defray the outstanding debt. To the annoyance of many in the town a solution to the problem of the grammar school eluded them. The rector and trustees leased a building in Brook Street but the school does not seem to have lasted long.[17]

When the trustees of the reorganised Bishop's Waltham Charities met for the first time on 8th December 1877 there is no reference to an existing school. The last reference to the grammar school is in the School Board Minutes for 1880 when it was estimated that the grammar school was educating 35 pupils.[18] It seems likely that it closed soon afterwards. The newly appointed trustees resolved that the income left when they had met their obligations to the poor of the parish should be devoted to establishing and maintaining a new school 'superior to a public elementary school'[19] They hoped to acquire a site and build a grammar school. They were discouraged by discovering that a similar school was planned for Winchester and seem to have seen this as competition which they were unlikely to overcome.[20]

Enthusiasm returned in 1885 when Charles Gunner reported to the trustees that a three acre field owned by Richard Austin in Botley Road was on the market at £100 per acre. Income accumulated over the years made its purchase possible. By 1887 things were even more hopeful. The trustees had saved about £1500 out of income, a considerable sum at that time, but not enough for the ambitious plans they had for a new school. However the town had resolved that its memorial on the occasion of the Golden Jubilee of the Queen should be the erection of a grammar school and £900 had been subscribed or promised. It was reported that 'Subscribers are anxious that the school should be commenced this year'.[21]

At last there seemed to be a sense of urgency. The trustees applied at once to the Charity Commissioners who agreed to draw up a scheme despite the smallness of the endowment. They forwarded to the trustees their first thoughts. The school would be a day and boarding school for boys and the course of study would be 'higher than an elementary school'. The tuition fees would be between £3–£6 per year and there would be at least ten scholarships 'to secure the interest of the poorer classes in the charities to be devoted to this purpose'. Scholarships would carry fee remission and some might carry a grant of £5 (presumably to cover uniform, books and stationery).[22]

The search was now on for a site and Richard Austin, estate agent was commissioned to identify possibilities. He came up with four overlapping sites each of about 4 acres on the Hoe estate then on the market. Each was valued at between £250 and £500 and there was a further possibility on the Hangars.[23] There can be little doubt that the trustees had every intention of going ahead. They devoted two whole meetings to examining the Commissioners' scheme in detail They added Bookkeeping, Land Surveying, Chemistry and Applied Mechanics to the proposed curriculum.

More ominously they wanted to change the basis of the Religious Instruction to be given in the school from 'the Christian faith', as specified by the Commissioners to 'the principles of the Church of England' and wrote to inform the Commissioners. Meantime they selected the first cooptative governors of the new school – William Brock, Walter Medlicott, Vicar of Swanmore and E.H.Liddell of Curdridge. On the religious issue however neither side would yield. The commissioners would not proceed unless the trustees gave ground. The trustees claimed that those who had promised money would only do so if the grammar school were a Church of England foundation and wrote to the Queen's Jubilee Committee to say that the proposed grammar school was in abeyance 'owing to differences of opinion regarding Religious Instruction'.

It seems to have been the new rector James Palmer Nash who revived the grammar school project soon after he arrived in Bishop's Waltham in March 1892 and became chairman of the trustees. His idea, put to the trustees at their meeting in August 1892, was to acquire a lease on Albert House (as the former Royal Albert Infirmary was now named) and once again to put a scheme to the Charity Commissioners. The trustees were favourable. Resources were not sufficient, they thought, to acquire land and build a grammar school but a less ambitious scheme to lease an existing building was desirable and this would be a school or department where older boys could receive education, some paying fees and some attending free and where there would also be evening classes and technical instruction. In October 1892 an assistant commissioner came to a meeting of the trustees and visited Albert House. [24]

The Commissioners supported the scheme but were doubtful whether more than 30 boys would be recruited from a place as small as Bishop's Waltham and this would be too few to make a viable grammar school. Since the charities mentioned children rather than boys how about a school with departments for boys and girls? Albert House was 'not unsuitable'. It would provide a residence for a man and wife or sister and brother who could run the two departments. There might then be 50 pupils and 'the project of a secondary school in so small a population be rendered less hazardous'[25].

Once more the trustees and the commissioners reached an impasse. The trustees were adamant: 'a girls school is not required' and even if it were 'it would not be advisable for boys and girls to be educated in the same building' and Albert House was 'specially unsuitable on account of its proximity to the Board School' Each of these resolutions was passed unanimously. The trustees concluded 'The need is really limited to boys'. Not surprisingly the scheme was turned down by the Commissioners as 'too hazardous to be made a scheme under the Endowed Schools Act.' Only 35–40 boys would come from Bishop's Waltham and the school would be unlikely to draw from more populous districts. [26]

Once more there was deadlock between the Commissioners and the Trustees. It was the commissioners who suggested that the Trustees might enlist the support of the County Council. The Council was interested in establishing a Higher Grade school or department to meet the needs of those who wanted to go beyond the level of education provided by a Board School.[27] After meetings in which the School Board, the Trustees, the Technical Education Committee of the County Council and the Charity Commissioners were all involved two proposals emerged: a Higher Grade school or department which would come under the School Board or an Educational Institute with provision for evening classes. An Institute would be 'easier to run and the chance of failure less than in the case of a secondary school or department'.[28]

The early months of 1894 saw a debate in the town about the two possibilities. On Wednesday 15th August 1894 a public enquiry took place in the Old Grammar School attended by Mr Selby Bigge, an Assistant Charity Commissioner and a decision was reached to go ahead with the Educational Institute.[29] Since charities were involved the Commissioners would have to draft a scheme. Once more the trustees debated the scheme in detail. Meantime the search was on for a site but this time not for a grammar school but for an institute. Caroline Gunner offered to give land which she owned opposite *The White Hart* (soon to become *The Mafeking Hero*) and it was here that the Institute was built. A new body of trustees was appointed with the charity divided between an educational branch and a branch for the poor. Architects were

35. The Educational Institute built partly from the grammar school endowments, opened 1899.

approached and tenders invited. The building eventually cost £2092 and was built by Hale Brothers a Bishop's Waltham firm.

At long last on 5th July 1899 the Bishop's Waltham Institute was opened by the chairman of the County Council, the Earl of Northbrook, in the presence of W.G.Nicolson the local member of Parliament. It had taken over 20 years to decide how to replace the old endowed grammar school. The facilities of the Institute included a reading room, library and recreation room equipped with chess boards, draughts, dominoes and bagatelle. It was open to parishioners of the 'ancient parish of Bishop's Waltham' (which included Curdridge and part of Swanmore) over the age of 14 for an annual subscription of 5/-. Opening hours were 10am to 10pm though the recreation room was only available from 6pm and from 3pm on Saturdays. Baths were available – a reminder that most houses in Bishop's Waltham had no bathroom – 2d for a cold bath and 4d for a hot bath. The bath on the first floor was reserved for ladies.[30]

From the beginning the Institute was a hive of activity. It was hoped to arrange gymnastic classes on two evenings a week. In June 1900 there was a successful visit by the County Travelling Dairy School. This was a large van drawn by two horses which spent ten days at the Institute when ten people – mostly aspirants to enter the dairy industry – attended classes on butter and soft cheese making. Three members of the class qualified for scholarships entitling them to five weeks free instruction as well as board and lodging at the county council Farm School at Basing – the forerunner of Sparsholt College.[31] There were demonstrations of 'poultry trussing' and ten lessons in dress cutting during the summer of 1900.[32] The Institute was to play an important part in the community life of the town in peace and war at least down to the 1960s when many of the classes were transferred to the newly opened secondary school at Swanmore. But there was a price to be paid. There was no secondary school in Bishop's Waltham. All pupils remained at the schools in Dodd's Alley and at Newtown unless they passed an examination at the age of 11 and went to a grammar school in Winchester or Fareham both some distance from Bishop's Waltham.

9

From the National School to the County Mixed School

AT THE beginning of the nineteenth century education for what contemporaries described as 'the labouring poor' was just beginning. The early years of the century saw the building in many parishes of schools funded by the parson or a leading lay person to provide elementary education, often supported by the National Society for Promoting the Education of the Poor in the Principles of the Established Church founded in 1811 (usually abbreviated to The National Society). Their purpose was to encourage literacy, to provide moral training and Christian instruction and as a spin off to keep the labouring poor out of the clutches of nonconformity which was thought to be subversive. One of the earliest local schools was opened at Upham in 1814, followed by one at Durley in 1823. At Swanmore the first school was built in 1833. The nonconformists replied with the British and Foreign Schools Society, abbreviated to British School but a British school was not founded in Bishop's Waltham until the 1860s.

At Bishop's Waltham it was James Ogle, the first resident rector for half a century, who provided the first elementary schools. In 1816 he rented a room in the Market House in the Square for a school for girls.[1] Six years later he built, at a cost of £236, a school in the churchyard close to the doorway in the brick wall which now leads to Roman Row. It seems to have provided for both girls and boys. In 1841 its master was Joseph Sparshott, a young man of 25, who had lodgings in French Street and the mistress was Jane Talbot aged 30 who lodged at the Rectory.[2] In the 1850s they appear to have been succeeded by Edwin and Eliza Stephens (aged 29 and 26) who had lodging with them John Mortimer a 16 year old pupils teacher from Portsea.

The census of 1851 is the first to indicate children who were on the books of a school describing them as 'scholar'. For the parish as a whole (excluding the tithing of Curdridge whose returns are not legible but which in any case had its own school) 250 children between the ages of four and twelve appear as 'scholar', whilst 152 have no such description. This suggests that about 62% attended school whilst 38% did not do so. Those not in school come substantially from the outlying areas of Ashton, Dean and Dundridge where almost all fathers were agricultural labourers who saw

Schools in Bishop's Waltham

Building in Churchyard/ Free Street

NATIONAL SCHOOL
1822 B G

Board School
1879 I
(Basingwell Street, 1877)

BOARD SCHOOL [1]
1896 I
(Free Street)

Council School
1903 I

Council School [2]
1909 -52 B 7-14/15

Council Infant School
1952-61 5-7

[County Library]

SWANMORE SECONDARY.
MODERN SCHOOL
1961-74 B G 11-15

Swanmore Comprehensive School [2]
1974 B G 11-16

Swanmore College of Technology
2002 B G 11-16

Building in Newtown

BRITISH SCHOOL
1866 B G I

Board School
1879 B G I

Council School
1903 B G I

Council School [2]
1909 -52 G 7-14/15   I 5-7

County Mixed School
1952 –61 G B 7- 15

County Junior School
1961- 69 G B 7 –11

County Infants School
1961-89 G B 5-7

RIDGEMEDE JUNIOR
SCHOOL
1969 B G 7-11

BISHOP'S WALTHAM INFANT
SCHOOL
1989 I 5-7

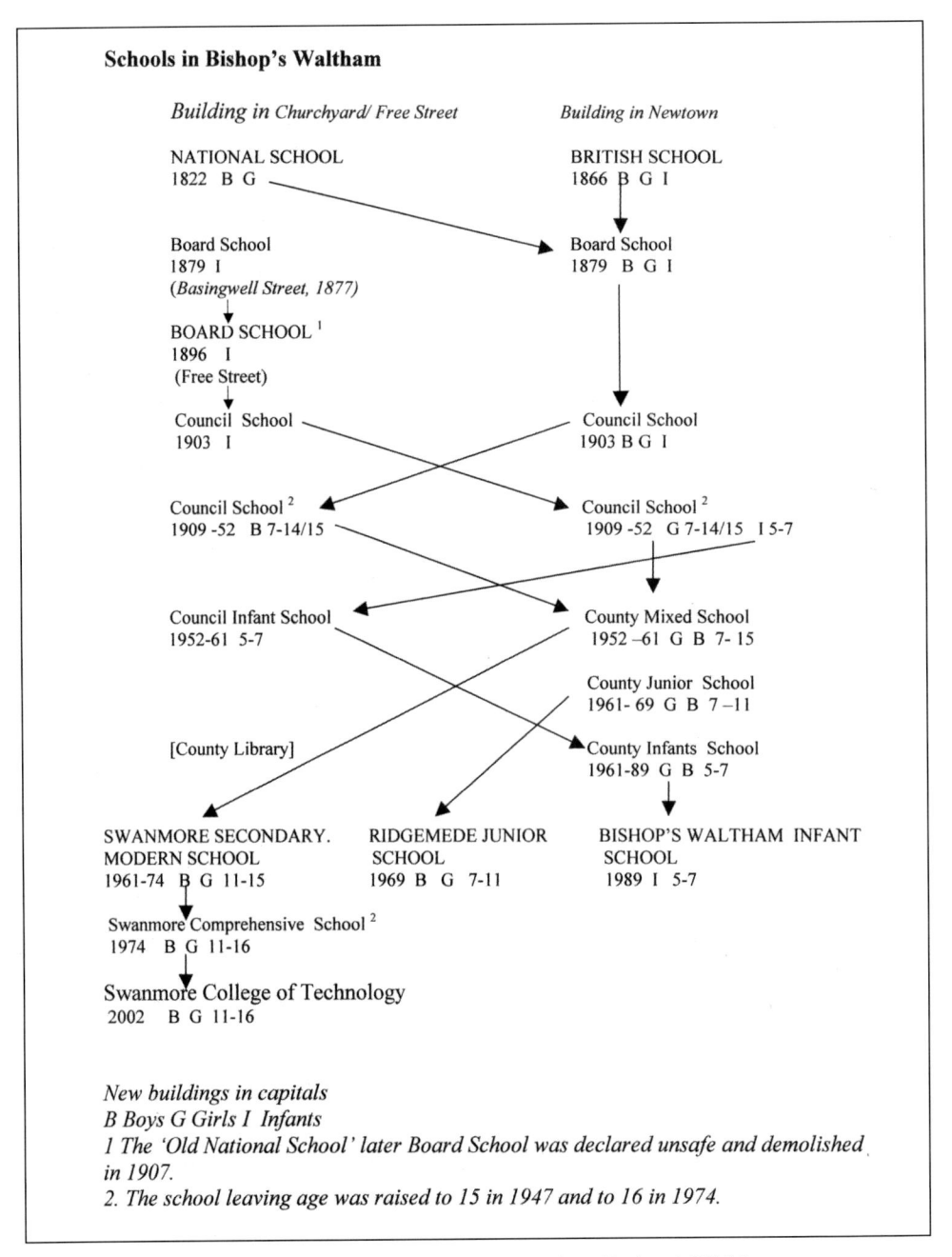

New buildings in capitals
B Boys G Girls I Infants
1 The 'Old National School' later Board School was declared unsafe and demolished in 1907.
2. The school leaving age was raised to 15 in 1947 and to 16 in 1974.

36. Diagram showing elementary schools in Bishop's Waltham.

little point in formal education and in any case lived a considerable distance from the school in the churchyard. The occupation of children as young as ten appears in the census. There was a ten year old agricultural labourer and another who was 'house servant'. At the age of 11 one boy was a 'letter carrier', another 'shepherd'. By the age of 13 there are errand boys, a shirt maker (girl), butcher boy and sawyer. Listing as 'scholar' does not mean regular attendance. Had the 250 children between the ages of four and thirteen attended regularly the National School would have been uncomfortably full.

That the literacy of boys and girls steadily improved is shown by the increasing proportion of brides and grooms who signed their name in the marriage register. The most significant progress comes in the 1860s – those who had attended school in the 1850s. By the 1870s it is rare for both partners to make their mark. By the 1890s inability to sign the register was confined to those married in their 30s or 40s who had been of school age before education was compulsory. The last couple, aged 49 and 50, made their mark when they married in 1889. The last woman to make her mark was a 25 year old married in May 1904 and the last man a 41 year old labourer married on 3rd August 1914.[3]

Dates	Proportion of brides and bridegrooms making their mark
1813–22	45.5
1837–45	41.1
1847–58	37.0
1859–67	19.3
1868–77	14.1
1877–85	8.7
1885–95	6.0

From 1871 the master or mistress of every school was obliged to keep a Log Book. It was a confidential document, strongly bound and provided with lock and key. The Log kept by the Bishop's Waltham school from 1872 to 1879 is in Hampshire Record Office and from it we catch a glimpse of the school in the decade in which there was a growing awareness nationally of the importance of elementary education.[4] The right to vote had been extended in 1867 and as Robert Lowe (an opponent of the Reform Act) told the House of Commons sarcastically while it was being debated 'You should prevail on our future masters to learn their letters'. The number attending the National School in Bishop's Waltham rose significantly from an average of about 50 in 1872 to 140 only five years later. For most of that time the master was Ebenezer Sims who arrived in March 1873, a young man of 23, who had recently obtained the coveted qualification of Certificated Teacher at the College of St Mark, Chelsea. He was to remain a teacher in the town well into the twentieth century retiring on the eve of the First World War after over 40 years service.[5] His memory has now passed beyond recall but he deserves to be remembered for the significant contribution he made to education in Bishop's Waltham.

Like most similar schools there was only one qualified teacher. Ebenezer Sims was assisted by two levels of apprentice-teacher: pupil-teacher and monitor, both grades recruited from promising pupils, not more than 14 or 15 years of age, who hoped in due course to go to college and themselves become certificated teachers. In 1872 the pupil teacher was expected to be at school each morning by 7am for his lessons.[6] Monitors were paid about 2/6 per week and pupil teachers £12.10.0 per year. In October 1872 the Log records: 'Henry H. Padwick completed his term of apprenticeship as a Pupil Teacher and leaves with the goodwill of Managers, Master and scholars. He sits his Queens Scholarship on Tuesday next at Winchester Training College.'[7] In May 1875 'Arthur Lomer the monitor, has left this week for the Grammar School' – later he was to return as a pupil teacher.[8] If the Master was absent the 'PT' (so described in the Log) was left in charge of the school, a daunting assignment for any boy or girl little older than some of the pupils they were required to teach – and control.[9] The only other assistance which the master received came from occasional visitors. William Brock, rector and chairman of the managers, looked in several times a week sometimes accompanied by his wife. They might bring apples or pears for the children or perhaps give a Scripture lesson, hear pupils read or inspect the girls' needlework.

Education was not yet compulsory but the 1870s saw a constant battle at Bishop's Waltham as elsewhere to get parents to send their children to school – and regularly. Attendance fluctuated according to the time of year and the exigencies of family life. Children walked to school, some a considerable distance from the outlying parts of the parish, along narrow country lanes and might be deterred by heavy rain or snow. Some were kept at home to look after younger children. Attendance dropped in March when children were needed in the garden, in June when they helped with hay making, in July when they gathered soft fruit and in September when they were needed for the potato harvest. The school broke up in mid-August for what was described as the Harvest Holiday but the ripening grain did not respect school terms. Harvest might begin before term ended or continue after the Autumn term began with consequent absence – 'Few children present. Harvest not over' (Log 22nd August 1874). In October children might go 'nutting or blackberrying' particularly on Friday afternoon when attendance was always lower (Log 25.10.74).

As well as absence, continuity of teaching was affected by the large number of whole or half holidays. 'Fete in the Palace grounds', the celebration of the anniversary of the Queen's Coronation, the Flower Show, the annual cricket match with Swanmore School, the School Treat, the Christmas Treat, the British School Treat, the Night School Treat, Ascension Day and St Andrew's Day were just a few of the occasions for a half day or whole holiday. Sometimes an infectious disease – scarlet fever, mumps or even flu – made the doctor close the school for as long as four weeks at a time.

Discipline too was a problem: 'Found the children very disorderly' (Log 1st July 1872). 'Punished a few for misconduct in Sunday School and church yesterday (8th July 1872).

Forster's Education Act of 1870 made the three R's – reading, writing and arithmetic – compulsory, as well as needlework for girls. Each day began with religious instruction when in a church school children were taught the Catechism, hymns, Prayer Book collects and passages from the Bible – all learnt by rote. 'Secular' instruction followed. The younger children used slates and the older ones pens and copy books. In July 1872 the Master ordered half a gross of penholders and a gallon of ink as well as one thousand slate pencils and two and a half dozen unframed slates.[10]

Inspectors visited the school regularly and usually felt that the standard of work left much to be desired. In July 1875 they wrote 'With the exception of the Reading which is good, the work is rough and inaccurate. The Writing is unformed, Spelling is bad, Arithmetic throughout is unsatisfactory and only two children out of 20 presented in Standards III, IV, V and VI passed in it.'[11] And yet it is perhaps surprising that the school could be run at all. Many children would prefer to be at home or in the fields and their parents had for the most part not attended school or had done so for a short time or irregularly and were not always convinced that more than basic literacy was needed. Teachers were battling against enormous odds. Reading the Log we are witnessing in one small Hampshire town the birth pangs of universal state education. The achievement of the school is measured in part in the gradual increase in literacy.

In 1877 the managers opened an infant department for pupils aged three to seven in a house in Basingwell Street. Inspectors refused to allow grant to be paid since it had no playground and only one 'office' (a Victorian euphemism for a lavatory) which was shared by the occupants of the adjoining house.

The Church of England may have been first in the field but the Congregationalists gained from their later start. Their building in Newtown was greatly superior to the National School in the churchyard. When the Congregational Church, built in Lower Lane (where the doctors' surgery is now), opened in December 1862, the Rector refused to admit to the National School children who attended the Congregational Sunday School so they opened their own school in a room at the rear of the chapel employing a mistress trained at the Home and Colonial College and drawing support from the British and Foreign Schools Society. Numbers grew rapidly and they resolved to build. Arthur Helps presented them with 'the beautiful and extensive site' on the hill at Newtown and here in June 1866 they opened a school with an adjoining Master's house.[12]

The Education Act of 1870 permitted the election of School Boards to supplement the provision made by the voluntary societies. Most Board schools were built in towns where the shortfall of school places was most serious. The Church of England was generally opposed to School Boards since the religious education provided in them might be Christian but must be undenominational. The small town of Bishop's Waltham was therefore unusual in having a School Board. (At Swanmore a School Board was held out as a threat by the Vicar to encourage generous support for the church school.)[13] The reason was the substantial cost which would be involved in improving the National School in the churchyard. The free churches had no objection on principle to a Board school and the Congregational church was no doubt pleased to be relieved of the cost of running a school.

The Board met for the first time in October 1878 at the Grammar School in Portland Square and was invited to take over three existing schools – the National School in the churchyard, the British School on the hill at Newtown and the National School at Curdridge. (Curdridge was until 1894 part of the parish of Bishop's Waltham.)[14] Ebenezer Sims (known to the children as 'Badger' Sims) was appointed Master of the school on the Hill, moved into the Master's house at the former British School and enjoyed a substantial increase in salary to £110 including a share of the government grant.[15] His school moved with him and infants from Basingwell Street were transferred to the school in the churchyard. The building was adapted for infants; it was repaired, refitted, a classroom added and a playground procured.[16] There was now twofold provision for infants: they might attend the school at Newtown or they could go to the school in the churchyard.

The School Board took advantage of the ruling that it could make education compulsory from the age of five to thirteen and appointed Edmund Nutley Garnett Attendance Officer at a salary of £12.10.0.[17] For many years attendance at Bishop's Waltham compared unfavourably with other local schools perhaps because the town was larger and more spread out than nearby villages and the distance to the school greater. The Board would warn parents and then bring them before the Droxford Bench where they were often fined 5/-, 2/6 or 1/- and had to promise to send their sons and daughters to school regularly.

Until 1891 when fees were abolished and education became free parents with several children in school at the same time pleaded poverty. They could not afford to pay School Pence – 2d per week which each child had to bring to school on Monday morning, It was reduced to 1d. if there were two whole holidays in any one week. The School Board was sympathetic and decided that a parent with seven children in school need pay for only five children (10p. per week), another with six paid for three whilst a third with three children would pay for only one 'until times are better'.[18]

In 1894 Curdridge became a separate civil parish and the Bishop's Waltham School Board was no longer responsible for its school. The newly elected Bishop's Waltham Board was faced with the need for additional accommodation. There were 276 children on the books but the average attendance was only 181 or 65%, far below the 80% which was the average for the country as a whole and below the average in local schools. The building at Newtown held 135 in the main school, 30 in a separate classroom and 26 in the infant room, a total of only 191 so if they were to succeed in raising the attendance level the school would be grossly overcrowded. The year 1895 therefore saw the provision of additional accommodation.[19]

At the infant school in Dodd's Alley there were problems too. In particular it suffered from frequent changes of staff. In its first ten years there were five mistresses as well as several temporary appointments. When Catherine Stocks returned from sick leave in May 1889 she found the children 'in a backward state'.[20] 'Not a child in the second class was taught to read a word during the nine months I was away' she wrote.[21]

Even more serious was the condition of the building. Inspectors pointed out that the school was cold in winter because the stove was too small, the furniture was not suitable for infants even when the desks had been cut down, the pump needed repair and the closets should be whitewashed. In July 1893 they were even more forthright. The site of the school in the churchyard was unsatisfactory, there was no classroom, the windows were too small, the floor was worn out, and the school was only 11 feet high. 'Are the managers,' they asked 'prepared to provide a new building?' A year later they asked what steps the managers had taken to build a new school.[22] The managers replied that they would repair the old one.

When their plans reached the Education Department, however, they were told that no renovation would be acceptable to a building whose walls were only nine inches thick.[23] At last the managers agreed to seek a new site – behind *The Wheatsheaf* stables perhaps or in Shore Lane – but their quest was at first fruitless. At last a ¼ acre site in Dodd's Alley was bought and the new school built.[24] 'Commenced work in the new school today' were the words inscribed in the Log for 30th November 1896. The old Infant School playground was sold to the rector to extend the churchyard whilst for the next ten years the building was used for meetings of all sorts. In September 1907 the rector reported that the school was no longer safe and within a month it had been demolished and the ground was incorporated into the churchyard.[25]

37. The demolition of the school in the churchyard, October 1907.

38. The British School opened 1866, often referred to as 'The School on the Hill'.

39. Group of pupils in the boys' department probably before 1910.

Elementary education in Bishop's Waltham had come a long way in the last 30 years of the nineteenth century. All children now attended school from the age of five or even earlier until they reached the age of 12. Literacy was universal. The 1890s saw the beginning of what we should call Adult or Further Education. The County Council, created in 1888, encouraged the formation of local committees to organise classes on technical subjects for older pupils and young adults. The Bishop's Waltham committee met at the Reading Room in St Peter Street and included many of the town's leading citizens. The chairman was H.W.Trinder of Northbrook House and the members included Thomas John Brown, soon to become the first chairman of the Parish Council, William Myers of Swanmore Park, Member of Parliament for Winchester, as well as the chairman and vice-chairman of the School Board. Even more significant the committee included three women – Mrs Austin of The Thickets, Mrs Brown of Mount House and Mrs Hurley of Albert House (the erstwhile Priory) wife of the chairman of the School Board.[26]

The first classes were held in the winter of 1891–2 and included cooking, woodwork, horticulture and agricultural engineering. The committee would like to have organised classes in brickmaking and clayworking as these were the main industries of the town. A Dairy School was planned for 'domestic servants and the industrial classes generally'. Vocational courses became a feature of each winter publicised in the Parish Magazine. From 1899 the parish had the enormous advantage of the Educational Institute which provided a modern venue and a focus for education beyond school

The Balfour Education Act of 1902 brought an end to the School Boards. In future school education would be the responsibility of the County Council which appointed an Education Committee. D.T.Cowan who since 1895 had been Director of Technical Instruction became the first Director of Education.[27] Bishop's Waltham Board School became Bishop's Waltham Council School. The difference was chiefly in final responsibility. Appointments for example were in the hands of the County Council Education Committee though the Managers could draw up a short list and make recommendations which the Education Committee would normally accept. The chairman of the Managers for the first 25 years of its existence was the minister of the Congregational Church, Samuel Longmore.

In April 1909 there was a further change. The infant school and the boys school exchanged buildings. For the next 40 years the boys were to use the building in Dodd's Alley. Whether this was a wise decision must be arguable. The building was cramped, there was no field and boys lacked the civilising influence of girls. There were often complaints about the behaviour of the boys – stone throwing and broken glass were among frequent complaints of residents and passers-by.[28]

National and local events formed part of the life of the schools. On 6th July 1891 there was a holiday to mark the marriage of the Duke of York and Princess Mary (later King George V and Queen Mary) When Pretoria was relieved during the

Second Boer War: 'Great excitement this morning. Children marched to the Square singing. School closed this afternoon and tomorrow' (31st May 1900). On Empire Day, 24th May: 'Children marched to the Square, saluted the Union Jack, sang several songs, marched to the field for sports.' The hot summer of 1911 when the wells ran dry is reflected in the Log. 'No physical exercise on account of the heat. … Temperature of room at 2.45pm 86 degrees.… The very hot weather seemed to take all the energy out of the children. … Still very hot, some of the boys seem quite overcome with the heat.' But the weather reverted to normal and on 24th November 'The first 30 minutes was devoted to exercises and running to circulate the blood'.

In the 1920s a major restructuring of state education was planned and had in many parts of the country been implemented by 1939. Sir Henry Hadow, Vice-Chancellor of Sheffield University and chairman of the Consultative Committee of the Board of Education, chaired a committee which published a report in 1926 entitled *The Education of the Adolescent*. It recommended the division of education into two phases, primary and secondary. Hadow hoped that in order to provide all children with four years of secondary education the school leaving age would be raised to 15. Local authorities embarked on what was called 'Hadow Reorganisation' and by the beginning of the Second World War only 22% of school children were still in 'all-age' schools, schools catering for all pupils from the age of five or seven to the school leaving age which was then 14.[29] The school leaving age was to be raised on 1st September 1939 but for obvious reasons this did not take place until 1947.

The area of which Bishop's Waltham forms part presented problems to Hampshire County Council. Neither Bishop's Waltham, Swanmore nor the Meon valley villages possessed a building which could be adapted as a secondary school so a new school would have to be built and that meant money. After the Second World War priority was given to building houses and to the needs of towns where bombing had taken place so it was not until the early 1960s that a secondary school for the district of which Bishop's Waltham formed part, could be provided.

In the meantime Bishop's Waltham schools were housed in sub-standard premises. The boys school in Dodd's Alley had been designed as an infants' school and built in 1896 (now the Library) and the girls and infants school in Newtown was in a building opened in 1866. The sites, particularly the boys', were cramped, and the facilities were basic. There were no science laboratories, no modern language teaching, no playing fields, no gymnasium or showers, and poor craft facilities. Large classes were taught in small classrooms. Cookery classes for girls were held at the Institute, netball took place in the playground and nature study was a substitute for science, toilets were noisome and the buildings cold in winter. In the late 1940s the rector allowed the boys to play tennis on the rectory court.[30] Conditions were accepted because they were not so very different from those in many rural schools in Hampshire and elsewhere. In the post-war years HMI had used the word 'anarchy' to describe the state of indiscipline which they encountered. at the boys' school in Bishop's Waltham.

40. Group of senior girls outside the School on the Hill c.1953
(Diana Gibson nee Chamberlain)
Back row: Margaret Privett, Patricia Bucksey, Diane Rogers, Glenis Holmshaw, Peggy Mills, Sylvia Thomas, Diana Chamberlain.
Centre: Wendy Stevenson, June Ellis, Sheila Pond, Sheila Coombs, Diane Bennett, Jane Russel, Ann Taylor, Joan Drakely, Ivy Mitchell.
Front row: Pamela Hammond, Doreen Stafford, Teresa Compton, ___ , Carol Hutchings, Doreen Pink.
Cross legged: Ann Todd, Josephine Pond

Teachers were dedicated to the welfare of their children but the academic ceiling was a low one. Some pupils took the 11+ examination which enabled a small number – perhaps two or three a year – to enter grammar schools. But not all who passed were able to go: uniform and travel were expensive particularly for the eldest children in large families. In 1943 two girls passed the examination for Winchester County High School and in 1944 one boy went to Taunton's School Southampton, still evacuated to Bournemouth and another to Gosport Central School.[31] In 1945 six boys transferred to Price's Grammar School at Fareham.[32]

The rest stayed at the all-age school until they were 15. In 1949 Mr Mann the headmaster of the boys' school reported that two boys had entered Price's Grammar at Fareham and a further three Southampton Technical School of Building. At the girls' school one girl had qualified for Winchester County High School for Girls. Limited horizons are well illustrated by the comments made by Miss Huffer the headmistress of the girls' school. In reporting the success of the girls who had qualified for a grammar school place she pointed out to disappointed parents that 'There are equally essential jobs to be filled where a grammar school education is not essential. Shop assistants and house maids are just as important members of the community as office girls and they are needed to work hard at school'.[33]

In 1951 HMI inspected the boys' school and reported that 'this school has not yet reached a creditable level in the education of its pupils'. By the more rigorous standards of the present Bishop's Waltham Boys School would have been judged a failing school, placed in Special Measures and threatened with closure. The retirement of the heads of both boys' and girls'schools gave the authority the opportunity to take decisive action. They closed both schools and opened a new one in September 1952 called Bishop's Waltham County Mixed School (for both boys and girls) in the Newtown buildings and appointed as headmaster John Gimblett a teacher from Eastleigh Secondary Modern School.

It was an inspired appointment. In a short time he had turned the school round. The curriculum was broadened, Priory fields and the Drill Hall were rented, the latter as a hall where the whole school could assemble. Out of school activities were encouraged. Both staff and pupils responded to a strong lead. John Gimblett was a disciplinarian but one who was respected. Pupils were expected to behave, to obey teachers, dress tidily with 'short back and sides' for boys and modest length skirts for girls – and generally they did. John Gimblett was a Welshman with high standards and the energy to implement them.

When HMI returned in 1958 they were loud in their praise of what had been achieved. They nonetheless recognised that the All-Age school was 'a relic of other days'.[34] Not surprisingly John Gimblett was appointed in November 1958 to be head-designate of the new secondary modern school at Swanmore. He gave it a flying start. By the time the purpose built secondary school opened in April 1961 only 2.4% of pupils nationally were in all-age schools. The area including Bishop's Waltham was the last in Hampshire to have all-age schools. It remains an extraordinary feature of the town that it has no post-primary education within its boundaries. All secondary and further education takes place at Swanmore where the school was successively a secondary modern school, a comprehensive school and early in the twentyfirst century became Swanmore College of Technology. Opened with 300 children and 15 staff it now provides education for over 1200.[35]

10

The Gunners of Bishop's Waltham

NOT SINCE Bishop Walter Curll escaped from the burning palace in 1644 has Bishop's Waltham had a resident Lord of the Manor. Nor can the town boast a leading family, perhaps titled, living in a medieval or Tudor house, related to the aristocracy and providing continuity through the generations. In the Gunner family however Bishop's Waltham has a dynasty, which was prominent through five generations from the late eighteenth century to the second half of the twentieth century. They are usually recalled as the proprietors of 'the last private country bank in England' but they were much more than that. Members of the family played a prominent part in the professional, business and social life of Bishop's Waltham over many years.[1]

The first Gunner to live in Bishop's Waltham was William Gunner I a solicitor who was born in Winchester in 1748 and moved to Bishop's Waltham about 1774. He appears in a Hampshire Directory of 1793 as one of the two attorneys in the town. [2] He died in 1797 and was succeeded as one of the town's lawyers by his son William Gunner II a young man of 20 when his father died. Some 14 years later, already a partner in the bank, he married Lucy Matilda Ridge one of the 19 children of Thomas Ridge, squire of Kilmeston Manor, near the small town of Alresford and a founder of the Hampshire Hunt, and set up house at Holm Oak in what was then French Street (where Roman Row now stands). Thomas Ridge was a landed gentleman and his family was thus a cut above the Gunners in the social hierarchy of the period. It was however the first of several alliances by marriage between the two families. The name Ridge has found its way into the town's history.

It was this William who, with three colleagues, signed Articles of Partnership on 4th October 1809 and a week later opened the bank for business in William Gunner's house, an event marked by a peal of bells rung from the tower of St Peter's church, the ringers' fee of £1 paid by the four partners – Thomas Fox (1765–1834) tanner and wine merchant, Stephen Steele (1763–1823) farmer, John Goulding Seymour (1773–1840) surgeon and William Gunner, solicitor and at 32 the youngest of the four. The bank went by a number of names, initially that of its four partners Fox, Steele, Seymour and Gunner but throughout its history the name Gunner always appeared. It was officially the Bishop's Waltham and Hampshire Bank but was known to all in the town simply as 'Gunners'.

41. William Gunner II 1777–1857 founder of Bishop's Waltham and Hampshire Bank.

42. Holm Oak and part of Gunners bank, Bank Street

Bishop's Waltham was, according to the Hampshire Directory of 1793, a flourishing small town with a grammar school and three fairs each year. Its amenities included 'Gunner's caravan from Portsmouth to Winchester twice a week' – what one wonders was its relation to William Gunner's other activities?[3] Gunner family legend has it that the farmers who came to the market in Bishop's Waltham were just sober enough, after visiting more than one of the local hostelries, to realise that they would be better advised to lodge their day's takings with Mr Gunner rather than take them home and hence his realisation that there was a place for a bank in the local economy.[4] For nearly a century Gunners was to be the only bank in Bishop's Waltham. It was used at first mostly by wealthy landowners and tradesmen but as confidence grew its customers were drawn from all sections of the community and it also held the accounts of local charities.

In the early years of the nineteenth century most small towns had one or more banks. By 1810 there were about 700, many opened in the previous 20 years. Provincial banks often provided the only available capital for the burgeoning businesses of the Industrial Revolution, then in full swing. Some were founded by a gold or silversmith but as often it was a solicitor who became the banker. Many were note issuing banks though the limits of issue were small and their notes circulated only locally. The heyday of the provincial note-issuing bank was from 1797 to 1836. Gunners bank is unique in surviving all the many crises arising from the fluctuating economic fortunes of the nineteenth century, in particular the collapse of the railway boom of the early 1840s, though note-issuing ended with the Bank Charter Act of 1844.

Each of the four partners in the Bishop's Waltham and Hampshire Bank made a contribution of £1000 to establish the bank and ensured that between twelve noon and three o'clock on most afternoons there was a partner available to interview influential customers and make decisions about investments. For the routine business they appointed a young man of 20 as clerk at a starting salary of one guinea per week paid quarterly. John Mansel (1789–1852) stayed with the bank for 42 years. His salary was raised in 1814 to £25 per quarter and in 1817 to £37 per quarter. Seated at a handsome circular desk on which he cut his initials, he used perhaps as many as five quill pens a day filling ledger after ledger in his neat copperplate handwriting. Shortly before he retired he was described by William Gunner as a man who was never found in error. He was deemed so trustworthy that he conducted some of the bank's correspondence and was the co-executor with William Gunner of the estate of Thomas Fox.[5] It was a typical small bank of the period with counter, cashier's desk, and partners' room. Throughout its life it operated from the mellow brick building in French Street with a frontage of 27 feet. Half the building was Gunner's Bank, the other half Gunners, Solicitors.

The original partners withdrew or died so that by 1841 William Gunner was the only survivor. He was joined by two of his sons. Thomas the eldest left soon afterwards. It was Charles James then aged 22 who would carry the bank into the next generation. The founder William Gunner II retired in 1851 and went to live in Winchester where he died in 1857 aged 80. He was buried in St Peter's churchyard and there is a memorial to him high on the north wall of the north aisle of the church. When John Mansel retired he was succeeded by his son-in-law James Lock at a salary of £150 still paid quarterly. By 1872 it had risen to £300 per year. In the census of 1851 James Lock aged 37 and born at Braunston in Devon was not only 'banker's clerk' but also a shirt merchant.

In 1850 Charles James Gunner married Caroline Hale and went to live at Holm Oak next to the bank where they had ten children, seven sons and three daughters. Charles James was far more than a banker and solicitor. He was registrar of the county court, then held at Bishop's Waltham, clerk to the Droxford magistrates, clerk to the trustees of the Bishop's Waltham to Fishers Pond turnpike, and a trustee of the London and Southampton turnpike. It was the firm of Gunner and Company, Solicitors who in the 1860s handled the many enterprises of Arthur Helps – gas works, brickworks and railway company among others. Letters survive from both Charles James Gunner and James Lock expressing concern about the viability of some of his business activities.

Not surprisingly involvement in so many and varied activities took a heavy toll on the health of Charles James. By early 1872 he was living at Ryde on the Isle of Wight and in June that year he died at the early age of 54. What was to happen to the bank and above all to the Gunner connection? The answer was an unexpected one. Caroline Gunner, the widow of Charles James took her late husband's place; a woman banker was highly unusual in the male dominated world of the nineteenth century. But Caroline was a remarkable woman whose business acumen was second to none. The increasingly valuable James Lock became managing partner and Thomas John Brown succeeded him as clerk with a salary of £8.6.8 per month which rose steadily to reach £200 per year in 1882. He was to stay with the firm for 43 years until his death in 1915. Meanwhile Charles Richards Gunner, the second son of Charles and Caroline was groomed to take over responsibility in due course. He was a promising school boy at Marlborough College and hoped to go up to Oxford. Instead it was decided that he should leave school in December 1871 and go to London to qualify as a solicitor and in due course to become a partner in the bank.[6]

In 1880 he married Jessie Kate Mason and they too had a large family – seven boys and two girls born in the 15 years between 1881 and 1896. They lived at first at Brook House where their first four children were born. They then moved to the nearby village of Swanmore living at Swanmore Cottage (the house is now named Swanmore Lodge) at the top of Hampton Hill. Needing however to be nearer to the bank Charles Gunner bought land behind Free Street in Bishop's Waltham and in 1897 built Ridgemede, where the Hambledon Hunt, with which he and other members of the family hunted, met several times a year. He enjoyed a daily cold bath in rain water and had a special tap in the bathroom from which he could draw water for this purpose.[7]

At the time of the 1901 census Charles Gunner now aged 48 and his wife Jessie were living at Ridgemede. Three of the boys were presumably at boarding school since their names do not appear in the census return. Charles and Jessie's eldest daughter Daisy was at home and so were the three youngest children – Benjamin (8), Edward (7) and Margaret (4). There was a staff of six servants – governess, nurse, cook, parlour maid, housemaid and nursemaid. [8]

Ridgemede stood in 18½ acres of ground.[9] It faced south and though the entrance was in Free Street the long drive led almost to Rareridge Lane. The Lodge was close to the entrance in Free Street and the drive was flanked by orchards. In the house itself was the drawing room (25 feet by 21 feet), a conservatory with centre pool and fountain off it, dining room (also 25 feet by 21 feet) and panelled study. On the first floor there were six principal bedrooms and dressing rooms and on the second floor housemaids' pantry, large bedroom, day nursery and four more servants' bedrooms. There were beer and wine cellars. The house was lit by gas 'from the mains of the Bishop's Waltham company'– electricity did not reach Bishop's Waltham until the 1930s.

43. Caroline Gunner 1829–1906.

Outside were coal shed and boiler house, stables, garage and room for the coachman. There were flower gardens, shrubbery and glasshouses, vinery and potting sheds as well as kitchen gardens. In the grounds was Ridgemede Cottage where in 1901 the coachman William Seward a young man of 28 and his wife Angelina lived with their children, boys aged two and seven days old.

At Holm Oak lived Caroline Gunner, now aged 71, the widow of Charles James, with her two unmarried daughters. It was she who made possible the restoration of the chancel of St Peter's church as a memorial to her late husband, in a style which would have been impossible without her substantial contribution. Her benefaction is noted on a small plaque at the entrance to the chancel. She also gave to the church the stained glass east window in the chancel and a carved wooden reredos (removed in the 1960s) in memory of one of her sons. That Caroline Gunner was an astute businesswoman cannot be doubted. What she described as her 'Schedule of Property', kept in a neat hand in a marbled exercise book is a list of her land, houses

44. Licence for a male servant 1905.

45. Licence for a carriage or motor car, 1905.

46. Charles Richards Gunner 1853–1924.

47. Some of the Children of Charles and Jessie Gunner c.1892 – Charles James, Daisy May, John Hugh, Thomas Ridge, Walter Robin and Benjamin George.

GUNNER FAMILY OF BISHOP'S WALTHAM

```
                    1770
      William      =    Mary              Thomas Ridge    =   Mary Ridge
      c.1748 – 1797     b.c.1750          1738-1801
      Solicitor                           Squire of Kilmeston
                                          21 children
                                                       1811
  Gertrude   Harriet    Elizabeth    William         =    Lucy  Matilda Ridge
  1771-1846  b.c 1771   1775 – 1861  1777-1857            1785 – 1859
  b.Winchester b. Winchester b. BW   b. BW                Kilmeston
                                     Lived at Holm Oak
                                     Retired to Winchester 1851
                                     P.1809-1851

                            1850
      Thomas       Charles James   =  Caroline Hale       Other children
      1815-1883    1818- 1872         1829 – 1906         2 sons, 3 daughters
      P.1841-1845  Holm Oak BW        P. 1872-1906        including 2 C.of E. priests
                   P.1841-1872

                                1880
  William Henry Ridge   Charles Richards  =  Jessie Kate Mason   Ernest John    George Herbert¹   Caroline
  1851 –1921            1853 – 1924          1860 – 1930         1862 –1925     1863-1897         Harriet²
  P.1883 -1921          Brook House BW                           P.1923 –1925                     1865-1934
                        Swanmore Cottage                                                          = Thomas
                        Ridgemede BW                                                              Archer-
                        P.1883-1924                                                               Shepherd
                                                                                                  1857-1908
  Frank Hugh
  1887 –1954
  P.1923-1953

  Charles James  Daisy May   John Hugh   Thomas Ridge   Walter        Richard     Benjamin  Edward     Elizabeth
  1881- 1893     1882-1924   1884-1918   1885-1910      Robin         Humphrey    George    Geoffrey   Margaret
                                                        1887- 1973    b.&d. 88    1892-1915 1894-1914  1896-1974
                                                        P.1918-1953
                                                        = Eleanor
                                                        Merewether
                                                        1884-1966

                                                        Harry   =  Sheila Brooks
                                                        b.1918     1916-2007
```

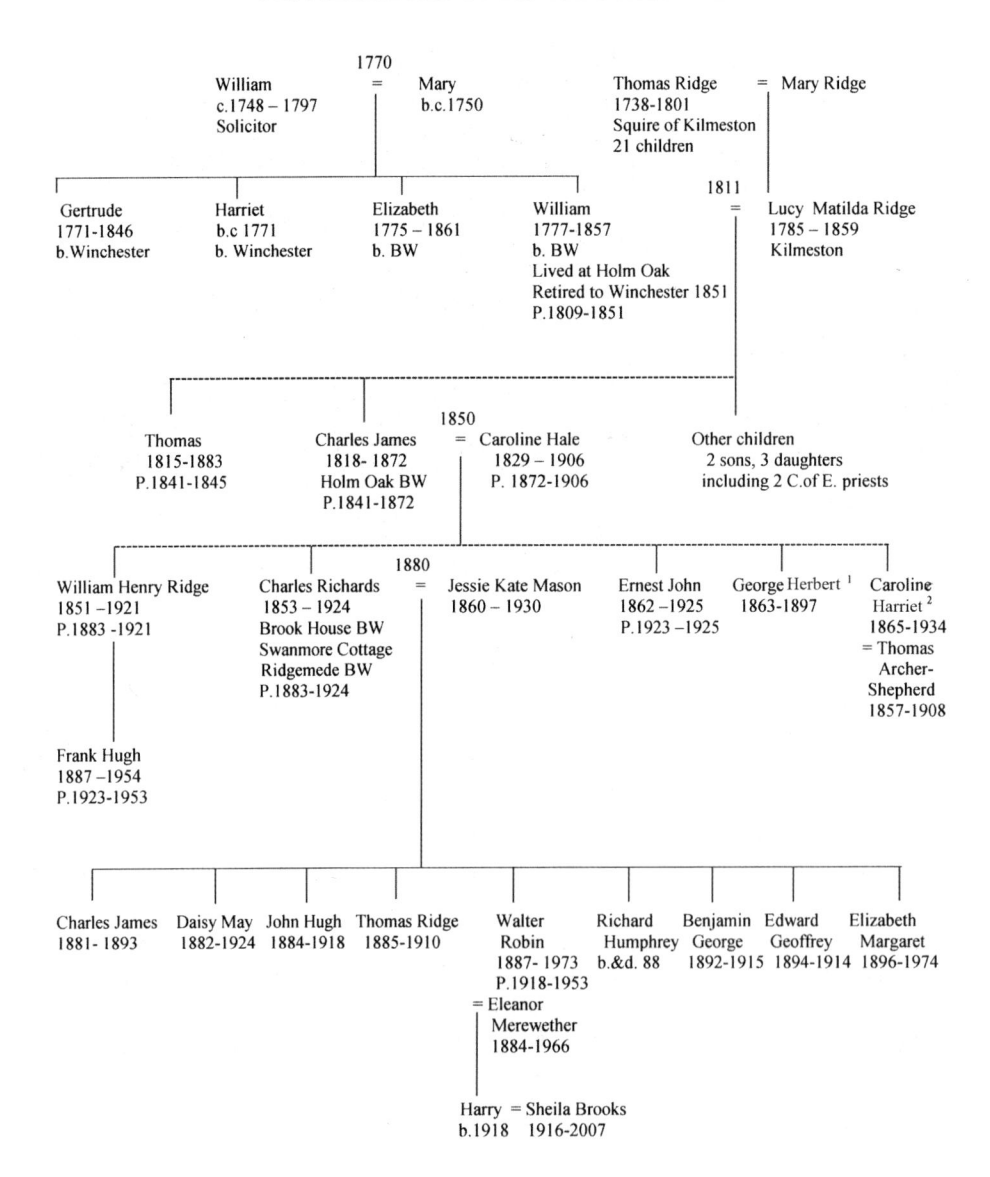

P. Partner in Gunners bank with dates.
1. The East window in the chancel of St Peter's was given in memory of George Herbert Gunner
2. Metal gates to the churchyard given by Caroline in memory of her husband, Thomas Archer-Shepherd

48. Family tree of the Gunner family of Bishop's Waltham.

49. Ridgemede House built 1897 by Charles Richards Gunner.

and investments. She summarised her estate as worth £42,884 which brought in an income of £1821. These are figures for 1904–1905, which would equate to capital worth something over £2 million and income of about £90,000 per year today. In addition to her own house, the bank and the adjoining office, she also owned the Grange, Hope House and about 17 other houses or cottages and a good deal of land in or close to the town. Caroline Gunner must have been the wealthiest citizen of Bishop's Waltham.

No account of the Gunners of Bishop's Waltham would be complete without reference to the devastating blows, which befell the family in the premature death of no less than six of the seven sons of Charles Richards and Jessie Gunner. In the south aisle of Swanmore church is a memorial window to five of their sons. Charles James, the eldest son, died of pneumonia at the age of 12 just after entering Marlborough College. Thomas Ridge Gunner was 25 and a lieutenant in the army in India when he died of enteric fever at Rawalpindi in 1910.

Three more sons died in the First World War and their names appear on the St Peter's War Memorial. The war had been in progress for only three months when, on 26th November, HMS Bulwark blew up in Chatham harbour, Sheerness. All but 12 of the crew of 800 were drowned. Among them was Sub-Lieutenant Edward Gunner, now aged 20, who had embarked on a naval career at Dartmouth as a 14 year old boy six years earlier. Less than a year later on 7th October 1915 Benjamin Gunner, a Captain in the Northumberland Fusiliers, who had already been awarded the Military Cross, was killed on the western front in Belgium aged 23. Just before the war ended on 9th August 1918 the eldest remaining son, John Hugh Gunner, Captain in the Hampshire Yeomanry, who lived in College Street, Winchester with the wife whom he had married in 1909 and two young sons, was killed also on the western front in Belgium. One son had survived for only a few days back in 1888.

By 1918 out of seven sons born to Charles and Jessie Gunner only one was left. He was Walter Robin Gunner who became a partner in the bank in 1918 and remained so until 1953. Frank Hugh Gunner, a cousin, joined him in 1921 and they remained partners until the bank closed in 1953. Robin Gunner was a member of St Peter's church throughout his life. He was scoutmaster for no less than 46 years from 1911 first at Shedfield later at Bishop's Waltham. Well into middle age he continued to take the Bishop's Waltham troop to camp at Swanage each summer.

When his father died in 1924 Robin Gunner and his family were living at West Hoe House. Ridgemede was placed on the market but it did not sell. Houses of this size were no longer desirable properties. Families were smaller, servants were now an endangered species and the fuel needed to heat a large house was expensive. Robin Gunner decided to move into Ridgemede with his family and they remained there until the 1950s when they moved to Mount House in Little Shore Lane. Ridgemede House then became a rest home. In addition to the house the Ridgemede estate totalled 44 acres, bordering Hoe Road, Rareridge Lane and Free Street. This now became available for development and it is on this land that the Ridgemede housing estate, Ridgemede primary school and Bishop's Waltham infant school were built.

The twentieth century in the banking world, as in so many other spheres, belonged to the big battalions. In 1899 the Capital and Counties Bank opened a branch in Bishop's Waltham claiming that it was at the request of local farmers. It was absorbed by Lloyds in 1918. Meanwhile in 1909 Gunners bank opened a short-lived branch at Wickham, open on Tuesday and Friday mornings, which closed on the outbreak of the First World War and did not reopen after the war. More surprisingly in 1921 Barclays who had been Gunners London agent since 1809 opened a branch at St George's House in the Square, Bishop's Waltham

By the early 1950s the partners in Gunners bank were in their 60s and no member of the next generation was available to take over. On 4th April 1953 Gunners bank closed its doors for the last time, taken over by Barclays and 144 years of banking history came to an end. There had been 15 partners in the bank's history and of these no less than nine had been members of the Gunner family. The firm of solicitors Gunner & Carpenter continued for another 20 years. The building, so long the headquarters of Gunners bank, is now the offices of the Registrar for Births, Marriages and Deaths, marked by a blue plaque placed there by the Bishop's Waltham Society to mark its 145 year association with the bank.

The death of Robin Gunner in 1973 brought an end to the firm which had been opened by his great-great grandfather William Gunner I over two centuries earlier. At the beginning of the twenty first century Robin's son Harry Gunner who lives in Swanmore is the sole representative of the family living locally.

11

Arthur Helps and mid-Victorian enterprise

IN THE EARLY 1860s Bishop's Waltham was a town bubbling with business enterprise. Within a few years it acquired its own railway line and station and became one of the first Hampshire towns to be lit by gas. Clay works and a water works were opened in the same period. The 1860s saw too the development of the suburb of Newtown to house the workers attracted to Bishop's Waltham by the prospect of employment in the clay works. A school was built and became a prominent landmark in the new suburb. The population grew faster in the 1860s than in any previous decade. The same group of men were involved in all these enterprises and at the centre was Arthur Helps, one of the few metropolitan figures to have lived in Bishop's Waltham.

Born in Streatham in 1813 Arthur Helps was educated at Eton and Trinity College, Cambridge. Still in his 20s he became private secretary to Thomas Spring-Rice, Chancellor of the Exchequer in Melbourne's Whig government. In 1847, now in his mid 30s, he moved to Bishop's Waltham with his wife and three young children and bought Vernon Hill House. Later he became private secretary to Queen Victoria and from 1860 until his death he was Clerk to the Privy Council. Arthur Helps also wrote and published a number of books among them *The Conquest of the New World* and *The Spanish Conquest of America* [1]

He cherished his links with the royal family, exemplified in the naming of Victoria and Albert Roads in Newtown, and in his scheme for the Royal Albert Infirmary soon after the death of the Prince Consort. He was knighted in 1872. Arthur Helps was an able and enterprising figure whose ambitious plans were never wholly matched to the resources needed to carry them out nor by the capacity to know when to stop. The railway was under-funded, Palace House which he bought was neglected because money was tight, the clay works flourished only under the later management of Mark Henry Blanchard and Vernon Hill House was let when he returned to London some years before his death.

Arthur Helps was described by William Houghton of Locks Farm who knew him: 'a kinder hearted, more lovable man never lived … [it is] much to be lamented

50. Arthur Helps. Portrait by George Richards, 1858.

51. Workmen at the clay works in Claylands Road 1922.

that his endeavour to lift Bishop's Waltham out of its sluggish inactivity resulted in so great a loss to himself'.[2] Arthur Helps died in debt in 1875. The Vernon Hill estate of 1280 acres was sold by auction at *The Crown* on 19th October.[3] Why Arthur Helps moved to Bishop's Waltham or how he combined his interests in London with his business interests in Hampshire we shall never know. He was however the catalyst of enterprises in Bishop's Waltham which would probably never have happened without him and without which the subsequent development of the town would have been very different.

Bricks had been made in Bishop's Waltham since the Middle Ages. The brickfield at Coppice Hill goes back at least to the fourteenth century and lasted until 1957.[4] It is however the clay works on the other side of the town, which is much the better known.[5] In 1859 Arthur Helps bought part of Pondside Farm. The land lay at the junction of the Reading Beds and London Clay and borings, which he asked Blanchards, a long established firm in Lambeth, to analyse confirmed that the clay was of high quality, later described as amongst the finest in the country. In 1862 Arthur Helps formed the Bishop's Waltham Clay Company whose £80,000 capital he used not only to open the works but to build houses in Victoria and Albert Roads in Newtown, for the workers which he hoped to attract to the town. The first products were black bricks and tiles used in the reconstruction of Blackfriars Bridge in London, which was then under way.

Early in 1866 Arthur Helps embarked on the production of terra cotta, decorated with scenes from Homer's Odyssey. It proved to be of fine quality, superior in hardness, texture, colour and finish to any other on the market.[6] It required the expertise of highly skilled workmen whom Arthur Helps brought from the Staffordshire Potteries. The enterprise proved however not to be profitable and in April 1867 after less than two years it was wound up and the company went into liquidation.

The clay works were rescued by another remarkable entrepreneur. In 1871 they were leased by Mark Henry Blanchard and nine years later he closed his Lambeth works and concentrated his business at Bishop's Waltham.[7] He built Claylands House, close to the works, a distinctive and ornate residence for himself and his family, but also a showcase for the products which his works were capable of producing. He used both red and blue bricks and the house was embellished with an impressive terra cotta coat of arms over the front door and a balustrade at the rear. Under Mark Henry Blanchard the clay works flourished and became 'the most important brickworks in Hampshire and acquired a first class reputation for its products not just in this country but in the whole world'.[8] The 1880s were its golden age. It covered 20 acres, employed 200 men in a town whose total population was less than 2,500 and was the most important brickworks in Hampshire. The brickworks produced red and blue bricks, roofing and floor tiles, terra cotta objects, art pottery, copings, channelling and drain pipes. In addition to a branch line from Bishop's Waltham railway station there was a narrow gauge tramway. The bell summoning men to start work or to break for lunch or at the end of the day could be heard all over the town and became a well-known time signal.

The bricks were widely used. Locally they supplied the brick skin for the Hockley Viaduct on the Didcot, Newbury and Southampton Railway line and bricks for the Prudential Building in Southampton.[9] In London Blanchards' bricks were used at Buckingham Palace, the Natural History Museum, Cannon Street station and the St Pancras Hotel, among other places. Abroad they were to be found in Poland and USA and in the Grand Hotel, Cairo.

When Mark Henry Blanchard died at the age of 76 in 1892 he was succeeded by his son Mark Henry II, a young man of 33 who was to live in Claylands House until his death at the beginning of the Second World War. He was not however as astute a businessman as his father and for this and other reasons the clay works began to decline.

There was a short-lived recovery in the 1920s when Elliotts, who bought the firm in 1919, provided additional buildings, installed new machinery and equipment and production increased. New methods however needed fewer workmen and Blanchards, as the firm was still called, now employed less than 100 men. The largest customer in the years before and after the Second World was the University of Southampton. Blanchard's bricks were also used in the Southern Evening Echo building and the Norwich Union offices in Above Bar, Southampton.

Two events contributed to a further decline in production – a fire in the early 1930s and a stick of German bombs dropped across the brickyard in August 1940. When war came the work force was about 40, young men were called up and there was little demand for bricks, since few houses were built during the war. In 1941 production ceased altogether. Part of the site was requisitioned and used to store aircraft parts and as a depot for emergency food supplies.

There was a further brief revival after the Second World War when the government embarked on a huge house building programme to make up for the backlog caused by cessation of building during the war. Blanchards Brick and Tile Works, to use its official name, closed in 1956. The last brickworks chimney, 130 feet tall, long disused but a prominent Bishop's Waltham landmark was demolished in July 1958.[10] Sadly Claylands House where Mark Henry Blanchard II lived until his death in 1940 was demolished in 1974.[11] Claylands Road is now the site of a small industrial estate, which most people enter only to use the recycling centre. They may not realise that they are close to the site which for nearly a century was the largest industrial undertaking which Bishop's Waltham has ever had and for which it was widely known.

Of all the reminders of bygone Bishop's Waltham none is more evocative than the railway line and station now recalled only by a plaque attached to the island where the roads from Corhampton, Winchester and Wickham meet – 'The Old Station Roundabout', it reads – and by the level crossing gates placed nostalgically where once there were real ones. The railway, which opened in 1863, just failed to reach its centenary. Passenger traffic ended on 31st December 1932, goods continued until 27th April 1962. In the late 1960s the rails were removed and the station was demolished soon afterwards.[12] Passenger services are now almost beyond living memory. It must have been one of the shortest branch lines ever opened: 4½ miles, 12 minutes running time, single track (though sufficient land was bought to provide a second track if it were ever warranted) and for much of its life no intermediate station.

The London and South West Railway (LSWR) opened its line from Bishopstoke (Eastleigh) to Gosport on 29th November 1841 with a station which, although named Botley, was actually in Curdridge, part of the civil parish of Bishop's Waltham until 1894. With easy access by rail to both London and Gosport, Botley was able to steal a march on Bishop's Waltham which was in danger of stagnating and already had considerable unemployment. Bishop's Waltham needed a railway line.

By 1860 the main towns of the country had been linked to the rail network. It was now the turn of the smaller towns and even villages which had been bypassed by the railway to lay claim to a line. This is the background to the plethora of bills laid before parliament in the 1860s to provide additional lines in Hampshire. A line from Petersfield to join the LSWR at Botley was proposed with stations at East Meon, Meonstoke and Bishop's Waltham. Another plan was to extend this line to Netley Hospital and Southampton. Both were opposed by the LSWR which wanted to keep its monopoly of the route to London. The bill authorising a Bishop's Waltham railway which received the royal assent in July 1862 encountered no such opposition since unless it was extended it would compete with no other line.

Arthur Helps, Bettesworth Pitt Shearer of Swanmore House and Charles Richards Gunner were among its supporters. As Gunner said 'For the last half century Bishop's Waltham has stood still whilst other town and neighbourhoods have prospered'. There would be obvious gains – coal would be cheaper and farmers would be able to bring in drainage pipes and lime for their fields. Once agreed the railway was built quickly. Though incomplete and with only a temporary station at Bishop's Waltham the line was opened on 1st June 1863 with appropriate celebrations. *The Hampshire Telegraph* reported:

> The Bishop's Waltham Railway was opened for public traffic on Monday last, which made the little town full of bustle and life. The beautiful toned bells of the old parish church were ringing a merry peal the whole day and a celebrated brass band paraded the town; the Bishop's Waltham Rifle Band also assisted. The principal gentlemen and tradesmen met at the Crown Hotel to inaugurate the opening of the railway. About 50 sat down to a first class meal, served up by Mr Pratt to the satisfaction of all present, the wines being first rate.

Arthur Helps was in the chair and proposed the Queen, the Prince and Princess of Wales and all the Royal Family. There follows a list of no less than eight men who made speeches. The report concludes: 'The proceedings were kept up with great

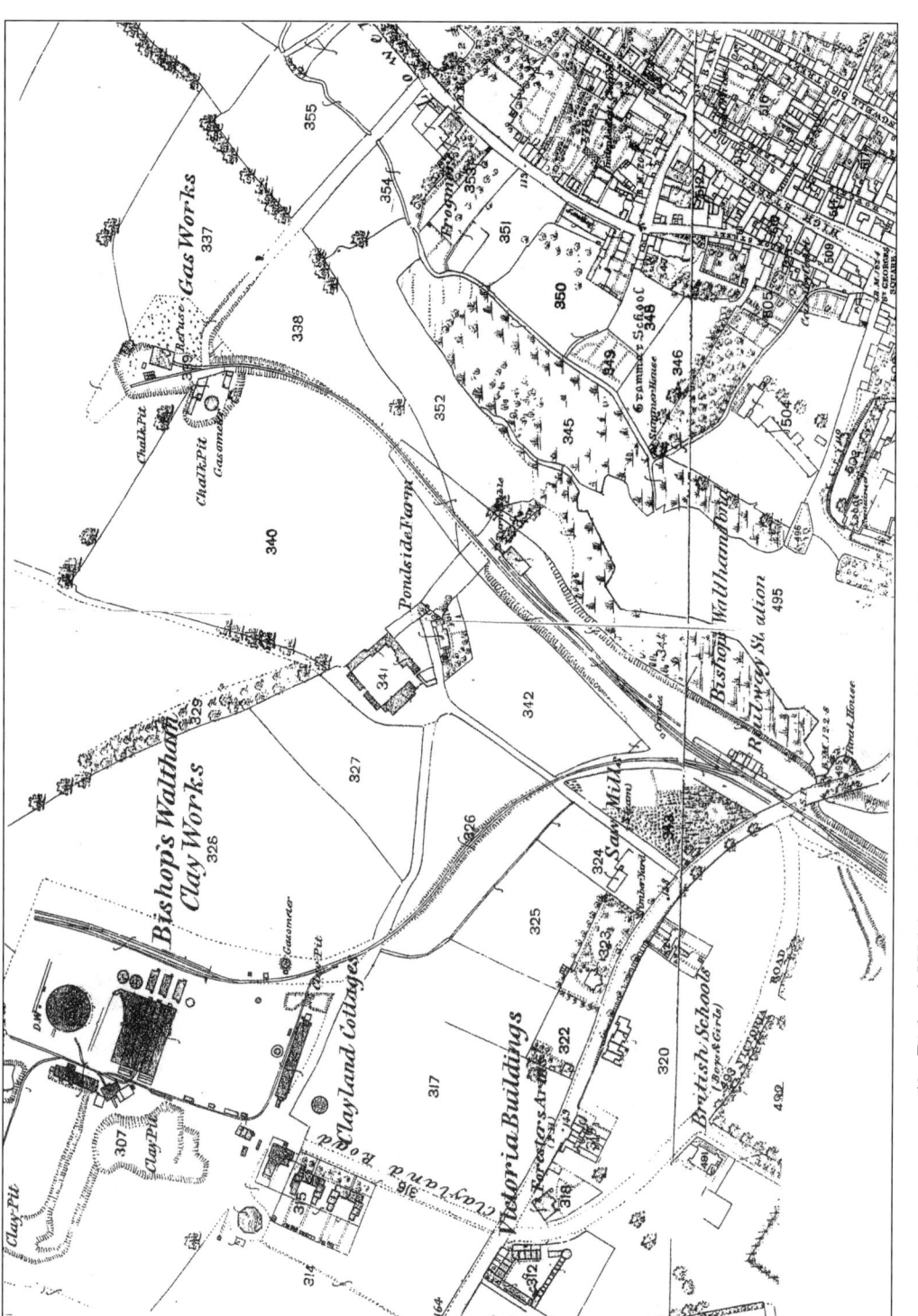

52. Bishop's Waltham Railway showing sidings leading to the clay works and gas works.

53. Timetable of the Bishop's Waltham railway June 1863.

54. Bishop's Waltham station.

spirit to a late hour ... The day concluded with the band playing 'God save the Queen'.

From the beginning the Bishop's Waltham Railway was in trouble. It was undercapitalised. The hope of a link to Petersfield was never realised. In 1866 Arthur Helps' clay company went into liquidation (though the situation improved when Mark Blanchard took over in 1871). Arthur Helps reported that the South of England Wagon Company intended to open its works at Bishop's Waltham and the siding which they requested was planned for an area south and west of the station. Had it done so Bishop's Waltham might have become a railway town as did Eastleigh in the 1890s. Instead the independent existence of the Bishop's Waltham line was in doubt from 1869. Finally it sold out to the LSWR in 1881.

Right to the end of the century there was hope of an extension of the line. There were a variety of plans: to build a line to Droxford, for a light railway to Brockbridge, and for a line to Winchester via Upham, Fisher's Pond, and Twyford. When the Meon Valley line was projected in the late 1890s the Parish Council asked for an extension to Brockbridge and were joined by other parishes. There was a public enquiry but nothing came of the proposal. [13]

The new century saw a moderate up-turn. Rail motors were introduced in 1904, a Sunday service was provided in 1907 and in 1909 a Halt was opened at Durley Mill. Before the First World War Sunday School outings were usually by train. In August 1898 the St Peter's Sunday School 'Treat' was to Portchester Castle. One hundred and seventy eight children travelled on the 1.30 train and arrived at Portchester at 2.45. Two months later the choir and bell ringers went to Bournemouth also by train and then by steamer to Swanage before beginning the return journey. [14] Ethel Cockle remembered the excitement of Sunday School 'Treats' in the Edwardian years. 'We would arrive at the station and our teachers would settle us in the carriages. Then the guard would lock us in and when we arrived at Lee on Solent he would unlock the doors and we would have a lovely day at the sea.'[15] During the First World War wounded soldiers came by train to convalesce at Northbrook House.

Throughout its life there were a few regular commuters (though they were not then called that) travelling to Botley or Southampton. When the passenger trains ceased there were just 25 holders of season tickets. Major Gunner lived at Portchester and travelled to the bank in Bishop's Waltham by train each day. If his train from Portchester were delayed the station master would hold the Bishop's Waltham train to await his arrival. [16]Before the days of the motor car commercial travellers used the line and stayed at *The Crown*. School boys going to Price's Grammar School at Fareham from Swanmore and surrounding villages or from Bishop's Waltham itself used the train. They cycled to the station, took the train to Botley where they changed to the Gosport line and walked up the hill to Price's, a circuitous route and a time consuming journey. [17] An expedition by train was an adventure for children. Ethel Cockle recalled visiting relations at Botley in the early years of the twentieth century. 'We would run from side to side to see the animals in the fields. Nearing New Arch we could see the river and the Botley Road as the train ran quite a way by the road.'

After the First World War the growing popularity of motor cars and charabancs and the beginning of bus connections to the neighbouring towns sounded the death knell for the line. The service was at first reduced but on 31st December 1932 it closed for passenger trafffic. As the reporter sent to cover the event for *The Hampshire Observer* commented: 'The service has had such an extended decline that the final passing was almost unnoticed as virtually the line has been a dying cause for years'. Somebody at least would note its passing. The same reporter quoted a well known market gardener and fruit grower who lived alongside the track: 'How on earth am I to know the time when the trains stop running?'[18] Reg Cockle, then a fifteen year old boy, was aware of the historic significance of the demise of passenger traffic and determined to travel on the last train. He loaded his bicycle into the goods van to cycle back from Botley and was put out when an officious ticket collector refused to allow him to keep his ticket as a memento of a nostalgic occasion.[19]

The railway staff was considerable: station master, porters, shunters, signalmen, guards, drivers and goods manager were among them. Goods traffic was always more important than passengers and the railway remained a vital link for goods for another 30 years. There were two goods trains daily, reduced to one later. The clay company received its coal and coke by train and sent its bricks, tiles and terracotta out by the same route. The gas company brought in coal and timber by rail. Grocers, millers and maltsters used the line. Coal merchants established their wharves at the station, received coal by train and transferred it to lorries for delivery to customers. The station was the railhead for farmers in the lower Meon valley. Following sales in the field below the station 600 cattle might be transported by rail. Horses came as far as Bishop's Waltham by rail on their way to Hambledon races. Surplus milk was sent out daily though not more than a few churns from any one farm. Sugar, hops and grain still reached the brewery by rail. The chemist received distilled water and drugs and machine tools and agricultural implements were also brought in by goods train.

During the Second World War the line was used to bring goods in bulk to the warehouse established at Swanmore House by Timothy White and Taylor, chemists, after their headquarters in Portsmouth was destroyed by enemy bombing. The Royal Engineers had a base at Hazelholt at which wire, pickets and steel hawsers were stored in case they were needed if the country were invaded. They too made use of the railway.

Memories of the goods trains were vivid. Ethel Cockle recalled the buzz of activity in the yard in her childhood:

> As we came from school …we would race down the hill to get through the big gates before the long goods train came through. Some of the trucks were loaded with bricks and tiles, shunted down the short line from Blanchards brickyard. … They were attached to other trucks loaded at sale times with cattle, sheep and horses which had been driven from the sale field in Bishop's Lane to the pens by the railway line… After shunting back across the line the signalman would open the small gates for us children to pass through. Then we would watch the long goods train on its way to Botley.
>
> The goods yard was a busy place. How we loved to see the horses which were used before cars took over. … The line carried on to the old lime kiln in Garfield Road. Trucks of coal were shunted down this line to the gashouse where we would see the retorts drawn and coke made from the coal, pour out red hot, and the water thrown over it would have a lovely smell.
>
> The goods yard was a very busy place. Goods came in from the outlying villages. Cabs and luggage vans from *The Crown Hotel* stables met every train. The coming of the buses killed the railway traffic.[20]

There was still a significant level of goods traffic after the Second World War but in 1956 the brickworks closed and in the early 1960s the daily goods train was reduced to two per week. On 24th April 1962 the last goods train ran.

The Bishop's Waltham Gas and Coke Company was inaugurated at a meeting held, like so many similar gatherings, at *The Crown Hotel* in St George's Square on 14th April 1863. The directors elected as chairman Bettesworth Pitt Shearer of Swanmore Park who was already chairman of the railway company. The site of the proposed gas works was agreed – Chalk Dell to which access could be made from Lower Lane – hence the origin of Garfield Road.

Just under a year later on 4th March 1864 the gas works opened and the town of Bishop's Waltham became the first small town in Hampshire to boast gas street lighting.[21] For the first 30 years of its existence the gas works was a profitable undertaking. Low costs and high output produced a good dividend for the shareholders whilst the company was able to reduce the price of gas to the consumer. A miners' strike in 1894 led however to a higher price for coal which had to be passed to the gas customer. The gas company continued to meet the needs of Bishop's Waltham until it was taken over by the Gosport and District Gas Company in 1931. The last gasholder remained an item of industrial archaeology until it was dismantled in September 1982.[22]

The final enterprise associated with Arthur Helps was his own brainchild. Bishop's Waltham, he concluded, needed its own hospital. Portsmouth, Southampton and Winchester each had its own but they were too far away for Bishop's Waltham people. Arthur Helps enlisted the interest and support of the Queen. He had at her request edited a volume of the Prince Consort's speeches and the Queen gave the profits – the substantial sum of £550 – to the institution which would be named The Royal Albert Infirmary. It was intended for about 20 patients and would include a dispensary to provide 'pure medicines to the poor at their own houses'. Sponsored by royalty, subscriptions were successfully elicited from distinguished backers from London as well as local subscribers.[23]

The foundation stone was laid on 4th August 1864 by Prince Leopold, Queen Victoria's youngest son, at the age of 11 fulfilling his first public engagement, assisted by Prince Louis of Hesse-Darmstadt, the husband of Princess Alice (daughter of the Queen). It was Prince Leopold who was the star attraction and an elaborate arch was erected across the High Street to welcome him.[24] It was a grand occasion. A Guard of Honour provided by the 3rd Battalion of the Hampshire Volunteers escorted the royal party to the site. After the ceremony they were entertained to lunch in the grounds of the Bishop's Palace. The day concluded with singing by a choir of 200, dancing and a firework display.[25] One newspaper reported 'Perhaps since the Knights Templars sojourned at the "praty tounlet" as Leland calls it, that place has not seen such an assemblage of people'.[26] The royal party returned after the ceremony to Osborne House.

The opening ceremony of the Infirmary held 15 months later was not so successful. It was a cold November day and as a consequence the crowds not as large. The royal party consisting of three of Queen Victoria's children – Princesses Helena and Louise, and Prince Arthur – were late arriving from lunch at Vernon Hill House. Nonetheless the ceremony went ahead. The now venerable Bishop of Winchester, Charles Sumner said prayers, the building was declared open and amidst a flourish of trumpets Princess Helena unveiled a statue of the Prince Consort. 'Rarely', says Peter Finn, 'can such a modest establishment have been launched with so much ceremony and national attention'.[27] Afterwards the royal party visited the British and Foreign School then being built on the Hill. A painting belonging to the National Portrait Gallery shows the royal party at the opening.[28]

55. Prince Leopold laying the foundation stone of the Royal Albert Infirmary 1864.

The difficulties at the opening were an omen of worse to come. The Infirmary was not complete and never opened as a hospital. It needed an annual revenue of £600 and this it never achieved. For a time it remained empty and by 1871 Arthur Helps had left Bishop's Waltham. When he died in 1875 the building was put up for auction. Intending purchasers were informed that it was built as an infirmary and that there were still four large wards, nurses' and matron's rooms as well as surgery and operating room and that it would make an infirmary or convalescent hospital. The first floor remained unplastered and unceiled. It must therefore appear that no further work took place after its opening by royalty twelve years before. Included with the building were the terraced grounds and an adjoining plot of 11 acres of pastureland.[29]

The intended infirmary became a private house. By 1884 it was occupied by Richard Hurley and named Albert House. It was next bought by Jacob Kalff who renamed it the Priory.[30] It changed hands several times but in 1902 was bought by Arthur Robinson who in 1908 put it up for sale as 'A gentleman's exceptionally well-built and substantial residence'. It included three acres of gardens and grounds.[31] It did not sell and Arthur Robinson continued to live at The Priory until his death in October 1911 when it was bought by the White Fathers and remained in their hands until the departure of the Order in 1967.

The Hampshire Police Authority bought the Priory as it was still called and estab-

56. The Priory, 1912. Built as the Royal Albert Infirmary but never used as a hospital. It became a private house until it was bought by the White Fathers in 1912.

lished a Police Training School which opened in 1972 but had a short life. The decision to move to Netley was made in 1980 but was not implemented until 1988. The building remained empty for several years, not surprisingly vandalised frequently. It was bought by developers and demolished in 1993; 42 houses were built on the site. Twenty one acres of playing fields were bought by the Parish Council for almost £120,000 and became Priory Park.[32] The writer of the Museum Scrapbook comments that Bishop's Waltham has a sports facility, a public house, retirement flats, and a housing estate all named after a Priory which never existed![33]

12

William Brock and the Victorian church

In 1827 Winchester had a new bishop. Charles Sumner was 36 when he was translated from Llandaff after only a year as its bishop, on the insistence of George IV: Sumner had been tutor to the son of George IV's mistress and through the king's favour enjoyed a number of lucrative appointments. Llandaff was the poorest of all the bishoprics in England or Wales (net income £1043 in 1835) and so its bishop was appointed also Dean of St Paul's. Winchester was worth over ten times as much as Llandaff (£10,654 in 1835)[1] Bishop Sumner's portrait hanging in Farnham Castle makes clear that he was every inch an aristocrat, the last of Winchester's prince-bishops. Winchester was the last diocese in the Church of England to be affected by the redistribution of church revenues carried out by the Ecclesiastical Commission in the 1830s, since it did not take effect while the incumbent bishop occupied the see. Charles Sumner, who was hostile to the work of the Commission, continued in office for 42 years until the Bishops' Resignation Act of 1869 enabled him to resign. By then he was incapacitated by age and infirmity. In the words of Owen Chadwick he survived 'in some cloud-capped Georgian Eden'.[2] He continued to live in Farnham Castle until his death in 1874.

But Charles Sumner was a conscientious bishop, the first for 300 years to be enthroned in Winchester cathedral, which impressed and excited his diocese.[3] He was opposed to clerical pluralism and non-residence, encouraged the building of new churches, parsonages and schools, revived the office of rural dean and met regularly those he appointed. John Haygarth rector of Upham and Durley was the first rural dean of Droxford North West.[4] In 1832 he built the large and magnificent rectory next to the church. Bishop Sumner was a convinced evangelical, one of the first to reach the episcopal bench, and would appoint only evangelicals to the livings where he had the presentation.[5] He made one exception – he appointed his relation and close friend Samuel Wilberforce to both the archdeaconry of Surrey and the important – and rich – living of Alverstoke.[6] He was a keen sabbatarian. He cannot however entirely escape the charge of nepotism since he appointed his son George Henry Sumner to the rich living of Old Alresford.

57. Charles Sumner, Bishop of Winchester 1827–1869.

58. William Brock, Rector 1833–91 wearing the academic gown and bands which he wore when preaching.

James Ogle died on 19th May 1833 at the age of 56 shortly after the death of two of his daughters, Elizabeth Lucy aged 19 and Jane Barbara aged 18, all three commemorated on a stone tablet in the sanctuary of St Peter's church, fulsome in his praise. His successor, appointed on 7th June 1833, was William Brock, a member of a leading Guernsey family born at St Peter Port in 1805. His father Thomas Brock was rector for over 50 years. William was married to Anne Magdalen Gosset at St Saviour's Jersey on 26th September 1828. He was aged only 28 when he came to Bishop's Waltham from a curacy at Highclere. He was to remain rector for 58 years until his death at the age of 86 on 21st November 1891.

William Brock had a total of 13 children over a period of 26 years by two wives. When they came to Bishop's Waltham he and his wife already had three children, Isaac (born in 1829), Emily (born April 1831) and George (born April 1833).[7] Within a year of arriving at Bishop's Waltham Anne gave birth to another boy, William, who lived however for only nine days. Between 1836 and 1844 Anne bore a further five children – Alfred (born 1836 died 1837), Martha Harriet (born 1838), Julia (born 1840), a boy also named William (born 1842) and Mary Elizabeth (born 1844).[8] Fifteen months later Anne gave birth to her tenth child in 16 years. Within a few days she was dead and the child, a girl named after her mother, Anne Magdalen, died when she was two years and ten months old. William remarried in 1848, Louisa Harrison, the 36 year old daughter of a clergyman who lived in Southwark. They had three further children, Louisa Wilhelmina (born 1849), Edith (born 1850) and finally Cameron (born 1855). By this time Louisa was aged 43 and there were no more children

The rector was one of the town's leading citizens known by all. He was chairman of the vestry at a time before elective local government had reached the countryside. He lived in some state in the rectory which had over three acres of gardens as well as stables and coach house. In 1851 in addition to his wife and seven children still at home there were no less than seven servants. Lucy Smith an unmarried woman of 34 was teacher of the three girls and one boy. There was a nurse for children of two and ten months as well as cook, parlour maid, housemaid, nursemaid and under nurse maid.

William Brock was, like his bishop, an evangelical who disapproved of deviations whether in a liberal or a catholic direction. In the Rare Books room at the British Library is a collection of his pamphlets. Some are sermons such as Victorian parsons were in the habit of printing for circulation to their flock and beyond. Others are writings called forth by crisis in the history of the Victorian church. In mid-century prominent Anglicans like John Henry Newman and Henry Manning became Roman Catholics and Pope Pius IX restored the Roman Catholic hierarchy in England to the consternation of the Queen and the Church of England. William Brock responded with a book *Tractarianism Schismatical and Dishonest* in which he denounced high churchmen. He pulled no punches, describing the writings of the Tractarians as 'a mass of blasphemous fables and dangerous deceits'. He continued 'the spirit of these misguided agitators is as deplorable as their teaching is heretical'.[9] He attacked particularly the bishops of Oxford and Exeter – Samuel Wilberforce and Henry Phillpotts.

The liberals too roused his ire. In 1865 the Privy Council dismissed the case against *Essays and Reviews*, a book widely reviled for its liberal views. William Brock preached a sermon at St Peter's which he subsequently had printed entitled *Infidelity in High Places*. He described *Essays and Reviews* as 'this wretched book', tracing 'all that has shamed the Christian public' to the writings of Thomas Arnold the famous headmaster of Rugby School.[10] In 1869 his wrath descended on no less a figure than the Liberal Prime Minister, W.E.Gladstone whose government had disestablished the Irish Church. William Brock responded by publishing six letters entitled *Mr Gladstone the Betrayer of the Religion and Liberties of the Country*.[11]

From the late 1820s there was a quickening of church life and it was recognised that people could not be expected to walk long distances to attend their parish church on Sundays, to have their babies baptised, to marry or to bury their dead. It was not yet possible to create new parishes but additional churches could be provided, described as chapels of ease (created for the greater 'ease' of parishioners).

At Shedfield a chapel of ease in the neighbouring parish of Droxford had been opened in 1829 to be followed by a church at Swanmore in 1845. The parish of Bishop's Waltham was also a large one. The tithing of Curdridge extended as far as the river Hamble at Botley. Until the end of the eighteenth century Curdridge was isolated since there was no bridge over the river Hamble at Botley but a ford usable only at low tide. As a Trade Directory of 1793 put it, perhaps overdramatically 'Botleigh (sic) is a small village, but lately emerged from obscurity and contempt, by the erection of a large brick bridge over the river; the fording of which was a terror to travellers, and caused many to prefer a long and circuitous route by Winchester, rather than trust themselves to its uncertain and fluctuating depth. This evil was effectually remedied by the establishment of a bridge and the improvement of the road'.[12]

William Brock was quick to respond to the request of the parishioners of Curdridge for a chapel of ease. He took the chair at a meeting on 11th June 1834 at which 'It was unanimously resolved that the piece of ground situated near Pound Farm be fixed for the site of the proposed Chapel of Ease at Curdridge in the parish of Bishop's Waltham'. Only three months later the rural dean John Haygarth, laid the foundation stone in a service conducted by William Brock. The chapel of ease was opened by Bishop Sumner on 27th August 1835 (following which Charles Walters took the bishop on a conducted tour of Bishop's Waltham parish, claiming that it was the first time a bishop had visited the parish since the sack of the Palace). Curdridge's chapel of ease was built of brick rendered with cement, had a spire with a bell and a gallery for the organ and the singers and a shallow chancel. There were pitch pine pews at the front to accommodate 118 people who paid pew rent and stained wooden benches for a further 215 people free of pew rent.[13] It had cost £1300.

The curate in charge was Richard Chenevix-Trench who stayed until 1841 and to whose stipend the rector of Bishop's Waltham contributed £100 per year. He came from a local family and lived at first at Sherecroft House, then at the house which is now called Beechcroft in what is still named Vicarage Lane. Trench moved in 1841 to become curate to Samuel Wilberforce in the large and important parish of Alverstoke.[14] He subsequently had a distinguished career becoming Dean of Westminster in 1856 and Archbishop of Dublin in 1864. Curdridge became a separate ecclesiastical parish in 1843 after the passing of the District Churches Act.[15]

William Brock had lost a quarter of his parish in the separation of the tithing of Curdridge and in 1845 he was to lose a further, though much smaller, part at the other end of the parish when a section of the tithing of West Hoe went to the making of the new parish of Swanmore.[16] Later in the century at both Shedfield and Curdridge more imposing churches replaced the earlier chapels of ease.[17]

The west gallery of St Peter's, built in 1733, lasted over 100 years but in October 1848 pew holders drew the attention of the churchwardens to the dilapidated state of the gable. The construction of an organ loft above the gallery had proved fatal to the structure.[18] Surveyors were called in and confirmed that the west wall was

18 inches out of upright, bowed badly over the window and the mortar was rotten. There was no alternative but to rebuild the west wall and to insert a new west window.[19]

Deaneries covered a much larger area than their modern counterparts. The Droxford deanery, since its medieval foundation, had consisted of all the parishes in the mainland part of what in 1927 became the diocese of Portsmouth, except for Botley which was in the deanery of Southampton. Soon after restoring rural deans Bishop Sumner realised that if they were to undertake the tasks he envisaged for them – comparable with work now undertaken by archdeacons – the deaneries must be smaller and more manageable. Instead of 10 deaneries in Hampshire from 1856 there were 24 including four Droxford deaneries – North East, North West, South East and South West. Bishop's Waltham was in Droxford North West.

A further reorganisation in 1871 reduced the number of deaneries to 21 and brought into existence the deanery of Bishop's Waltham. At the time of its creation the new deanery included, in addition to the parishes in the present deanery, eight parishes which remained part of the Winchester diocese when the Portsmouth diocese was created in 1927 – Bishopstoke, Fair Oak, Bursledon, Eastleigh, Hamble, Owslebury, Hound and Colden Common.

The only national census of church attendance ever held took place at the same time as the decennial census of population on 30th March 1851. It provides an invaluable snapshot of church attendance at a time when it must have been close to its Victorian high point. Attendance at St Peter's on census Sunday was: morning 461 adults and 140 children, in the afternoon 131 adults and 121 children, in the evening 437. At Curdridge there were 100 adults and 25 children in the morning and 120 adults n the afternoon. No other denomination had a place of worship in Bishop's Waltham and it is reckoned that on census Sunday 48.6% of the available population attended St Peter's.[20] The rector was asked in addition to estimate the capacity of the church. He gave the figure as 955, 'calculated at 20 inches per sitting excepting the space for the children', 493 of them were free and 462 were 'other', presumably meaning this was the number paying pew rent.

The rector was also asked the value of the living. Tithes were worth £1250, glebe £60 and fees £6 giving a gross value of £1316. Bishop's Waltham was a rich living. This was the period of high farming before agricultural depression set in during the 1870s affecting all whose income depended on land. William Brock appended a list of outgoings totalling £574 of which the most significant were poor rate £222.7.0, £100 to the curate of Curdridge chapel and £15 to Swanmore chapel.[21]

From time immemorial owners of property had been liable to pay the rate voted by the Vestry for the repair of the nave of the parish church and for other related purposes. The churchwardens collected the rate from each of the four tithings to meet capital costs for the repair of the building as well as running costs for the maintenance of the church and churchyard. The Churchwardens Account Book for the period 1823–77 has survived.[22] In 1823–4 the church rate amounted to £56.9.5, the outgoings to £52.1.2. Expenses included 'Beer for the weeders 2/-, Cooper for working in the churchyard 5/-, Parchment 10/-, For blowing the organ bellows 10/-, Looking after the boys at church £1, Attending the churchyard on Sundays during divine service £1–0–0'. In 1825 expenses included 'Beer for the men taking out the fire engine 7/-', and in 1826 'Mr Gunner on being sworn in Churchwarden 5/6' on 19th July 'Ringers for ringing the Coronation day 6/-' and on 4th September 'Dinner for the Ringers at the Dolphin £3–15–0'.

One of the first acts of Gladstone's first ministry in 1868 was the abolition of church rate. As the number of nonconformists had grown, particularly in the towns of the Midlands and North of England so resentment against the tax grew. In the rural south of England it was scarcely an issue but even so the change was symbolic. Together with the disestablishment of the Irish church in 1869 and the admission of dissenters to Oxford and Cambridge in 1871, it signalled that the Church of England was ceasing to be the church of the whole nation and was on the way to becoming a denomination. How then was the church in future to be financed? The long term answer would be church collections but not yet. The leading citizens again forked out. Their subscriptions tided the church over the next few years. (For church collections see pp 179–80.)

At Bishop's Waltham the abolition of church rate coincided with a further major and costly restoration of the parish church. In May 1867 the rector put his proposals to the Vestry. He wished to repew the whole church. He would like to have removed the south gallery, 'that unsightly erection', but recognised that the space could not be spared. He proposed however to replace the dormer windows erected in 1798 with ones 'of a more ecclesiastical character'. The porch and the tower needed work on them and he suggested the removal of the ceiling of the whole church so as to reveal the rafters.[23] Some money had already been given and the Vestry agreed to a church rate of 4½d. in the pound without demure even though they knew that in a matter of months it would no longer be compulsory.

From time immemorial the rector had been responsible for keeping the chancel in good order. William Brock seems to have acted on his own in removing the medieval stone piscina from the south wall of the sanctuary – used for washing the vessels at Holy Communion – and the aumbry from the north wall – in which the sacrament had in earlier years been reserved.[24] It was probably at the same time that he had a text from the New Testament painted above the chancel arch. All these acts were expressions of his strongly Protestant convictions.

In 1871 William Brock had the accounts printed and circulated. He was particularly grateful that the church rate had been 'both voted and paid with unanimity'. Bishop's Waltham 'is the poor man's church, the whole of the nave being free and unappropriated… the poor continue to occupy the same advantageous position as they did before'.[25]

There is a postscript to the story of the restoration of 1867–68. In 1873 a new organ was to be installed. Its location caused prolonged and fraught discussion recorded in great detail in ten pages of the Vestry minutes.[26] Eventually the rector got his way – but was soon proved wrong. Within a year the organ had to be moved. It had been placed against the outside north wall and was suffering from damp. The bellows were falling to pieces, the action was sluggish and it must be moved.[27] It was placed under the west arch of the north aisle arcade and there it stayed until it was moved again in the large-scale restoration of 1896–1897. The choir, not yet robed, occupied the pews immediately adjacent to it.

William Brock reached the age of 70 in 1875, but remained rector for another 16 years. By the late 1880s, now over 80 he was no longer capable of shouldering the work of a busy parish and more and more work fell on his curate, from 1889 Thomas Archer Meynell Archer-Shepherd. William Brock last appeared at the Easter Vestry in 1889 sending apologies on account of illness in 1890 and 91 [28] He died on 21st November 1891 and four days later was buried in the churchyard just over the wall from the Rectory where he had lived so long. His second wife died a year before he did in September 1890.[29] The funerals of Louisa and a year later William Brock were conducted by the rector's long standing friend George Hills whom he had presented to the living of Curdridge.

William Brock had been rector for an amazing 58 years, a record in the history of the parish. When he came to Bishop's Waltham William IV was on the throne; in his last years he witnessed the Golden Jubilee of Queen Victoria. Few parishioners could remember any other rector. He had lived through an era of unprecedented change. When he arrived the first Reform Act had recently been placed on the statute book. The Church of England had changed too. In the year he became rector John Keble's Assize sermon had begun the Oxford Movement of which William Brock disapproved so strongly. Halfway through his incumbency came Darwin's *Origin of Species* and the publication of *Essays and Reviews* which began what Matthew Arnold described as the 'melancholy, long withdrawing roar' of 'The Sea of Faith'.[30] By the time of his death William Brock was a figure from another age. His obituarist in the Parish magazine wrote:

> The Second Coming of our Lord was for many years a favourite topic of his study and the goal of his earnest expectations. He was at one time a member of the Prophecy Investigation Society. … Though he was an uncompromising Protestant he looked for a manifestation of a personal infidel Antichrist.
>
> Mr Brock read much and thought deeply and was thus able to consecrate to the ministry of Christ the ample resources of a richly furnished mind. Possessed of a commanding presence, a voice of exceptional richness and beauty and an acute and logical mind he was a power on the platform. Terribly in earnest he forced on his hearers the conviction that though they might not agree with his

particular views he thoroughly believed them himself and felt them to be of paramount importance.

In the pulpit he was very far above the average, thoroughly conversant with scripture and possessing a deep spiritual insight into the meaning of the more obscure passages With a choice and easy flow of words, his aptitude for expository treatment of the word of God was marvellous.

But it was in the presence of sorrow and suffering that the finest traits of his character revealed themselves. Naturally reserved he sometimes struck the superficial observer as being somewhat cold and unsympathetic; but in the presence of sorrow and suffering the ice of reserve at once broke down and revealed him as the warm and sympathetic friend, and the humble follower of Christ.

For several years past his powers had been on the wane; very gradually the silver cord was loosed, till at length the golden bowl was broken and he was admitted into the presence of the King.[31]

With the death of William Brock an era ended in the history of St Peter's. We should not see his like again.

13

Primitive Methodists, Congregationalists and Roman Catholics

THE EIGHTEENTH century belonged to the Church of England. With the return of Charles II in 1660 Protestant dissent – now divided between baptists, presbyterians and independents – had to accept defeat and for the next 25 years was persecuted. During these years John Bunyan wrote *Pilgrim's Progress* while in Bedford Gaol. The Toleration Act of 1689 was just that – toleration, no more. The Act allowed Protestant dissenters to have their own meeting houses – though they had to be licensed by the bishop – but they could not take part in local or national government or study at Oxford or Cambridge which remained exclusively Anglican until the mid-nineteenth century.

With the flight of James II in 1688 England resolved that it would not again have a Roman Catholic king though there were attempts made with French assistance to restore the Stuarts to the throne in the two Jacobite risings in 1715 and 1745. Throughout the eighteenth century Roman Catholics were proscribed though the penal laws were enforced only spasmodically. It was however well into the nineteenth century before either Protestant dissenters or Roman Catholics were granted civic recognition and even then they remained in the eyes of many second class citizens.

In preparation for his Primary Visitation in 1725 Bishop Richard Willis (1723–1734) enquired about the presence of dissent in his diocese. The rector of Bishop's Waltham, John Cooke, replied that there were 'four or five reputed papists in the parish, but of mean condition' and 'no meeting of Protestant dissenters … nor indeed any such dissenters in the parish'. In this part of Hampshire only at Hambledon were there many dissenters. There, according to the vicar, were '19 papists who openly profess themselves but of little consequence as to their estates'. There were in addition '14 Anabaptists who assemble once a fortnight in a house on the frontier of the parish which is rented for that purpose'.[1]

In 1767 there was a further enquiry about the number of 'reputed papists' in the parish. In two of the tithings – Waltham and Curdridge – there were none. In Hoe just one, a man of 67 who had lived in the parish from birth. In Ashton there was a papist family – a shoemaker aged 45, his wife, son of 12 who followed his father's trade and daughter aged four. In addition there was a 'widow woman' of 69 and a farmer who had moved from St Omer but who had lived in Hoe for 'upwards of 20 years'. The return was signed by the rector and the curate.[2]

The movement for Catholic Emancipation, allowing Roman Catholics to become members of parliament and to hold office, began in the 1780s and became urgent in the 1820s because of the situation in Ireland but it nonetheless provoked strong anti-Catholic sentiment. In Bishop's Waltham an Anti-Popery Petition to the House of Lords was presented by the Earl of Guildford. Its language is extreme but its sentiments were shared by many.

> 'Your petitioners view with feelings of indescribable anxiety the measures about to be laid before your lordships… to admit to further political power those persons commonly called Roman Catholics. They regard these measures as tending to remove the ancient bulwarks of the Constitution, to sap the foundations of the sacred edifice of the established government, the cornerstone of which is the Protestant faith. They view these proceedings as a fearful departure from the principles of sound policy and true religion which, excluding a popish tyrant from the exercise of abused authority, placed on the throne of these realms the sworn Protestant house of Brunswick.'

There follow a number of historical references: to 'the papal tyranny of the reign of John', 'the insurrection attempted to be incited by the Pope and his agents in Ireland in the reign of Queen Elizabeth'… 'the formidable Armada' and 'the tyranny exhibited by the bigoted James II'. It concludes 'We rely on your lordships to save us from these evils … the fate of your country is, as far as human agents are concerned, in your hands.'[3] The Catholic Emancipation Act was nonetheless passed by Wellington's Tory government in 1829.

Not until the second half of the nineteenth century do we have a record of the existence of Primitive Methodists and Congregationalists in Bishop's Waltham. The Congregationalist built a church in Newtown in 1862 and in the 1870s the Primitive Methodists rented what came to be called the Mission Hall in Free Street at the other end of the town. Roman Catholic worship began formally in Bishop's Waltham with the arrival of the White Fathers at the Priory in 1912.

Primitive Methodism started on the borders of Staffordshire and Cheshire at Mow Cop. Its founders, Hugh Bourne and William Clowes, were expelled by the Wesleyans for holding camp meetings – outdoor evangelistic services often lasting many hours. The name Primitive Methodists came from their claim to be returning to the evangelistic emphasis of the early Methodists.

The movement at first spread slowly but by the 1840s had reached Hampshire and in 1842 the Micheldever Circuit (a Methodist word for a group of churches which work together) established the Bishop's Waltham Mission.[4] Despite the name there is no record of Primitive Methodists in the town itself. There were small groups of

59. The Primitive Methodist Mission Hall (white building centre) 1871–1909.

Primitive Methodists in the surrounding villages, meeting in private houses but not registered for worship

When the census of religious worship took place on 30th March 1851 dissenting services are recorded locally only at Swanmore and Meonstoke, both Primitive Methodist and both in private houses.[5] The 1860s saw a spate of Primitive Methodist chapel building – Swanmore, Shirrell Heath, Hambledon, Meonstoke and Waltham Chase all had chapels by 1870 – but still nothing at Bishop's Waltham. It was in 1871 that the small band of Methodists rented a room in Free Street and the Mission Hall became their base for almost 40 years.

Primitive Methodism was very different from the established church. They used no Prayer Book, their prayers were extemporary, their preaching eloquent and fiery and their hymns evangelical. There was as yet scarcely any ministerial training. The clergy of the Church of England were gentlemen, educated at Oxford or Cambridge, enjoying the freehold of their parishes, living in substantial parsonage houses and employing servants. The Primitive Methodist minister or, as he was frequently called, the Travelling Preacher, lived often in a rented house, was paid a modest stipend and moved from circuit to circuit after one, two or three years. At that time he wore no clerical collar nor ecclesiastical robes. The contrast between the two was stark and there was scarcely any contact between them.

60 St Paul's Primitive Methodist Church opened in Basingwell Street 1909. Now the United Free Church.

Like all branches of Methodism the Primitive Methodists depended on local preachers, men and sometimes women who took services and preached on Sundays, and often walked great distances to do so. No local preachers from Bishop's Waltham appear on the Circuit Plan for 1883 but there are three men named as auxiliary preachers – people who sometimes took services and preached: William Pink, a builder living in Frogmore Cottages, Lower Lane; Henry Barclay, a young man of 27 who lived in Houchin Street and was postmaster and telegraphist and William Benham, a labourer who lived in Victoria Buildings.[6]

Analysis of the occupations of the fathers of children brought for baptism at the chapels of the Droxford Circuit between 1885 and 1900 shows that one third were labourers, and about 60% were engaged in some form of agriculture. They represented a different stratum of society from those who attended St Peter's. No less than 15 children are described as 'illegitimate', perhaps indicating that the Primitive Methodists were less judgemental than the established church or perhaps that illegitimacy was more likely to occur among the class to which Primitive Methodism appealed.[7]

In 1853 the chapels of the Bishop's Waltham Mission became part of the Winchester Circuit but were treated as a self contained section with a minister, usually a young man, responsible for the seven chapels of which Bishop's Waltham was one. From 1880 to 1883 the minister of the section was John Jopling, a young man of 25 who came from County Durham and who lived for a year in lodgings in Great Houchin Street, Bishop's Waltham. He described himself as 'Travelling Primitive Methodist Minister'.[8] On a Sunday he would take two or three services in one or more of the chapels spread between Hambledon and Bishop's Waltham, covering many miles probably on foot. In addition all the chapels had a week night service described at Bishop's Waltham as 'Wednesday Preaching' so on many evenings, winter and summer alike, he would again trudge many miles to preach at one of the chapels. In 1883 Bishop's Waltham had only 10 members though more would have attended the services. Before he left the Circuit in 1883 John Jopling had moved to live at Hambledon which was a stronger chapel with 29 members.

In the later years of the nineteenth century there were three specific causes of tension between dissenters and the established church – compulsory church rate, the use of parish burial grounds for the interment of dissenters by their own ministers and education. In 1868 Gladstone's first government abolished church rate. No longer would the repair of the parish church be paid for by a rate levied by the Vestry on all households. At Bishop's Waltham William Brock noted that although they knew abolition was in the offing nobody had refused to pay the rate needed for the major renovation of St Peter's in 1868.

The Burials Act of 1880 opened the use of parish graveyards to all. In future use of the Prayer Book burial service would not be obligatory nor need the Anglican parson conduct the service. In 1888 the Primitive Methodists were reminded of their rights and a list was drawn up of local preachers prepared to conduct funerals in parish churchyards. The first burial by the Congregational minister took place in September 1884.[9]

The education issue was altogether more fraught and proved to be the last great cause of tension between the free churches and the Church of England. Balfour's

Education Act of 1902 transferred the control of education in both board schools and voluntary schools to the recently created County Councils. Nonconformists were enraged. The great majority of voluntary schools were either Anglican or Roman Catholic which meant that free church parents would be required to pay through the rates for an education of which they disapproved. The slogan of the campaign was 'Rome on the rates' and the national agitation against the Act was led by the veteran Baptist minister Dr John Clifford.

It took the form of a campaign of passive resistance which led many free churchmen to withhold that part of the rate which was devoted to education. The resisters were liable to a gaol sentence. The Droxford Circuit (as it had become in 1892) had two ministers who took this extreme action. Walter Barnsley did so in 1906, though by then he had left the circuit and was serving in Southampton. John Leach, minister in the Droxford Circuit from 1908 to 1911, was a man of stern principle. In 1909 he was sentenced to a fortnight in Winchester prison for withholding part of the rate. He took advantage of the publicity which his case attracted and was photographed on Bishop's Waltham station on his way to prison accompanied by a policemen.[10] He wrote in the circuit newsletter:

> 'We are within eight hours of leaving home for Winchester gaol as we write this… It is awful to contemplate, that there are 16,000 schools in this land where no man or woman can become Head Teacher if they are Primitive Methodists. It is therefore to secure the rights and liberties of your children that your minister goes to gaol. Justice has been superseded by persecution and a scarcely veiled attempt to terrorise into submission to a diabolical law.'

Apart from his brief imprisonment John Leach deserves to be remembered in Bishop's Waltham as the minister who accomplished the building of St Paul's church in Basingwell Street. From being the Cinderella of the Circuit Bishop's Waltham came to have the most impressive building in the Circuit and the only one to be dedicated in Anglican style to a saint. As soon as he arrived in 1908 John Leach was on the look out for a site. The small society with only just over 20 members bought two cottages in Basingwell Street and demolished them to provide a prominent location in the middle of the town for the new church.

The stone laying took place in September 1909. Only five months later a procession marched from the Mission Hall in Free Street to the opening of the church in Basingwell Street. The building cost £672 and the whole scheme, including the purchase of the cottages, £1279. A decade later there was still a substantial debt on the premises. John Leach was rightly proud of the new church: 'The Circuit has only one town within its radius and in a sense had no head. Now it has', he wrote.[11] Yet his hopes for a numerically strong church, perhaps head of the Circuit, were never realised. There was a brief period in the late 1920s when membership rose to 56, second only to Shirrell Heath, but this growth was not sustained. Bishop's Waltham remained a predominantly Church of England town.

The First World War saw the beginnings of closer relations between the Christian churches. The appalling ordeal which the country suffered dwarfed the petty disagreements between denominations. When the Primitive Methodist District Synod met at Bishop's Waltham in April 1919 both the rector Edmund Sharpe and the Congregational minister Samuel Longmore attended one of its sessions. The Synod must have made its mark on the small town. On Sunday there was an outdoor service in the Square and an afternoon Camp Meeting in the Palace grounds. More open air services and meetings took place on the following days.[12]

Few if any other Methodist churches can claim to be the result of secessions from a parish church but that was the origin of the Methodist chapel at Curdridge.[13] When the chapel of ease at Curdridge was built in 1835 the Rector of Bishop's Waltham naturally became patron of the living, entitled to appoint its parish priest. He remained so until the 1880s when it passed first to the Bishop of Winchester and then to the Dean and Chapter of Winchester Cathedral.

The last vicar of Curdridge to be appointed by William Brock was George William Hills who came to the parish in 1867 at the age of 32 and remained there for 52 years until his retirement at the end of the First World War. He was, like his friend William Brock, a strong Protestant and low-church man. The services scarcely altered during his years at Curdridge and he preached right down to 1919 wearing a black Geneva gown, by then unusual in an Anglican church.[13] His successor was a minor canon of Winchester cathedral who made changes in a direction which the congregation thought of as 'ritualism'. A group of parishioners unable to accept the changes began to meet in private houses. They acquired a galvanised iron hut and 42 of them petitioned the Primitive Methodist minister, Alfred Clarke, to be recognised as a Primitive Methodist church. In 1925 the new chapel was opened with the Circuit band leading a procession from the Reading Room.

The Primitive Methodist church joined with the other Methodist denominations – Wesleyan and United Methodist – to form the Methodist Church in 1932. The Droxford Circuit favoured union and hoped for an enlarged circuit to include the Wesleyan churches in Durley and Wickham as well as the United Methodist churches in Soberton and Upham. In fact only Soberton joined the Droxford Circuit (in 1936). The Circuit was renamed the Meon Valley Circuit in 2000. It has retained its evangelical roots to the present day.[14]

The desirability of providing for Congregational worship in Bishop's Waltham was first aired in 1836. It was however another quarter of a century before a church was built. A legacy in 1849 made possible the purchase of a plot of land in Lower Lane and in 1856 a committee meeting at Above Bar chapel in Southampton began to explore the possibility of building in Bishop's Waltham The first service was held in a room made available by Mr Churcher on 31st March 1861 when the Revd Thomas Atkins preached 'to overflowing congregations'.[15]

Many Church of England clergy were hostile to dissent of any kind and William

61. The Congregational Church (United Reformed from 1972) Lower Lane, built 1862, demolished 1979.

Brock was no exception. 'A spirited opposition was manifested … by the Rector and several friends connected with the Established church'… to the existence of a 'dissenting place of worship' writes the chapel's chronicler. The Congregationalists were not deterred. They called the Revd William Maunsell of Yardley Hastings in Northamptonshire to the pastorate and he began his ministry in Bishop's Waltham on 27th April 1862. They had already opened a schoolroom for public worship in January 1862 and on 18th June laid the foundation stone of their new church. Those officiating dined at *The Crown* and a public tea was held in a barn in Botley Road made available by Mr Wyatt followed by an evening meeting attended, it was claimed, by about 400 people. The church which had cost £1600 opened on 11th December 1862. The building may not have the architectural distinction or the venerable associations of the parish church but it was an imposing building on a prominent site and inside had end and side galleries meant to hold a substantial congregation.

The rector was not at first reconciled to this rival to his ministry in the parish and refused to admit to the National School any child who attended the Congregational Sunday School. The Congregationalists' response was robust and immediate. On 9th February 1863 they opened a day school in a room at the rear of the chapel and employed a mistress from the Home and Colonial College. Two years later in July 1866 the new school at Newtown, on 'the beautiful and extensive site', given by Arthur Helps was opened under the auspices of the British and Foreign Schools Society.

The hostility of the rector towards the Congregational Church came to a surprising end. In 1875 without invitation or notice, it seems, the rector attended a meeting of the London Missionary Society (the Congregational missionary society), spoke a few words and at the end (presumably by invitation) pronounced the blessing, provoking this entry in the church book 'Behold how good and how pleasant it is for brethren to dwell together in unity'.

William Maunsell was a sick man and in 1875 he retired to Hereford and soon afterwards died. The church was now in financial difficulties: William Maunsell had private means – he had lived at Mount House in Little Shore Lane – so the church had not needed to provide either stipend or manse. Now if they were to call a full-time minister they would have to find both. In the next few years a series of ministers served the church none of whom stayed long. For a time there was a joint pastorate with Botley. The minister from 1879 to 1883 was the oddly named Melanchton Goody. (He must have been given this unusual if not unique Christian name after Philip Melanchthon the sixteenth century Lutheran theologian). In 1878 a School Board was formed and the British and Foreign School in Newtown came under its auspices thus relieving the church of further expense.

In 1894 the church called to its pastorate Samuel Longmore. Both he and his wife Kate came from the midlands. He remained minister until 1925 and played a full part in the life of the town.[16] He joined the School Board and for many years took a leading part in the work of the Parish Council. In 1903 he became the first chairman of the Managers of the Council School and remained so until he retired.[17]

The story of the later years of the Congregational Church is quickly told. In 1958 a church hall was built next to the church in Lower Lane which still exists, though put to other use. Only four years later the church was obliged to sell two houses which had previously been manses for the minister, unable any longer to support a fulltime minister and the minister of Fareham Congregational church undertook pastoral care and took some Sunday services. The upkeep of the building, now too large for the needs of a declining and ageing congregation, was too much. The membership was 37 in 1966. In 1975 talks began with the Methodists and in November 1978 the Lower Lane church closed and in 1979 was demolished. The United Reformed Church (the Congregational and Presbyterian churches united in 1971) joined with the Methodist Church in Basingwell Street to form the United Free Church in the Methodist premises.[18]

In the early years of the twentieth century anti- Catholic sentiment remained strong: there were few Roman Catholics in the rural south of England. The Boniface family who lived at Northbrook were the only Roman Catholics in Bishop's Waltham and they attended Mass at Eastleigh, the large parish of which the town formed part.[19] When soon afterwards Henry and Elizabeth Spurr moved to the *Mafeking Hero* they made an upper room available where a priest from Eastleigh could celebrate Mass on the rare occasions when he was able to visit the town.

It was the arrival of the White Fathers in Bishop's Waltham in 1912 that provided for the first time a significant Roman Catholic presence. The White Fathers were a French order, founded by the Archbishop of Algiers, Charles Lavigerie, which worked mostly in central Africa. They wished to establish a seminary in Europe for French students but were deterred from moving to France by the strong anticlerical sentiment there at the time. When they failed to find a suitable base in Jersey they came to England and the Roman Catholic bishop of Portsmouth suggested that they explore the possibilities of Bishop's Waltham.[20]

In 1912 they bought The Priory (the renamed Royal Albert Infirmary) which since 1875 had been a private house (renamed The Priory by Dr Jacob Ralff) now owned by Mrs Robson. Things moved swiftly and in October 1912 the first 12 boys arrived from France and in May 1913 building began to provide accommodation for about 60 boys. As a result of the disruption of the First World War numbers dwindled and it was not until 1919 that the seminary began to operate normally. The boys, no longer French, came mostly from the north of England, and spent five years in Bishop's Waltham before completing their training in Belgium. By 1925 there were 60 boys in residence and the seminary was full.[21]

The Chapel at the Priory became a chapel of ease for Roman Catholics in the district and in 1931 Bishop's Waltham was constituted a parish with the name Our Lady Queen of Apostles. The Father Superior of the White Fathers became titular parish priest. It was a large rural parish covering 100 square miles and in the early years, when few people had a car, Mass was said at a number of local centres.[22] In 1937 there were still only about 15 people attending Mass at Bishop's Waltham and it was not until 1955 that a resident parish priest was appointed, at first a member of the Order of White Fathers. During the Second World War the boys from the Priory were evacuated and the army requisitioned the residential accommodation. The Priory reopened in 1945 but the number of recruits to the Order declined and in any

62. Our Lady Queen of Apostles consecrated 1998.

case Junior Seminaries were phased out following Vatican II. The seminary closed in 1967 and the buildings were bought by the Hampshire Police Authority who in 1970 opened a college for the training of recruits to the police force.

The local Roman Catholics were once again without a home and for seven years Mass was celebrated, at first in the Drill Hall and then in the Youth Hall. The church had retained part of the grounds of the Priory and a new church was built on the site of the tennis court and consecrated at Easter 1977. Twenty one years later a church more in keeping with modern needs was opened and the church built in 1977 became a parish centre.[23]

In the meantime the churches had grown closer together. Invited by the rector to join other clergy in celebrations to mark the Coronation of Queen Elizabeth II, Father Donnelly had felt obliged to decline.[24] Nine years later during the Week of Prayer for Christian Unity in January 1962 Father Duffy was able to invite local clergy to a united service and to lunch afterwards.[25]

Three other branches of the Christian church were to be found in Bishop's Waltham. In the early years of the twentieth century there was a Salvation Army Citadel located at first in Houchin Street and later in Station Road close to where Budgen's

Supermarket was later built. It was demolished and replaced by the Youth Hall a functional but undistinguished prefabricated building.

The Gospel Hall in Basingwell Street was founded by Victor Madgwick, a remarkable man who had poliomyelitis and a serious kidney complaint from an early age. Sustained by his wife and three children he conducted an evangelical ministry in and far beyond Bishop's Waltham. He died in March 1972 in his 44th year.[26] Another evangelical body, the King's Church, bought the former Oddfellows Hall in the late 1990s and drew a congregation of strong evangelicals from Bishop's Waltham and the surrounding area.

Until the end of the nineteenth century the churches existed in isolation, viewing each other with a degree of suspicion and in some ways in competition with each other. The First World War saw the beginning of a rapprochement between the Free Churches and the Church of England. Not until after the Second World War was there greater cooperation and it was the 1960s before the Parish News included notice of the services of other churches in the town. In the late 1970s St Peter's held a joint evening service with the Methodist Church once a month. Later Roman Catholics were drawn in too when Churches Together replaced the British Council of Churches.

14

The Enclosure of Curdridge Common and Waltham Chase

BETWEEN 1850 and 1870 there occurred the last spate of enclosure and the consequent disappearance of thousands of acres of common land. Local parishes affected by what successive Acts described as 'Inclosure' included Droxford (1851), Upham (1852), Curdridge (1854), Durley (1856), Meonstoke (1856), Soberton (1858) and Bishop's Waltham (1863). (The dates are those of parliamentary authorisation, implementation often took place several years later).[1] Two schemes concerned the parish of Bishop's Waltham – the enclosure of 322 acres of Curdridge Common completed in 1856 and the enclosure of the part of Waltham Chase located in the parish in 1870. They were amongst the last parliamentary enclosures. Concern was already growing about the disappearance of commons and the movement for their protection was beginning

Curdridge Common was a plateau of gravel and clay which ran from near Botley station to Calcot Lane where the *Cricketers Inn* then stood on one side of the road and the tollhouse on the Southampton to London turnpike on the other. The turnpike bi-sected the Common though more of it lay south of the road than north. The surveyor of the Inclosure scheme was George Habin Appleby who had just completed the Droxford Inclosure. He laid out eight new roads across the Common which he described in names which indicate their location but do not leap off the tongue. They included what we now call The Plantation, ('Branch road from Curdridge lane to the church'), Chapel Lane ('the Middle road'), Reading Room Lane ('Wangfield and Kitnocks road'), Outlands Lane ('Curdridge and Swanwick road') Blind Lane ('Breach Hill road')as well as Church Road and School Road which are easily identifiable. Most new roads were to be 25 feet wide, Blind Lane and Vicarage Lane were to be 20 feet wide.

Watering places at *The Cricketers Inn* (on the corner of Calcot Lane), Wangfield Green and the Heart in Hand Farm in Curdridge Lane were to be maintained. Appleby allotted three acres of land for the use of the Surveyor of the Highways as 'a public quarry for supplying stones and gravel for the repair of the roads and highways' – no tar for another half century. The four acres in the triangle between The

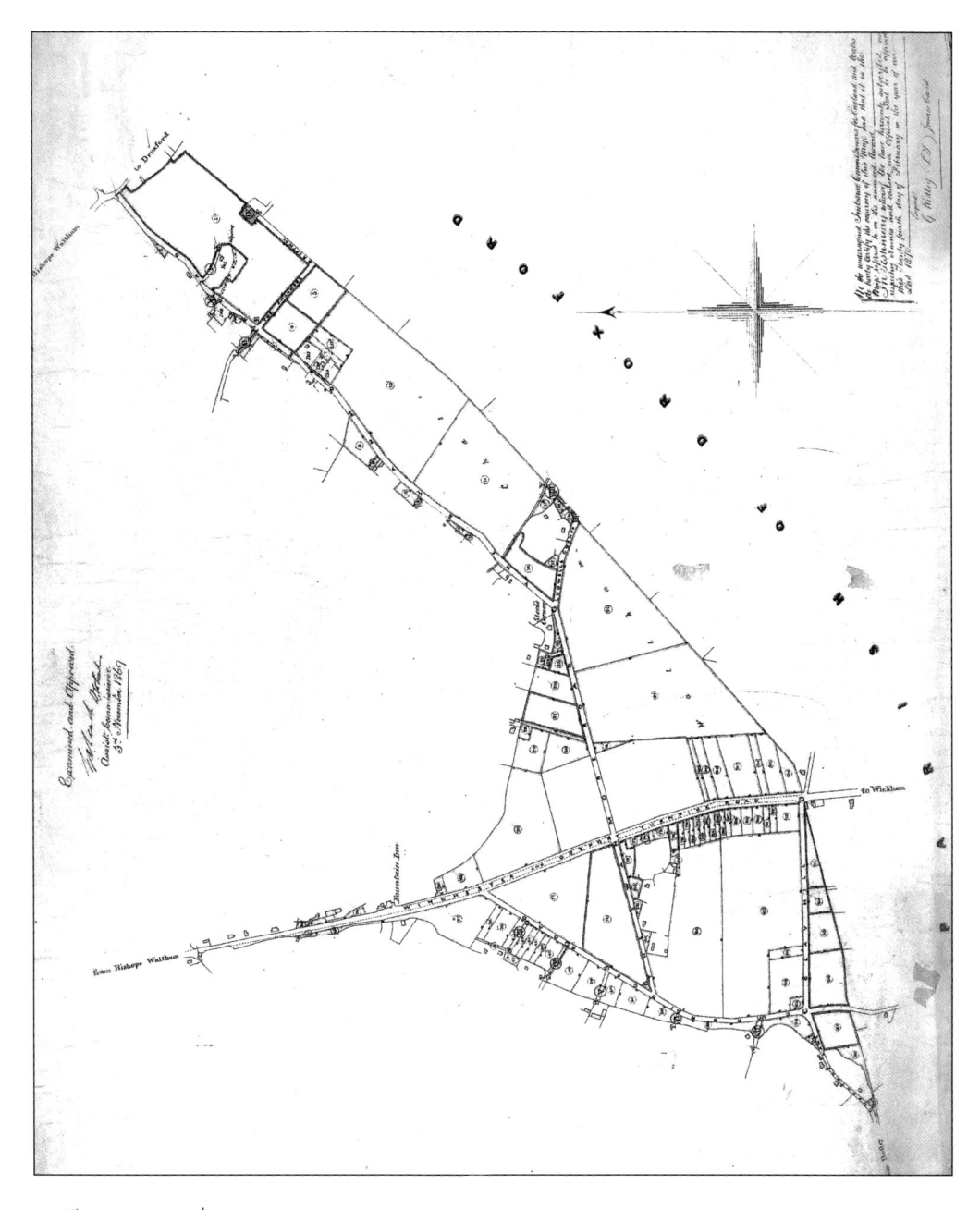

63. The enclosure of Waltham Chase 1870 showing the triangle of land allotted to the parish as a recreation ground.

Plantation and Curdridge Lane were for the churchwardens and overseers of the poor to provide ' a place of Exercise and Recreation for the inhabitants' and a further three acres where they must provide allotments for 'the Laboring Poor' *(sic)*. Three parcels of land close to the church totalling five acres were 'for supporting the National School' and a further five acres in three parcels of land were allocated to the parson as glebe and were situated close to the Parsonage (then in Vicarage Lane). Land was sold to defray the costs of enclosure, 20 acres was given to the Bishop of Winchester to compensate for the rights on the Common which he had lost. The remainder was allocated to the 47 copyholders who were entitled to a share of the common of whom James Warner of Harfield Farm was awarded 71 acres, the largest holding.[2]

The enclosure of Waltham Chase or Horders Wood had been on the cards since the beginning of the century.[3] William Cobbett who lived for a time in the parish of Bishop's Waltham and was a member of the Vestry disagreed with enclosure and wrote in the 1820s:

> 'I cannot quit Bishop's Waltham without observing that I heard last year that a Bill was about to be petitioned for to enclose the Chase. Never was so monstrous a proposition in this world … Here are a couple of hundred acres of land worth ten thousand acres of land in the New Forest … Besides the sweeping away of two or three hundred cottages; besides plunging into ruin and misery all these numerous families, here is one of the finest pieces of timberland in the whole kingdom, going to be cut up into miserable clay fields, for no earthly purpose but of gratifying the stupid greediness of those who think that they must gain, if they add to the breadth of their private fields'.[4]

But the arguments were complex and not all on one side. A pamphlet published in 1826 and entitled *An Appeal to the Bondland tenants against the Inclosure of Waltham Chase* had argued that forest was valuable unenclosed, that enclosure would increase the Poor Rate, that it would be injurious to the interests of small landed proprietors, would cost a great deal to accomplish, disadvantage the Bishop and once done could not be undone. A further pamphlet questioned all these conclusions and came out in favour of enclosure [5]. No action followed until 1851 when the enclosure of much of the Chase in the parish of Droxford was agreed and in effect created the modern parishes of Shedfield and Swanmore.[6]

Only a small proportion of Waltham Chase lay in the parish of Bishop's Waltham and much of what was enclosed in 1870 is now part of the parishes of Swanmore (as constituted when the civil parish was created in 1894) and Shedfield (as revised in 1967). The surveyor was James Harris who created two new roads. The first was what we call Clewers Hill continued across the Gosport turnpike in what we know as Lower Chase Road. He called the whole road The Swanmore Road. The second road he called Clay Hill; we know it as the part of Curdridge Lane from Clewers Hill to the traffic lights at Waltham Chase.

He also made what he called 'Swanmore Driftway'. A driftway was a route to enable cattle to reach a watering place, in this case Swanmore Pond. We know it as Broad Lane and its sharp left turn is to enable it to follow the original boundary between Droxford and Bishop's Waltham (before 1845) There was a further 'dipping place' in the Swanmore Road. Tracks from the bend in Lower Chase Road which the Surveyor called Steel's Corner to the Fountain Inn on the turnpike road were closed up. Twenty three acres were sold to defray the cost of enclosure and 65 copyholders received land mostly in small plots. The surveyor gave four acres for 'exercise and recreation for the inhabitants' of Bishop's Waltham. It was the triangle of land bounded by Clewers Lane and the turnpike road. It was inconveniently distant from the town but for many years remained the only public open space in Bishop's Waltham.[7] Today it is in the parish of Shedfield.

15

Houses, people and places in the late Nineteenth Century

IN THE last decades of the nineteenth century James Padbury was among the best-known citizens of Bishop's Waltham. When he died at the age of 81 in 1898 he had been churchwarden for 32 years but he was also a Poor Law Guardian, a member of the School Board, a Lighting Inspector and a committee member of the Volunteer Fire Brigade. He was a polymath, curious about a vast number of geographical, historical and scientific topics, exemplified by his collection of scrapbooks deposited in the Parish Chest and now to be found in the Hampshire Record Office.[1] But his fame arose from the family clock-making business in High Street of which he had been the proprietor since the death of his father in 1841. Although there is no longer a clockmaker in Bishop's Waltham, the house where he lived has a blue plaque erected by the Bishop's Waltham Society and a clock which he made and which has hung there since 1864 is displayed prominently on the wall, its mechanism concealed inside the building.

James Padbury was the fourth generation of Padbury clockmakers in Bishop's Waltham. His great-grandfather Andrew was born probably in London in 1718 and was apprenticed in 1735 to William Gunn a Quaker clockmaker at Wallingford in Berkshire.[2] He married Elizabeth Cammis, a Bishop's Waltham girl, at St Thomas's church Portsmouth (now Portsmouth Cathedral) They settled in Bishop's Waltham and it was here that seven out of their eight children were born between 1744 and 1760.

When he was still under 30 Andrew was commissioned by George Anson to make him a clock. Anson (1697–1762) was a famous man. He had sailed round the world and returned with booty from a Spanish treasure ship which he had intercepted, a share of which made him a rich man He lived at Soberton and it seems likely that is how he met Andrew Padbury. Anson beat the French off Cape Finisterre in 1747 in the War of the Austrian Succession and was raised to the peerage as Lord Anson of Soberton. In 1748 he married the daughter of Lord Chancellor Yorke. He was later twice First Lord of the Admiralty.[3] The clock is described in an inventory of his possessions as 'An old English black lacquer long case clock ... with gilt dial and

64. The Padbury clock, High Street.

65. The Palace House.

silvered chapter ring, the subsidiary dial with a model of the Prince George [a ship] inscribed 'Admiral Anson May ye 3, 1747'. The clock was a beautiful piece of work and established the reputation of its maker. Andrew lived to the great age of 94 and died in January 1812 at Wallingford to which he had apparently returned early in the nineteenth century.

Andrew's son Thomas was apprenticed to Henry Budden, a Bishop's Waltham blacksmith and became the second-generation of Padbury clockmakers. He is named in a Trade Directory of 1793 as 'clock and watchmaker'.[4] At least one clock made by Thomas Padbury is still in a private house in Bishop's Waltham.[5] Thomas's son John who carried on the family clock making business into the third generation was born in 1791 and moved from Great Houchin Street to High Street.[6]

James, the fourth generation of Padbury clockmakers, was born in 1816 at Yetminster in Dorset, married a Portsmouth girl, Mary Hannah Wills, in 1841, the year of his father's death at the age of 50. In 1864 he made the clock which hangs outside his premises in High Street. It is however the clock in the tower of St Peter's church with which he will always be associated. It was probably made for the Bishop's Palace in the fourteenth century and was rescued and installed in the parish church after the Palace was abandoned during the Civil War.[7] In September 1836 the churchwardens paid 1/- for digging in the belfry to find the weights. The following year they paid 'Padbury' £2.19.6 for the repair of the clock, perhaps John Padbury was assisted by his 19-year-old son James. In 1873 James Padbury converted the escapement from 'half dead' to 'double three-legged gravity escapement'. The pendulum now weighs 6 cwt 28 lbs 4 oz and is reputed to be the second heaviest in the world. It needs to be wound every three days, a duty at first performed by James Hall, one of Padbury's apprentices.

In the Bishop's Waltham Museum there is another Padbury clock. It was made in 1848 and was designed to show both London and Bishop's Waltham time, when London was four minutes ahead of Bishop's Waltham. The need for railway timetables, accurate at distances from London, lead shortly afterwards to the adoption of Greenwich Meantime throughout the country. The clock was bequeathed to Bishop's Waltham Combined Charities by its maker to be placed in the Institute 'now in course of erection'.[8] There it remained until 1987 when it came to the Bishop's Waltham Museum.

James Padbury was a well-known character in the town. Like William Brock, rector for much of Padbury's life, he was a strong evangelical though they did not always see eye to eye. 'He was', wrote his obituarist in the *Parish Magazine* ' a man of high principle, of strong religious conviction, fearless to express his opinions, as to what he thought right and wrong, perfectly straightforward, … perhaps a little too unsparing in his condemnation of opinions and practices of which he disapproved yet always kind and courteous to those from whom he differed'.[9] His views extended beyond death: he wrote in his will ' I especially direct that no floral decorations or papistical observances whatsoever be performed or used at my funeral'. James and his wife Mary had no children. He left his clockmaker's tools, existing stock and his bee keeping appliances and hives to his apprentice, William George Hedges. Hedges took over the shop, describing it as 'Late J. Padbury' and listing the services he provided 'Watch and Clockmaker, Jeweller, Silversmith and Optician. Church, Turret and Household Clocks, wound by Contract. All kinds of Repairs done on the premises. Established 1744.'[10] The business closed in 1909.

For four generations extending over 130 years Bishop's Waltham's medical practitioners have included at least one member of the Hemming family. Six generations have been doctors but the first and the last did not practise in Bishop's Waltham. The first, Dr John Hemming, was a doctor at Kimbolton in Leicestershire in the early years of the nineteenth century. The sixth generation is represented by Mr Stephen Hemming, who is a consultant in Salisbury. The four generations in between have all practised in Bishop's Waltham. It was Dr Charles Hemming born in 1829 who moved about 1877 from Abingdon to Bishop's Waltham. He and his family lived at Highfield, a substantial house on the Winchester Road, in the grounds of which part of the Battery Hill estate was built after the Second World War and whose lodge still exists.

Dr Charles Hemming and his wife Martha had five children, Clare born in 1858, Lucy Maud (born 1860), Agnes Blanche (born 1862), Philip Claude (born 1864) and Charles Horace, known as 'Archie' (born 1867). Philip Claude qualified as a doctor, moved into the town and was the second generation of Hemmings to practise in Bishop's Waltham. Two other members of the family are of interest to the historian of the town, Lucy Maud because she married Edward Falconer, curate of Bishop's Waltham and the cause of 'the beer riots' (see pp.168–9) and Agnes Blanche because she kept a diary for the year 1883 which remained in her family and has recently come to light through a great-grand daughter Jenny Maidment.[11]

The diary casts light on the life style of a young woman born into a professional middle class family in late Victorian Bishop's Waltham. Servants ran the household at Highfield supervised by the mistress of the house, who seems however to have been a semi-invalid, so there was no cooking or house keeping to be done. Few women had professions and Agnes Hemming

66. Agnes Blanche Hemming, diarist.

Parish [or Township] of Bishops Waltham	City or Municipal Borough of	Municipal Ward of	Parliamentary Borough of Bishops Waltham	Town of	Hamlet or Tything, etc. of						
No. of Schedule	Road, Street, &c, and No. or Name of House	HOUSES In-habited	Uninhabited (U), or Building (B)	Name and Surname of each Person	Relation to Head of Family	Condition	Age of Male	Age of Female	Rank, Profession, or Occupation	Where Born	
34	Northbrook Ho.	1		Lewis C. Corran	Head	Mar	40		Lt. Colonel Hants Volunteers	Suffolk Hoxton	
	Do Hendon			Catherine C. Do	Wife	Mar		29		Australia New South Wales	
				Thomas B. Do	Son		10		Scholar	Do Melbourne	
				Henry L. Do	Son		9		Do	Suffolk Cobham Hall	
				Charles J. Do	Son		6			Leicestershire Husting Hall	
				Marcel Do	Son		5				
				Maryanne Wells	Mother in law	Wid		59	Wife of a Landed Proprietor	Middlesex London	
				Maryanne Graham	Servant	Un		33	Nurse	Somerset Bath	
				Harriet Kent	Do	Un		28	Cook	Staffordshire Garnett	
				Maryann Gee	Do	Un		25	Ladies Maid	Oxfordshire Oxford	
				Ann Collins	Do	Un		26	House Maid	Wilts Hill Deverill	
				Jane Crombes	Do	Un		17	Under Nurse	Hants Southampton	
				Fanny Sparks	Do	Un		20	Kitchen Maid	Sussex Chiddam	
				Thomas Browne	Do	Un	27		Footman	Middlesex London	
				Benjamin Knight	Do	Un	28		Coachman	Staffordshire Stone	
35	Northbrook Cottage	1		Henry Heard	Head	Mar	46		Gardener	Hants Upham	
				Mary Do	Wife	Mar		48		Wilts Servant	
				George Do	Son	Un	18		Son	Hants Bishops Waltham	
				Henry Do	Son	Un	16		Bricklayer	Do	
36	Frogmore Lane	1		James Friend	Head	Mar	42		Tanners Labourer	Do	
				Hannah Do	Wife	Mar		43		Do	
				Henry Do	Brother	Un	28		General Servant	Do Hilsey	
37	Do	1		Ann Hickley	Sister in law	Mar		36	Seamans Wife	Devonportshire Devonport	
				Grace Reeves	Head	Wid		47	Wife of a Shipwright	Isle of Wight Ryde	
				Ann Browne	Mother	Wid		79	Wife of a Shoemaker	Do	
	Total of Houses...	4		Total of Males and Females...			12	13			

67. Page from the census return of 1861 showing the entry for Northbrook House with eight living-in servants. Not all entries in the Census are as legible and beautifully written as this one.

was no exception. She was probably afflicted by the boredom which was the lot of many middle class women in Victorian England. The initiative in love affairs was taken by men so a young woman could do little more than wait and hope. As Agnes confided to her diary: 'Played two sets [of tennis] with Francis Saunders and think I could quite fall in love with him, he is so jolly and a very graceful tennis player … Mr Saunders sang several songs and did not go until late in the evening' (21st May 1883).

The diary suggests a life of leisure enlivened by forays to London to stay with relations, weekly visits to church, where she appreciated the rector's 'energetic' sermons and Sunday School, where she taught a class of young girls. Agnes enjoyed the company of a limited circle of friends from the same social stratum who included two of the sons of the rector, 'Willie' (39 and unmarried) and Cameron the youngest son who was 25. He played the organ and published settings of church music. They all seem to have played cribbage, whist, chess and tennis a good deal and to have held musical evenings and supper parties. A number of Bishop's Waltham personalities have walk-on parts in the diary though none is described in detail. Ann Jenner who lived at Palace House, the Gunners and the Revd Melville Churchill aged 32, who had recently completed a stint as curate, and was a man of independent means planning to settle in Bishop's Waltham, all appear.

Dr Philip Claude Hemming moved about 1900 to Town View in Bank Street. According to the census of 1901 he was living there with his sister Agnes, the diarist, who was still unmarried and a 20-year-old 'general servant'. He owned several horses and rode on horseback to visit his patients. His wife founded the Guide movement in Bishop's Waltham about 1920; the four patrols each had a corner of the garden as their den. Her young son Charles was allowed to play tennis with the girls – though under strict supervision![12]

The third doctor Hemming-Dr Charles Hemming II – was born at Town View in 1914 and has lived there the whole of his life. After attending school at Epsom College he studied at the London Hospital, qualified in 1937 and at once returned to join the Bishop's Waltham practice where he remained until he retired.

Palace House and the Palace itself were owned by the bishop of Winchester until 1869 when it passed to the Ecclestical Commissioners who continued the bishop's practice of leasing it to successive tenants. In 1863 it was leased by Arthur Helps though he already lived at Vernon Hill House. Palace House was neglected. George Habin Appleby, surveyor to the bishop's estate, submitted a report in which he describes the house. It consisted of dining, drawing and breakfast rooms, four bedrooms and four attics, stable, chaise house, gardens, orchard and meadow together with soap and candle stores and walled garden. He valued it at £85. It had however, he continued, been neglected: 'The Palace House is a substantial building and genteel Residence with good gardens and grounds. In consequence of difficulties arising in the affairs of the late lessee it has not been inhabited for several years. It has become dilapidated and the garden and grounds run to ruin but it is capable of being restored at moderate expense. Meadow land alone is of considerable value and is enclosed with a high wall.'[13]

Though the lease was for 21 years Arthur Helps surrendered it in 1868 and the following year the Palace was granted to Kentish Jenner (1819–80) who lived there until his death at the house of his brother in Brook Street London in April 1880. He was buried in his brother's vault in Nunhead Cemetery. His sister Hannah continued to live at Palace House until her death in January 1887.[14] The house passed to Sir William Jenner and it remained in the hands of the Jenner family until it was leased by Admiral Cunningham in 1936. After the Second World War the Cunninghams were able to buy the house outright. It was they who in 1952 passed the Palace to the Ministry of Works, as it then was, now English Heritage, who cleared the undergrowth, made the palace ruins safe and opened it to the public. After Lady Cunningham left the Palace House in 1963 it was bought by the Martineaus and Monica Martineau set about collecting material for a history of Bishop's Waltham.[15] The present owners are Alan and Virginia Lovell who moved to Bishop's Waltham in May 1987.

Austin & Wyatt is a firm of surveyors, estate agents and auctioneers with offices in a number of towns in south Hampshire, as well as Bishop's Waltham. The firm began in Bishop's Waltham where three generations of Richard Austins were leading citizens for over a century.[16] The first Richard Austin was born in 1791 and lived at *The Crown Inn* in the Square with his wife Elizabeth (born in 1800) their son Richard (born in 1830) and five daughters. He described himself as wine merchant. He was a man of great energy and versatility and it was he who in 1836 founded the firm of estate agents. When he died in 1850 the family moved from *The Crown* to Coppice Hill House. In the Census of 1851 Richard's widow is described as 'brickmaker and farmer' – she farmed 30 acres with the help of six labourers – whilst her son Richard Austin II, aged only 20 when his father died, took over the estate agency and headed the firm for more than half a century.

He married Jane by whom he had two daughters and a son – the third Richard Austin born in 1866. The firm prospered and the name Austin figures prominently in the land and business transactions in Bishop's Waltham in the late nineteenth century. In the early 1880s Richard Austin II built himself an imposing residence on the Botley Road named The Thickets with a lodge and substantial land attached. His son Richard Austin III meanwhile bought Fernleigh an eighteenth century house in St George's Square.

Richard Austin II retired from the firm about 1903 and died two years later. His son Richard Austin III went into partnership with Archibald Wyatt of Fareham though he himself remained at the Bishop's Waltham office. On the death of his mother in 1924 he moved into The Thickets and Fernleigh became the Bishop's Waltham office of Austin and Wyatt. Between the wars Richard Austin III and his

68. Richard Austin III 1866–1945 wearing the bowler hat for which he was well-known, with his wife and recently widowed mother c.1905.

wife Maria Julia were at the apex of Bishop's Waltham society. Richard (Dickie) was always 'immaculately attired in well-cut breeches' whilst he and Maria 'rode to hounds two or three days a week in the season'. Invitations to tennis at The Thickets 'were much sought after'.[17] Richard Austin III was for many years a churchwarden at St Peter's and when he died at the end of the Second World War he was commemorated in one of the last plaques to be erected in the church. Maria lived until 1962 when she was 94. They had no children and so the Austin association with the firm ceased with his death.

The Chase Mill or as it was known in the middle ages the Est Myll probably existed even before Domesday. It is on the branch of the Hamble which rises on the Moors and flows under the turnpike road to Wickham and meets the branch which rises at Dean at Frenchmans Bridge on the Botley Road. From 1204 and for the remainder of the middle ages it appears regularly in the records of the bishops of Winchester kept

69. High Street c.1916. G.T.Floate was a photographer who published photographs of the town still available in 1944.

70. The town pump, Basingwell Street c.1912.

71. Two views of High Street before the road was tarred c.1910.

72. The Liberal Party campaigning in the General Election of 1906. The Liberals claimed to stand for cheaper food – the large loaf – and gained a landslide victory.

in the Pipe Rolls and Rentals.[18] For most of the period from 1613 to 1939 the mill was leased or owned by three families. The Colenutt family from 1613 to 1700 and the Willis family from 1700 to 1772 leased the mill from the bishop. In 1772 it came into the hands of the Jonas family and it was David Jonas who bought the mill from Bishop Brownlow North in 1806. In 1892 on the death of William Knapp Jonas the property passed to his cousin Arthur Hildyard Robinson who owned the mill and lived in the Mill House until 1939.

The mill itself was rebuilt about 1830 though parts are much earlier. It is unusual in remaining water powered until the end of its working life in 1955, largely because the supply of water from the river Hamble was then abundant at all seasons. In the nineteenth century the mill pond was perhaps three times as large as it is now. It was regularly cleared of weed using a punt and hook or scythe to cut the weed free and the sluices were then opened so that the weed could disperse down the river.

At the end of the nineteenth century Bishop's Waltham was short of meeting places. There was the Old Grammar School in Portland Square, which had ceased to be a school about 1880. Here the church held annual lectures and the county council held cookery classes. There was the old infant school in the churchyard which had been replaced as a school in 1896. The building had seen better days, became unsafe and was demolished in 1907 [19] (During demolition hundreds of slate pencils were found beneath the building dropped through the floor boards by bored pupils perhaps) Evening Continuation classes were held in the Council School in Newtown. There was the Workman's Hall in Basingwell Street and the small Reading Room in St Peter's Street. None was really adequate for the needs of the town. The curate was obliged to hold his confirmation classes in his rooms in Lower Lane.[20] Bishop's Waltham needed space for meetings small and large.

The first, and in some ways the most extraordinary, new meeting place in Bishop's Waltham was the Oddfellows Hall opened in High Street on 30th December 1895 with a spectacular flourish. Extraordinary first because of its size, out of scale with surrounding buildings and second because the Loyal Budd of Friendship Lodge of the Manchester Unity of Oddfellows was a strange organisation to build such a hall in a small Hampshire town. The Oddfellows Friendly Society was, however, a flourishing one with capital to invest. The building was the product of local skill and workmanship. The main hall and balcony could accommodate over 400 people. The outside was striking with a façade of white and red brick and white terra cotta mouldings, the latter supplied by Blanchards. The opening was yet another Bishop's Waltham occasion marked by a dinner at which William Myers of Swanmore Park, the local Member of Parliament, presided, attended by 170 local worthies. Music was provided by the Royal Marines Artillery Band who also gave a concert in the evening from which many had to be turned away when the hall was full to overflowing.

The hall was an asset to the town used for example for church services when the parish church was closed for restoration in 1896–1897. It was the venue too for the Sunday School treat when 200 children watched a lantern show on Palestine.[21] Dances, dinners and concerts were held there and Madam Lloyd brought a concert party once a year. On Sundays she held a concert of sacred music with a silver collection beginning at 8pm so as not to interfere with evening services at the church and chapels.[22]

After about 1920 the Oddfellows Hall became Bishop Waltham's first and only cinema, named the Palace and later the Classic. When in the 1960s cinema was giving way to television it became briefly a bingo hall. It was used as a furniture store until in 1995 it was bought by the King's Church as a Christian Centre.[23]

The Educational Institute, the second new public building in Bishop's Waltham, opened on 5th July 1899 (see pp. 95–6). It was the demolition of the old infant school in 1907 which seems to have accelerated the move to build a church hall.[24] In June 1910 part of the garden of Folly House with a frontage along the road from Free Street to the Mafeking Hero, backing on to the playground of the boys' council school was bought for £70 from the three Cobbett sisters. The Church Hall was built with the blessing of the diocesan architect Thomas Graham Jackson, well known to St Peter's through the restoration of 1896–97. It was extended in 1964 but as it approaches its centenary in 2010 it is reaching the end of its useful life and there are plans to replace it.

16

Pleasures and pastimes 1870–1914

IN THE SECOND half of the nineteenth century there was increasing concern about the evil effects of alcohol on society. In the view of many people some men spent too much time in public houses and too much money on beer to the detriment of wife and children, sometimes returning home drunk and violent. Churches of all persuasions – not just the free churches, which were traditionally associated with teetotalism – were united in opposition to drink. The Church of England Temperance Society was founded in 1862 and by the end of the century was the largest temperance organisation in the country with branches in most parishes.[1] Like many towns Bishop's Waltham was well supplied with public houses. The Census of 1881 listed no less than eight in the town itself, as well as the brewery in Lower Lane and a retail brewery in Brook Street: *The Wheatsheaf, The White Hart, The Swan, The Grapes, The Brewer's Arms, The Crown, The King's Head* and *The Forester's Arms* in Newtown. There were also pubs at Dundridge, Beeches Hill and Curdridge.

In September 1884 there occurred in Bishop's Waltham a spectacular confrontation between the beer interest and the temperance lobby which Frank Sargeant describes as 'The Beer Riots'. He tells in some detail of events on Friday night 19th September and what followed using a local paper and the evidence of eye-witnesses who were still alive when he was writing.[2]

The curate of the parish church Edward Falconer newly arrived in May 1884 was a headstrong young man, with strong views and firm evangelical convictions which led him to preach out of doors in the Square in a style which staid Anglicans were not used to.[3] He was a convinced opponent of alcohol whose zeal for the cause was not matched by tact or discretion. He appeared at sessions of the licensing magistrates and opposed the renewal of the licence of some of the many public houses in the town. Not surprisingly the campaign of a brash, recently arrived curate was resented by publicans and their customers alike. Encouraged or perhaps inspired by the town's publicans, a group planned to seize the curate when he returned to the parish on the last train from Botley on Friday night and teach him a lesson. They intended to throw him into the pond, which was conveniently close to the station.

Edward Falconer was warned what was afoot and so wisely did not travel on the train. Deprived of their quarry, frustrated of their plan and drunk on the free beer with which they had been plied by sympathetic friends and complicit publicans they rampaged through the streets of Bishop's Waltham. They burnt an effigy of the curate, threw stones and when the police attempted to intervene they were assaulted. Reinforcements arrived from Droxford but rioting went on until 3am.

The ringleaders were eventually arrested and brought before the magistrates the following week. They were refused bail and were kept in custody until Quarter Sessions when they were sentenced to a short term of imprisonment. On the day of Quarter Sessions a police superintendent and 25 police constables were sent to the town in case there was further trouble. There was none and the police spent a pleasant day quietly at *The Crown* with beer and sandwiches. So ended the Beer Riots. According to Frank Sargeant the story had a happy ending. When the malefactors were released from gaol they were met by the curate and they became firm friends!

73. The Revd Edward Falconer, curate 1884-7, the cause of the Beer Riots.

The campaign against alcohol took many forms most spearheaded by the churches. Young people – men in particular – were urged to 'sign the pledge', to abstain either permanently or for a period from alcohol. A Bishop's Waltham Jubilee Temperance Brass and Reed Band was formed in 1887 and named in commemoration of the Queen's Golden Jubilee. The bandsmen wore blue and gold uniforms and were available to lend sound and colour to local festivities.

The Band of Hope was a vigorous organisation for young people, formed to advocate temperance and to provide alternative activities for them. Those who joined undertook, 'By Divine Assistance to abstain from all intoxicating drink and beverages'. The Bishop's Waltham branch in which 53 children were enrolled met quarterly for tea in the Infant School. On 2nd January 1896 tea was followed by a magic lantern show. An alternative drink was recommended in the parish magazine which carried an advertisement for Fry's 'Non-intoxicating hop ale'.[4]

Later in the year the Band of Hope held a combined festival for the parishes of Bishop's Waltham, Swanmore, Soberton, Shedfield and Droxford. Over 270 children, 50 of them from Bishop's Waltham, assembled in the school yard at Swanmore and filled St Barnabas' church where a 'telling address' was delivered 'Urging courage and watchfulness to enable them to remain true to their promises to fight against the temptations of drink'. After the service the children marched to Swanmore House where Wiliam Myers entertained them to tea. Games lasted until 7pm when the evening concluded with hymns and prayers.[5]

In 1892, responding to the desire of the bishop that there should be branch of the Church of England Temperance Society in every parish, the new rector James Palmer Nash announced the formation of a Bishop's Waltham branch which would be open not only to total abstainers but to all 'who will in any way exert themselves for the suppression of Intemperance' and who will 'endeavour both by example and effort to promote the objects of the Society'.[6]

Harold Rycroft who arrived as rector in 1906 was also a keen advocate of temperance. Surveying the coming winter in the magazine for November 1906 and announcing a meeting to be held at the end of the month the editor wrote ' The rector…is very anxious that some good temperance work should be done in the coming winter and hopes that there may be a large and representative gathering from the parish'[7]. The Primitive Methodists were also keen abstainers. Any candidate for the Local Preachers' plan must be both an abstainer and a non-smoker.[8]

Alcohol was not the only social evil of which the parish was aware; tobacco was also a drain on money and health. *The Parish Magazine* for June 1907 describes a visit to Portsmouth dockyard by 60 'lads', arranged by the RED Brotherhood 'which exists for the purpose of helping to put down what is now without doubt a national vice, undermining the physique and character of the future men of England – juvenile smoking'. They visited the battleship *Glory*, and 'the latest leviathan the *Dreadnought*'. They were given the free run of the cruiser *Terrible*, 'and they made the most of it, some climbing the masthead, others diving into the stoke hole' – no Health and Safety legislation in those days, it appears.[9]

In December 1907 an anonymous correspondent (perhaps the rector himself) wrote in the *The Parish Magazine* that 'The evils of intemperance are so strikingly apparent in our parish that every opportunity must be used to bring home these evils and the blessed fruits of temperance to all the parishioners'. The committee of the Temperance Society arranged an entertainment in the Old Grammar School which would consist of part songs, solos etc and an address by Mr Tomson, the Church of England Temperance Society Police Court Missionary at Portsmouth.[10]

By 1900 almost all parishes had built Reading Rooms where books, newspapers, board games and other activities were available as a counter attraction to the society of the pub. Bishop's Waltham Reading Room was in a single storey building in St Peter Street. Although its rules do not mention alcohol the Bishop's Waltham Institute, opened in Bank Street in 1899, provided a host of educational and recreational activities for all ages meant in part to provide alternatives to public houses.

In the last years of the nineteenth century there appeared two means of transport which were to dominate the twentieth century, the bicycle and the horseless carriage, which we know as the motor car. Bicycles which became available in the early 1880s

74. The Bishop's Waltham Cycling Club outside Eastway House c.1898.

were the first democratic means of transport, relatively inexpensive to buy and maintain and equally suitable for both sexes. The first bicycle owner of whom we know in Bishop's Waltham was the rector's youngest son, Cameron Brock. 'Cameron came up on his bicycle' wrote the 21-year-old Blanche Hemming in her diary entry for 15th March 1883. It must have been a penny farthing since the so-called 'Safety Bicycle', with a driving chain to the rear wheel making possible two wheels of equal size, was not patented until 1885.[11] The photograph of the Bishop's Waltham Cycling Club taken outside Eastway House in 1892 shows some cyclists on penny farthings and some on safety bicycles and includes Francis Clark, owner of Eastway House and Thomas Archer-Shepherd the curate of the parish church, both keen cyclists.

Cycling clubs frequently met on Sundays and represented one of the first threats to the Victorian Sunday, providing an excuse not to attend church. At a time when most people worked at least on Saturday morning, Sunday was the only day for an all-day outing. In 1899 Bishop Davidson devoted part of his address to the Winchester Diocesan Conference to the threat to church attendance represented by the bicycle. One answer was to organise Cyclists Services at a central point on the likely route where riders might welcome a rest and at the same time maintain the habit of church attendance. A service held at Lyndhurst in May 1892 had apparently drawn 500 cyclists. The service held at Bishop's Waltham on 17th July 1892 unfortunately coincided with rain and only 50 cyclists turned up though many parishioners came to support the venture. The Dean of Winchester gave a 'helpful address' on

Isaiah 40 verse 4 'Every valley shall be exalted and every mountain and hill shall be made low; and the crooked shall be made straight and the rough places plain'.[12] In view of the state of the roads in the 1890s his address must have provoked some hilarity.

Early motorcars were the playthings of the rich. The first beneficiaries of the motorcar were however not its owners or even its passengers but the horses which it replaced. The first name for the motorcar was 'the horseless carriage'. A writer in the syndicated part of the *Parish Magazine* in September 1896 celebrated the emancipation of the horse: 'When we have unharnessed the toiling bus horse, taken the cab horse from the shafts of the four-wheeler, freed the cart horse from its straining load, and the drayman's horse from its exhausting labour, the autocar will have done its work of abolishing equine slavery'.[13] As the chairman of the Daimler Company informed his shareholders in 1897, 'There are no saddles to be rented, no feed, no trouble about the horse being out of order or sick. Looking after a motorcar is child's play compared with attending to a horse'.[14] Motor cars were however expensive, and as late as the 1920s relatively few tradesmen in Bishop's Waltham owned one. They ran on what was at first called Motor Spirit which was sold in a can by the chemist. Dr Claude Hemming claimed to be the first owner of a motor car in Bishop's Waltham when in 1908 he bought one from Peter Rooke who had opened a garage in 1899, one of the first in Hampshire.

The late nineteenth and early twentieth century saw an increase of recreational activities for boys and young men, less so for girls and women. Cricket and football clubs flourished and the Scout movement began.

Cricket was played in Bishop's Waltham in the eighteenth century. Together with the famous Hambledon Club and Alresford Cricket Club it was amongst the earliest in Hampshire. One of the first recorded matches took place on what is described as Stephen's Castle Green on 28th August 1775 when Bishop's Waltham lost to Alresford. In the next century Hampshire newspapers provide only occasional glimpses of matches.

A new start seems to have been made in August 1888 when what was described as the Bishop's Waltham Cricket Club was founded. It was the successor of the Swanmore Park Cricket Club which was dissolved in 1885.[15] Charles Gunner was treasurer of the Swanmore Club and it may have been he who initiated the Bishop's Waltham Cricket Club. The first Rules of the Club, drawn up in 1888, required a management committee of no less than 19 members. The annual subscription was half a guinea per year. Practices were held at 3pm on Tuesday and Friday which suggests that the members were men of leisure or at least controlled their own hours of work. Members must live within six miles of Bishop's Waltham though visitors could play for a subscription of 5/- per month.[16] Games were played at Swanmore Park on the ground and using the pavilion recently vacated by the Swanmore Park Cricket Club.

75. Bishop's Waltham Cricket Club no date.

76. Bishop's Waltham Football Club 1907-8.

The Gunner family were keen cricketers and a mainstay of the Bishop's Waltham club. C.R.Gunner played for Hampshire in 1878. His son John Hugh Gunner captained the Marlborough College XI in 1902, played for Trinity College, Oxford and in 1906 and 1907 for Hampshire. Later Robin Gunner was the club's wicket keeper though he had played hockey rather than cricket for Cambridge University and England. After C.R.Gunner acquired the Ridgemede estate in 1897 matches were played there. Later the club's home ground was at the Triangle at the Chase. It was however an unsatisfactory venue – small, badly drained and the club could not obtain permission to build a pavilion. The next move was to Hoe Road where the club remained until 2000 when at last it was able to lease land at Albany Road, lay out a ground and build a pavilion.[17]

When Robert Baden-Powell relieved Mafeking in May 1901 during the Second Boer war he became a hero overnight. Within months *The White Hart* at the end of Bank Street had been renamed *The Mafeking Hero*, perhaps because Baden-Powell had recently stayed there. (It remained so until the end of the twentieth century when it was renamed again *The Waltham Tandoori*). Baden-Powell's more lasting claim to fame came a few years later. In August 1907 he held his first experimental camp for 20 boys from a variety of backgrounds on Brownsea Island in Poole Harbour. In the following year came the publication of *Scouting for Boys*, one of the best sellers of the twentieth century. The Scout movement which resulted has been described as 'an overnight sensation'. It caught on both among the boys from all social classes who joined enthusiastically and the men who became its leaders.

Bishop's Waltham had one of the earliest Scout troops, founded in 1908. Camps were held at Peak Farm, West Meon and later at Swanage. The troop had three patrols and a fife and drum band. At the end of the annual camp at West Meon, the boys and their leaders would catch the train on the recently opened Meon Valley line from West Meon to Brockbridge and then march to Bishop's Waltham via Swanmore to enter the town with flags flying and band playing.[18] The first scoutmaster was Thomas Swinnerton-Hewitt assisted by Edgar Adams later Noel Stubbs, curate at St Peter's from 1909 to 1912. Robin Gunner was a scout leader, first at Shedfield and later at Bishop's Waltham, for 46 years.

The Wolf Cubs, as they were called in the early years, were started by Robert Baden-Powell in 1916 to provide for the younger brothers of Scouts. The first Bishop's Waltham Cub Pack was founded in 1919. One of the ten boys who attended a camp held at Weymouth in 1926 was nine year old Reg Cockle.[19] Cubs played an important part in the life of many boys growing up in Bishop's Waltham in the interwar years.

It was possible to be a spectator of sporting events as well as a participant. Ethel Cockle had a keen memory for events in the town of her youth in the early twentieth century. She recalled for example the day of the Hambledon Races held in April each year.

77. Bishop's Waltham Scout Troop with Thomas Swinnerton-Hewitt, scoutmaster and the Revd Noel Stubbs, curate and assistant scoutmaster c.1910.

'On our way to school we would see all kinds of horse drawn vehicles coming from all roads to pass through Bishop's Waltham then via Swanmore to Hambledon. We heard the post-horns coming long before we saw them and the four-in-hand coaches passed through, full inside and out. There were all kinds of people in them – ladies with leg-of-mutton sleeves in fashion then, large and small hats which fitted the ladies to perfection. The men all wore top hats and looked very elegant.... After five o'clock as the returning coaches came through some would throw cowslips, primroses and bluebells to us and money if they had a good day. Some of the four-in-hands, waggonettes, dog carts and brakes would fill the High Street and Square until there was no room left for late-comers.... We would be allowed to stay and watch them leave until the Square was empty and the sound of the horns had died away and we would go home in the dusk ... With the coming of the motor car the lively horses and the post-horns disappeared, much to our regret'[20].

In the early 1860s Bishop's Waltham was lit by gas for the first time and responsibility for collecting the rate was given to a body of lighting inspectors. A town meeting held in 1864 handed to this body the additional duty of supervising fire fighting in the town which had previously belonged to the constable. They in turn decided that the town needed two engines in working order which was achieved by repairing the two

78. Singing the National Anthem to celebrate the Coronation of King Edward VII 9th August 1902.

engines which it already possessed. James Padbury directed the repair and expenses were met by James Lock, treasurer of the committee who already had some cash in hand which was enhanced by donations from fire insurance companies which stood to gain from an effective fire service.

In 1891 the Volunteer Fire Brigade was formed with its own committee which would work in close collaboration with the lighting inspectors, an arrangement which lasted until the Fire Brigades Act of 1938 removed responsibility for the fire service from the parish.[21] The new brigade operated in two section each consisting of a captain, a lieutenant, an engineer, a foreman and five firemen. The two sections were on duty on alternate days. When there was a fire the section on duty 'would repair with all haste to the Engine House'. Notification of a fire depended on a runner, a cyclist or a man on horseback reaching the engine house. The firemen were then summoned by bugle sounded in three locations – the Square, Newtown and Bank Street. It is as well that there appear to have been few fires – only four in 1897–98 for example – since not only must there have been delay before the brigade appeared at the fire but the appliances available to fight the fire were antiquated. The brigade needed a modern fire engine. Subscriptions were solicited and as usual subscribers' names were publicised together with the amount of their contribution. In 1899 the committee bought a second-hand engine for £84 and had it brought down from London by train. It was still not self propelled but had to be pulled by horse or later car or lorry.

Fire fighting was not the only activity of the Volunteer Fire Brigade. It contributed an annual entertainment to the social calendar of the town. This took place for example in 1899 in the recently opened Oddfellows Hall in High Street. After a sit-down dinner and speeches there was 'A Good Programme of Vocal and Instrumental Music by Ladies and Gentlemen of the Neighbourhood'. This was followed by 'Mr Sydney Fielder, the Well-known Social Entertainer with his Remarkable Illusions and Hand Shadows'. Stalls cost 2/-, the Pit and Balcony 1/- and the Gallery 6d.[22]

17

The restoration of 1896–7 and the pre-war church

IN THE NINETEENTH century clergy came and stayed, in the twentieth century they came and went. Over most of the years of the nineteenth century St Peter's had two rectors, in the twentieth century there would be nine. Never again would a man (or a woman) be appointed rector in their twenties or stay for the rest of their life. William Brock's successor was James Palmer Nash who was just short of 50 when he came to St Peter's from Bishopstoke where he had been rector for five years following ten years as Vicar of Hedge End. He was instituted on 5th March 1892 and inducted six weeks later by George Sumner, Suffragan Bishop of Guildford.[1]

79. St Peter's church choir c.1892. The curate, the Revd T.A.M.Archer-Shepherd is on the left of the photograph.

There was need for change after such a long incumbency. For many years before his death the pattern of services favoured by William Brock was seriously out of date. He wore a black gown to preach, the Psalms were said not chanted, the choir, not yet robed, sat in the nave.[2] Holy Communion was celebrated twice a month, following Morning Prayer on the first Sunday and after Evening Prayer on the third Sunday.

The new rector introduced changes at once. Early Communion was held for the first time at 8.30am on Easter Sunday 1892. From May that year there was a weekly celebration. Evening Communion disappeared. By 1899 Holy Communion took place at 8.00am every Sunday as well as following Morning Prayer on the first and third Sunday. The clergy might teach the centrality of the Holy Communion but the laity remained unconvinced. To them Holy Communion must be taken seriously but not too often. It was the mark of the church's great festivals – Christmas, Easter and Whitsun. Numbers attending at 8am on other Sundays were in the low teens and after Morning Prayer between 25 and 40. Even on Easter Sunday there were only about 80 communicants though the number increased steadily up to the First World War and reached 229 in 1910.[3]

It was to William Brock's last curate Thomas Archer-Shepherd that we owe *The Parish Magazine*.[4] Parish magazines were the result of cheap paper and the spread of literacy following the Education Acts from 1870 onwards. By 1885 most parishes had a magazine; Bishop's Waltham's began publication in January 1890. 'The want of a Church periodical … has long been felt by the workers in connection with the Parish Church', were its opening words. It went on to announce a forthcoming confirmation, to appeal for more Sunday School teachers and to invite young men of 18 and over to a Bible Class to be held in the curate's rooms in Lower Lane.[5]

Early editions cost 1d, had a pink paper cover and consisted of a double page of mostly church news with advertisements for shops and businesses in the parish on the back. It was accompanied by a syndicated magazine entitled *Home Words for Heart and Hearth*, which contained improving stories suitable for Sunday reading, at a time when sabbatarian sentiment was strong and many homes forbade the reading of what they deemed frivolous fiction on Sundays. The circulation of the magazine in its early years was just over 300 copies.

Church collections were the invention of the late nineteenth century. Until 1868 the maintenance of the fabric of the nave of the church was the responsibility of the parish through a compulsory church rate voted by the Vestry. The end of church rate, the rising cost of running the church and obligations to the poor now required a regular and dependable income. The organist was now paid (£20 per year), so were the clerk (£5) and the organ blower (10/-). Gas and coke were needed to heat the church and from 1892 the choir boys were paid. In addition to the continuing generosity of better off parishioners more money was needed and so church collections began. In the 1880s collections were occasional – two in 1885, and three in 1887 and 1888. Once introduced the temptation to resort to collections was hard to resist particularly since accounts at the end of the year were often in deficit.

In the 1890s collections moved from occasional expedient to regular recourse. In 1891–92 there were six collections, in 1895–96 twelve, 1898–99 twenty two. At the Easter Vestry in 1899 it was resolved to take a collection every Sunday. They were however allocated to specific causes – on the first Sunday for the sick and needy, on the second for the restoration of the church still not fully paid for, on the third and fourth Sundays for church expenses and on the fifth for a specific project. The average collection was just over £2 per week and was still heavily outweighed by donations from richer parishioners whose

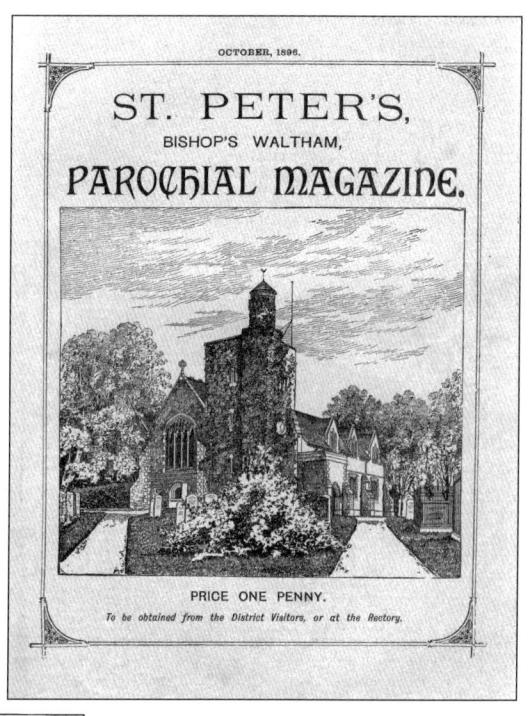

80. Two early Parish Magazines, the first shows the dormer windows placed over the south aisle to light the south gallery in 1797 and removed in 1896–7.

contributions were regularly published in the magazine by name and amount – a not so subtle form of blackmail in a good cause.[6]

The Mothers' Union was begun in 1876 by Mary Sumner, wife of George H. Sumner, then rector of Old Alresford. Her object was to bring together mothers of all social classes to sustain a sense of responsibility for the upbringing of their children. Twelve years later Harold Browne, bishop of Winchester (1873–91), made it a diocesan organisation and it soon took off nationally. 'Mary Sumner', wrote Owen Chadwick, 'was an aristocratic

Dr. ROGERS'
VEGETABLE BALSAM

will cure Coughs, Colds, etc. Dr. ROGERS' PILLS are the best remedy for all Bilious and Liver Complaints, Indigestion, etc.

Price 7½d., 1/1½ and 2/9 post free

From the Proprietor,

E. J. CAFFYN (late GEO. GOODLIFFE),

Dispensing Chemist,

BISHOP'S WALTHAM.

GILBERT WARE,
Hairdresser & Tobacconist,

BISHOP'S WALTHAM &
THE SQUARE, WICKHAM.

Private Hair-cutting Rooms. Hair Brushing by Machinery.

Choice Selection of Fancy Tobaccos and genuine Cigars. Walking Sticks and Canes in great variety.

HORACE H. HEAVER
(Late W. PAYNE & CO.),

HIGH STREET,
BISHOP'S WALTHAM.

GROCERY, DRAPERY,
AND
General Supply Stores.

A. W. GAMBLIN,
Decorator, etc.,

CROWN HILL,   ⋈

BISHOP'S WALTHAM.

Estimates Given.

W. WOODFORD,
Bootmaker,

HIGH STREET, BISHOP'S WALTHAM.

Repairs neatly and promptly attended to.

GRINDERY AND LEATHER STORES.

Good Class of READY MADE BOOTS kept in STOCK.

T. DUFFETT,
Boot & Shoe Warehouse,

High Street, BISHOP'S WALTHAM.

A Large Assortment of Chard's strong home-made BOOTS & SHOES at very low prices. Also a good Stock of Ladies' and Gentlemen's light Laced and Button Boots and Low Shoes. Orders punctually attended to.

Agent for Salmon & Son's Choice Teas, in 2 oz., ¼ lb., and ½ lb. packets. Salmon's French Coffee in ¼ lb. and ½ lb. Tins.

H. S. RICHARDS,
Ironmonger and Machinist.

BELL-HANGER, GAS, STOVE, AND RANGE FITTER.

Manufacturer of Steam and Hot Water Apparatus.

STEAM ENGINES, STEAM BOILERS.
BRASS, IRON, or LEAD PUMPS, etc., Erected New or Repaired.

NEWTOWN,
BISHOP'S WALTHAM.

W. LANG,
Family Draper, Milliner, and Outfitter,

BISHOP'S WALTHAM.

London Tailoring by Experienced Workmen.

A Large Stock of Manchester Linens, Calicoes, Sheetings, etc., etc.

The Largest Selection of Ladies' and Gentlemen's Boots, Shoes and Slippers in the Neighbourhood.

G. D. MARSH,
Tailor & Outfitter,

HIGH ST., BISHOP'S WALTHAM.

LIVERIES, ETC.

Your Patronage Solicited.

W. G. HEDGES
(Late J. PADBURY),

Watch and Clockmaker, Jeweller, = = Silversmith and Optician.

Church, Turret, and Household Clocks, wound by Contract.
All kinds of Repairs done on the premises
All Orders will receive Personal and prompt Attention
ESTABLISHED 1744

81. A page of advertisements in an early Parish Magazine.

philanthropist like Lord Shaftesbury….[she] was a great lady; taking cold baths daily; refusing to have a telephone and, when they came, a motor car or smoking in her home. She thought herrings were food for cats…and despite her early ignorance of working class mothers, she was wholly without patronage'.[7] The Bishop's Waltham branch was founded in December 1892 at a meeting held in the Rectory at which Mary Sumner was the speaker and has a continuous existence ever since.[8]

When James Palmer Nash became rector a further restoration of St Peter's was urgent. In partnership with T.G.Jackson, one of the best known and fashionable Victorian architects, James Palmer Nash carried through the restoration which created the church we know today. Thomas Graham Jackson (1835–1924, baronet 1913), began work in the offices of George Gilbert Scott in 1858. Much of his early work was done in Oxford where he was responsible for the Examination Schools. He became the Winchester diocesan architect in 1899. In Hampshire he built East Stratton and Northington churches for the Baring family and nearer home the new church at Curdridge opened in 1888 and extensions to All Saints', Botley. In the first decade of the twentieth century he was responsible for the underpinning of the foundations of Winchester Cathedral which saved it from collapse.[9] In the early 1890s Jackson was still at work at both Curdridge and Botley and this may be how James Palmer Nash obtained the services of this fashionable, busy and prosperous architect for St Peter's.[10]

Jackson's report on the parish church, hand written by his clerk in copperplate handwriting and dated 28th September 1894, was sent from his London office in Buckingham Street off the Strand. It falls into three parts: history, condition of the fabric and suggestions for improvement. It was accompanied by a plan of the church as it was and as it should be and an estimate of what the proposed restoration would cost. On the history he writes: 'The parish church of Bishop's Waltham has undergone so many transmutations, disasters and restorations that little remains to speak of from any date before the 15th century'. His remarks about the north nave arcade deserve quotation because they convey the character of the man: 'The North Nave arcade is of very simple and rude work but so devoid of detail that it is not easy to say whether its inartificial character bespeaks the primitive workmanship of the transitional period of the late 12th and early 13th century, or the clumsy hand of rustic masons in the 17th century when the aisle to which it opens was rebuilt.'[11]

Jackson goes on to report on the condition of the fabric, which was in better condition than might have been expected given its chequered history and the clay on which it was built. However the north nave arcade, the chancel arch and the junction of nave and chancel all gave cause for concern. The north nave arcade had settled outwards, the columns needed to be rebuilt on sound foundations and crushed stones in the shafts and capitals replaced. The chancel arch had been distorted on the south side in 1797 when the south gallery was built. It should be reconstructed, Jackson thought and he proposed to restore the squint, which he believed had originally

82. Thomas Graham Jackson (later Sir) architect of the restoration of St Peter's 1896–7, in his early 60s.

83. Plan of St Peter's church prepared by T.G.Jackson, showing the organ and choir in their original place and as Jackson proposed – organ at the end of the south aisle and choir in the chancel. He also proposed to move the pulpit steps but this was not achieved until later.

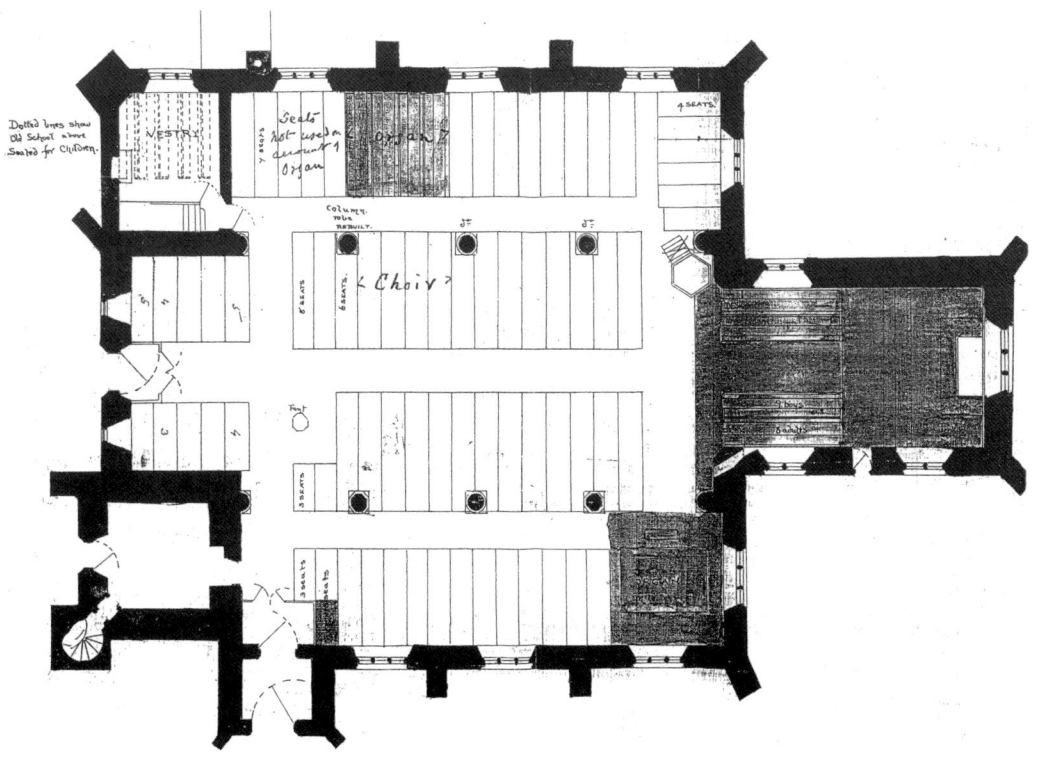

existed. The sidewalls of the nave where they met the chancel needed to be rebonded where cracks had occurred. Jackson would like to have lowered the tower removing 'the somewhat preposterous top of the turret' – the so-called 'pepper-pot', added he believed 'in modern times'.

So much for renovation. Jackson went on to recommend improvements. The south gallery could be dispensed with – a sign that congregations were already smaller than they had been in the 1860s. It should be taken down, the 'unsightly windows which light it' removed and the chancel arch and south arcade restored. The organ should be moved to the east end of the south aisle, not ideal but any alternative would mean building an organ loft. The tester above the pulpit had been removed in 1868, was now stored in the tower and was in a dilapidated state. Jackson wanted to repair and refix it in order 'to restore something of the picturesqueness and furnished appearance of which the interior of the church has in great measure been robbed by too sweeping a restoration'.[12]

Improvements to the heating were already in hand. Hot water pipes were above floor level, unsightly and an obstacle to entering the pews and in any case were inadequate to heat a building of this size. They were to be placed in a channel under the floor. The chancel was furnished with deal pews and had not generally been used. It should in future accommodate the choir and would need pews, 'which should be of

84. The south gallery built 1797, before its demolition in 1896–7.

85. Interior of St Peter's before the restoration of 1896–7. Note the distorted chancel arch with scriptural text, the old reading desk and central heating pipes above floor level.

oak and handsome'. There should be new steps of Portland stone, lower and more numerous than at present, at both the chancel arch and in the chancel itself.

Jackson's proposals would alter the appearance of the interior of the church significantly and for the better. The removal of the south gallery would lighten the church. Rebuilding the chancel arch, removing the New Testament text above it (*'The just shall live by faith'*) and refurnishing the chancel would restore the balance of the east end. Moving the organ, placing a robed choir in the chancel and restoring the canopy above the pulpit would change the focus of the building.

How was such an ambitious scheme to be afforded? Jackson's initial estimate including the heating was £1578. The modern equivalent would be at least £80,000 at a time when no central grants were available. Benjamin Hewitt a leading solicitor in the town and a church warden wrote to the rector in October 1894.' I herewith return the architect's report and suggestions for improvements to our grand old parish church ... but I fail to see where all the money is coming from to carry out the work recommended by Mr Jackson even excluding the estimates for Heating Apparatus' [13]

But it must be done and the rector determined that it should be and to the exacting specifications of Thomas Jackson. At a Vestry meeting held in June 1895

The Bishop's Waltham Parish Church Restoration Fund committee was set up.[14] It included the rector, the four churchwardens – Thomas John Brown, Charles R. Gunner, Basil Hewitt and the now aged James Padbury – and a further nine substantial citizens, all men of course. [15] Caroline Gunner was prepared to pay for the new chancel provided that the remainder of the work was carried out. A further £500 had already been promised by local well-wishers.

Work began on the north aisle in March 1896 but before long it was discovered that the roof had been weakened when the south arcade was dismantled in 1797 and now needed to be tied firmly to the nave walls. Thomas Jackson took a close personal interest throughout though day to day supervision was in the hands of the Clerk of Works Mr Mockford of whom he had a very high opinion.[16]

The correspondence addressed to the rector by Thomas Jackson has survived. Between September 1894 and January 1899 Jackson wrote over 30 letters – all handwritten since this was before the days of telephone or typewriter.[17] They convey a picture of a busy and committed architect with strong convictions. On the lead roof of the tower he wrote 'If you meddle with it I think you will have to put a new timber roof on as the present one is a very miserable affair. ... The tower itself is scarcely worth spending much money on.' – 8th October 1894. 'I shall arrive on the 4.2 at Bishop's Waltham; depart 6.50 for town' – 2nd July 1895. On the chancel 'I have ordered the pavement. Will it not be as well to have a pipe under the chancel seats back row? The fear however is that the heat will pull the oak to pieces. So if you are not afraid of being cold do it your way'. And finally ' I have an awful design for a lectern by Churcher. What can I do? It must be altered surely?' It was – Jackson himself designed the heavy but distinguished revolving lectern which was used in St Peter's until the 1990s.[18]

From the end of May 1896 the church was closed for a year to allow the restoration to be undertaken. Main services were held in the Oddfellows Hall though Holy Communion, baptisms and marriages took place in the blocked-off chancel. By December 1896 the new south arcade was complete and the wall plates and rafters of the nave and aisle roof had been repaired and bolted together. The whole chancel roof needed new lath and plaster and decayed rafters must be replaced. The estimated cost had now risen to £2200.[19]

By April 1897 the restoration was nearing completion. A gift had been received towards the £20 needed to equip the choir with the cassocks and surplices which would be worn once the new chancel was in use. Lectern, cross and pulpit fall were still needed and a new font – 'the present one is small and unsightly'. Still the bells had not been repaired – it had not been possible for them to be to pealed for over three years.[20] On 5th May 1897 the church was reopened with a great service at which the Bishop of Guildford preached. The final bill was £2560 of which £400 was still outstanding. (Modern equivalents about £125,000 and £20,000) Gunners bank gave the church an interest free loan. Not until 1901 were the bells fully restored and a service of celebration took place in December of that year.[21]

The death of Queen Victoria in January 1901 was felt by all in the country like a death in the family she had reigned so long. On the Sunday following her death the pulpit and reading desk at St Peter's were draped with crape relieved with lilies and ivy. 'The rector preached a most impressive and appropriate sermon from the text 'Her children shall rise up and call her blessed.' Proverbs 31.28…At the conclusion of the service which was a solemn and affecting one, the organist played The Dead March in *Saul* the congregation standing'.[22] The day of the queen's funeral Saturday 2nd February was observed as a day of mourning when shops and businesses were closed and a service was held in the parish church attended by a crowded congregation.[23] Bishop's Waltham was not alone. In London 'Even the prostitutes were clad in black and the street sweepers carried crepe on their brooms'.[24]

In August the following year came the coronation of Edward VII. Subscriptions were again invited to pay for the celebrations held on the cricket ground. Tea was served to 1332 people, and there were flags for the children, and prizes for the sports as well as £12 to compensate for the postponement of the event owing to the appendicitis suffered by the new king.

In the early years of the new century the church was the recipient of further gifts. First came stained glass for the east window of the south aisle given by Colonel Brine. Shortly before her death Caroline Gunner made two further gifts – stained glass for the east window in memory of her son George Herbert Gunner who had died in 1897 and a carved oak reredos erected behind the altar.[25] Soon after Caroline's death her daughter, also Caroline, married the former curate Thomas Archer-Shepherd, by now Vicar of Hedge End.[26] They were married for only a short time before his early death at the age of only 51 in 1908. Caroline gave two pairs of iron gates for the churchyard in his memory. Soon afterwards an inner porch to the south door of the church was given in memory of Benjamin Hewitt.

The parish was a flourishing one. Early numbers of the Parish Magazine convey a picture of a community centred on the parish church which provided worship, welfare, education and recreation for all ages. For the Church of England the period before the First World War was a golden age; the parish church enjoyed an unquestioned position. There were by now other churches in the town but they were for their adherents only and did not claim the wider responsibility expected of the parish church.

Services at St Peter's were well attended. There were in addition, what the magazine described as 'cottage services', at Dean, Ashton and Dundridge. The Sunday School was a large and flourishing organisation and there were classes at Dean and Ashton as well as the parish church. At St Peter's Sunday School teachers were allocated to the twelve classes and had their own outing – in 1891 to Netley Abbey – and there was a Sunday School library The school organised a winter 'treat' with tea, games and a magic lantern show. The infants met separately and as they left were each presented with an orange. In the summer there were more ambitious outings, to

Portchester Castle for example and for the younger children tea and games on Stephens Castle Down, then regarded as a public open space, to which they were conveyed in wagons lent by their owners.

On leaving school boys and girls felt they were too old for Sunday School and were urged to join organisations for their age group. For boys there was the 'Lads' Bible Class until they were 18 and then the Young Men's class held by the curate at 2pm on Sunday in his rooms in Lower Lane. Young women met separately in the Rectory. Confirmation classes too were held annually, separately for young men and women who were 15 or over. Ccnfirmation took place each year in one of the local churches on a weekday morning or afternoon. On 23rd June 1891 at 11am at the Confirmation held at St Peter's there were 86 candidates of whom 30 came from Bishop's Waltham. [27]

An alternative to the pubs was a priority and was provided at the Workman's Hall in Basingwell Street open during the winter months and available to 'young men who greatly need some such place of resort, where they may meet their friends and play games or read the newspapers after the day's work'. It was open each weeknight from 6pm to 10pm for men and lads over 16 for a subscription of 2d per week or 6d per month. Melville Churchill, a former curate who lived in the town took a special interest and provided an annual tea for members.[28]

The church choir and the ringers held an annual outing, maybe to Bournemouth, Brighton or London, usually travelling by train and returning in the early hours of the next day after 'a pleasant walk from Botley'.[29] Charles Gunner entertained the choir at Swanmore Cottage each year until he moved to Ridgemede. After tea there were races in the hayfield, and games 'which were entered into with great zest … until nearly dark'. Proceedings ended, as did almost all occasions, with the singing of God Save the Queen.[30]

In December 1894 the rector announced that he proposed to start a branch of the ponderously named Winchester Diocesan Society for Promoting Higher Education in Religious Knowledge. Each year a series of lectures given by local clergy was held in the Old Grammar School on topics such as Church History from 1604–40, Isaiah 1–39, or the Gospel of St John chapters 13–19. Each series concluded with an optional examination for which several entered. We do not know who attended the lectures but there are indications that the number reached between 30 and 40 and since they took place on weekday afternoons they must surely have been intended chiefly for ladies with the leisure and enthusiasm to attend. The success of the lectures is perhaps a commentary on the lack of education for women and the desire which many felt to remedy the defect.[31]

In addition to worship and education the parish operated its own welfare system. There were Coal and Clothing clubs which you could join on the recommendation of a District Visitor. Poorer parishioners were encouraged to save during the year and were rewarded with a bonus to which the better off subscribed. The amount of the bonus depended on the regularity of the deposits. At the onset of winter subscribers

86. The Rectory from the rear garden.

could buy subsidised clothing and coal available from recognised retailers. Blankets too could be borrowed from the rectory in November and must be returned in the spring for laundering and reissue next year. For the elderly Melville Churchill gave an annual tea and entertainment at his house at Southbrook. The Temperance Brass Band played during the afternoon. In August 1891 'most of the aged inhabitants' of the town, numbering 200, attended. Proceedings concluded at 9pm with the National Anthem.[32] In the summer the Rectory gardens were open to the parish on one evening a week.[33]

The rector needed a curate but the value of the living had declined with the agricultural depression. In 1835 its value had been assessed at £1250 per year and was among the richest in the diocese. In 1898 each £100 was worth less than £70 and was still falling. The rector had considerable outgoings including £200 towards the living of Curdridge, £15 to the living of Swanmore and £11.10.8 to St Cross. His net income was now only £398.5.11.[34] James Palmer Nash could not afford to pay and provide accommodation for a curate as his predecessor had done. In January 1900 he reported however that the bishop had offered him the chaplaincy of Preshaw House. It would involve little more than one Sunday service and Baron de Bush would pay a stipend which the rector would use to pay a curate. Shortly afterwards Gerald Thompson arrived from a curacy at Marlow, the first of a series of curates who served the parish until the Second World War.[35] Curates in those days were young men, almost invariably Oxford or Cambridge graduates, with a year or so at a theological college who would serve two or three curacies each lasting about three years before they could expect to be presented to a living.

Of Bishop's Waltham curates before the First World War two stand out. Noel Stubbs graduated from Queens' College, Cambridge, spent a year at Bishop's Hostel, Farnham and came to his first curacy at St Peter's in 1909. He was remembered because he married the daughter of Basil Hewitt, one of the town's most prominent citizens, who lived at St George's House in the Square and was a church warden. It was the wedding of the year, a grand affair recalled for many years by those who had witnessed it.[36] In 1931 Noel Stubbs was to return as rector.

His successor as curate in 1912 was John Wyndham Wayet. He had taken his degree at Emmanuel College, Cambridge, gone to Lincoln Theological College and came to Bishop's Waltham for his third curacy. He was remembered as a fine cricketer but even more for his response to the First World War. On 4th September 1914, with the war only a month old, he felt under a compulsion to join Kitchener's army as an ordinary soldier though with the intention of serving later as a chaplain. Many years later those who heard it recalled a sermon he preached at St Peter's to a packed congregation while he was on leave in December 1914. He quoted the words of Charles Kingsley which, though written in 1858, would have been familiar to his congregation: 'Men must work and women must weep'. Then he added 'Not a bit of it' and he went on to set out the active part which women could play in the war effort.[37]

18

The Parish Council and the town 1894–1914

THE POPULATION of Bishop's Waltham grew slowly during the nineteenth century, from 1,773 in 1801 to 3,028 in 1901, under 60% in a century or 0.6% per year.[1] This compares with 264% during the same period for Hampshire as a whole, 470% for Portsmouth and a remarkable 1212% for Southampton. Smaller towns such as Alton (270%), Andover (197%) and Fareham (270%) also increased far faster than Bishop's Waltham. The town had none of the qualifications for rapid or sustained growth – industry, communications, port, military establishment or seaside.[2] It remained a predominantly farming community with very little industry. Even brick making no longer absorbed as much labour as it had done in the 1870s.

The Census taken in 1901, the latest available for study under the 100 year rule, provides a fascinating snapshot of the town at the beginning of the twentieth century. It confirms that Bishop's Waltham was still an agricultural parish. No less than 254 men indicated that their occupations were concerned with the land. There were 24 farmers and a further 128 men describing themselves as either agricultural or general labourers. There were 40 carters, 13 dairymen, cowmen or cattlemen and nine shepherds. There was a traction engine driver, a sign that mechanisation was on the way, as well as gamekeeper, groom and farm bailiff. At Suetts Farm in West Hoe lived Alfred West (aged 30) who grew watercress on the nearby Moors. There were 30 gardeners, some of whom ran market gardens whilst others were gardeners at the big houses.

The second largest category – 70 men – owed their livelihood to the brick yards in the parish – at Coppice Hill and Claylands. Most were labourers or brickmakers (53), six were tile-makers, one was manager of the lime works, another a night watchman and a third a potter. Stephen Blanchard (aged 78) – probably a relation of the proprietor of the Claylands brick works – described himself as a retired modeller at a terra cotta works. He volunteered the information that he had been born 'on the High Seas between England and America'.

The railway provided employment for 17 men. Living in the parish were four engine drivers, four porters, two booking clerks, a guard and a signalman, whilst

Frederick Merritt (26) was 'a navvy' on the Meon Valley railway, then in course of construction.

Bishop's Waltham was self-sufficient. There was scarcely any commodity which you could not buy nor service you could not find within its confines. The outlying villages too – Swanmore, Shedfield, Durley, Upham and Curdridge – regarded Bishop's Waltham as their metropolis supplying what their more limited facilities could not. The centre of the town then as now was High Street. Here the main tradespeople lived and had their shops. Earlier it had contained a number of private houses; now almost all had been turned into shops. At the St George's Square end of the street was Christopher Eddolls (aged 30) harness maker, at the Bank Streeet end was Thomas Duffett, bookseller and stationer. William Hedges (27) had taken over from James Padbury and was the town's watchmaker. William Tickner (40) was one of several ironmongers. Other shopkeepers included cordwainer, draper, chemist, hairdresser, cabinet maker, several tailors and outfitters, butcher and of course the post office. The town had its own photographer in Paul Desa. There were shops too in other streets in the town and in Newtown.

Crafts were well represented – blacksmiths, coal merchants, carpenters, thatcher, carrier, woodman, harness maker, pedlar and hawker, pastry cook and bread maker, postmen, sewing machine agent, cutler and chimney sweep. There was in the town a 'fancy toy shop' run by Susannah Young who had been born in Tasmania. Bishop's Waltham had its own policeman – PC Matthew Mitcham (31) – living in the town.

Several people are reported as 'living on their own means' which means that they had saved for old age and were able to support themselves in a period before the Old Age Pension (introduced in 1908). Two sisters – Harriet Churcher (70) and Nellie Stroud (85) are described as living on parish relief. If you were physically capable you simply went on working. John Lock at 71 was still a pork butcher in Bank Street Frances Light (70) was still a charwoman and boarding with her was John Sutton (78) a labourer in the coal yard whilst Thomas Lamb at the age of 71 was still a railway engine driver. Almost nobody lived alone. A few worked away from their home village and boarded with a family which was glad of the small extra income. Young people of both sexes remained at home until they married sometimes still there into their thirties or even later. A widow or widower would be looked after in the home of a married son or daughter.

For women horizons had broadened but were still very limited by the standards of the twenty first century. On leaving school at 14 or even younger girls had a period of perhaps ten years employment before they married and entered their childbearing years. Only if they failed to marry or were widowed were they likely to remain in or to re-enter the labour market though a few were able to assist their husbands in a shop or trade.

On leaving school most girls obtained resident posts as domestic servants, some in the town though others left it for positions in houses in neighbouring towns or villages and were balanced by those who came from outside the town in response to advertisement. Sixty six households had one or more living-in servants – two had six servants and a further ten had three, four or five and 41 households had one servant. Nine households had two servants. One of them was the Revd Gerald Thompson, curate of the parish church, a young married man of 25 whose wife had a three month old baby. They lived at St Martins in Beeches Hill and had a nurse and a 'general servant'. At the Rectory there were three servants – a 46 year old parlour maid, a 21 year old cook and a 19 year old house maid. Just over 100 girls are listed in the Census as domestic servants, about half in their teens with a few starting as young as 13 and some coming from outside Bishop's Waltham. Some had a specialist function – there were for example 24 cooks. In the big houses such as Northbrook or Ridgemede – each with six servants – there was a hierarchy of servants each with her specific title – housekeeper, lady's maid, kitchen maid, parlour maid, a 'between girl' and, where there were small children, nursery maid or governess. But most people had one or two 'maids of all work' who are simply described as 'domestic servant'.

Few professions were as yet open to women but those that were included teacher and nurse. There were at least 15 teachers in the parish. They included Rhoda Sims (15) the daughter of Ebenezer Sims, headmaster of the board school at Newtown whose family lived in the School House and Katherine Longmore (20) the daughter of the Congregational minister. At Lithend Phoebe Wright (50) was Principal of a Ladies School assisted by her 18 year old niece Dorothy Buttifant described as 'governess' and Bertha Hull (24) music mistress. On the other side of the road was Mary Cobbett at Folly House where, assisted by her sister Rose, she too ran a girls' school.

If you were neither a domestic servant nor a nurse or teacher you could become a dressmaker (11) or a costume maker (5). Ethel Churcher (aged 24) whose father was Charles Churcher cabinet maker, shopkeeper and upholsterer described herself as 'upholstress'. There was also a demand for laundresses of whom there are 14 listed in the Census. A few girls were 'mother's help', for example 22 year old Eve Richards the eldest of nine children. Among the more exotic jobs held by women were pedlar/hawker, and poultry manager at Pondside Farm.

Curiously a number of public houses in Bishop's Waltham were managed by women, mostly widows – had they taken over from their husbands? Sarah Bywater a 49 year old widow was manager of *The Mafeking Hero*, Emma Foot was hotel keeper at *The Crown*, and at the age of 67 Harriet Wall was innkeeper at *The Grapes* whilst the 13 year old Florrie Young is listed as 'barmaid/barman' at *The Fountain* on the Chase.

Large families were still the rule in all social classes, birth control was either unknown or unreliable. Nothing is more striking to anybody studying the census returns than the inevitability of frequent childbearing. Only late marriage or infertility was likely to restrict the size of the family. Divorce was almost unknown. Many women must have spent years bearing children or nursing babies and often endured the desolation of infant death.

At Lodge Farm lived Alfred and Eliza West. At the age of 35 Eliza probably had several child bearing years ahead of her, yet there were already nine children aged 12, 11, 9, 8, 7, 6, 4, 2, and 10 months. At least they were reasonably well off and had three servants of whom one was a 16 year old nursemaid. John Nash was a thatcher and agricultural labourer living at Maypole Cottages in Free Street. At the age of 33 his wife, also Eliza, had already given birth to seven children, the eldest born when she was 20. Living on the Chase in a small cottage were Charles and Emily Emery with a family of ten children whose ages ranged from their eldest daughter Anne aged 21 to Eddie the youngest child who was ten months old. In between came daughters of 19, 16, 13, 10 and 4 and boys of 7, 3 and one. It is impossible for us to imagine what life must have been like for such families living in a small cottage on limited income. The house must have been intolerably crowded and in the winter dark Not only were families large but wives must have been pregnant for most of the years between marriage and their early 40s and sometimes later.

From 1890 the *Parish Magazine* published each month a list of those who had been baptised, married or buried at St Peter's. There were 288 deaths in the 1890s of which 18% or a total of 52 occurred in the first year or so of life. In 1895 and 1898 there were eight in each year, in 1892 seven, and in 1890 and 1891 six. Anxiety must have hung over each expected birth. A further twelve children died between the ages of two and ten and thirteen between 11 and 20. The infant death rate had changed little since the early years of the nineteenth century though it began to fall soon after the beginning of the twentieth century.[3]

Bishop's Waltham had a young population but this was in line with the national figures. The median age was still about 23 very little higher than it had been in 1841 (see pages 71–3) Bishop's Waltham had slightly more young people and slightly more elderly people than the national average.[4]

Age distribution of the population in the Census of 1901

Age	England and Wales	Bishop's Waltham
0–14	32.4	33.9
15–19	10.0	9.1
20–39	32.2	29.0
40–59	17.8	18.7
60–64	2.7	1.86
65–74	3.3	4.6
Over 75	1.4	1.7

Elective local government came to the towns in 1835 but the countryside had to wait for a further 50 years. Until the Parish Councils Act of 1894 rural parishes were governed by an oligarchy of parson and churchwardens meeting in the Parish Vestry.

87. Result of poll for the first Parish Council 17th December 1894 from the Council Minute book.

The Parish Councils Act provided for an elected council in all parishes with a population of over 300[5] The population of Bishop's Waltham was about 2,800 and even when the newly created civil parish of Curdridge and a small part of Swanmore were carved from it there was still a population of around 2,200. At first the Parish Council consisted of nine members – increased to 12 in 1897.[6]

The meeting to elect the first Parish Council was held, according to the requirement of the Act, on 4th December 1894 in the Old Grammar School in Portland Square. About 120 people attended and there were 19 candidates for 9 places on the Council. Nominations were received, placed in alphabetical order and a vote by show of hands took place. The chairman, Francis Clark, was required to allow ten minutes to elapse during which anybody dissatisfied with the result could demand a poll, Henry Hatch did, and the meeting dispersed without electing a Parish Council. The poll was held on 17th December also in the Old Grammar School and only four of those originally elected survived to become members of the first Parish Council. (This was not the only occasion on which a poll was demanded – 1896, 1910, 1913 and 1919 were other examples) Until 1899 elections were held each year; from 1901 every three years. Attendance at the annual meeting varied but was larger in election years, often exceeding 100.[7]

The Council met quarterly, unless there was a special reason for an additional meeting, at first in the Old Grammar School, but from 1899 in the newly built Educational Institute in Bank Street. Much of the Council's work was done by committees of which there were four: the Allotments and Recreation Ground committee, the Footpaths committee, the Sanitary committee and the Technical Education and Evening School committee. The chairman for the first twenty years of the Council's existence was Thomas John Brown, who died in office just before the annual meeting in 1915. He was a leading citizen of Bishop's Waltham who lived at Mount House in Little Shore Lane and worked for Gunners bank. He was also a bookseller and stationer, treasurer and secretary of the Penny Savings Bank, secretary of the Reading Room in St Peter's Street, Chairman of the Lighting Inspectors, a churchwarden for 37 years and organist of St Peter's church for 23 years.[8]

88. The front garden of Mount House, Little Shore Lane with Thomas John Brown, Chairman of the Parish Council 1894–1915 and his wife.

89. Dick Richards and the tank used to water the roads in summer.

The members of the first Council were leading citizens of the town. Three were farmers – Richard Westbrook of Hoe Farm, George Lock of Butts Farm and Edward Moldon. The Rector, James Palmer Nash, was a member and became the first vice-chairman as was his neighbour at Northbrook House, Henry W. Trinder, a solicitor but in fact man of leisure who had retired early. Alfred Weavil was a brickmaker who lived in Ladysmith Terrace, Newtown and Edward Clark who lived in High Street was a miller, maltster and coal merchant.[9]

The clerk of the Council was Charles Lipscomb Grossmith who lived at Mount Cottage in Little Shore Lane. He had been Assistant Overseer of the Poor since 1882 a post for which he was paid £50 per year and in which capacity he was responsible for collecting the poor rate twice a year. In 1911 this amounted to the considerable sum of £2,300. He also collected the sanitary rate and the lighting rate from those who lived in parts of the town lit by gas. His duties included preparing lists of jurors and registers of parliamentary and local government electors. With the formation of the Parish Council in 1894 he lost part of his job. Curdridge and part of Swanmore ceased to be in Bishop's Waltham. He was compensated by appointment as clerk to the newly elected Council with no reduction in salary – but no increase either. In 1906 his salary was raised to £70. There was of course no pension but in 1911 after almost 30 years service as Overseer of the Poor he resigned on account of being hard of hearing and finding Council minutes hard to write; scarcely surprising as he was aged 84.[10]

Bishop's Waltham was from 1894 to 1974 part of the Rural District of Droxford which consisted of the parishes which since 1835 had constituted the Droxford Poor Law Union.[11] The new Council consisted of two representatives of each constituent parish and its headquarters was initially at the Workhouse in Droxford. Edward Molden and Henry Trinder were the first councillors from Bishop's Waltham. The Council appointed a Medical Officer of Health and an Inspector of Nuisances to each of whom it paid a salary – £125 to the former and £85 to the latter. The responsibilities of the RDC included the roads of the district. It received complaints about the large stones put on the roads and thought they had not been through the stone gauge. It proposed to buy a steam roller but hesitated, deciding finally to hire one first. It should however be 'one of the newest pattern including all the latest improvements with one man in charge'.[12] A month later the council decided to hire a steam roller with 'a living van'.[13]

The Council noted the building of the Meon Valley railway and asked for a station at Mislingford as well as the station planned for Brockbridge – but was unsuccessful.[14]

The recreation ground at Waltham Chase allocated to the parish under the Enclosure Act of 1870, was inconveniently distant from the centre of the town. It consisted of a triangle of land measuring 4 acres just past *The Fountain Inn* (now named *The Chase Inn*) bounded by the turnpike road and Clewers Hill.[15] In 1897 the Parish Council had the opportunity to purchase 4½ acres near Cherry Gardens for £90 per acre. It was a controversial matter and the Council decided to hold a poll of the town. Of the 500 electors only 129 voted, 33 favouring the proposal. No reason is given in the Minutes for rejection of the proposal but it was probably cost. Anything which would increase the rates was likely to be voted down. The town had to wait until 1960 when at last the Hoe Road recreation ground was bought.[16]

In 1900 the Bishop's Waltham Waterworks was taken over by the Droxford Rural District Council, which extended its mains to Shedfield. Bishop's Waltham could be linked to mains water. This too was rejected – the town's wells and pumps were considered to be adequate and cheaper than any alternative.

The first episode of the long running Sewerage Saga began in 1903 and was still going when it was suspended during the First World War. The Medical Officer of Health of Droxford RDC had in 1899 prepared a report with the inviting title 'Water Supply, Sewerage and Scavenging in Bishop's Waltham'. When in 1903 the Parish Council received a letter from Lady Jenner who lived at Palace House complaining that the stream – the so-called 'River of the Lord' – which ran through her garden was polluted with raw sewage it felt obliged to take notice of the problem. The RDC had a scheme for emptying earth closets and cess pits but felt that now was the time to install mains drainage in the town with an outfall near the railway station where sewage would be treated using the septic tank system. The problem was money – the scheme would cost £5,905 which the parish would have to meet. In addition the

90. Station Road looking towards the Square c.1900.

91. St George's Square c.1900.

sewerage plant would require about two acres of land and a supervisor who would have to be paid.[17]

The scheme was rejected as far too expensive and a cheaper alternative requested. Drainage remained on the agenda and by 1908 the RDC was applying for a compulsory purchase order on land owned by Richard Austin for a sewerage farm behind The Thickets. The Council tried to persuade the RDC to drop the scheme. Prevarication paid off and in March 1915 the matter was closed until the end of the war.

Ethel Cockle remembered what the lack of mains sewerage meant. 'The landlord had to supply large buckets which were emptied twice a week on Tuesday and Friday. The alley door, [in Garfield Road where she lived], was left unlatched and you would hear the horse-drawn Ton (as it was called) coming down the street – you could hear the clip-clop of the horses' hooves and the iron bound wheels. The round usually started about 10pm and lasted well into the early hours of the next morning. In some streets – Houchin Street and St Peter's Street for example – buckets had to be carried through the house and left outside the front door'[18]

There were other examples of Council parsimony on behalf of its electors. The Council complained about the cost of street watering and the RDC pointed out that watering the streets actually saved money on road maintenance since it helped to compact the surface. In October 1907 the RDC wanted to put the open drain, which ran down Houchin Street, underground at a cost of £160. The Council urged the RDC 'to hesitate before such a heavy outlay'. A year later the Council decided it did not need additional fire hydrants for possible use by the Fire Brigade.[19]

One item which might involve money they did accept. The Post Office approached the Council in 1908 about extending the telephone system. It would, they said, 'Bring great benefits to the town of Bishop's Waltham'.[20] They would however require the Council to guarantee an income of £18.12.4 per year for the next seven years. If this figure were not reached the Council would have to meet the shortfall. In view of the benefits to the town the Council decided to risk it and their optimism was justified. Revenue exceeded the guarantee and was reduced for the following year when in any case the company was extending the telephone system to Botley. The new exchange, sited at the Bank Street end of St Peter Street, opened on 9th February 1910.[21] There was no subscriber dialling; the operator had to connect caller and called. The job of operator was popular; listening in to calls – strictly forbidden – gave you unrivalled access to town gossip.

19

The First World War and the inter-war years 1914–1939

'At August Bank Holiday 1914 the High Street was thronged with people all discussing one thing: the near certainty of war with Germany if the midnight ultimatum were ignored. The Reservists and the local company of the Hampshire Royal Garrison Artillery had already been called up to man the Sea Defence Stations. The evening wore on and the throng thinned. Midnight came but still no news. Next morning we heard that we were at war with Germany. Patriotism was high and young men in their thousands were clamouring to join the armed forces. ...'[1]

THAT NIGHT even before war was declared French boys from the recently opened Priory accompanied Fathers Godineau and Tessier who had been recalled to join the French army to the station and saw them off with rousing cries of *Vive la France* and a chorus of *La Marseillaise*. Others came from the town and joined in with *God save the King*.[2]

The first recruiting meeting in Bishop's Waltham took place in the recently built Drill Hall, Newtown. 'It was filled with young men from Bishop's Waltham and the surrounding parishes; influential local people filled the stage. ... After a few speeches about 30 or 40 young men walked to the stage to offer their services for King and Country. A few days later the Bishop's Waltham recruits left by train, seen off by friends, for the Drill Hall in Southampton. Recruits for the Rifle Brigade had left two days earlier.'[3]

What was seen in August 1914 as a great adventure turned into the nightmare of trench warfare, the slaughter of the Somme and the costly disaster of the Dardanelles. In 1916 the rector Henry Edmund Sharpe began to enter in the Burial Register the names of those killed in war, even though they had neither died nor were buried in Bishop's Waltham, under the heading 'European War – Parishioners who died for King and Country.' The first name recorded, under the 17th November 1914 was Charles Smith of Basingwell Street, who was serving in the First Dorset Regiment, then came Edward Gunner drowned on *HMS Bulwark* on

92. Two First World War fatalities: Sub-Lieutenant Edward Gunner drowned in HMS Bulwark 25th November 1914 and Sapper William Henry Richards (right) who died of wounds in the military hospital at Etaples, 1916. Three members of each family are commemorated on the War Memorial in the churchyard.

26th November and two days later Herbert Gibson of Bank Street killed at Meuville in France. Under 1915 the Rector noted the death of his son-in-law Major Andrew Buchanan King of the Argyll and Sutherland Highlanders, the husband of his daughter Evelyn Nina.

The Register of Church Services, normally a bare record of services held, initials of officiant and preacher and number of communicants, became a war diary in which the rector's emotions are scarcely concealed. On 3rd August 1914 he wrote 'Great Britain declares war on Germany for violation of the neutrality of Belgium and Luxembourg in response to appeal from Belgium'. On 11th September he wrote 'French take 150 guns. British take 16 guns and 6,000 prisoners. Great victory on the River Marne'. At Lent 1915 he wrote '*Deus misereatur – Six months of war*'. In April 1915, '280 men away serving in the war'; on 19th May, 'Memorial service for four parishioners killed in action'; on 9th June 1916, 'Memorial service for five parishioners killed in action in the great naval battle of Jutland in the North Sea'. At Easter that year the number of communicants was down, 'Most of our men are serving in the war' wrote the rector. In May 1917, 'King's royal proclamation read re economy of food'. He recorded allied triumphs and disasters alike. At Easter 1918, 'The eleventh day of the German battle on the western front'; on 17–18th July ' Franco-American forces drive back Germans in Champagne, France. 20,000 taken prisoner'.

By the end of what came to be called The Great War 58 men from Bishop's Waltham had died, ten in the Royal Navy, 47 in various army units and one in the Royal Air Force, which became a separate branch of the armed services just before the end of the war. Eight surnames occur twice on the War Memorial, men who were brothers or cousins and a further three occur three times – Andrews, Gunner and Richards. Ebenezer Sims the schoolmaster for over 40 years who had recently retired and his wife, lost two sons, Arthur and Oswald. There were men from all ranks in society and every profession and occupation. Not since the Black Death over 500 years before had death come to every village and town in the country at the same time and on this scale.

Of the 58 names on the War Memorial 48 appear in the Burial Register. The list in the Register records the growing death toll as the years went by –three in 1914, nine in 1915, thirteen in 1916, and nineteen in 1917. Most – 32 names in the rector's record, died on the Western Front in France or Belgium but almost every theatre of war was represented. Six served in the navy and five were killed at the battle of Jutland including the youngest victim from Bishop's Waltham 17 year old Robin Giffard-Brine, a Midshipman on *HMS Invincible*.[4] Frank Austin Stubbs, serving with the 29th Royal Fusiliers died in hospital in France three days after the end of hostilities whilst George Richards who had served in Egypt was buried in Gibraltar in November 1919. He was 42 and perhaps the oldest casualty of the war, the older brother of William Henry Richards who had died as a result of wounds on the Western Front in 1917 and a cousin of Esau Richards who had also been killed in the war, all members of a longstanding and well known Bishop's Waltham family.

The war had an impact on life at home. The work previously done by the men now in the forces had to be undertaken by others. Women made munitions and worked on the land. Mrs Wensley became postmistress. She and her three assistants, Kit Askew, Polly Aburrow and Sis Weavill were photographed wearing their long uniform skirts and carrying mail bags. Wounded soldiers came to the town and a hospital was established at Northbrook

93. Bishop's Waltham postwomen 1917. Postmistress Mrs Wensley with Kit Askew, Polly Aburrow and Sis Weavill.

94. Northbrook House used as a hospital during the First World War.

House. The Institute was opened during the day to provide recreational facilities and a fire was lit for them.[5]

It became vital to increase home food production. Allotment holders were encouraged to grow more and to take additional plots. The County War Agricultural Committee provided seed potatoes which the Parish Council was asked to distribute.[6] The Ministry of Agriculture made available 100 dozen glass jars for bottling fruit and vegetables, also distributed by the Parish Council, whilst the Council bought a pneumatic sprayer, designed to attack weeds, which could be hired for 1/- per day.[7]

The Womens' Institute was founded in Canada in 1897 and reached England in 1915. The first meeting of the Bishop's Waltham branch was held in the last year of the war, in February 1918. At the first full meeting, held in the Church Hall in early March, 38 members were enrolled. The programme included a demonstration of hay box cooking, a symposium on what to do in your garden in March and a display of economical dishes, which were later auctioned. There was a strong practical emphasis. At early meetings profitable poultry keeping, drying and preserving fruit, goat and rabbit farming were amongst the topics considered. Nurse Hearne of Shedfield Cottage Hospital gave a talk on 'Clothing, feeding and training young children'. In May wounded soldiers at the hospital in Northbrook House described the use of the weapons of war in the loan exhibition of war trophies. In November 1918 the meeting was cancelled because of the flu epidemic.[8]

At long last on 11th November 1918 the war ended and the rector was able to record: 'Great national and world-wide rejoicing'. That afternoon there was a service of thanksgiving in St Peter's at which the Congregational and Primitive Methodist ministers, Samuel Longmore and Herbert Stretch, took part – probably the first time free church ministers had ever joined in a service in St Peter's. 'Church completely filled', wrote the rector. In July 1919 there was a National Thanksgiving for the signing of the peace treaty when 1300 people 'partook of tea' at the Mill House, an occasion marred by heavy rain, – an omen perhaps of the tragic nature of the peace treaty which, as some people realised at the time, was a portent for the resumption of war almost exactly 20 years later.

In the euphoria of victory the government distributed captured German war trophies. The Parish Council decided to ask for a German machine gun to be placed in the Institute.[9] Such gifts offered to each parish exemplify the twin moods of exultation and revenge which characterised the period.

In addition to the peace celebrations held in July 1919 there was a banquet on 1st October to which 265 returning soldiers and sailors were invited. But what form should the town's War Memorial take and where should it be sited? There were a variety of suggestions including St George's Square and opposite Gunners Bank. Eventually the Memorial was erected at the entrance to the churchyard at the top of St Peter Street and was unveiled on 11th November 1921 by Charles Gunner, who had lost three sons in the war.[10] Two days later on 13th November the rector wrote 'A great congregation at this service. Every seat occupied by 3 o'clock. 150 standing and numbers outside'.

Throughout what later came to be called 'the inter-war years' there were two events held each year to commemorate those who had died in the Great War. At the eleventh hour of the eleventh day of the eleventh month Armistice Day was observed with wreath laying at the War Memorial attended amongst others by the schools in the town. The nearest Sunday to 11th November was Remembrance Sunday with an afternoon service in St Peter's to which all who had been involved in the war were invited and came in large numbers. At the last service before the Second World War held on 13th November 1938 'all the seats in the Church were occupied to overflowing'.[11] Even at the beginning of the twenty first century the First World War resonates. Families still treasure faded photographs and letters written from the front by grandfathers or great uncles which keep alive this most appalling of all wars. The Remembrance Service is still held in St Peter's at 10.50am when the names of the dead of the wars of the twentieth century are read. It is among the best attended services of the year.

Lloyd-George's post-war coalition government was committed to build 'Homes fit for heroes' and it was the job of Christopher Addison, the President of the Local Government Board to see that they were provided. Addison's Housing Act of 1919 required local authorities to survey their housing needs and to build accordingly, helped by government subsidy. Droxford RDC asked the Parish Council to report on how many houses 'for the working classes' it needed and where they should be built. The Council replied that it required 14 houses and settled eventually on Hoe Road as the best site and there they were built. The post-war council houses were – and are – easily identifiable, better planned and better equipped than any earlier housing for workers had been. There were also in the view of the council other needs. There was considerable overcrowding particularly in cottages at Ashton, Beeches Hill, Hoe and the Chase.[12]

Space in the churchyard was running out so a new burial ground was needed. George Garnett, a member of the Parish Council, offered land which he owned adjacent to the existing churchyard, as a memorial to his wife who had died in 1924.[13] The wall separating the new ground from the existing churchyard was removed and it was consecrated on 13th May 1926 and later an engraved stone was erected recording this gift to the town.

George Garnett was a considerable benefactor to the parish. For many years a recreation ground closer to the town than the one on the Chase had been sought. George Garnett offered to give land which he owned at Newtown to the parish.[14] It would be known as 'George Garnett's Public Recreation Ground for Bishop's Waltham Parish'. There were conditions: the parish would have to fence and drain it and provide entrance gates at a probable cost of £500 – and no games were to be played on Sundays. Following a town meeting at which the gift was narrowly rejected a poll of all ratepayers was held and this too voted for rejection this time decisively by 240 votes to 129. No reason is recorded but it seems almost certain that once again economy had won over a much needed amenity.[15]

When he died in January 1929 George Garnett left to the parish £100, then a substantial sum, to be invested and the income divided annually between five men and five women over the age of 60 selected by the parish council. It was known as the George Garnett Bounty and the council minutes record each year the names of recipients of 10/- gifts from the fund.

Poverty was a major social problem in the inter-war years and two constituencies were particularly affected: the unemployed and mothers with small children. There was as yet no welfare state and so the parish continued to organise its own welfare services, much of it through the initiative of the parish church.

Unemployment in the 1930s is usually thought of as the scourge of towns like Jarrow in the north of England. There was however much rural unemployment as the depression hit agriculture as well as industry. It was particularly bad in the winter when men were put off work on farms and the unemployed often congregated round the clock in the Square. A local relief organisation was started providing coal, food and clothes for the needy of which there were 71 beneficiaries. The scheme was soon expanded to provide alternative employment. The church, helped by an anonymous gift of £100, employed men to flatten grave mounds and to turf the ground in order to ease the task of mowing the churchyard.

In 1933 a more ambitious scheme was launched – the Bishop's Waltham Area Unemployment Association – with headquarters in Garfield Road. The Old Lime Kiln was prepared as a headquarters and men were employed cutting wood round the pond, allotment work, carpentry and arranging a Christmas party for members' children.[16] The parish was not unaware that things were much worse elsewhere and in May 1933 sent a consignment of clothes to 'the distressed areas of Yorkshire'.[17] By 1935 the economy was recovering, employment prospects improved and relief schemes were scaled down The rector wrote in his monthly letter in January 1935 of 'Bleak House giving way to Great Expectations'.[18]

March 1932 saw the launch at the Institute of the Infant Welfare Centre which included the parishes of Upham and Swanmore with 60 children under the age of three on the register. Dr Mitchell attended the monthly meetings to provide advice and help to mothers, the Red Cross served tea at 1d.per cup and there was a used baby clothes stall.[19] November 1933 saw the provision through a private gift of a parish ambulance to convey to hospital those who could not be taken by car.[20] The third initiative was the formation in January 1934 of the Bishop's Waltham and Upham Nursing Association, a more ambitious project since it involved considerable financial outlay. Subscriptions were invited towards the salary of Nurse Townsend and subsequently for the Austin Seven costing £121 which she needed if she were to cover the substantial distances in the parish. Sadly the scheme lasted only three years and was wound up in 1937 through lack of sufficient funds.[21]

Meanwhile Bishop's Waltham at long last had a library provided by Hampshire County Council. The branch of the County Library established at the Institute in March 1932 would be 'free to all Inhabitants of the Ancient Parish of Bishop's Waltham'. It would be open for one hour a week, from 6pm to 7pm on Fridays. Provided you were over the age of 14 you could join for 6d per year. If you were between the ages of 11 and 14 you needed a 'Certificate of suitability as a Reader', from your headmaster or headmistress. You could borrow two books at a time for fourteen days. Should there be an infectious disease in the family you must inform the librarian who would tell you how to dispose of any books you had on loan. The room at the Institute was used for other things so at the end of each hour long session the books had to be placed in boxes and locked up until next week.[22]

The year 1933 marked the beginning of episode two of the Sewerage Saga. This time the initiative in seeking a sewerage scheme came from the Parish Council which asked the Droxford Rural District Council to commission a scheme for their consideration. [23]It was not until 1936 that the scheme reached the council. The whole parish would receive the benefit of mains sewerage and the septic tank and filter beds would be built close to Locks Farm. It would however cost £34,515 which represented an additional rate of 3/- in the £. For a cottage whose rent was 15/- per week this would mean an increase of 1/3; for a cottage whose rent was 4/- the increase would be 4d.[24] The council was surprised at the cost of the scheme and asked for a cheaper one. They received a dismissive answer from the RDC. A parish meeting called to consider the scheme voted to reject it. Despite frequent complaints of overflowing cesspits particularly at the new council houses in Shore Lane, complaints about the pollution of the Pond and the unsavoury experience of the twice weekly emptying of cesspits in the centre of the town, the parish once more rejected a scheme for mains sewerage. Here perhaps is another indication of how close to the bread line many families were living as well as the high priority which the parish council continued to accord to keeping the rates down.

Motor traffic grew slowly in the inter-war years. The Bishop's Waltham to Wickham road was widened in 1927, the gradient of Coppice Hill was reduced and pavements constructed. Speeding was a problem particularly at the blind corner at the entrance to the town by *The Crown* where one door gained the unenviable nickname of 'the mortuary door'. As early as 1930 there was a plan for a bypass to eliminate this dangerous corner. It would run south west from the railway station, cut through the garden of Palace House, cross the Botley Road and rejoin the main Wickham road at Coppice Hill and would involve the demolition of Coppice Hill House.[25] Nothing came of it. Not for another 30 years was the traffic problem of Bishop's Waltham tackled.

Bus services to Winchester and Fareham began soon after the First World War, at first open topped, and charabancs, also open topped, were used for outings. Passenger services on the railway faded away so that when the final train ran on the last day of 1932 the demise of the service was scarcely noticed. The last Sunday School outing by train took place on 10th August 1932 when children, teachers and parents travelled to Hayling Island changing at Fratton. The following year 'Six coaches were needed to carry 80 children and their mothers to Hayling Island for their yearly treat'.[26]

In 1927 the long talked of division of the diocese of Winchester took place and Bishop's Waltham found itself in the new diocese of Portsmouth. The huge diocese of Winchester included the counties of Surrey, Hampshire, the Channel Islands and the Isle of Wight as well as south London. In 1877 south London parishes in east and mid Surrey were separated from the diocese of Winchester and added to the diocese of Rochester and in 1905 became part of the new diocese of Southwark. But the Winchester diocese was still unwieldy. In 1911 its population was over 1.3 million. There were 375 parishes in Hampshire alone and a total of 593 in the diocese. In 1914 the Tennyson Committee set up by the diocesan conference reported in favour of dividing the diocese but it was not sure how to do it – perhaps a Surrey diocese with Croydon as the see city. Portsmouth, it reported, did not want its own bishop and the Archbishop of Canterbury, himself a former bishop of Winchester, was against the division of the diocese.[27]

The war intervened and the matter was put on hold. By now it had been decided to create two new dioceses – Guildford and Portsmouth. Not everybody agreed. There were proposals for a diocese based on Bournemouth with Christchurch Priory as its cathedral. Perhaps the rest of Surrey could simply join the diocese of Southwark. The die was cast, an act of parliament passed in 1924 established the new dioceses and in October 1927 the dioceses of Guildford and Portsmouth came into existence. There was some disagreement about whether St Mary's Portsea or St Thomas's Old Portsmouth should become the cathedral. Portsmouth became a city on 26th April 1927 in keeping with its new dignity as the proposed seat of a bishop.[28]

In Bishop's Waltham there was regret that the link with the diocese of Winchester, which went back over 1000 years, was to be broken. The deanery of Bishop's Waltham lost five parishes which remained in the Winchester diocese. The first bishop of Portsmouth, Neville Lovett, was enthroned on 6th October. On the 8th October a service for children to join in the celebrations was held and Bishop's Waltham Sunday School was represented by ten year old Reg Cockle, Clarence Parsons, Joyce Tier and Kathleen Nicholson. After the service a somewhat sparse tea was provided for the children who sat at bare trestle tables – plates of sandwiches, an apple and orange. But Reg Cockle never forgot the occasion and recalled it vividly when in 2002 the diocese celebrated the 75th anniversary of its formation and he was again a guest at the service to mark the occasion.[29]

The Enabling Act of 1919 created the Church Assembly and took a small step towards self government of the Church of England. More important for most parishes was the creation of Parochial Church Councils (PCC). Many parishes including Bishop's Waltham already had an elected council. Now it was compulsory and the new PCC at St Peter's met for the first time on 6th July 1920. There was also to be a parish Electoral Roll. In order to qualify to join it you had to be baptised and to be a member of the Church of England. This was deliberately left vague and adults who felt themselves members whether or not they attended church regularly were free to join. The first electoral roll had 530 members and the number climbed steadily until 1931 when it reached a peak of 686 a high proportion of the adults in the town and a figure never since reached.[30] The new rector Noel Stubbs returning to Bishop's Waltham where he had been curate before the First World War was disturbed by evidence of smaller church attendances than he had expected which he attributed to 'indifference and laziness'. He brought changes, in particular the mixed chalice and wafers replaced bread at Holy Communion.[31]

Protection against fire remained a parish responsibility. By the late 1920s the Volunteer Fire Brigade needed a new Fire Engine, one which did not have to be towed to the fire by either horse or, more recently, by motor car or lorry, and whose water pump was automatic rather than manual. The impetus may have come from the attendance of the Brigade at the huge fire which completely destroyed Durley Sawmill in 1928. A new engine would also require the enlargement of the Engine House. If a more powerful and costly engine were contemplated it made sense to enlist the support of neighbouring parishes so approaches were made to Curdridge,

Durley, Shedfield, Swanmore and Upham all of which agreed to contribute.

The new Dennis Motor Fire Engine was bought and handed over at a ceremony in the Square on 15th March 1930. The first major fire it tackled was at Jervis Court Farm, Swanmore in June 1933 when four wagons and four petrol lorries as well as other vehicles and buildings were destroyed. The Brigade still owned two old engines, one bought in 1899, the other a vintage model going back to the eighteenth century. It was decided to offer the latter to the Institute 'as an interesting relic of the past'. The Institute declined the offer on the ground of its size, no doubt recollecting that it already had a First World War German field gun among its memorabilia. The old engine was eventually sold for £5. In 1938 the Fire Brigades Act handed over Fire Brigades to the RDC and the parish ceased to have direct responsibility.

Chase Mill remained open and by the inter-war years was producing animal feed. Ronnie Spratt worked at the mill from 1935 when he reached the age of 15 until 1942. He was paid 11/- per week for working from 7am to 5pm except on Saturday when work finished at 1pm. There was no overtime pay and he often had to stay at work to see a consignment finished which might be as late as 10pm. The animal feed was delivered in a 15 cwt. Ford van to farms within a radius of about 20 miles. Ronnie recalls being left alone 'in the big, noisy, splashing, whining, grinding, lifting, dark, dusty mill lit only by candles or the odd hurrricane light'. 'Can you imagine a dark January evening', he wrote, 'the lamps flickering, candles dancing in the wind, shadows everywhere, the only noise my deep breathing and the creaking of the doors in the wind? It's a good job it's time to go home.'[32]

There were bins of wheat, barley and oats, piles of sugar beet, bags of maize, ground nuts, alfalfa, sunflower seed, cotton cake and oyster shell. Each item had to be dragged to the hoist, put through the millstones until all was piled on the mill floor ready to be bagged up for delivery. Ronnie comments that in the years he was working at the mill he never saw a rat. Was it the effectiveness of the six cats belonging to the mill, or perhaps the appetite of the adders which lived in the surrounding fields? There was also a large family of owls in the trees and on the roof of the mill.

The Mill House next door to the mill is a handsome early Georgian building of about 1724 with grey and red brick façade and a porch surrounded by fluted columns and a tributary of the river Hamble flowing through the garden. There were 19 acres of land attached. Arthur Robinson died in 1939. The house was requisitioned during the war and troops camped in the surrounding fields.

The oldest citizens of Bishop's Waltham recall the years between the two wars with nostalgia. Life seemed simpler and the period is often suffused with a golden haze. Amy Harvey who was born in Southampton in June 1901 came to live in Bishop's Waltham in 1921. 'Life was spacious and secure, houses were always left unlocked and the children walked alone' she wrote. She lodged with Mrs Cobbett in Bank Street and worked at the Post Office in High Street which had a staff of postmaster, four clerks and a messenger boy In addition to the normal postal services there was a manual telephone exchange with 31 subscribers, the only public callbox in Bishop's Waltham and you paid for calls over the counter. There was a Morse key for telegrams. Upstairs there was a Labour Exchange. The Post Office opened from 8am to 7pm, as well as Sunday mornings from 9am to 10.30 for stamps and telegrams. Its business included the issue of motor and dog licences as well as the annual licence required to employ a male servant – female servants were tax free. In the late 1920s the telephone exchange moved to what is now called Exchange Cottage in Bank Street and the Morse key was no longer needed.

The town provided its own entertainment. The year was punctuated by a round of social occasions. The Firemen's Ball and the Hospital Ball were the highlights of the year. There was a weekly whist drive at the Institute for older people and a regular dance at the Oddfellows Hall which drew large crowds. On Bonfire Night there was a carnival with floats and fancy dress. The Salvation Army had a band which played in the Square and there was a town band too. During the 1930s an Agricultural Show was held on land close to Ridgemede. The football team was for players and supporters alike, the latter would cycle to away matches all over Hampshire. The Palace cinema at the Oddfellows Hall was a major attraction – nicknamed 'the bug hutch' by irreverent youth. Until about 1930 films were black and white, and silent, accompanied on the piano. The programme was changed twice a week and included a serial to encourage regular attendance.[33]

The Jubilee of King George V in May 1935 and two years later the Coronation of King George VI on 12th May 1937 were both marked appropriately. Jubilee celebrations began with sports and tea for the children held at Ridgemede followed by a carnival procession from Free Street to School Hill where there was a 'confetti battle', bonfire and fireworks followed by dancing in the streets from 10.30 until 1am. The Town Band played continuously from 2pm to 6pm and again from 8pm to 1am. On the previous Sunday there had been a Thanksgiving service held in the parish church in which all denominations joined and uniformed organisations paraded.[34] The parish marked the reign of George V by completing the peal of eight bells with two new ones and a peal was rung to celebrate the event. Empire Day, 24th May was also a significant event. In 1933 for example the children assembled on the Rectory lawn where Colonel Ricketts gave an address on the responsibilities of being a member of the British Empire and the assembled company sang the National Anthem and marched past the flag.[35]

The town boasted three private schools for girls. The Misses Cobbett ran a small school at Folly House (behind the Church Hall). Miss Wright was the headmistress of the school at Lithend in Free Street and Miss Johnson had a school in the Old Grammar school in Portland Square.

Amenities which had been taken for granted in larger towns had only just begun to reach the countryside. The main roads were tarmaced just before the First World War, road signs began to appear and mains water had reached Bishop's Waltham but

95. Miss Wright's school for girls at Lithend House, Free Street, 1920s.

not yet the outlying farms and cottages which still used rain water or depended on wells. Becketts Farm where Amy Harvey's father was born used rain water and if that failed water was drawn up by hand from a well 80 feet deep. Many houses were still lit by oil lamps, the copper was heated by a coal fire, and cooking was on an open range which had to be blackleaded regularly. Few houses had a flush toilet, most relied on either a cess pit or water closet emptied twice a week.

Electricity reached Bishop's Waltham in October 1932. Fred Locke who had a fish shop on the corner of Basingwell Street and Bank Street and was chairman of the Parish Council at the time was the first person whose premises were switched on. He was followed by the premises of Belton and Hall and Freemantles the butchers. In March 1933 *The Grapes* and in March 1934 *The Crown* public houses were lit by electricity. In September 1934 it was the turn of the Congregational Church equipped with electricity in memory of Ernest Gamblin and a bequest enabled St Peter's church likewise to have electric light in February 1935.[36]

There were plenty of small shops. Archers the bakers in Bank Street still used the time honoured method of making bread. Hazelwood bunts were placed in a brick oven to burn. When the oven was hot the ash was swept out and the dough placed in the oven to rise. Baking took place at midnight and the roundsman would deliver

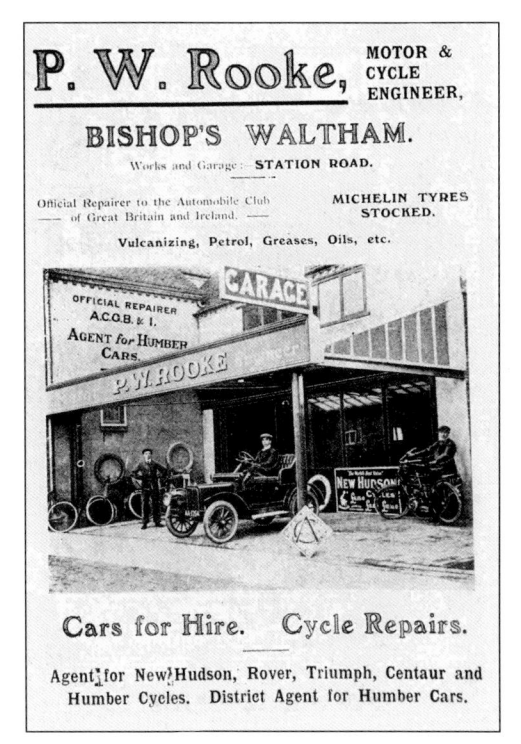

96. Advertising cards for two well known businesses from *Hampshire and the Isle of Wight by pen and camera* 1907.

fresh loaves in the early hours of the morning. Milk was delivered by horse and float and measured from a metal container direct into a jug. The wireless (*sic*) required an accumulator to be recharged weekly.

The surrounding country was still made up predominantly of working farms. Herds of cows making their leisurely way along the lanes from field to farm and farm to field for morning or afternoon milking were a common site. Most farms were mixed, with cattle, sheep, pigs and chickens as well as growing arable crops – barley, wheat and oats. Six times a year there was a cattle sale in the field close to the station where farmers would bring their cattle to be auctioned. When the sale was over the animals could be loaded on to the goods train and transported across the county. For buyers within ten miles radius there were drovers waiting to be hired to accompany the cattle to their new homes.

There were five dairy farms each producing their own milk, cream, butter and eggs for sale in shops in the town or delivered to the door step. Some people made their own cream, allowing the milk to settle, then skimming off the cream, pouring it into a bottle and shaking it until the cream was made. Excess milk was placed in labelled churns and delivered to the station for sale in the towns. One farmer was well known for his milk cart pulled by a temperamental mule which had a habit of stopping dead

97. Bishop's Waltham fire brigade first motor engine 1930.

as soon as it came within sight of the station with the milk train ready to depart. The engine driver would jam on his brakes and wait until the mule was ready to complete its journey and the churns were safely loaded.

The town had been lit by gas since the 1860s but the early burners emitted little more light than a carriage candle. The new gas mantles gave out much more light but were expensive to maintain since they were easily damaged in igniting the lamps. Later incandescent mantles were introduced protected by tubular fireproof glass. Edward Pitman was the last lamplighter in Bishop's Waltham In winter his round began in all weathers at 4pm and lasted until 6pm when the lamps had been lit. At about 10.30 his round began again putting out the lamps and ended at 11.30. He had two nights off per month when there was a full moon and the lamps were not lit. It was not unknown after the lamps had been lit for boys to climb the lamp standards, extinguish the light and chase after the lamplighter shouting :'You're lamp's out mister'. The game ended abruptly when the schoolmaster on his way home one night saw the malefactors at work and dealt with them appropriately.[37]

20

The Second World War and after 1939–1965

UNLIKE THE First World War, which came out of a clear sky, the storm clouds of the Second World War were gathering for several years before war broke out. From at least 1935 there was widespread foreboding that another war with Germany was inevitable. As early as July 1937 the RDC asked the Parish Council to appoint Air Raid Wardens.[1] In September 1938 war seemed imminent. At the Priory the boys who had just returned for the Autumn term received gas masks and spent two days digging trenches to provide emergency air raid shelters. They were joined by 100 pupils from Finchley Grammar School in expectation of the outbreak of war.[2] The Munich settlement postponed the inevitable. In July 1939 with war once more looming the Parish Council suggested drawing up a list of ARP workers and billeting officers, First Aid posts and buildings which could if necessary be requisitioned and the use for which they might be suitable.[3] There was almost a sense of relief when war was actually declared on Sunday 3rd September.

The government believed that the First World War and the more recent Spanish Civil War provided indications of what sort of war it would be. The civilian population would be involved from the start, there would be immediate and devastating bombing of major cities and poison gas might well be used on civilians as it had been on soldiers in the trenches in the First World War. The country must be prepared. Gas masks had been issued in September 1938, in Bishop's Waltham from the Drill Hall in Newtown. Detailed plans for the evacuation of schools were made and young men were urged to enlist in the reserves. A siren used to announce an imminent air raid or to signal the 'all clear' was erected on the Fire Station in Station Road.

On Friday and Saturday 1st and 2nd September 1939, 200 children and some parents arrived from Gosport to be billeted in Bishop's Waltham. The disruption delayed the start of the Autumn term at the schools and when it did begin buildings had to be shared with the Gosport schools – Brockhurst and Grove Road – residents and evacuees each working for half a day. But no bombs rained down and by the end of September the novelty of life in the countryside had worn off, to be succeeded by boredom and homesickness. Evacuees began to drift home. The Parish Magazine in

October warned 'We do think it is very short-sighted of many who have already returned to their home in Gosport. They should instead stay here where they are comparatively safe'.[4]

Blackout was imposed at once and strictly enforced by police and Air Raid Wardens. The parish church could not be blacked out so the evening service during the winter months took place at 3pm. School could not be made compulsory until air raid shelters were provided. When the siren sounded the boys' school in Free Street used the cellars of the *Mafeking Hero* but there were no shelters at the infants and girls school at Newtown. The Education Authority maintained that the building itself was sufficiently safe.[5] At Christmas 1939 the town sent each soldier from Bishop's Waltham serving in France a gift of cigarettes paid for by collections and the profits from Whist Drives.[6]

On two occasions during the war Bishop's Waltham was in the front line – in the summer of 1940 and again in the run-up to D Day in 1944. After the evacuation of the British Expeditionary Force from Dunkirk in June 1940 the Germans planned Operation Sealion, an invasion of England across the channel. If a landing were successful Hampshire would be an early target. All over the country the threat of invasion was taken seriously and resistance prepared. Tank traps and pill boxes were built, stop lines constructed and road blocks installed. In the summer of 1940 units of the Royal Engineers arrived in Bishop's Waltham from their depot at Chard, travelling by train as far as Romsey and marching to Bishop's Waltham. They set up a temporary tented camp, clearing the weeds and brambles from the grounds of the Palace. Eventually a Sergeants' Mess was opened at Claylands House, billets were provided by the White Fathers at the Priory and various locations in the town were commandeered for offices and headquarters. If invasion took place the Royal Engineers would ensure that Bishop's Waltham was impregnable. They set up road blocks on all the approaches to the town and at night these were manned, motorists were stopped and questioned about their identity and destination.[7]

Something of the urgency of those anxious days is conveyed by the fragment of War Diaries for August and September 1940 kept by 18 Field Park Company, Royal Engineers then stationed at Bishop's Waltham found in the War Office records at the Public Record Office at Kew:

> *Saturday 10th – Sunday 11th August* Erection of road blocks on the Wickham Road. This required the closure of the road whilst the work progressed. The weekend was chosen so as to disrupt transport as little as possible.
> *Monday 12th* – Unit witnesses action over Portsmouth and/or Southampton. … Scouting parties sent out to mount guard on crashed aircraft. …
> *Tuesday 13th* – Brickworks bombed by Heinkel iiiB.
> *Wednesday 14th* – Road blocks now established at Mafeking Hero and Winchester Road.
> *Thursday 15th* – Road parties find crashed Hurricane. Pilot was taken to Unit

Dressing Station and thence to Winchester hospital. At 2030 hours Sapper Withers reported Junkers 88 down at Morestead.
Sunday 25th – 1230 hours Bombs on Bishop's Waltham to Botley railway.
Monday 26th – Friday 30th LDV [Local Defence Volunteers later Home Guard] join Royal Engineers at road blocks round village.
Saturday 7th September – 'Cromwell' order received – manned Ops round village.[Cromwell meant invasion considered imminent.] Three bridges in and near Bishop's Waltham prepared for blowing.
Friday 20th – Stand Down [from Cromwell]
Wednesday 20th November – Air Raid on town.[8]

At the Priory it was decided not to open for the Autumn term in 1940. The building was requisitioned and until the end of 1944 service contingents were billeted there. The first to arrive in September 1940 was a detachment of REME who had been evacuated from Dunkirk. Next came an infantry unit which trained on the school field, followed by the Royal Engineers. The gymnasium became a social centre for the district. From 1942 onwards a small number of boys returned but the school was not fully in operation again until 1945.[9]

Anti-aircraft batteries were set up in Pondside Lane and Peake Copse and an ammunition dump in fields behind Coppice Hill. American soldiers were stationed at Preshaw and Hazelholt. The Royal Observer Corps used the tower of St Peter's church to keep a look out for enemy aircraft and their aircraft recognition chart is still on the wall of the ringing chamber as a reminder of those momentous days.

Bishop's Waltham also played its part in the 'secret' war, though not much was known about it at the time. The Royal Engineers' skill was enlisted to build hangars at the secret airfield at Marwell, not marked on any map, from which women pilots flew Lysanders, Mustangs and Tomahawks, taking secret agents to enemy occupied Europe. At Buryfield Farm at the top of Beeches Hill was a radio station which fed information to Bletchley Park, the requisitioned country house in Northamptonshire at which enemy codes were decrypted and which played such a crucial part in the achievement of victory. Mill House on Waltham Chase was requisitioned at the outbreak of war and was linked to the wireless interception station at Buryfield farm. In the summer of 1944 a V1 Rocket landed on the Mill House site killing or seriously injuring 17 of the soldiers stationed there and leaving a huge crater.

In June 1943 75 Italian prisoners captured at Tobruk and El Alamein arrived in Bishop's Waltham and were accommodated in a hutted camp in the fields between Albany Road and the Tollgate timber mill. Each Sunday they were marched with only minimal guard to the Priory for Mass and in the afternoon returned to play football. But Bishop's Waltham was no Colditz and the prisoners showed no inclination to escape and rejoin Mussolini's war. Life might be austere and monotonous but it was preferable to the battlefield and they were fed adequately and treated humanely. They were taken out each day to work on local farms and returned each night to their Nissen huts. In May 1944 they were given the option of returning to rejoin Italian forces now fighting on the allied side but preferred to stay in Bishop's Waltham and were now free to move about the town[10]

Later German prisoners were sent to Bishop's Waltham and were kept until 1947 to repair bomb damage and to help on farms where labour was scarce.

For almost six years the war was uppermost in the minds of all, from school pupils to pensioners, as well as those who joined the armed forces. From January 1940 food was rationed, at first only bacon, butter and sugar but later many other foodstuffs and clothes. The Food Office was at the Institute and ration books were issued from there for Bishop's Waltham and the surrounding villages. What was called 'The Home Front', was an aspect of war to which all contributed. In the winter of 1940 – 41 there were heavy German air raids on Portsmouth and Southampton: 'We watched the sky turn red as Southampton burned', recalled Amy Harvey.[11] In December 1940 the Church Hall, requisitioned earlier in the war, was used by 50 refugees made homeless by the bombing of Southampton. They were later found temporary billets in the surrounding villages.[12]

There was relief that the expected invasion did not materialise. As the rector wrote in January 1941, 'Six months ago there seemed the chance that England, like most European countries, might feel the weight of the aggressor's boot'.[13] So Bishop's Waltham settled down to the routine of a war which would last almost six years. The boys' school obtained the use of a field and set to work to 'Dig for Victory'. The Scouts collected waste paper and stored it in the stables at Northbrook House. The Guides resumed meetings but gathered in three groups in case of an air raid. They gardened, collected waste paper, made camouflage nets and wound packs. The Women's Voluntary Service (WVS) ran a canteen for servicemen and women each evening at the Institute.

ARP (Air Raid Precautions) had its headquarters in the dining room at the Rectory. Bishop's Waltham had its own Dad's Army commanded by Major C.V. Lanyon of Eastway House, a veteran of the First World War, assisted by Captain Nuttall and Lieutenant Billy Woods, which met in the Elms Hut in Malt Lane and used the Drill Hall in Newtown. Everybody took part in *Wings for Victory* Week in June 1943 when the town aimed to buy a Lancaster bomber for £40,000 and succeeded in raising £32,000. Each event was accompanied by a church parade however incongruous it might seem, for example for *Warship Week* in March 1943.

The Womens' Institute too was mobilised for war. In January 1940 members were reminded that in future they would have to bring their own sugar to meetings. Mrs Portal 'impressed upon members the need to produce all the food possible in village gardens'. The meeting in September 1940 was held in the Rectory garden and was broken up by the appearance of enemy planes overhead and the performance of a play was abandoned after act one. Members knitted for the troops of the Hampshire Regiment and made up parcels for prisoners of war. More knitters were needed. (13th November 1940). At the meeting in January 1941 Major Lanyon, CO of the Home

98. Civil Defence Workers marching to St Peter's for *Warship Week* service March 1943.

Guard, explained how to use a stirrup pump and Mr Bishop 'gave some useful information on dealing with incendiary bombs'[14]

There was a weekly dance for servicemen stationed in Bishop's Waltham to which local girls were invited, whilst some of the larger bases held their own dances and supplied transport to and from the camp to provide partners for the troops. When American soldiers arrived some were black, at that time organised in segregated units. For many people in Bishop's Waltham they were the first black people they had ever seen. At one often recalled dance, held in the Church Hall, an American Negro Jazz Band was scheduled to play. The crowd was so great that dancing was impossible and instead an enthralled audience enjoyed a unique experience listening to the band.

British and American soldiers, Italian and German prisoners and evacuees from Gosport were not the only newcomers to Bishop's Waltham during the war. Some came to escape bombing in Southampton and stayed. In October 1940 after prolonged heavy bombing of the city Austin and Elsie Chamberlain decided that Southampton was no place in which to bring up eight children during the war and a move to the country was essential even though Austin worked at Hamble and would have a long journey to work. After exploring briefly they settled on Bishop's

99. Admiral Andrew Cunningham 1942.

Waltham and, equipped only with a handcart for their belongings and bicycles for the family, they set out, reaching Bishop's Waltham at dusk. They were given temporary accommodation at a house in Lower Basingwell Street and gratefully slept that night on the floor. They were able soon afterwards to rent Folly House in Free Street with ample space for a large family and settled down in Bishop's Waltham for the duration of the war – and long after. When Austin returned to Southampton it was to find that their house had been gutted by incendiary bombs and their remaining belongings looted.[15]

Andrew Browne Cunningham, Admiral of the Fleet and First Sea Lord during the Second World War, was the most renowned national figure to live in Bishop's Waltham since the middle ages. He and his wife Nona leased the Palace House from Sir Walter Jenner when they returned from serving in the Mediterranean in June 1936 and, as far as service life allowed, it was their home for almost 30 years.[16] Regular visits to Bishop's Waltham in the later years of the war gave Admiral Cunningham much appreciated respite from the pressures of London and the war. He would drive down on Saturday afternoon, garden vigorously and return to London in his Bentley on Sunday afternoon.[17] At Churchill's insistence a scrambler telephone was installed at Palace House so that the First Sea Lord could receive confidential calls at any time.[18] Bishop's Waltham was conveniently close to Southwick House where General Eisenhower established the Supreme Headquarters Allied Expeditionary Force (SHAEF) in preparation for the allied invasion of Europe in 1944. In the run-up to D Day Admiral Bertram Ramsey the Chief of Naval Operations was a frequent visitor to the Palace House for lunch or dinner.[19]

Nobody living in this part of Hampshire in the spring of 1944 can have doubted that the long expected allied invasion of the European continent was imminent, what the historian G.M.Trevelyan described as 'the Second Battle of Britain'.[20] Every road, lane and lay-by was occupied by military vehicles – tanks, lorries, guns, jeeps, ambulances and amphibious landing craft. There was even an ENSA unit (Entertainments National Service Association) to maintain the morale of troops waiting for Operation Overlord to begin. King George VI, Winston Churchill, General Smuts and General De Gaulle visited General Eisenhower's headquarters at Southwick House in the early days of June 1944 and spent a night in a siding on the Meon Valley railway.

Late on the 5th June the sky was full of aircraft, some towing gliders, all showing navigation lights. Next morning there was more movement and the troops and vehicles disappeared from the lanes towards the coast and across to the Normandy beaches. Radio broadcasts confirmed that the Second Front had begun. These were days which nobody who was living at that time will ever forget. Bill Drake, stationed at HMS Kestrel at Worthy Down recalled seeing 'the vast Armada of ships in Southampton Water, a truly memorable sight'.[21]

Not all Bishop's Waltham's citizens were spectators on D Day, some were participants. Among these Ron Paterson (later ordained and Vicar of Swanmore from 1962–85) was a Beachmaster on Juno Beach, George Bladon landed on Gold Beach and Bert Gee on Sword Beach whilst Hugh Knollys was on board HMS Harrier off Sword Beach. Some spent D Day in other theatres of war. Alf Bowers was in a prisoner of war camp in Thailand, Reg Cockle likewise a prisoner but of the Germans, spent D Day on a farm in Austria ploughing with two horses watched over by a German guard whilst John Humphreys was at Monte Casino in Italy taking part in one of the most keenly fought and bloody battles of this last phase of the war. Les Powell was a fire-fighter in the naval dockyard in Portsmouth. All now in their eighties recall D Day vividly as though it were yesterday.[22]

By 1943 the tide had turned. Church bells were rung for the first time since 1939 at Easter that year. In October 1944 black-out was abandoned; night raids were no longer a threat and Evensong at St Peter's went back to 6.30 pm. At Christmas 1944 greetings and a present of a 10/- note were sent to each of the 335 men of Bishop's Waltham serving in the services of whom 150 were abroad.[23]

The war with Germany ended on Tuesday 8th May 1945 – VE Day –Victory in Europe Day. At 3pm a service was held in St George's Square which was decked with flags and bunting, and at 8pm St Peter's was full for a service of thanksgiving. That night there were bonfires all over the town. From their vantage point high above the town the boys at the Priory enjoyed a huge bonfire around which they sang far into the night. As it got dark they could see the searchlight displays and other bonfires twinkling in the night sky.[24] On the following days there were street parties and plans were made for Welcome Home gifts and celebrations for returning service men and women.

In the New Years Honours list in 1946 Andrew Cunningham, in common with the other Second World War service chiefs – Tedder and Portal – was made a Viscount. He retired later that year at the age of 63 and led an active life at Bishop's Waltham with frequent visits to London and further afield.[25] The Cunninghams were enthusiastic gardeners, played croquet, owned dogs, cats, geese and poultry and took an annual fishing holiday in Sutherland. They had a living-in gardener, cook and house maids. Andrew Cunningham died in his 81st year in June 1963 and was buried at sea. Nona, Lady Cunningham left Palace House and moved to Beeches Hill. She remained active in the Red Cross and in St Peter's church until her death in 1978.[26] Meanwhile in 1974 the west end of the north aisle of St Peter's church was designated

The Admiral's Corner in honour of Bishop's Waltham's most distinguished citizen of modern times.

In the town thoughts were turning to the future, to 'post-war reconstruction'. As early as April 1943, a full two years before the end of the war, the Parish Council was asked to compile a wish list for the post-war town. There would, thought the Council, be need for 16 houses for agricultural workers built near the farms where they were employed and others to replace cottages now 'unfit for habitation'. Piped water should be extended to remote parts of the parish still dependent on wells or pumps. The collection of house refuse should be improved and a sewage disposal scheme implemented. The town would lend itself to the development of light industry. Gas and electricity should be available to all. Finally the town needed a central recreation area where organised games could be played and a hall to seat up to 500 people where drama could take place. Post-war idealism was as characteristic of Bishop's Waltham as it was of so many places in town and country and as hard to translate into reality.[27]

Despite victory the country was slow to recover from the war. Rationing continued for no less than nine years after the war and some shortages actually got worse. Not until the summer of 1954 was rationing finally ended. In July 1946 the Parish Council agreed to undertake the distribution of 'gift parcels' of food from 'the Dominions and Colonies'[28] They decided that the most needy were those with a 'single ration book' – those living on their own – and they made a list of 64 recipients. Each was to receive tins of jam and meat, raisins and an allocation of fat. One hundred pounds of fat had to be cut up and 18 lbs of raisins weighed and bagged into 2 oz. packets. Each person would also receive one other item – chosen from canned beans, carrots, beetroot, pineapple and honey. Nor was this a one-off gift. For several years the distribution of food parcels from the Dominions was a regular item on the agenda of the Parish Council.

The year 1945 was a landmark in the history of the Parish Council. After 50 years it saw the appointment of the first woman councillor. Women had been eligible for election to parish councils since their inception, half a century earlier, but few had successfully stormed this male bastion. As late as 1935 only 3% of councillors nationally were women. At its meeting on 28th January 1943 the Bishop's Waltham Council received a letter from the local branch of the Women's Institute asking with amazing restraint that in future at least one councillor – out of twelve members of the Council – should be a woman. The point was taken. When the next cooptative vacancy occurred in May 1945 Mrs Henry Smith (sic) of Coppice Hill was elected. She served on the Council for less than a year but at the next elections in 1946 two women were among the successful candidates – Mrs Gunner and Mrs H. Storey and in 1948 Hilda Storey became the first woman chairman of the Council. Nationally the picture changed slowly. By 1966 only 13 % of councillors were women and by 1991 27%.[29]

But this was not the only sign of progress and greater professionalism. From April

100. The Mill Pond and the Mill on the Chase.

1945 the Council met monthly instead of quarterly. In 1947 the clerk asked for a typewriter for correspondence. By 1949 members resolved to have minutes – still handwritten – duplicated and circulated and so to eliminate the longwinded procedure of reading minutes at the beginning of each meeting.

After the war some Italian prisoners remained in England and settled in Bishop's Waltham including Carmelo Jacobucci and Angelo Arigo They were related to each other and their friendship led to an extraordinary and moving love story. Carmelo who came originally from Iquila san Pio in northern Italy worked at Hill Farm, Botley. One Sunday he was invited to lunch by Angelo and Stellina, his wife who had recently joined him from Italy. Shown family photographs 30 year old Carmelo was at once attracted by Gilda the niece of Stellina, one of six daughters from a poor home at Monjana, Calabria in southern Italy. Carmelo asked permission to write to 23 year old Gilda and, since she had not been to school and could not read or write, her aunt read his letters and wrote her replies. Carmelo and Gilda fell in love without ever having met and decided to marry. They did so with papal permission in two simultaneous ceremonies, one in Gilda's home village in Calabria and the other at the Priory in Bishop's Waltham on 16th October 1951.

Just before Christmas Gilda set off to join her husband in England accompanied as far as Rome by her father and brother. Carmelo was to meet her in Paris and arrived with presents for his new wife, but through a mix-up of dates they missed each other and Carmelo returned to England alone. Gilda with the help of sympathetic fellow travellers found her own way to Waterloo station and then to the obscure little town of Bishop's Waltham in Hampshire. Travelling by ferry and train she eventually reached Botley station where an ancient taxi took her to Hill Farm. Carmelo was working in the fields on that cold, dark December afternoon and the taxi driver set out to find him. 'I saw my husband coming across the fields towards me carrying a tilly lamp.' she wrote. They were united and the tilly lamp is among Gilda's most precious possessions to this day.

Gilda and Carmelo had two sons Nicky and Johnny both of whom live nearby. Carmelo subsequently went to work in the Claylands brickyard and when it closed was employed by Pirelli in Eastleigh for 29 years. Gilda worked at the Priory and later was house keeper to a succession of Roman Catholic priests and in 2001 was awarded a papal medal for her work. Meantime they had moved to Albert Road where Gilda still lives – a keen Anglophile with a strong Italian accent – the subject of a recent television programme about her life.[30]

In October 1948 Noel Stubbs who had been rector since 1931 moved to the smaller and less demanding parish of Soberton. His successor was Frank Sargeant. The new rector had read history at Cambridge in the 1920s and was a keen local historian. Drawing on information collected by Admiral Dampier in the 1930s and by Admiral of the Fleet Lord Cunningham more recently he wrote a series of articles for the

101. Aerial photographs c.1938 a) The Palace in the foreground and Coppice Hill brickyard in the background. b) Palace and Pond in the foreground, also includes the railway station.

Parish Magazine which he made into three booklets on the history of the church, the palace, and the town of Bishop's Waltham which together constituted the first history of the parish since the lecture given by Charles Walters over a century earlier.

We also owe to Frank Sargeant two of the best loved Christmas services at St Peter's. In December 1949 he introduced Midnight Communion. Five years later came the Service of Nine Lessons and Carols, an increasingly popular service in all denominations held originally after Christmas so as not to affect the observance of Advent.[31]

Frank Sargeant was a keen Scout. Early in his ministry he revived the Scout troop of which he became Scoutmaster and each year accompanied the troop to camp. The church was a flourishing one. There was a strong Sunday School and youth club, boys joined the choir in some numbers and in 1951 there were 35 confirmation candidates. In 1962 the electoral roll was still 484. The rector brought with him from Southsea Deaconess Mary Taylor who remained in the parish and lived at the rectory throughout his ministry.

Towards the end of Frank Sargeant's ministry the future of the rectory came up for discussion. As early as 1913 Hugh Rycroft had felt that it was too large and too grand for a modern rector.[32] In 1931 Noel Stubbs, returning as rector to a parish where he had been curate 20 years earlier, realised that the house was too big for the needs of a twentieth century parson and had the ancient kitchen quarters and the rooms above pulled down leaving only four staff bedrooms.[33] The house was still a substantial one with ample grounds. It was too large for a family no longer able to employ servants. Heating costs were prohibitive and the upkeep of a large garden not possible without help. It was decided to sell the land for housing and to build a modern rectory in the grounds which would be occupied by Frank Sargeant's successor.

What was life like for a boy growing up in Bishop's Waltham during the war and reaching manhood in the years following? Don Cole was a well known figure in the town, one of the village postmen from 1956 until he retired in 1990. He was born in Basingwell Street – Nurse Jarman the midwife for no less than 40 years cycling through a thunder storm to be there in time – and still lives there though in a different house. One of his early memories is the scarlet fever epidemic of 1934 when half the town seemed to be infected with what in the days before antibiotics was a life threatening disease. They were taken by ambulance to the Treloar Isolation Hospital at Alton.

Don transferred from the Infant School on the Hill to the boys' school at Dodd's Alley in 1937 and here he stayed until he left school in 1944. He recalls 'Tinker' Blunden, the headmaster and Mr Peterson who wore plus-fours, had an old motor-bike and was a 'really good teacher' from whom Don learnt much. There were three classes covering the whole age range from 7 to 14 with an average of 35 in each class. Physical Training, as it was then called, took place only when the weather was fine

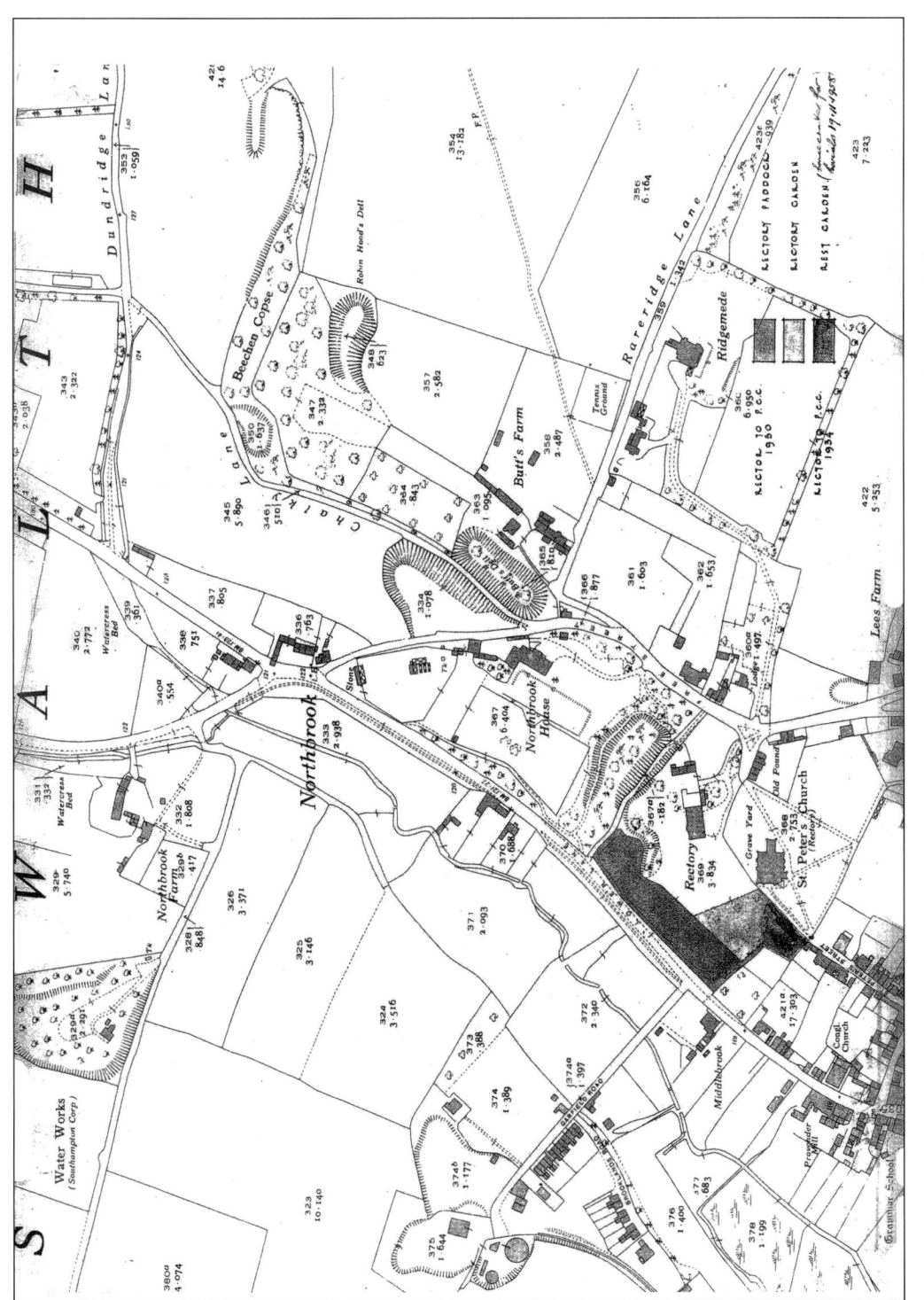

102. The Rectory and Northbrook House c.1958. Rectory land bordering on Lower Lane was then intended as an extension to the graveyard, later sold for houses. Also shows Ridgemede House with drive from Free Street.

with pupils wearing school clothes and outdoor shoes. 'Gardening' was on the curriculum on a patch of land off the footpath between the Rectory and Lower Lane.

When war came all had to carry gas masks and if the siren sounded the school was evacuated to the cellars of *The Mafeking Hero* where in the half light boys would while away the time consuming beer purloined from the pub stock. Don recalls the arrival of evacuees bombed out in the raids on Southampton in the winter of 1940–41 with little more than the clothes they stood up in. The school was overcrowded and the Church Hall next door took the overflow. He remained at the Dodd's Alley school until he reached the school leaving age which was then 14.

He left school in the 'Doodle bug' summer of 1944 and went to work at Vecks in the High Street to learn the boot repair trade, a shop at which he had been working after school since he was 13. He earned the princely sum of 11/- per week. Determined to improve his income he became at the age of 17 a milkman at Wickham where he started work at 5am. And there he stayed until he was called up for National Service joining the Royal Engineers at Aldershot for 'square bashing' and trade training. He spent the remainder of his 18 months service in North Africa returning to be demobbed in 1950.

As both a school boy and youth Don played football for Bishop's Waltham. The club had no headquarters and no changing facilities. Teams played at Pondside Farm in the field next to the gasometer on Saturday afternoons erecting their own goalposts and net and then trying to avoid the cowpats. He, like other contemporaries, remembers the 'bucket men' calling twice a week The dentist worked from home in Bank Street as did the doctors – no group practice nor purpose built surgeries in those days. The doctor was also prepared to remove a loose or bad tooth, quickly even if not entirely painlessly. Don was one of the regulars at 'the bug hutch', the affectionate nickname for the Palace cinema, where 7d. was sufficient to buy a ticket and where during the war a red or green light indicated whether or not the air raid siren had sounded.

Soon after returning from National Service Don Cole joined the Fire Service, then commanded by Godfrey Pink, and remained a member until he retired in 1985 and was awarded the British Empire Medal. He was what was called a 'retained fireman', meaning that if a fire broke out he was called by siren or house bells to the Fire Station behind the *White Swan* in Basingwell Street and later to the new fire station in Lower Lane. (When he was a boy firemen were called by the firing of a maroon at the fire station then in Station Road) In the mid-1950s he became a postman and cycled 32 miles delivering letters twice a day to the outskirts of the town In those days there were two deliveries each day so no sooner had he completed the first delivery than he was off again, this time also collecting the mail from country letter boxes. Not until the early 1970s was Bishop's Waltham allocated vans which made life much easier.[34]

In the 1950s Bishop's Waltham seemed to be facing a series of problems which it had no means of solving. It needed a transformation such as had been achieved in the

103. Demolition of last brickworks chimney (130 feet high) Claylands July 1958.

1860s under the stimulus of Arthur Helps when the railway, the brick works and the gas works had all opened within a short time of each other and the new suburb of Newtown had been built. Bishop's Waltham had then become – if only briefly – a vibrant, forward looking town.

The plight of the town at the mind-point of the twentieth century was highlighted by an article published in the picture magazine *Illustrated* in April 1953.[35] It was occasioned by the closure of Gunner's Bank on the retirement of Robin Gunner and was headed provocatively *Town that is dying*. 'Young people who live in Britain's small towns are apt to complain that these days such towns are dying on their feet.' said the writer, who continued, 'That unfortunately is exactly what seems to be happening to Bishop's Waltham in Hampshire and nobody can do anything to stop it'. In addition to the closure of the bank the writer pointed out that the brewery (in Lower Lane) and the mill (at the Chase) had recently closed, the town's ambulance had been withdrawn and so had the local fire brigade. The County Court was no longer held at Bishop's Waltham. Shops were for sale and there seemed to be an air of resignation. 'Thus a town which was thriving in the time of the first Elizabeth faces disintegration at the beginning of the reign of the second Elizabeth.'

What should the Parish Council do? 'Stand on its dignity and ignore the report', said one. 'Call a town meeting', suggested a second. It was decided to invite the writer of the article to a meeting of the Parish Council. The features editor of *Illustrated* replied to the clerk's letter saying that the piece had been written by a freelance writer to whom the letter had been forwarded. Not surprisingly the author chose not to enter the lion's den and with Coronation celebrations in the offing nothing further was heard of this storm in an Elizabethan teacup.[36]

Despite the righteous indignation of the Council and the town, the 1950s were a watershed decade in the history of Bishop's Waltham. Within a few years the brickworks at Claylands and Coppice Hill had both closed down, goods traffic dwindled and the railway line was finally closed in 1962. The cinema closed too. The town still had no mains sewerage and there were constant complaints of overflowing cesspits. Motor traffic was in danger of throttling the town. Buses and cars choked the High Street and there was still no provision for off-street parking in the centre. Provision of a bus station, a public convenience and a meeting place were still on the agenda of the Parish Council. Bishop's Waltham was one of the very few places in the entire country where education was still in all age schools.[37] The town needed radical change but few can have anticipated how radical it would be.

21

Growth and renewal since 1965

WHEN DAVID LLOYD wrote the entry on Bishop's Waltham for the Hampshire volume of the Pevsner *Buildings of England* series in 1965 he described the town unflatteringly. 'It has the atmosphere of a half stranded town in, say, Shropshire, rather than of a place easily accessible from twentieth century Southampton and Portsmouth', he wrote. He concluded his piece 'Much of Bishop's Waltham gives one the impression that decay is incipient if not imminent; whole stretches of street frontage look as if they will not last much longer… the traffic problems thanks to the extreme narrowness of the streets and the frequency of right-angle corners, seem to be even more acute than usual … The town has belatedly to come to terms with the twentieth century'.[1] The theme of this final chapter is rejuvenation and expansion so that, however justified David Lloyd's strictures may have been in 1965, they are no longer even remotely appropriate. Bishop's Waltham has come to terms with the twentieth century and successfully entered the twenty-first. It is a very different place from the town which he castigated in the 1960s.

There was a price to be paid and not all Bishop's Waltham residents, particularly the older ones, believe it was worth it. Between 1965 and 1970 the topography of the town changed more than it had done at any time since it was first laid out in the twelfth century. The planners had in mind two related objects: first to create space for the parking of cars which were threatening to stifle the town and second to provide a by-pass so that the increasing number of vehicles passing through no longer need enter the town centre itself. The problem was acute, the solution drastic.

Almost all the town's main streets were narrow, adequate for pedestrians, cyclists and horse drawn vehicles but unfit for motor cars. It was said for example that the occupants of a car travelling down Houchin Street could touch the houses on each side. Brook Street was narrow too particularly at its southern end where the 'river of the lord' still ran. As long ago as 1917 premises in Cross Street were so badly damaged by a lorry attempting to round the corner that they had to be demolished.

Space must be cleared for a car park and the decision was made that this should be as near the centre of the town as possible. The solution involved the demolition of almost the whole of Houchin Street, much of the west side of Basingwell Street and Red Lion Street including some houses which were of historic and architectural interest and a townscape which had lifelong associations for many as well as some houses which had reached the end of their useful life. They were small and damp; some still depended on wells for water, none had bathrooms or indoor toilets. To the planners the solution was obvious. To those who had lived for many years in this close knit community it was less so. They were nonetheless rehoused in modern houses on the newly built Ridgemede estate. The west side of Brook Street too was demolished in 1963, 'the river of the lord' was placed in a culvert and new houses built further from the street. Demolition revealed timber-framed houses some first built in the sixteenth century.

The by-pass meant new roads round the west and north of the town. The road from Wickham which until now had entered the town at *The Crown* corner and left from St George's Square, would in future avoid the town altogether, sweeping through the outer court of the Bishop's Palace involving the destruction of its historic barn. Initial surveys showed 17 feet of mud so a foundation of brushwood was built and allowed to settle before the road was built across what had once been the ten acre Bishop's pond dividing it into two separate ponds, one of which soon became derelict. A large traffic island was built where the railway station had stood and led to a new road round the north of the pond to connect with Lower Lane which was realigned to meet the Corhampton road. Whereas once all through traffic was obliged to enter the town, now the only people who need come into the town centre were those who wished to use shops, post office or banks in the High Street and surrounding streets. Everybody else could avoid the centre altogether.

There are two fundamental facts about Bishop's Waltham in the last 40 years of the twentieth century which are cause and effect of each other. The first is the provision at long last of mains sewerage. This essential amenity so long postponed was at last provided in the mid-1960s. Without it the growth in population which took place from the 1960s is inconceivable. In those years the population more than doubled, from under 3000 in 1961 to 6538 in 2001, 6747 by 2007, and grew far faster than at any time in the whole history of the town (see Appendix B). By the year 2000 at least half the population of the town were newcomers since the 1960s with roots elsewhere in the country. Some came to retire, others because Bishop's Waltham was an attractive place to live and they could easily commute to work in Winchester, Fareham, Southampton, Eastleigh or Portsmouth or in a few cases London. The pace of expansion is slackening but in the first decade of the twenty first century new housing developments are still springing up on vacant plots

There has as a result been a transformation in the nature of Bishop's Waltham unequalled in all its long history. Yet the town remains cohesive. Families who have lived locally for generations, or even centuries and newcomers both feel loyal to the town and prepared to take part in its life and activities. But there has been a price to pay. The obvious changes were the new by-pass road and the town centre car park which took an inordinate time to complete. Demolition began in 1965 and the new road and the town centre car park were not in place until the early 1970s. The site of

104. Aerial photograph of reconstruction in progress 1966. Central area has been cleared for a car park. Building of road across the pond, traffic island and new Corhampton Road in progress.

the proposed central car park looked for over five years, in the words of John Bosworth, 'like a gigantic bomb site', an image which resonated with the generation which recognised it from the Second World War.[2]

There were other less noticeable but in the longer run equally significant changes. Houses which may not have been ancient or architecturally distinguished but had earned a place in the history of the town were demolished and their once extensive

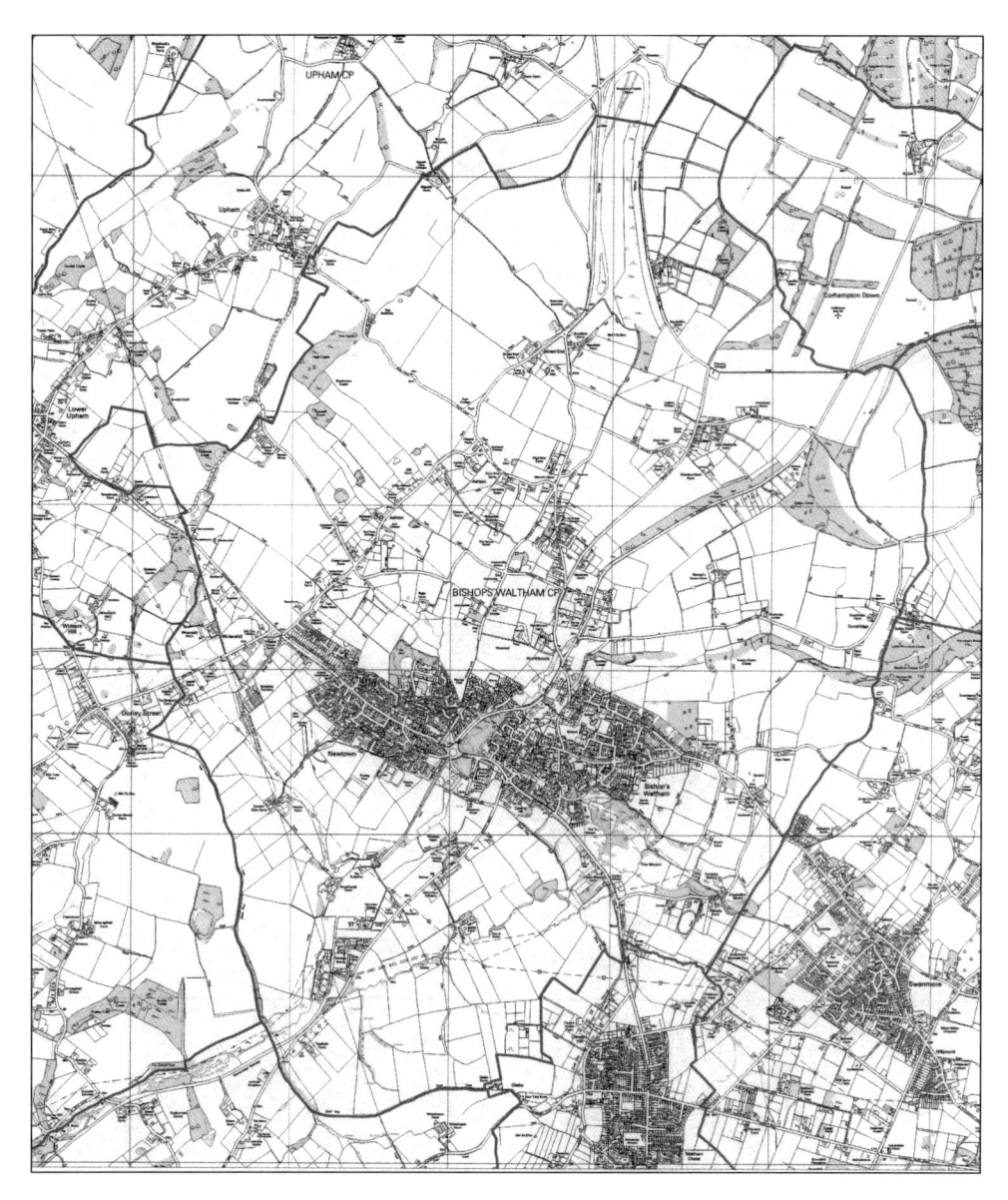

105. Boundaries of the parish of Bishop's Waltham after the 1967 adjustment.

gardens and grounds built on. The greatest losses included The Priory, built as a hospital, more recently a Roman Catholic seminary and then a police training centre, Claylands House the distinctive if eccentric house built by Mark Henry Blanchard, Mount House in Little Shore Lane, Eastway House, replaced by a housing estate, and Holm Oak with historic associations with Gunners bank in whose grounds Roman Row and Malvern Drive were built. The United Reformed church in Lower

Lane was a vast Victorian edifice which lay across the road from the equally large Duke's Mill. The church was replaced by the Bishop's Waltham doctors' surgery and car park; Duke's Mill made way for a housing estate which tried vainly to retain architectural echopes from the lost mill building.

Some large houses survived but were no longer private. Northbrook House had since 1937 been the headquarters of the Droxford Rural District Council. In 1974 the RDCs of Droxford and Winchester were united to form Winchester City Council. Northbrook House was no longer needed and became the offices of a firm of civil engineeers. After several years when it was empty it was bought by a firm of developers and at the beginning of the new century became the centrepiece of a substantial development of 30 houses and flats.

Ridgemede, an elegant late Victorian mansion built by C.R.Gunner in 1897, now provides sheltered accommodation for elderly people and its extensive grounds have given the name Ridgemede to an estate of over 300 houses and bungalows, as well as the newly built Ridgemede Junior School and Bishop's Waltham Infant School. A few of the prominent houses have survived as private residences. Vernon Hill House in Ashton, The Thickets in Botley Road, Palace House close to the former Bishops' Palace and the Rectory (though now the Old Rectory and no longer the home of the rector of Bishop's Waltham), are examples. Houses in St Peter's Street too are largely unaltered and the street continues to be a pleasant approach to the parish church.

Some changes are harder to catalogue. Bishop's Waltham has lost what Trevor Harvey, then chairman of the newly formed Bishop's Waltham Society, described in 1986 as its 'quality of cosy enclosure.'[3] Streets have been widened and straightened. Traffic roundabouts have been created – where the railway station stood, where the Wickham Road enters the town and at the Hoe Road end of Crickelmede. In a number of places the line of the road has for safety reasons been curved so that roads no longer meet each other across a main road – Garfield Road and Lower Lane, Free Street and Corhampton Road and Wintershill and Ashton Lane are examples. Kerb stones and pavements are needed for safety but create a suburban rather than a rural ambience.

Free Street is an example of a road changed from the lane it had long been, into the highway it has become by widening, adding pavements, and new roads opening from it. The Methodist Mission Hall has gone, the grass triangle outside the rectory has been tarmaced and the drive into the Rectory realigned The Old Grammar School, admittedly derelict, was demolished in 1964 and the name Portland Square has gone. Station Road, one of the town's main streets before 1965, no longer leads anywhere, appropriately since the station no longer exists, and is recalled now only by a plaque high on a wall. The town's wish to keep it as a link road on to the new by-pass was rejected by the planners.

Not all has been disaster. The High Street is relatively unaltered though traffic calming and one way traffic has been introduced. Many buildings are better cared for

106. The Church Hall, Free Street opened 1910 enlarged 1964.

than they were in the 1960s whilst historic features such as the Padbury clock, the eighteenth century fire medallion, and the plaque commemorating the 1887 Jubilee of Queen Victoria remain and wells have been preserved in some houses and shops.

The single biggest change is the installation of mains sewerage. It is hard to remember that until the early 1960s houses depended on cesspits or earth closets and the Council's 'violet cart' made its rounds twice a week to empty the buckets of effluent. Concern about the danger represented by open sewers was first expressed by the Parish Vestry in the 1830s. In the early 1900s the Parish Council begrudged the expense and fought off the wish of the Rural District Council to install mains sewerage. In the 1930s the Council again decided against the expense. Bishop's Waltham was fortunate to escape a major epidemic. At long last in May 1962 the sewerage plant was opened at Brooklands Farm costing £250,000 and was expanded later in the 1960s. The streets were dug up to connect most if not all houses to the new system. In most parts of the parish what the children had called 'the poo lorry' was no longer a familiar sight.

The feature which a visitor returning to Bishop's Waltham after an absence of 40 years notices first is the number of new roads lined with houses. The biggest estates of local authority housing are at Battery Hill off the Winchester Road and Ridgemede off Hoe Road. The largest private estate is at Pondside, started in the early 1970s with phase two in 1978, the roads named after bishops of Winchester. A third area of development has been off Hoe Road and the newly constructed by-pass road named Cricklemede. Most recently land near the town centre in Hoe Road and open spaces close to the Old Station roundabout have been built on. Provision for the elderly has become a concern and the late 1960s saw the building of Bishop's Waltham House in the grounds of Northbrook House, as a County Council home for the frail, Greens Close and Cunningham House in Claylands Road (opened by Lady Cunningham) and Priory Court Rest Home.[4]

The town's footpaths remain important in preserving the past and the outdoor heritage. At a meeting at the Institute, held in March 1970, to enable the Council to report on its stewardship during the past year and chaired by the Chairman of the Council Godfrey Pink, a speaker from the County Council explained that landowners were not permitted to keep bulls over one year old in a field through which a right of way passed. Whether in response to a question or spontaneously she went on to explain that if you were doubtful about the age of a belligerent bull then the way to check was to inspect its teeth! There is no record of audience reaction to this presumably facetious reply.[5] It may perhaps have led later to the appointment by the Parish Council of a Footpath Warden.

Some open spaces have gone for good. No longer could the Hambledon Hunt meet in the fields behind Ridgemede nor a fete be held at Holm Oak.[6] The Rectory no longer opens its garden to parishioners on summer evenings. But some open spaces have been preserved or even enhanced. When the police sold the Priory in 1971 the Parish Council bought land which became Priory Park a large open space close to the town. It is a feature of Bishop's Waltham that almost everybody lives within easy reach of paths which quickly lead out of the town to Ashton, Dean, Dundridge, West Hoe or the Moors.

The last third of the twentieth century also saw development in the town's facilities. In 1969 Bishop's Waltham at last obtained an adequate branch of the county library, though not a purpose built one. From 1932 until the 1950s the library consisted of shelf space at the Institute. The stock was renewed periodically from the depot at Fareham but at the end of each session the books had to be stored in boxes since the room was used for other purposes. In the 1950s the library moved to a room above the post office where at least the books could be left on the shelves between sessions. When the infant school moved from Dodd's Alley to Victoria Road the library was able to occupy the premises at Dodd's Alley where, in addition to room for 10,000 books, the mobile library which served the surrounding villages could be parked. A new Youth Hall was opened in 1970 to replace the one demolished to make way for the new road across the pond. Flat roofed and unimaginative in construction its life span was short and it is likely to be replaced by the end of the first decade of the twenty first century. When Droxford RDC was merged with Winchester RDC and vacated Northbrook House the Registry Office was moved to the premises of the former Gunners Bank. For the rest of the twentieth century the Parish Council fought off repeated attempts to close the Registry Office which would have meant that people could no longer register births, marriages or deaths in the town.

The closing years of the century saw the creation of a Bishop's Waltham branch of the Citizens' Advice Bureau (CAB). It was at first based in a corner of the library but in 1988 received CAB status and its own premises in the library building. It provides advice not only for the town but for the surrounding area and the Meon valley.

The churchyards of the parishes of Swanmore and Bishop's Waltham were both almost full. At Bishop's Waltham land belonging to the Rectory skirting Lower Lane had been designated for churchyard extension but had not been consecrated. By the late 1950s it was more valuable as building land and was sold for that purpose. Joint facilities for burials with Swanmore were treated with reserve: the two communities had traditionally regarded each other with suspicion. In 1978 however eleven acres of land at West Hoe was purchased. Bishop's Waltham met two thirds of the capital cost, £16,500, and a joint committee of management was set up representing the two parishes[7]

The Ridgemede Swimming Pool was the inspiration of John Watts headmaster of Ridgemede School. Conceived in 1975 it took four years to raise funds and build. It is a major amenity used by people of all ages and by a variety of organisations.

In 1980 the Jubilee Hall at last gave Bishop's Waltham a large hall and meeting rooms as well as catering facilities. In the early 1970s when the Council sold 1.22 acres of the allotment site at Claylands for £133,000 there was a town debate about how this windfall should be spent. It was decided to build the meeting place the town had needed at least since the Second World War. Though not opened until 1980 it was intended to mark the Silver Jubilee of Queen Elizabeth II. It had cost £116,000 to build and a further £24,000 to furnish.

The future of the Educational Institute had been in doubt ever since provision of adult education moved to Swanmore Secondary School (now Swanmore College of Technology) when it opened in 1961. The Institute had not been brought up to date and was running at a loss. Despite efforts to give it a new lease of life its closure became inevitable and took place in July 2001. Two years later it was sold by auction for £401,000 to a developer who converted it into flats with the misleading name of The Old School House.[8]

At the beginning of the third millennium the clock in St George's Square was built to mark the Golden Jubilee of Queen Elizabeth II. The inspiration was that of W.E.Walmsley and it was built by Christopher Baldwin, a local clockmaker, its design deliberately reminiscent of the work of James Padbury the nineteenth century Bishop's Waltham clockmaker. It cost £13,000 raised by local people with a substantial contribution from the Parish Council and was dedicated on a wet June day in 2002 by the Lord Lieutenant of Hampshire, Mary Fagan, who commented that in view of the weather she was not so much dedicating it as baptising it. The accompanying celebrations were transferred to the Jubilee Hall.[9]

The years since 1970 have seen the establishment of a number of organisations which have enriched the corporate life of the town. The Bishop's Waltham Carnival which had not been held for many years was revived to celebrate the Silver Jubilee of Queen Elizabeth II and has remained an annual event. In 1991 when its future was in jeopardy it was taken over by the newly formed Rotary Club which has continued to organise the Carnival ever since. In 1980 came the twinning association. Bishop's Waltham was linked with St Bonnet le Chateau, a small town of 3000 people in the Loire region of France, 2800 feet up in the foothills of the Massif Centrale, half an hour's drive from St Etienne. Though it is 450 miles from the English Channel it is easy to reach by road, rail or air and there have been regular and varied contacts, for all ages many involving young people, in the quarter of a century since the exchange began.[10]

The Bishop's Waltham Society was founded in 1986 to keep a watching brief on planning applications and so ensure that the views of ordinary citizens were placed before the planners when new developments were under consideration. In addition to a monthly meeting with a speaker often on a local topic the Society has encouraged conservation. Its first venture was the publication of a book of photographs by John Bosworth comparing scenes of 25 years before with the town as it had become. Perusal of that book still surprises the reader with the extent of the change which had come about in almost every part of Bishop's Waltham.[11]

Later the Society erected three blue plaques on buildings of historical interest – the shop in the High Street where James Padbury ran his clock making business in the nineteenth century, the *Crown Hotel* where Admiral Villeneuve lived briefly in 1805 and the site of Gunners Bank from its foundation in 1809 to its demise in 1953. To mark the millennium the Society installed a replica of the town pump in Basingwell Steeet and a copy of the ropemakers' post in Houchin Street.[12] The Society ensured the preservation of the traditional red telephone box in St George's Square which British Telecom was proposing to replace with an anodised aluminium telephone box.[13]

The Museum Trust had two sources: the 'town treasures', and the Historical Society. The 'town treasures' as they were known were memorabilia, some documentary, others larger and more varied, some of historical value and others ephemeral curiosities accumulated over the years. They were stored in cupboards and corridors in the Institute and rarely exhibited.

The Historical Society arose from the heightened awareness of what had been lost when the centre of the town was reconstructed and many houses demolished in the 1960s. Amongst the artefacts which had recently come to light was the tollboard from the Park Gate toll house on the Fishers' Pond turnpike. It had for 40 years been in a builder's yard in Lower Lane covered with a layer of whitewash beneath which the tolls could be dimly discerned. The first meeting of the Historical Society was held at the Institute in October 1972. Among the artefacts brought by enthusiasts attending were boot blacking bottles from the early nineteenth century and clay pipes made to celebrate the battle of Trafalgar, both found in demolished houses. The idea of a museum was aired at this first meeting but was not realised for another fifteen years [14] Enthusiasm was not sustained and the Historical Society languished.

The scheme for a museum came to fruition in June 1987 and owed much to the enthusiasm and hard work of John Bosworth. A room at the rear of their premises in Brook Street was made available by Barclays Bank at a peppercorn rent and the Museum opened.[15] Though smaller than many would have liked it was a beginning.

At the end of the twentieth century came the Bishop's Waltham Festival taking place in June or July with a week long programme of concerts, drama and events for all tastes many of them held in the grounds of the 900 year old Bishops' Palace. Since 1997 Bishop's Waltham in Bloom has encouraged many participants to provide displays of plants and flowers which each year have won a variety of awards.

An issue which concerned many people was the fate of the historic bishop's pond. The South Pond was restored in the early 1970s. It now contained enough depth of water, was restocked with fish and became the base for the Bishop's Waltham Fishing Club. Meanwhile the North Pond deteriorated; it contained between 10 and 16 feet of silt, as well as fallen and decaying trees and only in wet winter months did it contain much water. Meetings to confront planners with the concern felt by residents were many but all in the long run abortive. When Portsmouth Water Company took over from Gosport Water Company in 1955 it was licensed to abstract up to 4.5 million gallons of water per day through the Northbrook Pumping Station with a maximum of 6.2 milllion gallons on any one day. The result was to reduce the Hamble to a trickle with insufficient water to sustain the pond. Where there used to be watercress, fish and abundant wild life there was now a stagnant and sometimes foul smelling marsh. Restoration it was reckoned would cost as much as £4 million. The pond belongs to James Duke and Son who offered to rehabilitate part of it in return for access to the town centre facilities they had long wanted. This site has been part of the scenery of Bishop's Waltham for approaching 900 years and threats to its continuing existence were resisted strongly by the Council and the people of the town. Despite suggestions that part of it might be turned into a car park it has survived as an open space and a home for a variety of bird and animal species though not the extensive pond it had once been.

In the 1990s the Moors was designated a Site of Special Scientific Interest (SSI) on account of its rich ecology. It consists of a mixture of woodland, fen, grassland and open water characterised by a series of springs bubbling up through the clay from chalk aquifers below. The best known feature is the 'sand boils', where water with swirling sand rises under pressure. As part of the preparation for the Second World war the Gosport Water Company built a pumping station at Hoe drawing a substantial amount of water from the river Hamble. It was intended to provide an emergency supply should the existing waterworks at Soberton be disabled by enemy action but also to provide the extra water which mains burst by enemy action might necessitate. The Hoe Pumping Station was made permanent after the war but it closed in 2003: the Moors will take many years to recover from the prolonged period of reduced water supply.

Town centre shops continue to thrive despite the opening of two supermarkets in Bishop's Waltham and the attraction of branches of large supermarket chains at Hedge End, only four miles away. The Cooperative store in High Street was the first supermarket in the town whilst Budgen's, built on the site of the outer courtyard of the Bishop's Palace was the first to be purpose built. Bishop's Waltham still has a surprising variety of specialist shops. What has disappeared for ever is the old fashioned grocer serving customers at the counter with sugar in blue bags, loose biscuits out of a tin, butter off a pat and bacon sliced to order. The last such store in Bishop's Waltham was the Country Stores which is now the Wine Shop and claims a continuous existence since 1617 – a national record.[16] Its last proprietor was Charles Livermore who retired in 1980. It is unlikely that the town will ever again have a 'sweet shop' selling unwrapped sweets, weighed out from large glass bottles and sold in triangular shaped bags yet until her death in the early 1990s Madeleine Griffiths had such a shop in High Street. On the corner of Bank Street and St Peter's Street was an old fashioned general store run by Eleanor Askew who retired in 1984 at the age of 86. The counter now forms part of an exhibit in the Bishop's Waltham Museum.[17] Meanwhile cinema, launderette and bingo hall have come and gone.

The Church of England has changed more in the last 40 years than in the previous 500 years. Since 1960 all the churches have experienced declining and ageing congregations. The number attending St Peter's at services held at 8am and 9.15 may not have declined significantly since the 1960s but since then the population of the town has more than doubled.[18]

In the mid-1960s the Church of England embarked on major changes to its services. Prayer Book Mattins and Evensong, which had been the staple of worship since the sixteenth century Reformation, were gradually phased out and replaced by new services in modern English and Holy Communion became the norm in most churches.

At St Peter's change was begun by Christopher Biddell who was appointed rector in 1962. He introduced Family Communion at 9.30, designed to appeal to younger people and to families. For a time it ran alongside the time honoured 11 am Mattins to which older, more traditional churchgoers came in some numbers. Gradually the number attending Mattins declined. Mattins required a choir but increasingly members of the choir were drawn to Family Communion. From October 1980 Mattins was no longer held every Sunday, but twice and later once a month instead. But once a month and with no choir meant inevitable decline and the last regular Mattins was held in July 1993.

Until the 1960s Evensong was a popular service, sometimes fully choral and on occasion attracting a visiting preacher. It appealed to those who were used to attending church twice on a Sunday but they were a dwindling band. Many people including the rector of Bishop's Waltham held that it was the BBC which killed it off, not just at St Peter's, but at churches all over the country. From October 1967 *The Forsyte Saga* was serialised on television on Sunday evenings and attendance at evening services plummeted – there were as yet no video recorders – and never recovered.[19] Few people any longer attended church twice and in 2003 the last Evensong (except for special occasions) was held at St Peter's.

The new emphasis in worship needed a different approach to the church buildings. The rector no longer celebrated Holy Communion facing the altar with his back to the congregation. So the altar was moved and the president faced the people from behind the altar. But the altar in the chancel was a long way from the people so the next stage was a portable altar closer to the congregation on the steps under the chancel arch. This began to be used at first on one or two Sundays each month in 1981 when John Willard was rector and became more frequent in the early 1990s. In 2005 a permanent dais was installed with an altar at which the whole congregation now receives Holy Communion. Both altar and rails were movable so that the area could be used for concerts or drama.

By the 1960s the Church of England was divesting itself of its substantial Georgian and Victorian parsonages. Large rectories in spacious grounds conveyed an impression which the Church of England no longer wished to encourage. One of the first local parsonages to be replaced by a more modest house was the Rectory of St Peter's. Discussions were under way by 1960 and when Christopher Biddell arrived as rector with his wife and three small children in 1962 the decision had already been taken to sell the rectory though as yet the new house had not been built. They moved into the new rectory in June 1964. The garden was wonderfully productive, made on soil enriched by years if not centuries of manure from the stables.[20] The new rectory was built to the side of the old rectory stables, which were adapted in the early 1990s as a Parish Centre with office, quiet room and meeting room.

The last 40 years have seen a dramatic change in the status of women in almost all walks of life and the Church of England has followed if somewhat belatedly. During the incumbencies of Frank Sargeant and Christopher Biddell two deaconesses served the parish – Mary Taylor and Mary Dee. Not until the coming of John Willard was the first woman churchwarden appointed. Joyce Sansbury (later Law) became a warden in 1976 and was succeeded by Peg Price in 1980. The practice of having two men and two women churchwardens, one elected each year who each normally hold the office for four years was established by Simon Wilkinson in the early 1990s.

Meanwhile the Church of England nationally was taking slow steps to extend the role of women. In 1969 the office of Reader – lay people trained for preaching and teaching – was opened to women. From 1987 women could be ordained deacon and

107. *Parish News* June 1976. Former rectors *Top row*: William Brock, James Palmer Nash; *Second row*: Harold Rycroft, Henry Edmund Sharpe; *Third row*: Noel Stubbs, Frank Sargeant; *Bottom row*: Christopher Biddell, John Willard.

in 1994 the first women were admitted to the priesthood. The first full time woman curate at St Peter's was Jane Hemmings who came from Hackney and was ordained in 2003.

Children could no longer be sent to Sunday School so that parents could have a peaceful hour on Sunday afternoon. The only children likely now to be found in church were those whose parents were churchgoers. The name Sunday School – itself badly dated – was abandoned finally in the 1990s in favour first of Junior Church and later Sunday Club. Afternoon activities for children ceased at St Peter's in 1965 though at that time the number attending Sunday School was still substantial. It has since dwindled in number and reduced in age.

The Church of England now has many fewer stipendiary clergy than in the 1960s and it was no longer possible for every parish to have its own parish priest. From 1977 there were plans to create a single benefice for the parishes of Bishop's Waltham and Upham and in 1979 John Willard became rector of both parishes. Full time clergy are now assisted by an increasing number of men and women ordained as NSMs (non stipendiary ministers) and by Readers. Jane Beloe admitted a Reader at Upham in 1986 was ordained an NSM and returned to the benefice of Bishop's Waltham and Upham as part-time NSM in 2006. Bishop's Waltham's first Reader was John Read who came to live in the parish in 1971.

In the late 1950s the *Parish Magazine* was renamed *Parish News* but it was more than its name which changed. Though still run by St Peter's church with the rector as its editor, it became and has remained no longer exclusively a church periodical but community oriented including a regular report of the doings of the Parish Council. In 1997 the format changed from the small pages of the traditional parish magazine to a larger format and at the beginning of the new millennium began to use colour. By general consent it became one of the best parish publications in the country with attractive presentation, professional style, varied content and rising circulation, an important town amenity.

The Friends of St Peter's was the brainchild of John Willard, rector from 1975 to 1987. In 1986 the church and town celebrated the 850th anniversary of their foundation by Bishop Henry of Blois and joined in national events held to mark the 900th anniversary of the making of the Domesday Book. A fete in the Palace grounds, a flower festival and a pageant of the history of Bishop's Waltham were among events held during the year. Partly as a result John Willard suggested the formation of the Friends of St Peter's to draw into support of the church people who might not be regular church goers but who recognised the place in the community of the historic parish church. The Society has been a great success Over the last 20 years under the chairmanship of Nick Jonas and then Alan Lovell it has raised £150,000 towards the costly maintenance of the fabric of St Peters', as well as contributing to the social life of the town a host of activities including visits to places of interest, concerts, talks and art exhibitions.

108. St Peter's church with dais for nave altar completed 2005.

In the second half of the twentieth century the nature of the country town changed and Bishop's Waltham no less than others in Hampshire and beyond. Earlier Bishop's Waltham had been a large village, often so described by people who couldn't quite believe it was a town. Many of its citizens come from families who had lived here for generations or even centuries. Some were farmers, shopkeepers, professional people or country craftsmen. They lived, worked, shopped, and worshipped in Bishop's Waltham and their children went to the all-age schools. The town was self-sufficient; you scarcely needed to go beyond its boundaries for the necessities of life.

In the second half of the twentieth century all that changed. The population increased by 227% (2883 in 1951 to 6538 in 2001) over four times as fast as it had done in the first half of the century (see Appendix B). New people moved in for whom the town was a dormitory. They slept here but worked elsewhere often in Fareham, Winchester, Portsmouth, Southampton or even London. Households were now much smaller than they had been in the early years of the twentieth century. In 2007 Winchester City Council estimated the population as 6747 in 2884 households an average of 2.33 people per household. There was a good balance of ages with a median age of about 33. The population was over 99% white and of British origin. Under 50 people originated outside the British Isles, a few from the Caribbean or Indian, Asian or African continents. The largest minority – only 29 – had been born

109. The Jubilee Clock in St George's Square, erected 2002.

in Ireland.[21] Agriculture was no longer prominent in the town's economy. Shops survived but many people went out of Bishop's Waltham to supermarkets and superstores elsewhere.

Newcomers, some of whom came to retire to an attractive community, contributed to the range and variety of town life. There are activities for all ages – from senior citizens to children of nursery school age – and all interests whether sporting, cultural, ecological or general. After half a century of rapid expansion and seemingly inexorable growth the town has in the first decade of the twenty first century reached equilibrium. Winchester City Council forecasts that the population will remain close to the present figure to 2012 though the number of dwellings is expected to rise from 2884 to 2937.[22] Bishop's Waltham is a pleasant place to live. It has absorbed the shock of 50 years of growth and change.

Continuity remains a strong feature of the town. Many of its citizens take a strong interest in its folklore and history. If the DNA of the present population were to be analysed some of the citizens of Bishop's Waltham would perhaps show descent from the Saxon settlers who reached Waltham and surrounding villages 1500 years and some 60 generations ago.

Appendices

A. Landmarks in the history of Bishop's Waltham

c.500	Waltham (OE woodland estate) settled by Saxons invaders.
Early 700s	Willibald attends monastic school at Waltham.
720	Willibald leaves for Rome from Hamblemouth.
904	King Edward the Elder exchanges Waltham for Portchester with Bishop Denewulf. Episcopal ownership of the manor continues until 1869 (with short breaks).
1001	Town burnt by the Danes.
1086	Domesday Survey suggests a population of about 660 for whole manor. Priest is named Radulf.
1136	Henry of Blois (bishop 1129–1171) starts to build the Palace, founds the church on its present site and lays out the town outside the walls of the Palace.
1208–09	Pipe Rolls of the Bishops of Winchester begin.
1324	Birth of William of Wykeham.
1348	Black Death.
1378–1401	Bishop William of Wykeham (1367–1404) extends the chancel of St Peter's, makes doorway from the chancel to churchyard and builds the south porch. He is the second builder of the Palace.
1404–47	Henry Beaufort bishop of Winchester.
1522	Henry VIII meets the Emperor Charles V at the Palace.
1551–8	Manor of Bishop's Waltham owned by William Paulet, Earl of Winchester; returned to the bishop by Queen Mary.
1554	Mary I waits for Philip of Spain at the Palace before their marriage in Winchester Cathedral.
1582	(31st December) Tower of St Peter's collapses.
1584–89	Tower rebuilt and two bells placed in it.
1612	Parish Registers begin.

1626	Bishop Lancelot Andrewes (1619–28) presents the pulpit for St Peter's to Dr Robert Ward, Rector.
1637	North aisle of church built including schoolroom with external entrance.
1644	Palace sacked by Cromwellian troops. Bishop Walter Curll escapes to Soberton, dies 1647.
1647–60	Manor of Bishop's Waltham owned by Robert Reynolds, returned to the bishop at the Restoration.
1651	Bells added probably using metal from the Palace.
1652	South aisle of the church rebuilt using stone from the Palace.
c.1658	Market House built in St George's Square.
1662	George Morley becomes bishop, abandons the Palace and rebuilds Farnham Castle as bishop's main residence.
1679	Bishop George Morley (1662–84) founds the Free Grammar School.
1722	Passing of the Waltham Black Acts.
1733	West gallery of the church built. Father Smith organ installed in the gallery (1734).
1741	Pest House built on the Chase.
1758	Gosport to Chawton, Bishop's Waltham to Odiham and Winchester to Stephen's Castle Down turnpikes authorised by Act of Parliament.
1759	Common Fields in Ashton enclosed.
1762	Workhouse opened in Basingwell Street (also called Workhouse Street) in the building now the Barleycorn Inn.
1780	The Revd Charles Walters I becomes headmaster of the grammar school. Dies 1811.
1793–1812	Bishop's Waltham a parole town for French and Spanish prisoners during French Revolutionary and Napoleonic Wars.
1797–8	South gallery added to the church.
1801	Curdridge Common to Corhampton turnpike added to the Southampton to London turnpike.
1801	First national Census of population.
1802	James Ogle aged 25 presented to the living by Bishop Brownlow North, first resident rector for half a century.
1809	Gunners Bank opened.
1811	The Revd Charles Walters II becomes headmaster of the grammar school (to 1822).
1822	The National School built in the churchyard.
	The Revd. Thomas Scard becomes headmaster of the grammar school.
1833	Death of James Ogle; William Brock aged 28, becomes rector, presented to the living by Bishop Sumner.

APPENDIX A LANDMARKS IN THE HISTORY OF BISHOP'S WALTHAM

1834	Turnpike from Bishop's Waltham to Fishers Pond opened with branch to Fair Oak.
1834	*Our Town* published by 'Peregrine Reedpen'.
1835	Chapel of ease built at Curdridge.
1837	Opening of the Union Workhouse at Droxford.
1841	Tithe map of the parish. First Census to contain names.
	Demolition of the Market House in the Square.
1844	Charles Walters delivers lecture on the History of Bishop's Waltham, subsequently published.
1847	Arthur Helps comes to live at Vernon Hill House.
1848	Rebuilding of the west wall of St Peter's church.
1851	Census of church attendance 30th March.
1856	Enclosure of Curdridge Common.
1859	Arthur Helps buys Pondside and finds rich clay.
1862	Arthur Helps founds the Bishop's Waltham Clay Company.
	Building of houses in area named Newtown.
1863	Railway line from Botley to Bishop's Waltham opened.
1863	Congregational church built in Lower Lane.
1864	Town lit by gas.
	Foundation stone of the Royal Albert Infirmary laid by Prince Leopold.
1866	British and Foreign School built in Newtown ('The school on the Hill') by the Congregational church.
1868	Abolition of compulsory church rate.
1869	Under Bishops' Resignation Act the Palace becomes the property of the Ecclesiastical Commissioners.
1870	Enclosure of Waltham Chase. Land allocated for a recreation ground.
1871	Primitive Methodist Mission Hall opened in Free Street.
	Purchase of the brickworks by Mark Henry Blanchard I.
1872	Arthur Helps knighted.
1875	Death of Sir Arthur Helps. Vernon Hill estate sold at *The Crown*.
1878	Bishop's Waltham School Board formed. Ebenezer Sims headmaster of the British & Foreign School (retires 1914).
1884	The 'Beer Riots'.
1887	Search for a site for the grammar school.
1890	(January) First Parish Magazine published.
1891	(21st November) Death of William Brock, rector since 1833 at age of 86.
1892	Death of Mark Henry Blanchard I.

1894	(December) First Parish Council elected. Parish included in Droxford Rural District Council.
1896–97	Restoration of St Peter's under the direction of Thomas Graham Jackson.
	Samuel Longmore becomes minister of the Congregational Church.
1897	Building of Ridgemede House by C.R.Gunner.
	Oddfellows Hall opened in High Street.
1899	(5th July) Bishop's Waltham Educational Institute opened by the Earl of Northbrook chairman of Hampshire County Council.
1910	Primitive Methodist Church opened in Basingwell Street.
	St Peter's Church Hall opened in Free Street (extended 1964).
1912	White Fathers buy The Priory (former Infirmary) as a Roman Catholic seminary.
1914–18	First World War – 58 men from Bishop's Waltham killed in action.
1927	Diocese of Portsmouth separated from Winchester – Bishop's Waltham in the new diocese.
1932	(31st December) Bishop's Waltham railway closed for passenger traffic.
	Electricity supply reaches the parish.
1937	Northbrook House becomes headquarters of Droxford Rural District Council.
1939–45	Second World War – 32 men from Bishop's Waltham killed in action.
1953	Gunners bank closes - taken over by Barclays.
1956	Blanchards Brick and Tile Works closes.
1961	Opening of Swanmore Secondary School (later Swanmore College of Technology).
1962	Sewerage plant opened at Brooklands Farm - mains sewerage comes to Bishop's Waltham.
	The Old Grammar School in Portland Square demolished to provide a car park.
	Bishop's Waltham railway closed to goods traffic – demolished 1965.
1963	Portland Square car park opened with 60 spaces.
1964	New Rectory occupied. by the Revd Christopher Biddell.
1964	The Classic Cinema in High Street (formerly Oddfellows Hall) closed and building sold as furniture store.
1965	Building of the new road across the pond begun. Demolition of much of Houchin Street and Basingwell Street to make town centre car park.
1966	Free Street widened – former Methodist Mission Hall and cottages demolished. Grass triangle outside the Rectory tarmaced.
1969	Eastway House demolished, road widened and new houses built on the site (later).

APPENDIX A LANDMARKS IN THE HISTORY OF BISHOP'S WALTHAM

1969	Ridgemede House opened as an Old People's Home. Ridgemede estate – 300 houses – and Ridgemede Junior School built on the fields.
	Bishop's Waltham House Rest Home opened in the grounds of Northbrook House.
1970	By-pass road opened.
1971	Boundary of the ecclesiastical parish adjusted to include Waltham Chase in parish of Shedfield.
	The Priory bought by Hampshire Police Authority for a police training school, Priory Park bought by the town council as a recreation ground.
1974	Claylands House demolished.
	Bishop's Waltham comes under the new Winchester City Council.
1975	Mount House, Little Shore Lane demolished.
1976	New Roman Catholic church opened in Martin Street.
1978	West Hoe Cemetery opened jointly with Swanmore.
1979	Congregational Church in Lower Lane demolished.
	Ridgemede Swimming Pool opened.
1980	(June) Jubilee Hall opened in Little Shore Lane.
1982	Last gasholder dismantled at Garfield Road.
	The Bishop's Waltham Society founded.
1987	Friends of St Peter's founded.
1994	Stables of the old Rectory of St Peter's refurbished as The Stables Parish Centre.
1997	Consecration of new Roman Catholic church.
2001	Sale of the Educational Institute.
2002	The Jubilee Clock erected in St George's Square.

B. *Population of Bishop's Waltham*

Estimates of population before 1801.

1086	600	Domesday Survey for Bishop's Waltham Manor.[1]
1603	687	Compton Census[2]
1665	1300	Hampshire Hearth Tax Assessment[3]
1676	1258	Compton Census.
1725	1400	Estimate of the rector John Cooke[4].
1760	1647	Hoskins Formula[5]
1790	1689	Hoskins Formula.

National Census of Population.

1801	1773		1911	2488
1811	1830		1921	2597
1821	2126		1931	2782
1831	2181		1941	No census
1841	2193		1951	2883
1851	2265		1961	3171 [2923]
1861	2267		1971	4055[7]
1871	2618		1981	5189
1881	2484		1991	6032
1891	2842		2001	6538[8]
1901	2309[6] [3028]			

Notes.

1. Estimated population based on Domesday (1086) is 600 for Bishop's Waltham manor which included Durley, Upham and Bursledon. Domesday gives only heads of households so the total population is usually reckoned to be about six times the number given in the survey.
2. Estimates for 1603 & 1676 are based on *The Compton Census of 1676.* (Appendix E The population of market towns in 1603,1676, 1811 p.cxvi.) The figure for 1603 looks too low & not consistent with other figures for later seventeenth and eighteenth centuries.
3. *Hughes & White* 1991 p.xiv suggest a multiplier of 4.5 to translate households into individuals.
4. Estimate for 1725 is that of the rector John Cooke (see Ward p.20).
5. *Hoskins* 1959 p.143 suggests that total baptisms taking place in a decade divided by 10 and multiplied by 30 produces a population estimate. Figures for 1760 & 1790 using this formula look convincing.
6. By the time of the 1901 Census Curdridge had become a separate civil parish so is no longer included in the Bishop's Waltham total. Curdridge figures are: 627 (1901), 805 (1911), 852 (1921), 838 (1931), 1036 (1951), 1232 (1961) 1284 (1971).

7. In 1967 there was a small boundary change affecting the civil parishes of Bishop's Waltham, Curdridge, Swanmore and Shedfield in order to include the whole of Waltham Chase in the parish of Shedfield. The ecclesiastical boundaries were adjusted to conform in 1971. The figure in brackets for 1961 is that of the reduced parish of 1967.
8. Winchester City Council estimates the population in 2007 as 6747 and for 2012 as 6727.

C. *Rectors of Bishop's Waltham*

[1086]	Radulf	Domesday book.
– c.1160	Walter	Charter of Henry of Blois [7].
c.1160 –	Christopher	Charter of Henry of Blois.
–1289	Peter de Wynton	Died 1289.
1289–1321	Edmund de Maydenestane	Collated 10 March 1289. Bishop's chaplain. Resigned from North Walsham & Lasham 1289.
1321–1346	John de Erdeshope	Dispensations January 1321, November 1324, December 1328. Probably non-resident.
1346–1366	John Payn	Collated 20th June 1346. Parson of South Waltham, appointed Bailiff of the Manor 10th July 1347.
1366–1404	Hugh Craft	Died 1404.
1404–1409	John Wykeham	Collated on death of above 19th June 1404.
1409	Thomas Marchell	Rector of West Turoyle exchanged with above 28th November 1409.
1409–1412	Henry Langham	
1412–1447	John Milon	Rector of Kennet diocese of Norwich, exchanged with above 3rd August 1412.
1447–1453	Robert Langthorne	Resigned 5th December 1453.
1453–1487	Nicholas Belle	Collated 5th December 1453. Rental 1464.
1487–1497	John Mytton	Collated 19th June 1487 on death of the above.
1497–1504	Alexander Blenkensopp [8]	Collated 6th June 1497 (in place of Benedict Dodyn who resigned and was presented to Wyke Regis). Died.
1504–1509	Ralph Upton (Lepton) [9]	Collated 22nd December 1504 on the death of the above. Instituted to St Nicholas', Guildford 8th December 1504. Probably non-resident. Resigned.
1509–1525	Robert Walshe	Collated 2nd January 1509 on the resignation of the above.

1525–1566	Gilbert Burton	Collated 29th September 1525 on the death of the above. Also rector of North Waltham from 21st April 1524, where he lived, & of two other parishes.
1566–1576	John Bridges	Collated 17th February 1566. Dean of Salisbury 1577. Bishop of Oxford 1604–18. Non resident.
1576–1619	William Singleton [10]	Collated 12th February 1576. Buried BW 2nd December 1619.
1619–1622	Nicholas Fuller [11]	Collated 21st February 1619. Died 10th February 1622, buried at Allington, Wiltshire. Non resident.
1623	John Moulton	Collated 29th March 1623.
1623–1629	Robert Ward [12]	Collated 30th August 1623. Buried BW 23rd May 1629.
1629–1642	Benjamin Lang	Collated 21st May 1629.
1642–1668	Joseph Goulston	Collated 20th January 1642. Canon of Winchester 1660. Died 10th April 1669. Rate Book 1653-1668. Also Precentor & Dean of Chichester Cathedral 1663–9.
1669–1684	Robert Sharrock	Collated 8th May 1669. Rate Book 1669–1684. Archdeacon of Winchester 21st April 1684 but died and was buried in chancel BW 13th July 1684.
1684–1696	Francis Morley	Collated 4th July 1684. Rate Book April 1684-November 1696. Nephew of Bishop Morley.
1696–1705	John Duke	Collated 6th October 1696. Rate Book April 1697–1705.
1706–1717	Thomas Browne	Rate Book March 1706–1717.
1717–1744	John Cooke	Collated 4th January 1717. Rate Book 1717. Buried at Winchester 5th July 1744.
1744–1750	Peter Maurice	Collated 20th July 1744. Buried in London 5th April 1754.
1750–1753	Robert Ashe	Collated 3rd May 1750. Resident (son, Benjamin, born to Robert and Hannah 8th June 1752).
1753–1782	James Cutler	Collated 12th April 1753. Rate Book 1761–64. Also Rector of Droxford. Non-resident.
1782–1794	Henry Ford	Collated 2nd April 1782. Cession. Non-resident. Professor of Arabic at Oxford.

1794–1797	Edmund Poulter	Collated 13th April 1794. Other appointments. Non-resident. Cession.
1797–1802	Edward Salter	Collated 13th February 1797. Non-resident Rector of Stratfield Saye where he lived & Stratfield Turgis. Resigned 9th March 1802.
1802–1833	James Ogle	Collated 10th March 1802. Died 19th May 1833. Also Rector of Crondall 1811-33. First resident rector since 1753, last pluralist rector.
1833–1891	William Brock	Collated 7th June 1833. Died 21st November 1891, buried BW 25th November 1891.
1892–1905	James Palmer Nash	Collated 7th March 1892. Resigned 24th September 1905.
1905–1913	Edmund Hugh Rycroft	Collated 5th November 1905. Cession 2nd November 1913.
1913–1931	Henry Edmund Sharpe	Diocese of Portsmouth from 1927. Collated 15th December 1913. Resigned 30th June 1931.
1931–1948	Noel Howard Stubbs	Collated 16th September 1931. Resigned October 1948.
1949–1962	Frank Hubert Sargeant	Collated 5th January 1949. Resigned 10th June 1962.
1962–1975	Christopher David Biddell	Collated 5th October 1962. Rural Dean. Resigned 28th September 1975.
1975–1987	John Fordham Willard	Collated 14th November 1975. Resigned 1st March 1987.
1987–1988	Paul Wilfrid Howlden	Collated 29th November 1987. Resigned 23rd October 1988.
1989–1997	Simon Evelyn Wilkinson	Collated 3rd September 1989. Resigned 14th September 1997.
1998–2007	Andrew George Davis	Presented by the Lord Chancellor 13th November 1998. Resigned 8th June 2007.

Notes.

1. E.W. Benson (Archbishop of Canterbury 1883-96) suggested that churches should display lists of past clergy in order to emphasise the continuity of the English church. The list of rectors of Bishop's Waltham was compiled by the Revd. James Palmer Nash about 1905. He was assisted by the Revd Francis Thomas Madge, Rector of St Swithin's, Winchester, who provided information about incumbents up to 1525 drawing on the Registers of the Bishops of Winchester available from the time of John of Pontoise (bishop 1282-1305). I have followed this list but made some corrections after checking entries in the Bishops' Registers (1282-1684) and Act Books (from 1743) or transcripts in HRO and the Parish Registers. I have discovered the names of two hitherto unknown rectors c.1160, Walter and Christopher. (see note 7 below) [J.P.Nash's drafts are in HRO 30M77/P135 and there is additional information in Hampshire Notes and Queries Vol.2 1884].

APPENDIX C RECTORS OF BISHOP'S WALTHAM

2. In 1835 a chapel of ease dedicated to St Peter was built in the tithing of Curdridge and an ecclesiastical district, later designated a parish, was carved out of the ancient parish of Bishop's Waltham. In 1845 a small part of the tithing of West Hoe with the tithings of Hill and Swanmore in the parish of Droxford were constitited the new ecclesiastical parish of Swanmore. In 1894 both Curdridge and Swanmore became civil parishes in the Droxford Rural District. In 1971 the boundary of the ecclesiastical parish of Bishop's Waltham was adjusted to include Waltham Chase in the parish of Shedfield and to conform to the civil boundaries revised in 1967.
3. From 1979 the Rector of Bishop's Waltham was also Rector of Upham. The Lord Chancellor now has the presentation to the living one turn in three.
4. *Collation* - admission to a benefice where the bishop is patron. *Cession*–'the vacating of a benefice by taking another without dispensation'. SOED.
5. In the early 18th century there are several appearances of a 'curate' who signs the Poor Rate book apparently in place of the rector for example William Bronne (or Browne) 29th April 1709, 3rd April 1711 and Robert Knapp 19th April 1715, also 1716 and 1718. In 1723 the Rate Book is signed by 'Wm Pearse, Minister'. The rector may have been non-resident or a curate may have had temporary charge of the parish in the absence of the rector.
6. Until 1752 the Julian Calendar was in use and the year began on 25th March. Dates from 1st January to 24th March appear as the year before we should recognise them eg John Bridges –old style 1566, new style 1567; William Singleton old style 1576, new style 1577. This is sometimes written e.g.' 1566/67. I have adhered to the style in use at the time.
7. *Walter* and *Christopher* Two 12th century parsons of Waltham are named in a Charter of Bishop Henry of Blois, granting permission to the monks of Hamble to build a chapel at Bursledon in the *parochia* of St Peter at Waltham. See pages 5–6 and chapter 1 note 17.
8. *Alexander Blenkensopp* according to Spaul (J.E.H.Spaul *The Reformation in the diocese of Winchester 1538-1616 based on the Registers of the bishops of Winchester*) was appointed in place of Benedict Dodyn who had resigned but there is no other reference to Dodyn as rector of Bishop's Waltham.
9. *Ralph Lepton*. Spelling uncertain may be Upton.
10. *William Singleton* according to *Alumni Oxoniensis* he was rector of Bishop's Waltham from 1577-1620, of Baughurst 1578-79, of Chilcomb 1598-1601, & Millbrook 1601-24. His burial is recorded in the Parish Register: 'Mr William Singleton person [parson] was buried the 2 day of December [1619]'. His successor was collated on 21st February – ten weeks later.
11. *Nicholas Fuller* was rector of Allington in Wiltshire. He died in February 1622 and was buried at Allington. It seems likely that he was presented to Bishop's Waltham but continued to reside at Allington. There is no reference to his being rector of Bishop's Waltham in DNB. Further research needed perhaps at Allington.
12. *Dr Robert Ward* The entry in the Parish Register reads : 'Robert Ward Doctor of Divinity was buried the 20 [?] of May [1629]'. There is a note initialled by Charles Walters reading 'Rector of Waltham and one of the Translators of the Bible in King James's time. C.W.1819'.

D. *Chairmen of the Parish Council*

1894–1915	Thomas John Brown *
1915–1919	Arthur Francis Hardy
1919–1921	Frank Hale
1921–1923	Arthur Francis Hardy (2)
1923–1926	Zebulon Andrews
1926–1927	E. Sydney Trigg
1927–1928	V.G. Primmer
1928–1929	Thomas Pink
1929–1930	James Duke
1930–1931	William Henry Terrey
1931	Henry Edmund Sharpe + (Revd.)
1931–1932	H.W. Watson
1932–1933	Frederick.G.Locke
1933–1934	G.H. Putnam
1934–1935	C.V. Lanyon (Major)
1935–1942	Frank Hugh Gunner (Major)
1942–1947	D.P. Blunden
1947–1948	W.J. Sprinks
1948–1949	Hilda Storey (Mrs)
1949–1950	W.J. Sprinks (2)
1950–1951	D.P. Blunden (2)
1951–1952	A.J. Marsh
1952–1953	H.M. Privett
1953–1954	George Hall
1954–1955	William S.A. Warren
1955–1956	H.M. Privett (2)
1956–1957	C.L. Askew
1957–1958	George Hall (2)
1958–1959	R.V. Cartwright (Major)
1959–1960	H.M. Privett (3)
1960–1961	W.J. Taylor
1961–1965	R.V. Cartwright (Major) (2)
1965–1969	Peter H. Weeks ^
1969–1979	Godfrey E. Pink
1979–1983	Christopher J. Bigham
1983–1985	Peter H. Weeks (2)
1985–1986	Christopher J. Bigham (2)
1986–1987	Dorothy Quiney

1987–1990	Trevor J. Fletcher
1990–1991	Jean Hammerton
1991–1993	Trevor J. Fletcher (2)
1993–1994	Linda Banister
1994–1997	David Wright
1997–1998	David Rees
1998–1999	Rex Blundell
1999–2000	Brian Blunt
2000–2006	Eric C. Birbeck
2006–	David McLean

* Died in office 30th March 1915.
+ Resigned owing to ill health October 1931.
^ Resigned owing to ill health January 1969; Godfrey Pink elected in his place.

Numbers in brackets indicate second or subsequent terms of office.

Abbreviations

CUP	Cambridge University Press.
DNB	Dictionary of National Biography.
HCC	Hampshire County Council.
HFC	Hampshire Field Club.
HFCAS	Hampshire Field Club and Archaeological Society.
HRO	Hampshire Record Office.
Log	School Log Book.
Nd	No date.
Np	No publisher named.
ODCC	Oxford Dictionary of the Christian Church.
OUP	Oxford University Press.
Op	Out of print.
PCC	Parochial Church Council.
PCM	Parish Council Minutes.
PMM	Parish Meeting Minutes.
PMag	Parish Magazine.
PN	Parish News.
Registers	Registers of baptisms, marriages and burials at St Peter's from 1612.
RDC	Droxford Rural District Council.
SOED	Shorter Oxford English Dictionary.
SPCK	Society for the Promotion of Christian Knowledge.
VCH	Victoria County History of Hampshire & the Isle of Wight Volume 3.

Bibliography

UNPUBLISHED

Unpublished sources include documents which were once printed but are no longer available in libraries. Most of them can be found in the Hampshire Record Office in Winchester. Where it is obvious the name Bishop's Waltham has been omitted as a title word.

Brock William Sermons and lectures. Copies in the rare books room at the British Library.

Census returns 1841–2001 (on microfilm HRO).

Fryer Priscilla Nd *A short history of Vernon Hill House* Np.

Hase P.H. 1975 *The development of the parish in Hampshire particularly in the eleventh and twelfth centuries* Cambridge University PhD thesis. Copy in Cambridge University Library.

Parish Council Minutes 1894–.

Parish Meeting Minutes 1894–.

Parish Magazine 1890– (renamed in early 1950s).

Parish News 1950s– (Parish Magazine, renamed).

School Log Book: National School 1872–79 (HRO).

School Log Book: Board School / Council School (Infants) 1879–1912 (HRO).

School Log Book County Mixed School 1952–1961(held privately).

Walters Charles 1844 *History of the town, church and episcopal palace of Bishop's Waltham from the earliest period to the present time in a lecture delivered before the Literary Institution of that town.* Jacob & Johnson, Winchester.

PRINTED

Albert W 1972 *The Turnpike Road System in England 1663–1840* CUP.

Aston Michael & Lewis Carenza eds.1994 *The Medieval Landscape of Wessex* Oxbow Monograph Number 46.

Barstow Harold G.1992 *Rentals of Bishop's Waltham Manors 1332 & 1464* Published privately.

Barstow Harold G. 1993 *Rental of Bishop's Waltham Manors 1550 Part 1* Published privately.

Barstow Harold G.1994 *Rentals of Bishop's Waltham Manors 1630 & 1693; Bursledon 1550, Bitterne and Weston 1550, Ashton 1573 Parts 2 & 3* Published privately.

Barstow Harold G. 1998 *Pipe Roll of the Bishopric of Winchester a translation* Published privately.

Beeson Trevor 2002 *The Bishops* SCM.

Beeson Trevor 2004 *The Deans* SCM.

Bennett H.S. 1937 *Life on the English Manor* CUP

Best G.F.A.1964 *Temporal pillars* CUP.

Bettey J.H. 1986 *Wessex from AD 1000* Longman.

Bettey J.H. 1987 *Church and Parish* Batsford.

Biddell Barbara 1999 *The Jolly Farmer? William Cobbett in Hampshire, 1804–1820* Hampshire Papers 15 HCC.

Biddell Barbara 2002 *Bishop's Waltham, a history* Phillimore.

Biddell Barbara 2007 *Napoleonic prisoners of war in and around Bishop's Waltham* Two plus George.

Blair John ed.1988 *Minsters and parish churches: the local church in transition 950–1200* Oxford University Committee for Archaeology Monograph No.17.

Blair John 2005 *The church in Anglo-Saxon society* OUP.

Bosworth J.S.R. 1985 *Bishop's Waltham in old picture postcards* European Library, Netherlands o.p.

Bosworth John 1986 *Bishop's Waltham and Newtown 25 years of change* Bishop's Waltham Society.

Bosworth John 1988 *Bishop's Waltham a pictorial record* John Bosworth Publications.

Bosworth John 1991 *Bishop's Waltham Fire Brigade centenary 1891–1991* John Bosworth Publications.

Briggs Asa 2003 *Victorian things* New edition Sutton Publishing.

Brooke Christopher 2006 *The rise and fall of the Medieval monastery* New edition Folio Society.

Chadwick Owen 1966 *The Victorian Church Part 1* A.& C.Black.

Chadwick Owen 1970 *The Victorian Church Part 2* A.& C. Black.

Chapman John &Seeliger Sylvia 1977 *Formal and informal enclosures in Hampshire* Hampshire Papers 15 HCC.

Coates Richard 1989 *Hampshire place names* Ensign publications.

Cobbett William 1886 Rural Rides 2 volumes.

Cochrane C. 1969 *The lost roads of Wessex* David & Charles.

Collins F.B.& Hurst J.C. 1978 *Meonstoke & Soberton* Winton Publications.

Cross F.L. & Livingstone E.A.eds.1997 The Oxford Dictionary of the Christian Church Third edition.

Cunningham Andrew 1951 *A Sailor's Odyssey* Hutchinson.

Dickens A.G. 1964 *The English Reformation* Batsford 1964.

Emery Grace 1991 *Some of the history of Shedfield parish* Paul Cave.

Finn Peter 2002 *History of the Priory, Bishop's Waltham* Hedera Books.

Fitzhugh Terrick V. H. 1998 *The dictionary of genealogy* Fifth edition A.&C.Black.

Foster Joseph 1887 *Alumni Oxonienses* Joseph Foster.

Hewlett G.P. & Hassell Jane 1973 *Bishop's Waltham Dikes* HFCAS 1973.

Hodgson R.A. 2006 *Gunners Bank* Np. Reprinted from Portsmouth Archives Review.

Hogg John 1988 *Curdridge and St Peter's Church* Np.

Hope Gordon 1980 *1000 years in Droxford* Np.

Hoskins W.G. 1959 *Local history in England* Longmans.

Hoskins W.G.1988 *The making of the English landscape* New edition with new material by Christopher Taylor Hodder & Stoughton.

Hughes E. & White P 1991 *The Hampshire Hearth Tax Assessment 1665* HCC.

Hughes Michael 1976 *The small towns of Hampshire* Hampshire Archaeological Committee HCC.

Jackson Nicholas ed. 2003 *Recollections: the life and travels of a Victorian architect* Unicorn press.

James Tom Beaumont 1999 *The Black Death in Hampshire* Hampshire Papers HCC 1999.

Kitching R.J.2001 *No longer poor old Droxford* n.p.

Knight Frances 1995 *The nineteenth century church and English society* CUP.

Knowles Dom David 1950 *The monastic order in England* CUP.

Law Leslie 1980 *The history of Upham* Upham PCC.

Lennard Reginald 1959 *Rural England 1086–1135* OUP.

McIlwain. John ed. 1992 *The house of Elliotts* Elliott Brothers.

Marsh David C. 1967 *The changing social structure of England and Wales 1871–1961* Routledge & Kegan Paul Second impression.

Moore Pam 1988 *The industrial heritage of Hampshire and the Isle of Wight* Phillimore.

Newsome David 1966 *The parting of friends* John Murray.

Nicolson Adam 2003 *Power & Glory: Jacobean England and the making of the King James Bible* Harper Collins.

Page M. ed. 1996 *The Pipe Roll of the Bishopric of Winchester 1301–1302* Hampshire Record Series Vol.14 HCC.

Page M. ed. 1999 *The Pipe Roll of the Bishopric of Winchester 1409–1410* Hampshire Record Series Vol.16 HCC.

Paul John E. 1959 *Hampshire recusants in the time of Elizabeth I, with special reference to Winchester* HFC pp. 61–81.

Pevsner Nikolaus & Lloyd David 1967 *Buildings of England Hampshire and the Isle of Wight* Penguin.

Pitman Trevor 1977 *Newtown and clay 1860–1957* n.p.

Poole K.P.& Keith-Lucas B.1994 *Parish government 1894–1994* National Association of Local Councils.

Powicke F.M.& Fryde E.B. eds.1961 *Handbook of British Chronology* 2nd Ed.

Riall Nicholas 1994 *Henry of Blois, Bishop of Winchester a patron of the twelfth century Renaissance* Hampshire Papers 5 HCC.

Roberts Edward 1986 *The Bishop of Winchester's Fishponds in Hampshire, 1150– 1400* in HFCAS Vol.42 HCC.

Roberts Edward 1988 *The Bishop of Winchester's Deer Parks in Hampshire 1200–1400* in HFCAS Vol.44 HCC.

Rosman Doreen 2003 *The evolution of the English churches 1500–2000* CUP.

Rushton Gillian A 1989 *100 years of progress* HCC.

Sargeant F.H.1955 *The story of the church of St Peter, Bishop's Waltham* n.p.

Sargeant F.H.1958 *The story of the Bishop's Palace, Bishop's Waltham* n.p.

Sargeant F.H. 1961 *The story of Bishop's Waltham ancient and modern* n.p.

Simmonds R.& Robertson K. 1988 *The Bishop's Waltham branch railway* Wild Swan publications.

Simpson Michael 2004 *A Life of Admiral of the Fleet Andrew Cunningham* Frank Cass .

Smith Mark ed.2004 *Doing the duty of the parish: surveys of the church in H ampshire 1810* HCC .

Talbot C.H. 1954 *The Anglo-Saxon Missionaries in Germany* Sheed & Ward.

Tate W.E. 1983 *The Parish Chest* Third edition CUP.

Turner B.Carpenter 1978 *A history of Hampshire* Phillimore.

Venn J. & J A 1927 *Alumni Cantabridgienses* CUP.

Victoria County History of Hampshire and the Isle of Wight Volume 3 1908 Institute of Historical Research .

Vickers John A.ed.1993 *The religious census of Hampshire 1851* HCC.

Walmsley W.E. compiled 2004 *Some memories of Bishop's Waltham during the early 1940s* and *D Day 6th June 1944 Where was I?* Bishop's Waltham Society.

Ward.W.R.ed. 1995 *Parson and parish in eighteenth century Hampshire: replies to bishops' visitations* HCC.

Wareham John 2000 *Three palaces of the bishops of Winchester* English Heritage.

Watkins Peter R 2001 *Swanmore since 1840* Swanmore books.

West John 1982 *Village Records* Second edition Phillimore.

Whiteman Anne ed.1986 *The Compton Census of 1676* OUP for British Academy.

Whyte William 2006 *Oxford Jackson* OUP.

Notes

Numbered references are to documents in Hampshire Record Office unless otherwise indicated.

Chapter 1 Palace, park and ponds to 1644 Pages 3–17

1. Coates 1989 p.169.
2. Fifth century pagan cemetery at Droxford.
3. Blair 2005 p.49.
4. Ib.p.74.
5. Hase 1976 Preface 'All mother churches discovered were on royal estates'.
6. Blair 2005 p.79.
7. *Ad monasterium quae vocatum Waldheim* in the *Hodoeporicon of St Willibald* in Talbot ed.1954 pp 155–7.
8. I can find no evidence to support Frank Sargeant's claim that St Boniface came to the monastery at Waltham in 715. Sargeant 1955 p.1.
9. Talbot 1954 p.175, Blair 2005 pp.162,227 & ODCC p.1750.
10. Birch Anglo-Saxon Charters Vol.2 p.274. Hughes 1976 p.48.
11. In the 12th century the town was described as Waltham Episcopi Wintoniensis (Waltham belonging to the bishop of Winchester), Walters 1844 p.19.
12. The Winchester Manuscript Corpus Christi College Library, Cambridge MS173.
13. Hase 1976.
14. In a Charter of the Hospital of St Cross quoted by Henry of Blois, Bishop's Waltham and Upham are described as *ecclesiae* while the Palace chapel, Durley and Bursledon are described as *capellae*. See BM Harley 1616 Liber Primus Sancti Crucis.
15. Lennard 1959 c.10 and particularly p.307.
16. Quoted by Hase in Blair 1988 p.61. The Charter, 10629 in the archives of Winchester College, is undated. The catalogue gives a date between 1153 and 1171 (letter to the author from the College archivist Miss S. Foster dated 12.7.2007). The Charter was probably issued after the return of Henry of Blois from France in 1158.
17. Blair 2005 pp 69, 442.
18. Parish Register for 1736 & VCH Vol.3 pp.184, 281.
19. Page 1996 p.ix.
20. Knowles 1950 p.287, Brooke 2006 p.78.
21. Riall 1994 p.3.
22. For family tree see Riall 1994 p.4.
23. Knowles 1950 pp.285–93, Riall 1994 pp.3–8.
24. For map of the bishop's estates Riall 1994 p.8.
25. For the Palace see excellent guides by J.N.Hare & John Wareham to which this account owes much.
26. See Register of Bishop Edington 1344–1366 Hampshire Record Series Vols.7&8 1986–7.

27. Quoted in Sargeant 1958 p.12.
28. R.Hilton *The marriage of Mary I to Philip of Spain* in HFCAS Vol.14 part I 1938 pp.46–61.
29. I owe this reference to Alan Lovell who lent me a letter written to Lord Cunningham of Hyndhope dated 26th April 1960 drawing his attention to the quotation in A.L.Rowse *The expansion of Elizabethan England.*
30. For the Park and Ponds I have made substantial use of Roberts 1986 & 1988.
31. Page 1996 p.255.
32. Roberts 1988 p.73.
33. Quoted in Sargeant p.18.
34. Walters 1844 p.76, Sargeant 1958 p.17, Biddell 2002 p.61.
35. VCH Vol.3 p.278.
36. Walters 1844 p.76.
37. Collins & Hurst 1978 p.34. There is a Curll chapel in Soberton church.

Chapter 2 Manor, town and church to 1644 Pages 18–30

1. VCH Vol.3 p.275.
2. Barstow 1992.
3. List of the manors of the bishop of Winchester in Page 2002 p.6.
4. Ib.p13.
5. Ib. pp 20–21.
6. Page 1996 & 1999.
7. Barstow 1988,1992,1993,1994.
8. Page 2002 p.8.
9. For an example of villains electing the reeve see Bennett 1937 p.170.
10. Page 1996 pp.249 ff.
11. Ib. p.249.
12. Ib. pp.252–3.
13. Ib. pp.254–55.
14. Ib. p.249.
15. Bettey 1986 pp.62–3.
16. Ib.p41.
17. VCH Vol.3 p.278.
18. Bettey 1986 pp49–50.
19. Ib.p.85.
20. Beaumont James p.9.
21. Ib.p.22.
22. E.M.Stevenson Hampshire Field Club Newsletter 42/51 p.28–9, using Barstow 1998.
23. Cochrane 1969 c.9 pp167–70.
24. Law 1980 pp8–9.
25. Page 2002 p.20.
26. Pevsner & Lloyd 1967 p.107; David Lloyd *Report on Bishop's Waltham 7th September 1971* typescript in HRO 5M87/49. Hughes 1976 p.50.
27. Biddell 2002 quoting 11M59/E1/123/10 & 11.
28. Hughes in Aston & Lewis 1994 p.204 also Hughes 1976 p.50.
29. Barstow 1992.
30. Pevsner & Lloyd 1967 p.104.
31. VCH Vol.3 & Charter of 1138 in British Museum Harleian MS 1616 fol.9. A hide was about 100 acres.

32. Page 1996 p.259.
33. Aumbry – a recess with a door in which the consecrated elements at Holy Communion were kept. Piscina – a small bowl for washing the vessels used in Holy Communion and the priest's hands before he consecrated the elements. Walters 1844 pp.25–8.
34. Of the 31 parishes in the Droxford deanery (much larger than it is today and covering almost all the parishes in what became in 1927 the diocese of Portsmouth) the richest was Meonstoke, worth £46.2.10½. Bishop's Waltham ranked fifth.
35. See J.E.H. Spaul *The Reformation in the diocese of Winchester 1530–1616*.
36. VCH Vol.3 p.281.
37. Registers of Stephen Gardiner & John Poynet Canterbury & York Society 1929–30.
38. A.W.Goodman The Catholic church in the archdeaconry of Winchester in 1562 in HFC Vol.14 1938 pp 63–85. Archbishop Parker's Questions to the diocesans of the southern province 1561 and Bishop Horne's reply 1562. Original in the library of Corpus Christi College, Cambridge.
39. Sargeant 1955 p.14.
40. Spaul op.cit.
41. Paul 1959 p.65 & Collins & Hurst 1978 p.44.
42. Walters 1844 p.31.
43. Venn 1927.
44. HFC Vol.14 Part 1 1938 for Liber Actorum 1574.
45. Paul 1959 p.78.
46. Tate 1983 p.43 ff & Fitzhugh 1998 pp.204–17.
47. The earliest Registers kept by a local parish were at Soberton – burials from 1538, marriages from 1540 & christenings from 1546. For details of other parish registers in Hampshire see C.R. Humphreys-Smith *The Phillimore Atlas and Index of Parish Registers* 3rd edition 2003.
48. According to the Julian Calendar in use until 1752 New Year's day was 25th March so dates from 1st January to 24th March are usually written eg 1612/13.
49. The Parish Registers were kept in the Parish Chest until 1977. In 2.1977 they were displayed in the Church Hall before deposit in HRO PN 2,4.1977.
50. 30/M77PR1. JW was John Wallis of Salisbury VCH p.281.
51. For Andrewes see ODCC p.61 & Nicolson 2003 p.187 ff. For Prynne ODCC p.1342.
52. Walters 1844 p.30.
53. The tester over the pulpit was probably a 19c. addition.
54. Walters 1844 p.30.
55. PN 5.1976.
56. VCH Vol.3 1908 p.280.

Chapter 3 After the Palace 1644 –1760 Pages 31–42

1. Walters 1844 p.8.
2. Dr Goulston's name is spelt in a variety of ways. I have adhered to the spelling he used in the Poor Rate book. (see page 35)
3. Walker Revised p.179 John Walker *Sufferings of the clergy*. Law pp.10–11.
4. *Chichester Cathedral* ed.Mary Hobbs 1994 Phillimore p.101.
5. For references to the first Register see 30M77PR1.
6. Book of Common Prayer as printed from 1662–1859.
7. 5M87/42/1–2.
8. For the Park leases see Biddell 2001 c.7.
9. 16/17 Carolus II c.13. The regnal years of Charles II were counted from the death of Charles I rather than his return in 1660.

10. Moore 1988 p.89.
11. HFCAS Vol.46 pp33–4.
12. Hughes & White 1991 Introduction & pp.15–25.
13. Walters 1844p.28.
14. The bishop's letters are inside the front cover of the Parish Register (from 1737) 30M77/PR3. Frank Sargeant refers to the incident but dates it incorrectly 1681.
15. Copy of the faculty dated 1768 is in HRO 30M77PW5.
16. Quoted in HNQ Vol.VI p.44.
17. Pevsner & Lloyd p.109 but the house was not built after the battle of Porto Bello.
18. DNB.
19. Information about Vernon Hill House from Priscilla Fryer *A short history of Vernon Hill House* nd,np.
20. Priscilla Fryer in conversation with the author April 2007.
21. Emery 1991 p.22.
22. Chapman & Seeliger 1997 p.1.
23. Ib.p.259.

Chapter 4 Poverty, pestilence and fire 1644–1840 Pages 43–54

1. Tate 1983 p.12.
2. Ib.pp 29–35, Biddell 2002 pp70–3.
3. 30M77/PO1.
4. Biddell 2002 particularly chapters.12–19.
5. 30M77/PO1–9.
6. 30M77/PO1.
7. 30M77/PK3.
8. Poor Rate 10. 10 – 6.12 1759.
9. Rate Book 22. 6. 1762.
10. 30M77/PV1 25. 9. 1808.
11. 30M77PO8.
12. 30M77/PVI.
13. 30M77/PV1 19.11.1809,26.11.1813,7..4. 1816, 6.6.1817, 28.4. 1820.
14. 33M77/PV1 7.9, 1819.
15. 33M77/PV1 29.1.1835.
16. 29M48/1.
17. 29M48/1 17.5, 24.5, 9,30.8. 1836.
18. 29M48/1 14.2. 1837.
19. PLIII7/1 pp.231–8.
20. I.Anstruther 1973 *The scandal of the Andover workhouse* Bles.
21. 30M77/PV2 3.1.1839.
22. 29M48/1 30.5.1837.
23. 77M30/PR4.
24. 'Goody is short for Good Wife; applied to a married woman in humble life' SOED.
25. 30M77/PO3 5.6.1724.
26. 30M77/PO3 5.6.1726.
27. Parish Register for 1740.
28. 30M77/PV1 19.4.1818.
29. 30M77/PV1 27.4.1828.
30. 30M77/PV2 10.12.1831.
31. 30M77PV1 20.2.1814.

32. 30M77/PO3 &PO4.
33. 261M86/6.

Chapter 5 The Turnpike Roads Pages 55–63

1. Albert 1972 p.45.
2. Ib. p14.
3. Ib. Appendix B pp.202–23 is a list of turnpikes authorised by act of parliament between 1663 and 1836.
4. 36M72A1/2.
5. 44M69/91/130.
6. 4M30/1–4.1758–91,1791–1820,1820–44,1844–75.
7. 5M54/112 contains the plan of the road from Botley to Corhampton.
8. *The Times* 7th September 1874. Copy in HRO 5M54/139.
9. *Hampshire Chronicle* 1.1.1810.
10. 5M54/144.
11. 44M73E/P17 contains a map of the projected route.
12. Moore 1988 c.7.
13. 5M54/118.
14. 5M54/67.
15. 78M73A/DH1.

Chapter 6 From the French wars to the Census of 1841 Pages 64–76

1. 30M77PO7.
2. TOP5/3/26.
3. In her latest book based on research much of it in the Admiralty records in the Public Record Office at Kew Barbara Biddell casts much new light on the prisoners held in Bishop's Waltham and elsewhere during the Revolutionary and Napoleonic Wars. Biddell 2007.
4. Biddell 2007 c.2,3.
5. Ib.c.5.
6. Ib Foreword & c.9.
7. Seen by Peg Price in 1963. The present owner of Hope House, David Ellis Jones, kindly showed the author the wall on which the pictures were originally painted.
8. Biddell 2007 c.11.
9. Sargeant 1961 p.40.
10. 30M77PR3 & PR11.
11. Catalogue of Sale 1884.
12. DNB & 30M77/PZ35.
13. PN 10.2002.
14. VCH Vol.3 p.278.
15. Alan Lovell.
16. Grose *Antiquities of England: Hampshire* 1784 p.284.
17. I am grateful to Barrie Cross for lending me his copy of *Our Town* & drawing my attention to aspects of it.
18. *Our Town* Vol.1 p.iii.
19. Ib. Vol.1 pp.8, 10.
20. Ib Vol.2 pp1–40.
21. Ib.Vol.1 p.17.

22. Ib. Vol.2 pp.157,159,140.
23. Ib.Vol.2 42–3,51.
24. FitzHugh 1998 pp.60–64 for Census returns & p.281 for Tithes.
25. The Census names French Street and St Peter Street whilst Pigott's Dirctory of 1844 describes the same streets as Bank Street & Church Lane. I have followed the Census to avoid confusion.
26. Pigot 1844 pp.12–3.
27. Bettey 1986 p.242.
28. Walters 1844 Title page.
29. Ib. p.30,71.
30. HNQ Vol.II p.48.
31. Best 1964 pp.187–9.
32. PV2 15.12.1837.
33. PV2 29.9.1841,F723/1, 21M/65.
34. HNQ Vol.VI 1892 p.64.
35. VCH Vol.3 p.278.
36. 30M77A/PV2 26.11.1841.

Chapter 7 Registers and rectors 1737–1833 Pages 77–86

1. 30M77/PR3.
2. Based on analysis of 400 marriages recorded in the Register from 1754–88.
3. 30M77PR5.
4. Ward 1995 pp.172–3.
5. Details of non-residence in Hampshire are in Ward 1995. See also Collins & Hurst 1978 pp.50–6 for a neighbouring parish.
6. 21M65A2/1 Register of Benjamin Hoadly.
7. Pevsner & Lloyd 1967 p.194, Hope 1980 p.30.
8. Walters 1844 p.33.
9. Smith 2004 p.xxiii.
10. Winchester Act Book 1802–23 & Beeson 2006 p.4.
11. Collins & Hurst 1978 pp.56–8.
12. Smith 2004 p.110.
13. The Poor Rate book for 1788–9 includes three payments to 'Sir C.Ogle's Boy',30M77PO7.
14. Smith 2004 pp.xxviii,xxxv,xli,lx, 23, 68, 76, 134.
15. Ib.pp.xxx & 34. for Crondall just before Ogle became rector.
16. Chadwick 1966 p.34.
17. 30M77/PB6.
18. 30M77PB9 dated 1960 when sale of the Rectory was first considered.
19. Description of the Rectory from a letter from Barbara Biddell to the author 29.8.2006.
20. 30M77PV1 6,8,23.1.1822.

Chapter 8 From the Grammar School to the Educational Institute Pages 87–96.

1 Barfoot and Williams Dirctory 1793.
2. HFCAS Vol.45 1989 pp.148–56.
3. HNQ Vol.6 p.44.
4. Turner 1978 pp.91–3.
5. 30M77PK3.

6. Hurst 1980 p.21.
7. 21M65/A2/1.
8. HNQVol.II 1884 pp.49–52 also Hampshire Miscellany.
9. Quoted in Biddell 2007 p.66.
10. HFCAS Vol.45 1989 pp 148–51.
11. 30M77PZ28, DNB, J.Webb et al. *The Spirit of Portsmouth* 1989 pp.157–9.
12. 30M77PZ28.
13. 261M86/8–9.
14. 261M86/1–16.
15. HNQVol.I pp49–52.
16. Census of 1851 contains information about parents and places of birth.
17. Biddell 2001 pp.123–4.
18. 378M87/1 3.7.1880.
19. 84M76A/PK38.
20. Ib.26.4.1878.
21. Ib.6.9.1887.
22. Ib.27.7.1887.
23. 84M76A/PK83 & 84M76A/PK39 1.11,6.12.1887 & 3.1.1888.
24. Ib.28.10.1892.
25. Ib.29.11.1892.
26. Ib.29.12.1892.
27. 261M86/2/36 Letter dated 9.5.1893.
28. Ib.16.5,27,10 1893; 13.1, 15.2.1894,.
29. Ib.15.8.1894.
30. P.Mag.8.1899.
31. Ib.7.1900. See Rushton 1989 p.27 for photograph of the travelling dairy van.
32. P.Mag.7.1900.

Chapter 9 From the National School to the County Mixed School Pages 97–108

1. 5M54/71.
2. Census of 1841 & Pigot's Directory 1844.
3. Marriage Registers. Each cohort contains about 100 weddings.
4. 216M86/LB1.
5. P.Mag. 4.1914.
6. Log 1.7. 1872..
7. Log 23.10. 1872. Winchester Training College was later renamed King Alfred's College and is now part of the University of Winchester.
8. Log 28 .5.1875, 13.3 1877, 2.5. 1879.
9. For example Log 17.9.1872.
10. Log 15.7.1872.
11. Ib.28.7.1875.
12. 128M88/1.
13. Watkins 2001 p.31.
14. 378M87/1 17.10. 1878.
15. Ib.12.5.1879.
16. Ib. 7.7 1879.
17. Ib.6.1. 1879.
18. Ib. 2.1. 1882.

19. *Hampshire Chronicle* 12.1 1895, offprint in HRO 30M77/PJ6.
20. Log 8.5.1889.
21. Ib.14.10 1889.
22. Ib. 10.7 1893,11.7 1894.
23. School Board Minutes 13.12.1893.
24. Ib.18.10 1895.
25. P.Mag. 9 &10 1907. 30M77/PZ11.
26. 84M76/PK40.
27. Rushton c.2 & Appendix 11.
28. 378M87/12. Letter Book 21.12.1911& 1.2. 1913.
29. Statistics from B.Simon *Education and the Social Order 1940–1990* pubd.1991Table 2a p.516.
30. P.Mag. 9.1949.
31. Ib.7. 1943 & 8. 1944.
32. Ib.9. 1945.
33. P.Mag. 9. 1949.
34. Log of Bishop's Waltham Mixed School 1952–61 particularly HMI report reproduced on pp.220–9.
35. Log of Swanmore Secondary School 6.9.1961 reports 329 pupils; by 9.1970 there were 572.

Chapter 10 The Gunners of Bishop's Waltham Pages 109–118

1. I am indebted to Harry Gunner for lending me family papers and photographs.on which this chapter is largely based as well as sharing reminiscences with me. Also R.A. Hodgson *Gunners Bank* reprinted 2006.
2. Barfoot & Williams Directory 1793 & Hampshire Directory 1784.
3. Barfoot & Williams op cit.p.399.
4. Hodgson 2006 p.4.
5. Ib.pp11–12.
6. *The Marlburian* 5.3. 1924 made available by Harry Gunner,.
7. Information from Harry Gunner.
8. Census 1901.
9. Catalogue of Sale 1925.

Chapter 11 Arthur Helps and mid-Victorian enterprise Pages 119–131

1. DNB.
2. HNQ Vol.VI 1891–2 p.64.
3. 30M87/9.
4. Bosworth 1988 p.97.
5. Pitman 1977, Simmonds & Robertson 1988 pp.80–1.
6. HFCAS Vol.28 1971 pp.81–97.
7. Pitman 1977 no page numbers.
8. HFCAS op.cit. p.94.
9. Moore 1988 pp.38,81–2. The Hockley Viaduct is still visible from the motorway link road south of Winchester. McIlwain 1992 p.85.
10. McIlwain 1992 p.85.
11. Bosworth 1986 p.86.
12. Simmonds & Robertson 1988 pp.19,79.

13. PCM 14.6.1899.
14. P.Mag.8,10.1898.
15. PN 11.1975.
16. Harry Gunner.
17. Watkins 2001 p.115.
18. *Hampshire Telegraph and Post* 6.1.1953 The Last Train.
19. Reg Cockle.
20. PN 9.1975.
21. Simmonds & Robertson 1988 pp.83–4.
22. Bosworth 1986 p.100.
23. James Padbury's Scrapbook contains a great deal about the Infirmary including lists of subscribers and press cuttings. 30M77/PZ54.
24. Bosworth 1985 p.6.
25. *HampshireChronicle, Southampton and Isle of Wight Courier* 6.8.1864.
26. Quoted in Sargeant 1961 p.50.
27. Finn 2002 p.20.
28. Biddell 2002 p.44.
29. Catalogue of Sale 3.11.1877.
30. Finn 2002 pp.23–4.
31. Catalogue of Sale 5.1908.
32. Finn 2002 p.223.
33. Scrapbook BW Museum Trust 4.2004.

Chapter 12 William Brock and the Victorian church Pages 132–139

1. Best 1964 p.545.
2. Chadwick 1966 p.116.
3. Beeson 2002 p.17.
4. Winchester Act Book 1824–44 21.8.1829.
5. Beeson 2002 pp.17–8.
6. See Newsome 1966 p.25 for family trees of Wilberforce and Sumner families.
7. Baptismal Register of parish of Highclere.
8. I have found no entry for George Brock in any census. It seems likely that he died in infancy away from the parish and was buried elsewhere.
9. BL 4107.bb.20.
10. BL 4478cc (9).
11. BL4107.bb.20.
12. Barfoot & Williams Directory of Hampshire 1793 p.399.
13. TOP87/1/1 & Hogg 1988 pp.7–8.
14. Newsome 1966 p.282.
15. Hogg 1988 pp.7,10.
16. Curdridge parish contained 2174 acres out of the 8325 in Bishop's Waltham. For the creation of Swanmore see Watkins 2001 pp.16–7.
17. Shedfield 1880, Curdridge 1888.
18. 30M77PV2 25.10.1848.
19. Ib.13.11.1848.
20. W.N.Yates *Victorian church attendance the evidence* in Hampshire Studies ed.J.Webb et al Portsmouth City Record Office.
21. Vickers 1993 p.140.

22. 30M77/PW1.
23. 30M77PV2 7.5.1867 ?.
24. Sargeant 1955 pp.6–7.
25. *Restoration of Bishop's Waltham Chursh* Printed pamphlet dated August 23 1871 with statement of accounts and list of contributors
26. 30M77PV3 20.9,10.10.1873.
27. M77PV3 6.11.1874.
28. Ib. 23.4.1889,21.3.1990 & 21.3.1891.
29. Obituary of Louisa Brock P.Mag.11.1890.
30. *Dover Beach* 1867.
31. P.Mag.1.1892.

Chapter 13 Primitive Methodists ,Congregationalists and Roman Catholics Pages 140–151

1. Ward 1995 pp.20 & 65.
2. 21M65F4/2 List of reputed Papists in the Parish of Bishop's Waltham, Hants.
3. 62M73M/F19 Anti-Popery Petition to the House of Lords presented by the Earl of Guildford 1829.
4. Some material on Primitive Methodism in the Droxford Circuit from Kitching 2001.
5. Vickers 1993 pp.141 & 144.
6. Primitive Methodist Circuit Plan & Census 1881.
7. Kitching 2000 pp.68–9.
8. Census 1881 & Primitive Methodist Preachers Plan January to March 1883 in Kitching 2000 pp.6–7.
9. Burials register.
10. Kitching 2001 p.18 & Watkins 2001 p.95.
11. Kitching 2001 p.21.
12. Ib.pp27–8.
13. Hogg 1988 pp11–2. Kitching 2001 pp.34–5
14. For list of Primitive Methodist ministers in the Droxford Circuit see Kitching 2000pp74–5 & Watkins 2001 pp.155–6.
15. 128/M88/1. Bishop's Waltham Congregational Church Book pp.1–36 contains an account of the period 1836–94 written by a contemporary from which much material in subsequent paras. comes.
16. He died in 1926 and is buried in the churchyard.
17. PM 4.3.1901.
18. Kitching 2000 p.61 also TOP31/1/16.
19. Census 1901. Boniface family: Ernest (28), Annie wife (24) born in Ireland, Kathleen (1), Percy (19, Ernest's brother).
20. Finn 2004 pp.25–6.
21. Ib. pp 62–75.
22. Ib.p.89.
23. I am indebted to Bunny Thornton for use of material which she has collected on the history of the Roman Catholic parish. Also HFCAS Vol.46 p.28, PN 4.1977.
24. Finn 2004 p.127.
25. Ib.pp135–6.
26. *Faithful Victor*, a memoir of Victor Madgwick, lent to the author by Dr Nick Lalor.

Chapter 14 The Enclosure of Curdridge Common & Waltham Chase Pages 152–155

1. Chapman & Seeliger 1977 p.20. For Meonstoke see Collins & Hurst pp.114–7.
2. Q23/2/34.
3. Horders Wood was the older name for Waltham Chase. *Hordareswode 1301*, Coates p.169.
4. HRO Cobbett Vol.2 p.261. Cobbett greatly underestimated the extent of the Chase –it is closer to 2000 acres in extent.
5. The first pamphlet has not survived but its contents are summarised in order to be contradicted in HRO 44M69/121/18.
6. For details see Watkins 2001 pp.23–5.
7. Q23/2/14.

Chapter 15. Houses, people and places in the late nineteenth century Pages 156–167

1. 30M&&PZ53–9.
2. I am grateful to Neil Padbury of Bath for permission to use the research he has undertaken on his family history.
3. DNB also Collins & Hurst 1978 p.146.
4. Barfoot & Williams 1793.
5. Seen by the author.
6. Pigott 1831.
7. Sargeant 1955 p.13.
8. 125M85/18/5 is a codicil to Padbury's will dated 27.7.1898 about a fortnight before he died.
9. P.Mag. 9.1898.
10. Ib.eg. 12.1899.
11. Diary by kind permission of Jenny Maidment.
12. Dr Charles Hemming II in conversation with the author.
13. 11M59/E2/155472, 115M91W/9/39.
14. St Peter's Churchyard records.
15. Monica Martineau's papers are deposited in HRO 5M87.
16. I am indebted to a brief history of the firm entitled *Austin & Wyatt 1836–1986*. Since there is no named author or publisher; I refer to it as 'AW'.
17. AW p.5 P.Mag.1896.
18. Information drawn from research by W.E.Walmsley and written up in his *Chase Mills of Bishop's Waltham, Hampshire*, 1999 unpublished to which the author kindly gave me access.
19. P.Mag. 9 & 10.1907.
20. Ib. 1896.
21. Ib.2.1896.
22. PN 2.1976 article by Ethel Cockle.
23. Museum Scrapbook No.7 Spring 1996.
24. P.Mag.9 &10 1907.

Chapter 16 Pleasures and pastimes 1870–1914 Pages 168–177

1. ODCC p.1584.
2. Sargeant 1961 pp52–6.
3. Jenny Maidmant – family folklore.
4. P.Mag.2.1896.

5. Ib. 9.1896.
6. Ib.11.1892.
7. Ib.11.1906.
8. Plan of the Droxford Circuit 7–9.1910.
9. P.Mag.6.1907.
10. Ib.12.1907.
11. Diary by kind permission of Jenny Maidment whose great aunt was Blanche Hemming.
12. P.Mag. 8.1892.
13. Ib. 9.1896.Home Words p.210.
14. Briggs 2003 p.370.
15. See Watkins 2001 pp.46–8.
16. PN 1.1977.
17. I am indebted to David Williams for information on which this account of cricket in Bishop's Waltham is based.
18. *Portsmouth Evening News* 28.11.1972).
19. PN 2.1972 in article by John Cornell then Group Scout Leader.
20. Ib.2.1977.
21. Bosworth 1991 p.5.
22. Ib. p.9.

Chapter 17. The restoration of 1896–7 and the pre-war church Pages 178–190

1. P.Mag. 3 & 4.1892.
2. PN2.1972. 'The parson retired to the vestry at the west end of the church and shortly reappeared wearing a black academic gown instead of his surplice'. From *Memories of childhood spent in Bishop's Waltham.*
3. Service registers from 1892.
4. 30M77/PV3 19.4. 1892.
5. P.Mag. 1.1890.
6. For example Ib.5.1892.
7. Chadwick 1970 pp.192–3.
8. P.Mag. 1.1893.
9. See Pevsner & Lloyd 1967 for Jackson's work in Hampshire.
10. For T.G.Jackson see Jackson 2003, Whyte 2006 & DNB.
11. The aisle was built not rebuilt in 1637.
12. 30M77PW29.
13. 30M77PW42.
14. 30M77PV3 27.6. 1895.
15. 30M77/PW30.
16. Mockford was also Jackson's clerk of works at Brasenose College, Oxford & Eltham Palace.Whyte 2006 p.59.
17. 30M77SW38.
18. 30M77PW43.
19. P.Mag. 12.1896.
20. Ib.4. 1897.
21. Ib. 1. 1902.
22. Hampshire Chronicle.
23. P.Mag. 3. 1901.
24. Quoted in Whyte 2006 p.199.
25. P.Mag 5.1904 & 1.1905.

26. Ib.10. 1906.
27. Ib. 7.1891.
28. Ib.2.1893 & 11.1894.
29. Ib. 8. 1890.
30. Ib.7. 1890.
31. Ib.7.1894,96,98.
32. Ib.8. 1890& 8 1891.
33. Ib. 6. 1907.
34. Ib. 4.1898.
35. Ib.1.1900.
36. Ib. 1. 1953.
37. ODQ p.437.12. Service register 1913–20, 30M77P1/14 & P.Mag.1.1953.

Chapter 18. The Parish Council and the town 1894–1914 Pages 191–200

1. For 1901 I have added figures for Bishop's Waltham and Curdridge together in order to provide comparison of 1801 & 1901. See Appendix B.
2. Bettey 1986 pp 230–2.
3. P.Mag.1890–9, Marsh 1967 pp.10 & 63.
4. National figures Marsh 1967 p.24.
5. For background to the Act of 1894 see Poole & Keith-Lucas 1994 cc.1&2.
6. PM 18.3. 1897.
7. Ib.4.12. 1894 & 4.2. 1895.
8. Plaque to his memory on wall of the south aisle of St Peter's.
9. Warren's Directory 1893 & Census 1901.
10. PCM 12 & 19.10 1911.
11. 78M73A/DDC1.
12. PCM 1.6. 1897.
13. Ib.27.7. 1897.
14. Ib. 30.4. 1897.
15. Q23/2/14.
16. PM 7.10. 1897.
17. Ib.24.3. 1903.
18. PN. 7.1977.
19. PCM 21.7.1908.
20. Ib. 21.1. 1908.
21. Ib.22.7. 1910.

Chapter 19 The First World War and the inter-war years 1914–1939 Pages 201–214

1. Based on PN 3.1972.
2. Finn 2002 p.48. In France priests were not exempt from military service.
3. PN 3.1972.
4. Son of Admiral and Mrs George Giffard who erected a plaque in St Peter's in his memory.
5. PCM 23.3.1917.
6. Ib.19.1.1917.
7. Ib.20.7.1917,22.3.1918.
8. 118M98/A1.
9. PCM 17.1.1919.

10. 30M77PV3 24.4.1919,4.11.1920.
11. P.Mag.12.1938.
12. PCM22.4,2,5.1919.
13. PMM 8.10.1924.
14. P.Mag.7.1925.
15. PMM 13.1.1926.
16. P.Mag.10&11 1934.
17. Ib.5.1933.
18. Ib.1.1935.
19. Ib.9.1933.
20. Ib.11.1933.
21. Ib. 9.1934, 5.1936, 3.1937.
22. Flier distributed with P.Mag.3.1932.
23. PCM 22.9.1933.
24. Ib.21.12.1936.
25. PCM 17.1,17.10 1930, 3.6.1932.
26. P.Mag. 9.1932, 9.1933.
27. 44M68/G3/1, P.Mag.7.1914.
28. P.Mag. 5.1927.
29. PN 5.2002.
30. P.Mag.2.1932.
31. Ib.4.1932.
32. Walmsley 1999 no page numbers.
33. Amy Harvey PN 1.2000 p.13.
34. P.Mag.6.1935.
35. Ib.6.1933.
36. Memorial brass now in Bishop's Waltham Museum & PN 6.1976.
37. Last three paragraphs based on reminiscences of Charles Pitman, son of last lamplighter, made available to the author by Peg Price.

Chapter 20 The Second World War and after 1939–1965 Pages 215–230

1. PCM15.7.1937.
2. Finn 2002 p.93.
3. PCM 21.7.1939.
4. P.Mag. 10.1939.
5. Ib.10.1940.
6. Ib.12.1939.
7. For this paragraph and material later in this chapter see Walmsley 2004.
8. PRO WO166/3565 slightly edited.
9. Finn 2002 pp.97–117.
10. Ib.p.116.
11. PN 1.2000p.13.
12. P.Mag.3.1941.
13. Ib.1.1941.
14. 118M98/A3.
15. Diana Gibson nee Chamberlain in conversation with the author.
16. I am grateful to Alan & Virginia Lovell the present owners of Palace House for drawing my attention to and lending me copies of Lord Cunningham,'s autobiography *A Sailor's Odysssey* 1940 and the biography by Michael Simpson 2004.].

17. Simpson 2004 p.175.
18. Cunningham 1940 pp.581–2.
19. Simpson 2004 p.1175.
20. Quoted in David Cannadine *G.M Trevelyan, a life in history* Harper Collins 1992 p.24.
21. PN 6.2001.
22. Walmsley 2004 pp.3–10.
23. P.Mag.12.1944.
24. Finn 2002 p.116.
25. Simpson 2004 p.219.
26. Ib. pp 224–6.
27. PCM 22.4.1943, 14.5.1943.
28. PCM 26.7.1946.
29. Poole & Keith-Lucas pp.156–7;PCM 28.1.1943,25.5.1945.
30. Gilda Jacucci in conversation with the author, 7.2007. Carmelo died 3.2003 aged 82.
31. P.Mag. 11.1949, 1.1955.
32. Finn 2002 p.37.
33. 30M77/PB6.
34. Don Cole in conversation with the author, 1. 2007.
35. *Illustrated* 25.4.1953 pp.39–42.
36. PCM27.4.1953, 21.5.1953.
37. Ib.28.3.47, 30.5.47.

Chapter 21 Growth and renewal since 1965 Pages 231–246

1. Pevsner & Lloyd 1967 pp.104, 109.
2. Bosworth 1986 Introduction.
3. Harvey in Bosworth 1986 Foreword.
4. PN 6.1969, 8.1970.
5. Ib.4.1970 .
6. The Hambledon Hunt no longer exists. It was merged with an adjoining Hunt.
7. PN 5,12.1978.
8. Ib. 9.2002, 5.2003.
9. Ib.7–8. 2002.
10. Ib.2.1997,6.2000 & others.
11. Bosworth 1986.
12. PN 9.2000 p.28.
13. Ib.6.1987.
14. *Hampshire Chronicle* 27.10.1987.
15. PN 9,10.2004.
16. Research undertaken by *Off Licence News* concluded that this is the oldest shop in the country on the same site which has sold alcohol continuously (since 1617).
17. Bosworth 1988 p.29.
18. St Peter's Annual Report 2006: Average Sunday Attendance (ASA) in 2006 was 162. This comprised 140 adults and 22 children.
19. PN 9,10.2004.
20. Ib.
21. Population statistics from Census of 1991.
22. Winchester City Council Population forecasts 2001–12.

A note on pre-decimal coinage

The pound was decimalised in 1971. Until then it had been divided into 20 shillings each of which consisted of 12 pence so a pound (£) was 240 pence which was abbreviated d. for denarius (Latin). A shilling was written 1/- and a penny 1d. One shilling and sixpence was therefore written 1/6. I have used the old currency descriptions throughout this book until 1971.

Units of pre-1971 currency with approximate post-1971 values.

Unit	Written	Value post-1971
1 farthing	1/4d	just over 0.1 of a penny.
1 halfpenny	1/2d	just over 0.2 of a penny.
1 penny	1d	0.4 of a penny.
6 pence	6d	2½ pence.
1 shilling	1/-	5 pence.
2 shillings (florin)	2/-	10 pence.
2 shillings and 6 pence (half a crown)	2/6	12½ pence.
1 pound	£1	1 pound.
1 pound 1 shilling (guinea)	£1.1.0	1 pound 5 pence.

Index

This index covers the text of the book but does not include illustrations, appendices, bibliography or notes. Names appearing only in the decennial census are not usually included.

Adams Edgar 174
Addison's Housing Act 205
Admiral's Corner (in St Peter's) 222
Adult education 105
Air raid wardens 215
Aisle North 29
Aisle South 32
Albert House (see Royal Albert Infirmary)
Albert Road 119, 121
Alcohol 168–70
Alfred the Great 4
Alice (Princess) 129
Allen William 91
Allington 28
Alresford 15, 58, 59
Andrewes Lancelot 28–9
Anglo-Saxon Chronicle 5
Anglo-Saxon colonisation 1
Anjou, Margaret of 10
Anson Admiral George 156
Anti-popery petition 141
Appleby George Habin 75, 152, 161
Archer-Shepherd Thomas 138, 171, 179, 187
Arigo Angelo & Stellina 224
Armistice Day 205
Arnold Matthew 138
Arnold Thomas 134
ARP 215, 218
Arthur (Prince) 129
Ashe Robert 80
Ashton 40, 41, 44, 71–2
Ashton Farm 71
Ashton Thomas 29
Attendance officer 102
Aumbry 137
Austin & Wyatt 162
Austin Richard
  I 162
  II 162
  III 93, 162–3, 200
  Mrs 105

Baden Powell Robert 174
Band of Hope 169
Bank Charter Act 1844 111
Bank Street (also French Street) 21, 22, 109–10, 170, 192, 212
Banns (of marriage) 80
Baptisms 77
Barclays bank 118
Barleycorn Inn 47
Barnsley Walter 145
Barstow Harold 18, 22
Barton Robert 66
Basingwell Street 2, 21, 22, 65, 201, 212, 231
Battershell Sarah 88
Battery Hill 236
Beaufort Henry 9, 10
Becketts Farm 212
Beer Riots 168
Belfry 84
Belle Nicholas 22
Bellringers 84
Bells (St Peter's) 28, 32, 211
Beloe Jane 244
Belton & Hall 212
Bicycles 171
Biddell Barbara 2, 16, 22, 44, 65
Biddell Christopher 241–2
Bishop's Waltham & Upham Nursing Association 207
Bishop's Waltham in Bloom 240
Bishop's Waltham & Hampshire Bank 109
Bishop's Waltham Carnival 239
Bishop's Waltham Clay Company 121
Bishop's Waltham Cycling Club 172–3
Bishop's Waltham Deanery 136
Bishop's Waltham Educational Institute 158
Bishop's Waltham Festival 240
Bishop's Waltham Gas & Coke Company 128
Bishop's Waltham Historical Society 239
Bishop's Waltham Jubilee Temperance Brass & Reed Band 169, 189
Bishop's Waltham Palace 158
Bishop's Waltham Society 156, 235, 239
Bishop's Waltham Waterworks 198
Bishopsdown Farm 72
Black Death 20
Blackout 216
Blanchard Mark Henry I 119, 122
Blanchard Mark Henry II 122, 234
Blanchard Road 2
Blanchard's Brick & Tile Works 122
Bletchley Park 217
Blois Henry of 1, 5–6, 14, 22
Blue plaques 239
Blunden D.P. 226
Bone Mary 89
Boniface family 149
Book of Common Prayer 25, 26, 31, 32, 77, 101
Bosworth John 233, 240
Botley 1, 21, 75, 135, 188, 224
  (road) 65
Boys School (Dodd's Alley) 105, 108
Bradwardine Thomas 20
Bramdean 90
Bridges John 26
British & Foreign Schools Society 101, 102, 129, 148
Brock Ann Magdalen (Gosset) 133
Brock Cameron ` 161, 171
Brock family 133–4
Brock Louisa (Harrison) 133, 138
Brock Thomas 133
Brock William 48, 51, 73, 94, 100, 133, 135, 137–9, 144, 146–7, 158, 178–9
Brook House 11, 112

Brook Street 22
Brooklands Farm 236
Brown Thomas John 105, 112, 186, 196
Browne Harold 180
Buchanan-King Andrew 202
Budgen's supermarket 150, 241
Bulwark (HMS) 201
Bunyard Reg 2
Burials Act 1880 144
Bursledon 5, 6, 18, 22
Burton Gilbert 24-6
Buryfield farm 217
Bus services 208
Bush Baron de 189
Bypass 208, 232

Catholic Emancipation 1829 141
Census 1831 70
Census 1841 70-1
Census 1851 73-4, 97-9, 162
Census 1861 160
Census 1901 161, 191
Census of church attendance 1851 136
Chadwick Edwin 49
Chadwick Owen 180
Chalky Lane 16
Chamberlain family 219
Charity Commissioners 92, 93, 95
Charles II 31-3
Charles V (emperor) 11
Chase Inn (also *Fountain Inn*) 39, 40, 193, 198
Chase Mill (also Est Myll) 210
Chawton 80
Chelsea 33
Chenevix-Trench Richard 135
Cheriton Battle of 16
Cherry Gardens 198
Cholera 53
Church Ales 35
Church Hall 167, 218, 236
Church rate (abolition of) 136-7
Church wardens accounts 137
Churches Together in Bishop's Waltham 151
Churchill Melville 161, 188, 189
Churchwardens 43-4
Churchyard (St Peter's) 206, 238
Citizens Advice Bureau 238
Civil War 16
Clark Edward 197
Clark Francis 171
Clark George & Maria 69
Clarke Alfred 146
Clay Hill 154
Claylands brickyard 191, 224, 230
Claylands House 121-2, 216, 234
Claylands Road 122
Clewers Hill 154, 198

Clock in the Square 238, 246
Clothing Club 188
Cluny 7, 8
Coaches 61, 73
Coal Club 188
Cobbett William 60, 154
Cockfighting 75
Cockle Ethel 127-8, 174, 200
Cockle Reg 127, 174, 209, 221
Cole Don 226-7
Colenutt family 166
Collections (church) 179, 180
Collins Frances 84
Colpoys family 66
Colpoys J.A.G. 66
Common fields 22
Commonwealth 32
Confirmation 188
Congestion (traffic) 208
Congregational church (United Reformed 1972) 101, 102, 146, 205, 212, 234-5
Constable (parish officer) 43, 53
Cooke John 140
Cooperative store 241
Coppice Hill 49, 208
Coppice Hill brickfield 72, 191, 230
Coppice Hill House 162
Corhampton 80, (road) 232-3
Corn Laws 48
Coronation of Elizabeth II 230
Coronation of George VI 211
Council houses 205
Council School 105
County Mixed School 108
Cowen D.T. 105
Crickelmede 235, 237
Cricket 172
Cricketers Inn, Curdridge 152
Cromwell Oliver 1
Cromwell Thomas 25, 27, 43
Crondall 85
Cross Street 231
Crown Inn (Hotel) 65, 73, 75, 127, 128, 169, 212, 232
Cunningham Andrew Admiral of the Fleet (Lord) 162, 220, 221, 224, 226
Cunningham House 237
Cunningham Nona (Lady) 220, 221, 224, 226
Curates 82
Curdridge 1, 21, 40, 41, 44, 52, 53, 72, 75, 97, 102, 135, 146, 152, 197 (chapel of ease) 135-6
Curdridge Common 72, 75, 152
Curdridge Lane 20
Curdridge Methodist Chapel 146
Curll Walter 16, 17, 29, 31, 109
Cutler James 58, 82

Cyclists service 171

D-Day 216, 220, 221
Dairy school 96, 105
Dampier Admiral 224
Danish raids 5
Davidson Randall 171
Dean 72
Deanery of Droxford North West 136
Dee Mary (deaconess) 242
Deer 14
Deer Park (bishop's) 12, 14
Denewulf, bishop of Winchester 4
Desa Paul 192
Dig for Victory 218
Diocesan Conference (Winchester) 171
Disestablishment of Irish Church 134, 137
Dissenters admitted to Oxford & Cambridge 137
District Churches Act, 1843 135
Dodds Alley 96, 103.105, 106, 108, 226, 228
Domesday book 5, 14, 75, 244
Donniger Ezekiel 37
Dowse family 72
Drill Hall 150, 201, 215
Droxford 22, 26, 126, 169
Droxford Primitive Methodist Circuit 144
Droxford Rural District Council 198, 206, 207, 235
Droxford Union Workhouse 50, 51, 53
Duffett T. 213
Duffy Father 150
Duke James and Son 15, 235, 240
Dundridge 16, 71, 72
Dunkirk 216-7
Duppa Brian 33
Durley 18, 21, 22, 27, 50, 82, 90, 97, 132, 153, (sawmill) 209
Durley Mill 126

East Meon 3
Eastway House 171, 234
Edington William 20
Education Act 1870 (Forster) 101
Education Act 1902 (Balfour) 105, 145
Educational Institute 88, 95, 96, 105, 167, 170, 238, 239
Edward III 9
Edward IV 10
Edward the Elder 4
Edward VI 12, 25, 26
Edward VII (Coronation) 176, 187
Egwald (Abbot) 4
Eichstatt Bishop of 4

Electoral roll (St Peter's) 209
Electricity 212
Eliot George 39
Elizabeth I 12, 18, 25, 43
Elizabeth II (Silver Jubilee)239, (Golden Jubilee) 2, 238
Elkington Major-General F.R. 39
Elliotts Brick Company. 122
Enabling Act 1919 209
Enclosure (Parish of Droxford) 152, 154, 198
Enclosure Acts 40–1, 152–5
English Heritage 1
Essays and Reviews 133, 138
Estmylle (see Mill House) 22
Evacuation (World War II) 215
Evans John 89
Evensong (St Peter's) 242
Excommunication 35
Exton 25

Fairs 73
Fairthorn 72
Falconer Edward 159, 168–9
Falconer Lucy Maud (see Hemming)
Family Communion 241
Fareham 51
Fareham Congregational Church 148
Farham Geoffrey de 19
Farms 74
Farnham Castle 33
Father Smith organ 37
Felpham 32
Fernleigh 162
Finn Peter 129
Fire Brigades Act 1938 177, 210
Fire Service 54, 195, 209, 210, 214, 228
Fishers Pond Turnpike 61–3
FitzAdderley Charles (Peregrine Reedpen) 69–70
FitzAdderley Sarah 70, 88
Flynn Peter 92
Folly House 167
Font (Saxon in St Peter's) 4
Food Office 218
Food parcels 202
Football 173, 228
Ford Dr.Henry 82
Fountain Inn (see *Chase Inn*)
Fox Thomas 109.111
Free Street 235
French prisoners in Bishop's Waltham 64–6
French Street (see Bank Street)
Frenchmens Bridge 65, 163
Frensham Great Pond 15
Friends of St Peter's 244
Frogmore House 73

Frogmore Lane 73
Fuller Nicholas 28
Fulling mill 19

Galleries (in St Peter's) 37, 84, 86, 184–5, 135
Gardiner Stephen 25, 74
Garfield Road 128, 200
Garneray Amboise-Louis 65
Garnett George 206
Garnier William 82
Gas lighting 128, 175, 214
Gas masks 215, 228
George V(Jubilee) 211
George VI (Coronation) 211
German prisoners of war 218
Gibbet (on the Chase) 40
Gibson James 89
Giffard-Brine Robin 203
Gimblett John 108
Girl Guides 161, 218
Glastonbury Abbot of 7
Glebe 24
Godineau (Father) 201
Goody Melanchthon 148
Gorham John 90
Gospel Hall 151
Gosport 215
Gosport Central School 107
Gosport Turnpike 58, 63
Goulston Dr Joseph 31–2, 34, 44
Grammar School (Bishop Morley's) 44, 92, 100, 102, 235
Grammar schools in Hampshire 88–9
Great Pond (the bishop's) 12, 15–6, 75
Greens Close 227
Griffith-Colpoys Sir Edward 66
Grog 38
Grose Francis 68
Grossmith Charles Lipscomb 197
Guildford (diocese of) 208
Gunner Benjamin 117
Gunner Caroline (Hale) 95, 112, 113, 186, 187
Gunner Charles James (1818–72) 111–2
Gunner Charles James (1881–93) 117
Gunner Charles Richards 93, 112, 117, 123, 174, 186, 188, 205, 235
Gunner George Herbert 188
Gunner Harry 118
Gunner Jessie Kate (Mason) 112
Gunner John Hugh 118
Gunner Lucy Matilda (Ridge) 109
Gunner Sub.Lt.Edward 117, 201–2
Gunner Walter Robin 118, 174, 229

Gunner William I 109
Gunner William II 60, 61, 69, 109, 112 (Shooter)70
Gunners Park 2

Hadow reorganisation 106
Hamble (river) 1, 5, 6, 16, 33, 163, 166, 240
Hambledon 14, 27
Hambledon Hunt 112
Hambledon races 174–5
Hamblemouth 4
Hampshire County Council 105
Hampshire Police Authority 130, 150
Hamwic 4
Hardwick's Marriage Act 1754 77
Harvey Amy 210, 212, 218
Harvey Trevor 235
Haygarth John 82, 132, 135
Hearne (Nurse) 204
Hearth Tax 33–4
Helena (Princess) 129
Helps Arthur (later Sir) 39, 68, 93, 101, 112, 119–21, 123, 126, 161–2, 229
Hemming Agnes Blanche 159, 171
Hemming Dr Charles 159, 172
Hemming Dr Claude 159, 161, 172
Hemming Dr Philip 161
Hemming Lucy Maud (Falconer) 159
Hemmings Jane 244
Henry II 8
Henry III 9, 15
Henry of Blois 1, 5, 6, 7, 22, 244
Henry VI 10
Henry VIII 11
Hewitt Basil T. 185–6–7
Hewitt Thomas Swinnerton 174
Highclere 133
Higher Grade School 94
Highfield 159
Highways Act 1835 63
Highways Board 1863 63
Hills George W. 138, 146
His Majesty's Inspectors 106, 107, 108
Hoadly Benjamin 89
Hockley Viaduct 122
Hoe (tithing of) 44, 53, 72, 93, 140
Hoe estate 93
Hoe Road Cemetery 238
Hoe Road recreation ground 198
Holm Oak 109, 112, 113, 234, 237
Home Guard 218
Hope House 65, 69, 85
Horders Wood (see Waltham Chase)

Horne Margery 26
Horne Robert 26, 28
Horner William 37
Horseless carriage (motor car) 172
Houchin Street 2, 21–2, 200, 231
Hurley Mrs 105
Hydrants (fire) 204

Illegitimacy 77
Illustrated (1953) 229
Ine (king of the West Saxons) 3
Infant school 101, 102 (demolition)103
Infant Welfare Centre 206
Infidelity in high places 134
Italian prisoners of war 217, 219

Jackson Thomas Graham (later Sir) 167, 182–6
Jacobite risings 140
Jacobucci Carmelo & Gilda 224
James II 140
Jarman (Nurse) 226
Jefferys Samuel 88
Jenner Anne` 161, 198
Jenner Kentish 162
Jenner Sir William 162
Jennings William 88
Jervis Court Farm 210
Jonas family 166
Jonas Nick 244
Jopling John 144
Jordan the Otter Hunter 14
Jubilee Hall 238
Jubilee of George V 211
Jubilee of Queen Elizabeth II 238, 239
Jubilee Temperance Brass & Reed Band 169
Jutland (battle of) 202

Kalff Jacob 130
Kerby Robert 89
Kilmeston Manor 109
King James Bible
King's Church 167
Kings Head 69

Lanfranc 24
Langton Thomas 10, 11, 67
Lanyon Major C.V. 218
Lavigerie Charles 149
Law Joyce (Sansbury) 242
Leach John 145
Ledwell William 46, 47, 52
Legh Peter (Lord Newton) 39
Leland John 12, 40.129
Leopold (Prince) 129
Lewes George 39
Library (county) 207, 237
Liddell E.H. 94

Literacy 80, 99
Lloyd David 21, 22, 231
Lock George 197
Lock James 112, 177
Locks Farm 207
Lodge Farm 74, 194
Log books (school) 99, 100, 101
Lomer Arthur 100
Lomer Arthur 100
London & South Western Railway 123
London Missionary Society 148
Longmore Samuel 105, 146, 148, 193, 205
Louis Prince of Hesse-Darmstadt 129
Lovekin Louis James 50, 5172
Lovell Alan & Virginia 162, 244
Lovett Neville 209
Lovett Neville 209
Lowe Robert 99
Lower Lane 167, 232

Madden Frederick 90
Madgwick Victor 151
Mafeking Hero (*White Hart*) 59, 67, 95, 149, 174, 193, 216, 228
Malvern Drive 234
Mansel John 111, 112
Market House 75, 97
Market House 75
Marriage of D. of York & Princess Mary 105
Martineau Monica 162
Mary I (Queen) 12, 25, 26, 74
Mass 26
Maunsell William 147, 148
Maypole 75
Maypole Corner 73
Maypole Cottages 194
Medlicott W.E. 94
Meon Valley Circuit (Methodist) 146
Meon Valley Railway 126, 192, 198, 220
Meonstoke 26, 34
Mews Peter 35
Midnight Communion (Christmas) 226
Milestones 61
Militia 64
Mill House 37, 205, 210, 217, 223
Mitford Mary Russell 69
Mockford Mr 186
Molden Edward 198, 197
Moore Robert 29
Moors (Nature Reserve) 39, 240
Morley Francis 34, 35
Morley George 33, 89
Mother churches (also *parochia*) 5
Mothers Union 180

Motor car 172
Mount House 118, 148, 196234
Munich settlement 215
Museum (Scrapbook)131 (Trust)239
Myers W.H., MP 105, 167, 170

Nash James Palmer 94, 170, 178, 182, 189, 197
National School (Bishop's Waltham) 99, 101, 102, 148
National School (Curdridge) 102
National Service 228
National Society 97
Nave altar 242
Negro Jazz Band 219
Neile Richard 29
Nelson Admiral Horatio 65
Newton (Lord) see Legh Peter
Newtown 101, 102, 106, 121, 148
Nine Lessons and Carols 226
North Brownlow 82, 83
North Francis 82
North Waltham 24
Northbrook Earl of 96
Northbrook House 66–7, 73, 105, 127, 193, 203, 204, 218, 235, 237,
Northbrook tollgate 60, 63
Nursing Association 206
Nursling 25

Oddfellows Hall 151, 167, 177, 186, 211
Odiham 58
Ogle James 47, 48, 85, 97, 133
Ogle Sir Chaloner 85
Old Grammar School 166, 170, 188, 195
Old Station Roundabout 122, 237
Open fields 21, 40
Operation Overlord (1944) 220–1
Organ (in St Peter's) 37, 138
Origin of Species 138
Our Lady Queen of Apostles 149
Our Town 69–70
Overseers of the Poor 43, 44, 64, 197
Overton William 25
Oxford Bishop of (John Bridges) 26
Oxford Movement 138

Padbury family 156–58
Padbury James 156, 157, 158, 177, 186, 192, 238, 239
Padwick Harry H. 100
Padwick Henry H. 100
Page Mark 21
Palace (of bishops of Winchester) 1, 8–12, 16, 17, 28, 33, 75, 232

INDEX

Palace Cinema (also the Classic) 167
Palace House 64, 67, 119, 157, 161, 162, 220, 235
Paper makers 72
Parchment 27
Parish Chest 2, 44, 156
Parish Council 126, 131, 148, 194–5, 196, 197, 205, 222, 224, 229, 230
Parish Councils Act 1894 194–5
Parish Magazine (from 1950s Parish News) 170, 172, 179, 180, 181, 194, 215, 226, 244
Parish Registers 27, 44, 77
Park 33
Park Lug 13, 14
Parker Matthew 24
Parochia 3, 5, 6, 22
Parochial Church Council 209
Parochial Registers & Records Measure 2
Parole town 64
Parole towns 64
Parry Sir William 67
Paulet William 12
Paupers 49
Payn John 20
Peak Farm 174
Penny John 64–5, 66, 68
Pest House 47, 49, 52, 53
Peter's Pence 6
Petersen (teacher) 226
Petersfield 39, 123, 126
Pevsner *Buildings of England:Hampshire* 21, 231
Philpotts Henry 134
Pigot's Directory 70, 71, 72, 73
Pipe Rolls (of bishops of Winchester) 16, 18–20, 24
Pipe Rolls (of the Bishops of Winchester) 18, 19
Piscina (removal of) 137
Pitman Edward 214, 218
Poll (at Council elections) 195–6
Pondside estate 236
Pondside Farm 121
Poor Bargain 87
Poor Law Amendment Act 49
Poor Rate book 44
Population 20, 191, 232, 245 (age distribution of) 194
Portchester 1, 2, 4, 65
Portchester Castle 65, 188
Portland Square 195
Portsmouth diocese of 1, 136, 208–9
Post office 211
Postman 228
Poulter Edmund 82, 83–4, 85
Poynet John 25

Preshaw 189, 217
Pretoria (relief of) 105–6
Price Peg 242
Price's Grammar School, Fareham 107, 127
Primitive Methodist church 141–6, 170, 205
Primitive Methodist District Synod 146
Primitive Methodist Mission Hall 142, 235
Priory (see Royal Albert Infirmary)
Priory Park 131, 237
Priory The (see Royal Albert Infirmary)
Provincial banks 116
Public houses 73, 168, 193
Pulpit (St Peter's)` 28
Pupil teachers 100
Puritans 26

Radulf (Domesday) 5
Railway (Botley to Bishop's Waltham) 122–8, 208
Raleigh William 15
Rationing 222
Rationing 222
Reading Room 105, 167, 170, 196
Recreation ground 198
Rectory (St Peter's) 85, 97, 189, 235, 237, 242
Recusants 26, 27
Red Lion Street 231
Reedpan Peregrine (see Fitzadderley Charles)
Reeve 19
Reformatioin 25, 27
Registers (parish) 27, 28, 32, 37, 77, 78, 79
Registrar of Births, Marriages & Deaths 72
Registrar of births, marriages & deaths 118
Registry Office 237–8
Remembrance Sunday 205
Restoration (of Charles II) 32
Restoration of church 1896–7 182–7
Revolutionary & Napoleonic Wars
Reynolds Robert 32, 44
Richard I 8
Richards family 203
Richardson F.W. 92
Ridge Thomas 109
Ridgemede 112, 113, 118, 188, 193, 211, 235
Ridgemede Cottage 113
Ridgemede housing estate 118, 232, 235, 236
Ridgemede Primary School 118
Road blocks 216

Robed choir 186
Robert of Waltham 19
Robinson Arthur 130
Robinson Arthur Hildyard 166, 210
Roman Row 234
Rosewell Maria 69, 70, 88
Royal Albert Infirmary (also The Priory & Albert House) 75, 92, 93, 94, 105, 119, 129, 130, 149, 201, 215, 217, 234
Royal Engineers 216–7
Royal Engineers 216–7
Rycroft Harold 170, 226

Salisbury (Dean of)26, (Bishop of) 33
Salter Edward 84
Salvation Army 150, 211
Sandale John 15
Sansbury Joyce (later Law) 242
Sargeant Frank 168–9, 224, 226, 242
Saxon settlement 1
Scard Eliza 90
Scard Thomas 69, 90
School (Infants)
School attendance 99–100
School Board 93, 94, 101, 102, 148
School pence 102
Scouting for Boys 174
Scouts 174–5, 218, 226
Sewerage Saga 198, 207–8, 232, 236
Seymour Thomas Goolding 69–70, 109
Sharpe Henry Edmund 201–3
Sharrock Robert 34
Shearer Bettesworth Pitt 63, 123, 128
Shedfield (chapel of ease) 134, 135
Sheep 20
Sherecroft House 135
Sims Arthur 203
Sims Ebenezer 99–100, 102, 193, 203
Sims Oswald 203
Singleton William 27, 31
Siren (Second World War) 215
Slates (school)`101
Smallpox 52, 53
Smith Bernard (Father) 37
Soberton 17
South Downs 1
Southampton 21
Southampton Technical School of Building 108
Southampton to London turnpike 60, 152
Southampton University 122

Southwick House 33, 37
Sparshott James 97
Spratt Ronnie 210
Spurr family 149
St Bonnet le Chateau 239
St Cross, Winchester 24, 29
St George's House (Barclays Bank)` 37
St George's Square 2, 22, 75, 199, 232, 238
St Paul's Methodist Church 135
St Peter Street (also Church Lane) 2, 4, 88, 200, 205
Stake William 21
Stakes farm 21, 74
Stares Robert Hatch 50
Station Road 235
Steam roller 198
Steele Stephen 109
Stephen of Blois 7
Stephen the Huntsman 14
Stephens Edwin & Eliza 97
Stockbridge, Winchester & Southampton Turnpike 59
Stocke Matthew 31
Stocks Catherine 102
Storey Hilda 222
Stretch Herbert 205
Stretthe Robert 19
Stubbs Noel 174, 190, 209, 224, 226
Suetts farm 191
Summer of 1911 106
Sumner Charles 129, 132, 133
Sumner George Henry 132, 178, 180, 186
Sumner Mary 180
Sunday School (Church of England) 100, 126, 187, 188, 244
Sunday School (Congregational) 101
Surveyor of the Highways 44, 55
Swanmore (parish of)37, 97, 101, 135, 169, 197
Swanmore Cottage 112, 188
Swanmore Driftway 155
Swanmore Park House 63, 128, 169, 170, 172
Swanmore Secondary School (Swanmore College of Technology) 108, 238

Swanmore St Barnabas 117, 135

Tangier Farm 33
Taylor Mary (deaconess) 242
Telephone 200
Temperance Society 170
Tessier (Father) 201
Thickets, The (also *Thickets House*) 162, 235
Thompson Gerald M. 189, 193
Titchfield 3, 20, 21, 90
Tithe map 15, 74–5
Tithings 18, 44
Toleration Act 1689 140
Toll houses 1–2, 59, 61, 75
Tractarianism Schismatical & Dishonest 134
Travelling Dairy School 96
Tremlett Bruce 2
Triangle (recreation ground on the Chase) 155, 174, 197, 198
Trinder H.W. 105, 198
Turnpike Trusts 55, 56
Twinning Association 239

Unemployment 206–7
Uniformity Act of 1559 26
United Free Church 149
Upham 5, 18, 21, 22, 25, 50, 80, 82, 132, 152, 244

Vaccination 52, 53
Valor Ecclesiasticus 24
VE-Day 221
Vernon Admiral Edward 37–8
Vernon Hill 21
Vernon Hill estate 121
Vernon Hill House 37–8, 65, 119, 129, 235
Victoria Queen (Golden Jubilee) 138, 169 (death of) 187
Victoria Road 119, 121
Villeneuve Admiral 65, 239
Volunteer Fire Brigade 177, 209

Walmsley W.E. 238
Walters Charles I 87, 88, 89
Walters Charles II 17, 28, 31, 48, 74, 90, 226
Walters John Vodin 88, 89
Waltham Black Act 39–40
Waltham Blacks 39

Waltham Chase 75, 154–5
Waltham Episcopi 5
Waltham Treaty of 11
War Memorial 203, 205
War trophies 205
Ward Dr Robert 28
Water supply, Sewerage & Scavenging in Bishop's Waltham 198
Wayet John Wyndham 190
Wayferer Myrh 31
Wayneflete William 10
Wealdham 3
West Hoe 135, 191
West Hoe House 118
Wheatsheaf 103
Wheatsheaf The 22
White Fathers 130, 149
White Gilbert 82
White Hart (see *Mafeking Hero*)
White John 25
White Swan 228
White's Directory of Hampshire 92
Wickham 21, 80, 232
Wilberforce Samuel 132, 134, 135
Wilfrid St 3
Wilkinson Simon 242
Willard John 242, 244
William III 38
Willibald St 3, 4
Willis Richard 140
Winchester County High School for Girls 107–8
Winchester diocese of 1, 33, 208, 209
Wine shop 241
Wolf Cubs 174
Wolvesey Palace 15
Women's Institute 204, 218, 222
Womens Voluntary Service 218
Woodlock Henry 15
Workhouse 47, 50 (street)47
Workmans Hall 167, 188
World Wars I 146, 201–5, 215 II 215–22, 233, 238
Wyatt Archibald 162
Wykeham William of 9, 10, 21, 24, 68

Youth Hall 237